James Macdonald, James Sinclair

History of polled Aberdeen or Angus cattle

Giving an Account of the Origin, Improvement, and Characteristics of the Breed

James Macdonald, James Sinclair

History of polled Aberdeen or Angus cattle
Giving an Account of the Origin, Improvement, and Characteristics of the Breed

ISBN/EAN: 9783337139728

Printed in Europe, USA, Canada, Australia, Japan

Cover: Foto ©ninafisch / pixelio.de

More available books at **www.hansebooks.com**

HISTORY

OF

POLLED ABERDEEN OR ANGUS CATTLE

GIVING

AN ACCOUNT OF THE ORIGIN, IMPROVEMENT,
AND CHARACTERISTICS OF THE BREED

BY

JAMES MACDONALD

EDITOR 'IRISH FARMERS' GAZETTE,' AUTHOR OF 'FOOD
FROM THE FAR WEST,' ETC.

AND

JAMES SINCLAIR

SUB-EDITOR 'IRISH FARMERS' GAZETTE'

ILLUSTRATED WITH NUMEROUS ANIMAL PORTRAITS

WILLIAM BLACKWOOD AND SONS
EDINBURGH AND LONDON
MDCCCLXXXII

HISTORY

OF

POLLED ABERDEEN OR ANGUS CATTLE

GIVING

AN ACCOUNT OF THE ORIGIN, IMPROVEMENT,
AND CHARACTERISTICS OF THE BREED

.

BY

JAMES MACDONALD

EDITOR 'IRISH FARMERS' GAZETTE,' AUTHOR OF 'FOOD
FROM THE FAR WEST,' ETC.

AND

JAMES SINCLAIR

SUB-EDITOR 'IRISH FARMERS' GAZETTE'

ILLUSTRATED WITH NUMEROUS ANIMAL PORTRAITS

WILLIAM BLACKWOOD AND SONS
EDINBURGH AND LONDON
MDCCCLXXXII

CONTENTS.

CHAPTER I.

ORIGIN OF DOMESTIC CATTLE.

CHAPTER II.

ORIGIN OF POLLED RACES OF CATTLE.

CHAPTER III.

ORIGIN AND EARLY HISTORY OF THE POLLED ABERDEEN OR ANGUS CATTLE.

CHAPTER IV.

IMPROVEMENT OF THE BREED.

CHAPTER V.

CHARACTERISTICS OF THE BREED.

CHAPTER VI.

NOTES ON SOME EARLY POLLED CATTLE.

CHAPTER VII.

EXTINCT HERDS.

CHAPTER VIII.

EXTINCT HERDS—*continued.*

CHAPTER IX.

EXTINCT HERDS—*concluded.*

CHAPTER X.

EXISTING SCOTCH HERDS.

CHAPTER XI.

EXISTING SCOTCH HERDS—*continued.*

CHAPTER XII.

EXISTING SCOTCH HERDS—*continued.*

CHAPTER XIII.

EXISTING SCOTCH HERDS—*continued.*

CHAPTER XIV.

EXISTING SCOTCH HERDS—*concluded.*

CHAPTER XV.

THE BREED IN ENGLAND AND IRELAND.

CHAPTER XVI.

THE BREED IN FOREIGN COUNTRIES.

CHAPTER XVII.

THE LEADING FAMILIES.

CHAPTER XVIII.

SYSTEM OF MANAGEMENT.

CHAPTER XIX.

THE BREED IN THE SHOW-YARD.

CHAPTER XX.

CHAPTER XXI.

THE BREED IN THE SALE RING.

LIST OF ILLUSTRATIONS.

THE POLLED ABERDEEN OR ANGUS
BREED OF CATTLE.

CHAPTER I.

ORIGIN OF DOMESTIC CATTLE.

Disagreement as to origin of domestic cattle—The ox in prehistoric times
—The *Bos urus*—The *Bos longifrons*—Domestic cattle descended from
one or the other, or from both—Opinion of various naturalists : Rütimeyer, Cuvier, Bell, Boyd Dawkins, Darwin, Storer, Owen, Dr John
Alexander Smith—Are the *urus* and the *longifrons* really distinct
species?—Practical value of the discussion—Probability of domestic
cattle coming from "one common source"—Low on variations in
cattle.

IT is probable that complete agreement may never be
arrived at in regard to the origin of the domesticated races
of British cattle. There has been much discussion as to
whether they ought to be looked upon as the conglomerate
produce of two or more distinctly different species of the
genus *Bos*, or as the variegated offshoots of one great
parent stem. The subject, like most other questions re-
ceding far into the mists of prehistoric times, would seem
to be almost hopelessly entangled in the meshes of scientific and theoretical speculation.

The combined researches of the geologist and the archæ-
ologist have proved that the genus *Bos*—the generic appel-

lation of the ox and kindred species—had lived in Britain
at the time of the Mammoth, sharing with many varieties
of extinct mammalia the luxuriant herbage that distinguished the flora of Northern Europe prior to the glacial
period. Its fossil remains, along with those of the elephant, rhinoceros, &c., have been dug up from the drift
and fresh-water deposits of the Newer-Pliocene formation.
There is little doubt that, outliving many of its earlier
associates, and finding new companions as it passed from
age to age, the ox, of one or other variety, has since that
remote period had constant existence in Northern Europe.

The varieties of the ox which in the prehistoric era
roamed in the sweet freedom of nature through the British
forests and marshes have been arranged by palæontolo-
gists into two main divisions. The line of demarcation—to
minds of a practical turn somewhat arbitrary—seems well
enough understood by naturalists. The two types or
species differed materially in size, and also, to a varying
extent, in some other points of lesser importance. In the
strictest sense of the term, however, they presented no
structural differences. The larger was named the *Bos primigenius* by Bojanus, and is likewise known as the *Bos urus*.
To the smaller, Owen gave the designation of *Bos longifrons*. Other species of fossil European oxen are spoken
of by various writers, notably the *Bos frontosus* and the
Bos trochoceros, but all these are now generally regarded
as identical with either the *Bos primigenius* or the *Bos
longifrons*. Rütimeyer considers the *Bos trochoceros* to be
the female of an early domesticated form of the *Bos primigenius*, and to be the progenitrix of the *Bos frontosus*.

The *Bos urus* is described as having been an animal of
enormous size and ferocious temper. When the Romans
first penetrated into the heart of Britain, more than half
a century before the dawn of the Christian era, they
found the great *urus* roaming wildly through the forests
and marshes. Cæsar describes this animal as being in

size little inferior to the elephant, but in colour, form, and
general appearance resembling the common bull. "Great
is their strength, and great their swiftness," says the Roman
leader, "and they spare neither man nor wild beast that
comes within their view. The Germans take and kill
them in pitfalls made with great care and trouble. Their
young men inure themselves to this labour, and exercise
themselves in this kind of hunting ; and they who have
killed the most, publicly produce their horns in testimony
of their exploits, and receive praise. But it is impossible
to accustom them to man, and to tame them; and to this,
even the very young ones are no exception. The great
size, form, and beauty of their horns make them differ
much from the horns of our oxen: these they collect with
great care, and, surrounding the margin of them with
silver, use them as cups at their largest banquets." This
is an interesting picture drawn by a graphic writer who
had seen the huge monster careering wildly in all its pris-
tine majesty. Pliny describes the *urus* as an animal of
"excessive strength and swiftness," and states that both
the *urus* and the bison were conveyed from Germany to
Rome, and "viewed by the people in the circus."

Numerous skeletons, or parts of skeletons, supposed to
belong to the *Bos urus* type, have from time to time
been discovered in the British Isles, and elsewhere in
Europe, and from these various scientific observers and
celebrated naturalists have given us sketches of this
ancient variety of cattle. Professor Nilsson, writing of
the *urus*, says: "The forehead is flat, the edge of the
neck is straight, the horns very large and long, near the
roots directed outward, and somewhat backward; in the
middle they are bent forward, and towards the front
turned upward. This colossal species of ox, to judge from
the skeleton, resembles almost the tame ox in form and
the proportions of its body; but in its bulk it is far
larger. To judge from the magnitude of its horn-cores, it

had much larger horns, even larger than the long-horned breed of cattle found in the Campania of Rome. According to all accounts, the colour of this ox was black; it had white horns, with long black points; the hide was covered with hair like the tame ox, but it was shorter and smooth, with the exception of the forehead, where it was long and curly." Rütimeyer, Owen, Bell, Boyd Dawkins, Smith, and others, give similar descriptions of the *urus*, differing slightly in minor details. There is uncertainty as to the colour of the *urus*. Some say it was black; others believe it to have been white.

By various writers elaborate measurements are presented of the *urus*, showing that the animal must have been of huge dimensions, far exceeding any living variety of cattle. The length of the body "from the nape to the end of the rump-bones," is stated at about 9 feet; and the length of the head "from the occipital ridge to the anterior border of the intermaxillary bones," at 2 feet 4 inches, making the entire length of the animal no less than about 11 feet 4 inches. Then the height over the mane is said to have been 6 feet to 6 feet 6 inches. The horns carried by the *urus* must have been of great size. The horn-cores of the various skulls found in Scotland and elsewhere measure, along the outer curvature, about 2 feet or 2 feet 2 inches in length; while the span between the tips of the horn-cores is stated at 2 feet 2 inches, and their circumference at the base at 1 foot 2 inches. The breadth of the forehead, between the horn-cores, would seem to have been about 9 inches.

The *Bos longifrons* has been represented as smaller in size than many of the existing varieties of cattle. Professor Owen, in his work on 'British Fossil Mammals and Birds,' says: "This small but ancient species or variety of ox belongs, like our present cattle, to the sub-genus *Bos*, as is shown by the form of the forehead, and by the origin of the horns from the extremities of the occipital ridge; but it differs from the contemporary *Bos primigenius*, not only by its great inferiority of size, being smaller than the ordinary breeds of domestic cattle, but also by the horns being proportionately much smaller and shorter as well as differently directed, and by the forehead being less concave. It is indeed usually flat; and the frontal bones extend farther beyond the orbits, before they join the nasal bones, than in the *Bos primigenius.* The horn-cores of the *Bos longifrons* describe a single short curve outwards and forwards in the plane of the forehead, rarely rising above the plane, more rarely sinking below it: the cores have a very rugged exterior, and are usually a little flattened at the upper part."

The accounts of other writers differ but little. The *Bos longifrons* would seem to have been short in the body, and to have had legs almost as slender as those of the deer. Professor Nilsson, in a paper "On the Extinct and Existing Bovine Animals of Scandinavia," published in the 'Annals and Magazine of Natural History,' says that, as far as he knew, the *Bos longifrons* was "the smallest of the ox tribe that had lived wild in our portion of the globe;" the whole length, "from the muzzle to the end of the rump-bone," having been "about 6 feet 8 inches." The skull would seem to have been long and narrow. The various specimens found and preserved measure in length from the supra-occipital ridge to front edge of intermaxillary bone about 16 to 18 inches; from roots of horn-cores to upper edge of orbits, about $3\frac{1}{2}$ to 4 inches; breadth of forehead between roots of horn-cores, from 5 to $6\frac{1}{2}$ inches; breadth of skull across middle of orbits, from 6 to 7 inches; circumference of horn-cores at base, from 4 to 7 inches; length of horn-cores along outer-curvature, from 3 to 7 inches; and span from tip to tip of horn-cores, from 9 to 16 inches.

From the bison and other varieties of humped cattle— *Bos priscus, Bos babulus, Bos indicus,* &c.—these two types,

just described in detail, are generally regarded as specifically distinct. It is not denied that the *Bos urus* and
Bos longifrons, as well as the existing races of non-humped
cattle, all come within the one generic—or rather sub-
generic—distinction, the *Bos taurus*. Naturalists, however,
as we have seen, have arranged the ancient varieties of
humpless cattle into two main species or types, the *Bos
urus* and the *Bos longifrons;* and while they would seem
to agree that these two species represent the sub-generic
division to which domesticated cattle belong, they have
been unable to arrive at anything like unanimity of opinion
as to which type or "species" has been perpetuated in
existing races, or as to whether both have been so preserved; and, if both have been preserved, in what varieties
each type has its purest representatives. Some naturalists
tell us that our living races of domesticated cattle are pure
but modified descendants of the huge *urus*. Others claim
the deer-like *longifrons* as the progenitors of existing races.
Perhaps the most generally accepted notion is, that existing
domesticated cattle are the intermixed descendants of the
two ancient types.

Rütimeyer gives it as his belief that some of the larger
domesticated races on the Continent and in England, as
well as the semi-wild cattle in Lord Tankerville's Park at
Chillingham, are the descendants of the *urus*. The Chillingham cattle, he says, are less altered from the true *urus*
type than any other known breed. Cuvier, Bell, and
others, would seem to go the length of believing that our
entire stock of living cattle are " the degenerate descendants
of the great *urus*." Nilsson considers that the existing
races of cattle may probably have been derived from the
Bos urus, the *Bos longifrons*, and the *Bos frontosus*. Boyd
Dawkins and Darwin are of opinion—and the one quotes
the other to this effect—that " European cattle are descended from two species"—namely, the *urus* and the
longifrons. In his interesting work on 'The Wild White

Cattle of Great Britain,' the late Rev. John Storer devoted himself mainly to the substantiating of his belief that the semi-wild cattle confined in the Chillingham and Cadzow and some other parks were the progeny of the great *urus;* and that the *Bos longifrons,* having been " driven with its master, the Celt, to the remote and inaccessible parts which the English could not reach," has been preserved in the Kyloe of the Highlands of Scotland and in the smaller cattle of Wales.

Owen considers it highly improbable that the enormous and savage *urus,* spoken of by Cæsar, was ever tamed so as to be fitted for the uses of man. He believes that the progress of agricultural settlement had caused its "utter extirpation," just as similar progress in North America is fast driving out the bison, and as it drove out the Aurochs in Europe, and that our knowledge of the *urus* "is now limited to deductions from its fossil or semi-fossil remains." Owen suggests that the early domestic cattle in Britain, more particularly in Roman Britain, had been derived mainly from importations of breeds "already domesticated" by the founders of the new British colonies. But, he remarks, "if it should still be contended that the natives of Britain or any part of them obtained their cattle by taming a primitive wild race, neither the bison nor the great *urus* are so likely to have furnished the source of their herds as the smaller primitive wild species or original variety of *Bos,*" the *longifrons.* Winding up his concise and complete description of the *longifrons,* the same writer says: " In this field of conjecture the most probable one will be admitted to be that which points to the *Bos longifrons* as the species which would be domesticated by the aborigines of Britain before the Roman invasion." Dr John Alexander Smith, of Edinburgh, who has given much attention to the subject, and whose papers on the "Ancient Cattle of Scotland," published in the 'Proceedings of the Society of Antiquaries of Scotland,' are full of interest,

expresses his entire concurrence with Owen's belief as to
the extirpation of the *urus*.   Dr Smith adds : " To suppose
beasts like these not only tamed, in opposition to such
decided evidence to the contrary, but also so strangely
degenerated into the comparatively small-sized and placid
ox of the present day, seems really past belief." He is
inclined to regard the *longifrons* as "the true origin of
our domesticated cattle," and presents strong evidence in
support of the contention.

These extracts from noted writers, not by any means
comprising all the different views that have been expressed
by men entitled to be heard on the subject, will serve to
indicate how hopelessly involved the question of the
"true origin" of our domestic cattle has become.   But
while we despair of the discovery of facts calculated to
bring all investigators and thinkers to full agreement, we
indulge the comfortable conviction that for every practical
purpose it matters little which of the varying "beliefs,"
"opinions," and "contentions" referred to is really the
correct one.   We shall not seriously raise the question
as to whether the two recognised types of ancient humpless cattle, the *urus* and the *longifrons*, should properly
be regarded as "distinct species," or merely as varieties
of one species, the sub-genus *Bos taurus*, modified in form
by food, climate, and other changing conditions.   That
is indeed a question upon which some pertinent considerations might be submitted; but for our present purpose it
will suffice to assure the reader that whether the existing
races of domesticated cattle are the descendants of the
huge long-horned *urus*, or the slender short-horned *longifrons*, or of both combined, the material of which these
races are composed and the forces bound up in them are
still the same.   If (as the late Mr Storer would have us
believe) at Chillingham we might look upon a pure
descendant of the *urus*, and in the Highlands of Scotland
upon a living specimen of the ancient *longifrons*, we would

in the two cases have before us material of almost complete sameness—animals so entirely identical in structure,
although slightly modified in form by different usage, that
in spite of all the arbitrary and fanciful distinctions that
naturalists have endeavoured to set up, we would still feel
constrained to regard them as having had a common origin
in one well-defined if somewhat varying species of the
genus *Bos*,—those wild humpless cattle that browsed on
the luxuriant plains in this country during the Newer-
Pliocene period.

In leaving this subject, we may present an apt quotation from a footnote in Professor Low's admirable work
on the 'Domestic Animals of Great Britain.'   In referring to the huge oxen whose skeletons were found in
various parts of Europe, Professor Low says these skeletons indicate an animal nearly three times the bulk of
the oxen of the present day, and adds that the skeletons
have been found "in the same situations as the great
extinct Irish Elk, and thus seem to have survived various
species with which they were associated, and even perhaps to have survived till within the historic era."   Continuing, he says: "A question, however, which has been
agitated by naturalists is, Whether these huge animals
are the origin of the domestic races, and may not even
have been the *uri* described by Cæsar?   The question is
one which bears less than is assumed upon the origin of
the existing races.   We can, by all the evidence which
the question admits of, trace existing races to the ancient
uri which, long posterior to the historical era, inhabited
the forests of Germany, Gaul, Britain, and other countries.
It is a question involving an entirely different series of
considerations, whether these *uri* were themselves descended from an anterior race, surpassing them in magnitude, and inhabiting the globe at the same time with
other extinct species.   While there is nothing that can
directly support this hypothesis, there is nothing certainly

founded on analogy that can enable us to invalidate it.
There is nothing more incredible in the supposition that
animals should diminish in size, with changes in the
condition of the earth, than that they should be extinguished altogether, and supplanted by new species. The
fossil *urus* inhabited Europe when a very different condition existed with regard to temperature, the supplies
of vegetable food, and the consequent development of
animal forms. Why should not the *urus*, under these
conditions, have been a far larger animal than he subsequently became? We know by experience the effects
of food in increasing or diminishing the size of this very
race of animals. The great ox of the Lincolnshire fens
exceeds in size the little ox of Barbary or the Highland
hills, as much as the fossil *urus* exceeded the larger
oxen of Germany and England; and we cannot consider
it as incredible, that animals which inhabited Europe when
elephants found food and a climate suited to their natures,
should have greatly surpassed in magnitude the same
species under the present conditions of the same countries."

CHAPTER II.

ORIGIN OF POLLED RACES OF CATTLE.

Speculation as to origin of hornless cattle—Their antiquity—Their distinctiveness—Letter from Darwin on loss of horns—Letter from Dr John Alexander Smith—Professor Low's opinion—Absence of horns —Deviation from original form—Loss of horns before and after domestication—Preserved and fixed by selection in breeding — Acquaintance with principles of breeding in early times—Advice of Palladius, Columella, and Virgil—Distribution of polled cattle—Polled cattle in Austria, South America, Norway, and Iceland—In Cheshire, Lancashire, Nottinghamshire, Norfolk, Yorkshire, Devonshire, in England—In Ayrshire, Lanarkshire, and Isle of Skye, in Scotland— In Ireland—Existing polled breeds in United Kingdom—The Galloway breed—Norfolk and Suffolk polls.

REGARDING the probable derivation of the polled varieties of cattle, there has been considerable speculation. As far as our present knowledge extends, the subject is found to rest mainly on conjecture. By some it has been seriously argued that polled cattle are entitled to be ranked as an original and distinct species. We have even met with the assertion that their polled progenitors first saw the post-diluvian world at the "general dispersion on Mount Ararat"! Without going either so far back or so high up for their origin, the majority of thoughtful writers who have given attention to the subject are prepared to assign to the principal living varieties or breeds of polled or hornless cattle a separate existence for a long period of time. The idea which finds most favour—and we believe the correct one—is that the aboriginal cattle from which existing races are derived were all originally provided with horns, and that, therefore, the many varieties of hornless cattle which have from time immemorial existed in various parts of the British Isles and elsewhere must be regarded as forming distinct departures from the ancient or original order of things. How and when these departures may have been effected must be left in a large measure to conjecture.

That eminent philosopher and naturalist, Dr Charles Darwin, who has so recently gone the way of all the living (he died at Down, Kent, on April 20, 1882, aged 73 years), and whose works, notably those on the 'Origin of Species' and 'Animals and Plants under Domestication,' mark him out as at once the most gifted and most far-reaching inquirer into matters connected with the origin, formation, and deviation of species, confessed frankly that he could not account for the loss of horns on certain races of cattle. In his last-named work, he says he has "often speculated on the probable causes through which each separate district in Great Britain came to possess in former times its own peculiar breed of cattle;" and yet he had not been able to arrive at a confirmed conclusion as to how the horns may have disappeared, and how the hornless breeds have sprung up. He thinks "it is probable that some breeds," and "some peculiarities, such as being hornless, &c., have appeared suddenly, owing to what we may call in our ignorance spontaneous variation," and that through selection in breeding, either skilled or rude, the results of these "spontaneous variations" have come to possess a powerful hereditary tendency. In a courteous communication to us, dated January 23, 1882, this gifted naturalist expresses his regret that he had "not had time during several years to attend to the very interesting subject of domesticated animals;" and adds: "No one can give any explanation—although no doubt there must be a cause—

of the loss of horns, any more than of the loss of hair, both losses strongly tending to be inherited. It is, I think, possible that the loss of horns has occurred often since cattle were domesticated, though I can call to mind only a case in Paraguay about a century ago. Is there not a sub-breed of the so-called wild park cattle which is hornless ? "

In a communication to the authors, dated March 1, 1882, Dr John Alexander Smith of Edinburgh, whose interesting 'Notes on the Ancient Cattle of Scotland' have already been referred to, also expresses his belief that the absence of horns in certain breeds of cattle is " an accidental variety or peculiarity which might occur in any domesticated herd." Professor Low evidently regards the absence of horns as a departure from the original condition of things, but protests against the application of the term "accident" to the organic change that gives rise to such peculiarities. " There is nothing," he says, " in the phenomena of nature to which the term accident can be justly applied. The characters were doubtless the result of some organic change proper to the animals in which they appeared, and their transmission to their progeny is only the exemplification of a law common to other cases of transmitted characters. . . . In the case of the domesticated animals, we find similar evidences [as in regard to the human race] of the wonderful permanence of characters once acquired and imprinted on the animals. In certain breeds of oxen and sheep, the animals retain from generation to generation their distinctive marks, the presence or absence of horns, the length and peculiar bending of these appendages, and even the minutest variations of colour, as spots of white and black on certain parts of the body."

Other writers have expressed themselves in similar terms ; and in the absence of proof to the contrary, the conclusion would seem justifiable, that the want of horns constitutes a deviation from the original form of the ox ; that the deviation has been due in the first place to sudden organic changes — whether "spontaneous," "accidental," or " proper," we need hardly inquire ; and that by selection in breeding, the new feature has come to possess the fixity of an original character. But while we believe that the absence of horns may have arisen from some such sudden variation as has been indicated, we nevertheless maintain that the principal races of polled cattle are quite as well entitled to be classed as distinct breeds as any of the horned varieties, and that their chief distinguishing feature, the absence of horns, is now as firmly established as any of those varying characters, either in colour, form, or attributes, that distinguish from each other the leading horned tribes.

Among those who regard the polled varieties as departures from the original form, it is generally considered as more than probable that these offshoots had appeared after the wild horned cattle had become domesticated. This idea is supported by the fact, that all those fossil and semi-fossil skulls and skeletons which constitute almost the sole witnesses we possess of the existence of wild cattle in Britain itself, as well as in Europe generally, prior to the historic era, would tend to prove the constant presence of horns. Even in the face of these considerations, however, we are not prepared to admit that no such variations as the sudden loss of horns had ever occurred among cattle while they roamed in their natural wildness. From all we know, the conditions under which cattle lived before domestication were scarcely less favourable to the occurrence of spontaneous variation than after they had been tamed ; and following the law of analogy, and recognising an inherent power in nature to give forth modified variety—we regard such deviation as the fulfilment, rather than as the breach, of nature's laws—we are constrained to assume that among the wild progenitors of our domesticated cattle there may have appeared an occasional hornless animal. But while we think it more than probable that that may have been the case, we are nevertheless inclined to regard the common belief as accurate in at least one sense.

There is, we conceive, ample proof in support of the conclusion that those sudden losses of horns—those spontaneous variations, or proper organic changes, which have given us our known polled varieties—have really occurred since domestication took place. It is admitted by all authorities—Darwin clearly enforces the point — that while deviations from the original or typical form of races of animals may arise spontaneously, some sort of artificial method or selection in breeding is necessary in order to impart to those spontaneous and isolated deviations such fixity of character, or such strong hereditary power, as would insure their perpetuation. Among cattle completely wild, no artificial selection could take place ; and therefore any such sudden and radical variation as the loss of horns which may have occurred among ancient wild cattle, would in all probability have been rapidly obliterated by the undirected flow of long-sustained natural forces. With cattle under domestication the case is different. The appearance of new characters, whether the loss of horns or some other feature, might be taken advantage of by the owners, who, by isolating the animals possessing the peculiarities desired to be perpetuated, and breeding from none but these, would succeed in stamping with less or more hereditary fixity those favoured features or changes which at first were but transitory, and which, had not artificial means been taken to preserve them, would have quickly disappeared, merging again, as it were, into the main current from which they had temporarily strayed.

In this connection it should be remembered that, although the general principles which regulate the laws of heredity are now better known, and have been made to produce more remarkable results in late years than at any former age, yet those laws were recognised, and to some extent observed, even in the earliest historic times. In all the ancient nations the ox was the principal beast of burden, and the works of most of the early writers who deal with industrial subjects show clearly that in these nations the power of selection in breeding had been known and employed. This was notably the case among the Romans. Palladius gives explicit directions as to the selection of bulls. "The bull," he says, "should be tall, with huge members, of a middle size, rather young as old, of a stern countenance, small horns, a brawny and vast neck, and confined belly." Columella's description of the best cow is still more minute. He most approves of cows that "are of a tall make, long with very large belly, very broad forehead, eyes black and open, horns graceful, smooth, and black, hairy ears, straight jaws, very large dewlap and tail, and moderate hoofs and legs." Virgil discourses at some length on the breeding of both horses and cattle, remarking that "if any one, fond of the prize at the Olympic games, breeds horses, or if any one breeds stout bullocks for the plough, he chiefly attends to the make of the mother, who ought to be large in all her parts." In Dryden's Virgil (Georgics, Book III.) we come across this piece of sound advice amongst directions for the management of cattle:—

> " Distinguish all betimes with branding fire,
> To note the tribe, the lineage, and the sire ;
> Whom to reserve for husband of the herd ;
> Or who shall be to sacrifice preferred ;
> Or whom thou shalt to turn thy glebe allow,
> To smooth the furrows, and sustain the plough :
> The rest, for whom no lot is yet decreed,
> May run in pastures and at pleasure feed."

Darwin says he has found that the degree of care—the selection and isolation—necessary to perpetuate peculiarities in races of stock "has sometimes been taken even in little-civilised districts, where we should least have expected it, as in the case of the *niata*, *chivo*, and hornless cattle in South America." These facts indicate that in the earliest historic times selection in the breeding of cattle had been practised with considerable skill. Along with other known circumstances, they also seem to justify the conclusion that almost ever since cattle were thoroughly domesticated and fitted for the uses of man, they have been submitted to some kind of selection, perhaps in remote ages more rude than skilled, but still sufficient to stamp with permanency such an exceptional character as the absence of horns.

Polled varieties of cattle have been more widely spread than is generally supposed. No traces have been discovered of the existence of any polled cattle prior to the historic era—although, as we have already remarked, an occasional hornless animal may even then have appeared. Then, as far as we are aware, no reference to polled cattle is made by any of the early writers excepting Herodotus, who describes the domestic cattle of the Scythians as having been hornless. But passing to more recent times, say within the past two hundred years, we gather from sufficiently reliable evidence that, in the British Isles and elsewhere, a great many varieties of polled cattle have existed. A number of these varieties have disappeared, but several still survive. It is known that on the estate of Prince Leichtenstein in Austria a herd of red polled cattle has been in existence from time immemorial; and we are told by Darwin that in Paraguay in South America a variety of hornless cattle originated little more than a hundred years ago. The latter case Darwin, in his communication to us, mentions as the only instance he had ever come across in which the origin and formation of a polled race were fully known. In his work on 'Animals and Plants under Domestication,' he states (and he takes

B

his information from Azara, the author of 'Des Quadrupeds du Paraguay'), that amongst a horned race a polled bull had been born in 1770, and that, having been preserved, the animal founded a hornless breed.   There are also polled cattle in Norway ; while Dr Uno von Troil, writing in 1772, says Iceland is " well provided with cattle which are generally without horns."

It is not necessary to state all that is known regarding the many varieties of polled cattle that have at one time or other existed in the British Isles. It will suffice to mention where the more important have been found. Several of the herds of semi-wild cattle which existed in the parks around the seats of country gentlemen in England and Scotland early in the present century, but which have now, with two or three exceptions, wholly disappeared, were destitute of horns. At Somerford Park, in Cheshire, England, there has existed from time immemorial a pure herd of white polled cattle. Writing of this herd in 1875, the late Rev. John Storer said it then numbered twenty head; that it was of great though unknown antiquity, having been at Somerford Park for several hundred years ; that it had undoubtedly been at first derived from the wild herds of South Lancashire ; and that it had been long domesticated, but was probably the best representative extant of the hornless and tame variety of the original wild white breed. The semi-wild herd "of unknown origin but great antiquity" which was formerly kept at Wollaton Hall, Nottinghamshire, England, becoming extinct nearly sixty years ago, was without horns; as also were a similar herd at Whalley Abbey, Lancashire, which is said to have been transferred to Gisburne Park, Yorkshire, where it remained till about twenty-five or thirty years ago; and another at Middleton Hall, Lancashire. Dr Charles Leigh, in his work on the 'Natural History of Lancashire and the Peak of Derbyshire,' published in 1700, mentions the Middleton Hall herd, and presumes that the

cattle had first been brought there from the Highlands of
Scotland, although he does not state the grounds upon
which that assumption was based. According to Mr
Storer, this herd was in 1765 transferred to Gunton Park
in Norfolk, where it existed till some thirty-five or forty
years ago, having thrown off several branches which are
still represented by polled herds, at Blinkling, Woodbast-
wick, Brooke Hall, and other places in Norfolk.

In other districts in England there would seem to have
been races of polled cattle which have long ago disappeared.
Youatt, writing nearly fifty years ago, says, "The *Devonshire nats,* or polled cattle, now rapidly decreasing in
number, possess the general figure and most of the good
qualities of the horned beasts of the district;" while, in
reference to the "Northern or Yorkshire polled cattle," or
"Yorkshire polls," he says, they "are almost as large as
the horned beasts of that county, and as good for grazing and for the pail. Many breeders pay particular attention to the shape of the head of these polled cattle, and to
a certain extent also in the horned ones."

Passing into Scotland, we have several extinct as well
as two living races of polled cattle to note. The herd
of wild white cattle which existed at Ardrossan Park,
Ayrshire, for centuries, and became extinct about 1820, is
described as having been originally horned, but latterly
polled. Then it is clearly established that the Duke of
Hamilton's celebrated herd of semi-wild cattle, which has
existed at Cadzow Park, Lanarkshire, from the remotest
antiquity, although now horned, was formerly polled.
This latter curious and significant circumstance is authen-
ticated by the facts, that there is in preservation the
skeleton of a Cadzow ox showing the animal to have been
hornless, and that at the show of the Highland and
Agricultural Society of Scotland at Glasgow in 1844, two
polled specimens of the Cadzow herd were exhibited.

From a very peculiar source we have interesting testi-

mony of the existence of polled cattle in the Western Highlands of Scotland more than a hundred years ago. Dr
Samuel Johnson, in his published account of the journey
which he and Boswell, his faithful follower, made through
the Western Islands of Scotland in 1773, says: "The cattle
of Skye are not so small as is commonly believed. Since
they have sent their beeves in great numbers to southern
markets, they have probably taken more care of their
breed. Of their black cattle, some are without horns,
called by the Scots *humble* cows, as we call a bee *humble*
that wants a sting. Whether this difference be specific or
accidental, though we inquired with great diligence, we
could not be informed. We are not very sure that the
bull is ever without horns, though we have been told that
such bulls there are. What is produced by putting a
horned and unhorned male and female together no man
has ever tried that thought the result worthy of observation." When or how the polled cattle of Skye became
extinct, we unfortunately know nothing, for the earlier
writers on agricultural matters in the north of Scotland,
as elsewhere, describe cattle so generally, that any reference to such points as horns is very rare.

Pennant has left us interesting notes on his tours in
Scotland during the years 1769, 1772, and 1773, but only
in a few isolated cases does he give a minute description of
the cattle he had seen. He travelled through Sutherlandshire in 1769, and he tells us that it is " a country abounding in cattle, and sends out annually 2500 head, which
sold at this time [August 1769] (lean) at from £2, 10s. to
£3 per head. They are very frequently without horns,
and both they and the horses are very small." Of the
Sutherlandshire polled cattle we have also lost all trace.
In other parts of Scotland, polled strains which are now
extinct would seem to have existed in former times, but
we have mentioned the more important varieties known
to us.

It is well known that, although the native breeds of Ireland are now horned, there was at one time a polled race in that country. The most interesting and valuable testimony of this fact is the following extract from a review of a work on agriculture which appeared in the 'Irish Farmers' Gazette' in August 1847. The reviewer says: "A relative of our own, deceased a few years ago at the age of 114, had polled cattle in Ireland, and stated that the same breed had been in possession of his great-grandfather over 200 years before our informant was born. These cattle were chiefly black, and black and white on the back; occasionally red, and brindled with white stripes; in some cases all white but the ears, which were red; and he believed there was never any intermixture of English or Scotch blood amongst them for the period he alluded to. They possessed the characters of being great milkers and good butter-producers."

At the present time three distinct and well-defined breeds of polled cattle exist in the United Kingdom. Two, the Aberdeen or Angus, and the Galloway breeds, have their headquarters in Scotland; and the third, the Norfolk and Suffolk, in England. The first forms the subject proper of this volume. As to the others, a few sentences here may be of interest. There is hardly any doubt that the polled Galloway cattle are the direct but modified descendants of the horned race that formerly occupied the old Galloway district, which comprised an extensive tract of valuable grazing-land in the south-west of Scotland. According to Youatt, the "greater part" of the Galloway cattle were horned—some had medium horns and some were polled—about the middle of the eighteenth century; while Dr Bryce Johnstone, in his view of the agriculture of Dumfries, written in 1794, George Culley (who died in 1813 in his 79th year), in his works on live stock, and Aiton, Smith, and Singer, in their views of the agriculture of Ayrshire, Galloway, and Dumfriesshire, pub-

lished towards the end of the first decade of the nineteenth
century, all testify that, at the time they wrote, the majority of the cattle in these districts were hornless. The
Rev. Mr Gillespie, editor of the 'Galloway Herd Book,'
says: "I think there can be very little doubt but that
the Galloway and the West Highland breeds of cattle
have sprung from the same parent stock at a very remote
date. There is a close resemblance, even at the present
day, between a well-bred polled Galloway and a West
Highlander *minus* the horns. Indeed the similarity is so
great, that when we bear in mind the fact that previous
to the close of the eighteenth century almost all the
Galloways were horned, it is easy to understand how any
difference between the two types of animals may have
been produced by the different circumstances in which
they have long been placed, and the different treatment
to which they have been subjected."

These and other considerations support the conclusion
that the polled Galloway cattle had originated in the
manner already set forth as the most likely source of hornless cattle—*i.e.*, by the sudden appearance of one or more
animals without horns, and the preservation of the new
feature through selection in breeding. At what time the
first hornless animals may have appeared in Galloway we
cannot presume to say. We know from Youatt that about
1750 "only some of them were polled," and from the
several other writers named, that fifty or sixty years thereafter only a "very few" had horns. We may thus infer
that the absence of horns had been favoured by the Galloway farmers, and that they had so managed their herds
as to ultimately "breed out" the horned strains. Indeed
we know, from authentic sources, that the farmers of
Galloway had strong inducement from exterior quarters
to cultivate and extend their polled herds. Shortly after
the union of England and Scotland in 1707, there arose
an active trade in cattle between the two countries; and

in the exportation of lean cattle from Scotland to England, Galloway participated to a large extent. By the end of last century as many as 20,000 head of cattle were annually sent from Galloway to England—chiefly to Norfolk—to be fattened there for the southern markets. It is stated that the English buyers preferred the hornless cattle; and no doubt, this fact had induced the enterprising Galloway farmers—who had been taking advantage of the new outlet for the produce of their herds—to strive more anxiously than ever to get rid of the horns and to enlarge the ranks of their polled stocks. About twenty-five or thirty years ago, mainly through the encroachments of those excellent dairy cattle, the Ayrshires, and the changing of grazing-lands into tillage farms, the Galloway polled breed became greatly reduced in numbers. Indeed had not some enterprising gentlemen, who knew well the value of the race, taken active steps in the matter, it might have soon become extinct. Since the commencement of the 'Polled Herd Book' in 1862, the breed has regained much of the popularity it worthily enjoyed in bygone days. It is now reared extensively, and with much success, in Dumfriesshire, Kirkcudbrightshire, and elsewhere. In general appearance the Galloway resembles the polled Aberdeen or Angus breed, although we believe the one to be almost, if not indeed quite, as far removed from the other in kinship as from any of the other British breeds. The Galloways are handsomely formed, all black in colour, slightly ranker and coarser in the hair, rather thicker and stiffer in the skin, and also somewhat slower in maturing than the polled Aberdeen or Angus cattle. They are, however, justly celebrated as graziers, and are well deserving of the increased and growing attention now being bestowed upon them. They are noted for remarkable fixity of type.

The origin of the Norfolk and Suffolk polled breed has been the subject of considerable discussion. By some it is regarded as indigenous to the district it now occupies.

Others believe that it had sprung from Galloway polled
cattle introduced in the last century, probably soon after
the union of England and Scotland, when, as has already
been stated, a large number of cattle were driven every
year from Galloway and elsewhere in the south of Scotland into Norfolk and other parts of England. Youatt
in particular adopted the latter notion as to the origin
of the breed. He says that the polled cattle which he
found in both Norfolk and Suffolk (about 1832 to 1835),
and which are recognised as one breed, had " undoubtedly
sprung from the Galloway." It has been stated that in
1765 a herd of semi-wild polled cattle was introduced
to Gunton Park, Norfolk, from Lancashire. These wild
cattle became domesticated in Norfolk ; and it is believed
by some that they also have had a share in the building up of the improved Norfolk and Suffolk polls. In
a volume published a few years ago at ' The Field ' Office,
London, Mr John Coleman—the editor of the work, who
is himself a Norfolk man, and one of the best living
authorities upon the subject—in his article on this breed,
admits the probability of the Galloway polls being in the
main its progenitors, but claims part of the credit to an
" old native race." He says : " From a very early period
large numbers of polled Galloway cattle were brought
into the counties of Norfolk and Suffolk. There can be
little doubt that these were crossed with one or other
(probably both) of the native races, and that thus the
present breed of Norfolk and Suffolk red polled cattle
was called into existence." The characteristic colour of
this breed is a deep blood-red. Formerly, according to
Youatt, some were black, some red mixed with white, and
some black mixed with white, all having a " golden circle
about the eye." In recent years the breed has been greatly
improved, and it now ranks creditably among English
cattle.

CHAPTER III.

ORIGIN AND EARLY HISTORY OF THE POLLED ABERDEEN OR ANGUS CATTLE.

Scotch domestic cattle derived from aboriginal wild breed—All one variety
—Differing according to conditions of life—Origin of polled Aberdeen
or Angus breed—Natives of their present home—Loss of horns—
When ?—Probably centuries ago—Polled cattle in Angus in 1752, in
1757, in 1797, and in 1813—Youatt on Angus polled cattle—Polled
Galloways in Angus—Polled cattle in Aberdeenshire in last century—
Keith and Williamson on Aberdeenshire cattle—Youatt on ditto—
"Native low country" and "Buchan humlies" the same breed—
Letter from Mr Macpherson, Huntly, in 1832—Polled Galloway cattle
in Aberdeenshire—Early polled breeders in Aberdeenshire—Improved
breed direct descendants of Angus doddies and Buchan humlies—The
latter two same variety—Loss of horns.

WE have already indicated that, among naturalists and
other persons of distinction, there has been much discussion upon points connected with the origin of
domestic British cattle. It has been disputed whether
they should be regarded as the degenerate descendants
of the great *urus*, the magnified progeny of the slender
longifrons, or the composite product of these two.
There has also been discussion as to whether they have
been derived solely from the aboriginal wild cattle of
ancient Britain, or partly from these and partly from
domesticated cattle introduced from the continent of
Europe. There would seem to be strong reason to believe
that the latter idea may be applied correctly to several of

the English breeds. With the more truly Scotch races, however, the case is different. It is hardly possible, we think, for any one who has become acquainted with the early history of the country, and with the works and circumstances bearing upon the origin and domestication of British farm stock, to avoid arriving at the conclusion that the foreign element could have had but very little to do with the formation of the existing races of Scotch cattle.

At present four distinct breeds have their headquarters in Scotland—namely, the Ayrshire, the polled Galloway, the polled Aberdeen or Angus, and the Highland or horned breed. The first—a valuable dairy breed—has undoubtedly been to a large extent, if not wholly, derived from the introduction of foreign cattle, probably either of the Alderney or Holderness races. The other three are in the fullest sense of the term native Scotch cattle. It is right, we think, to regard them as the true lineal descendants of those wild aboriginal cattle that roamed through the forests and marshes of ancient Caledonia. Whether those wild aboriginal Scotch cattle, from which the existing races were derived, were of the *urus* or the *longifrons* type we need not, perhaps could not, determine. It is at any rate tolerably clear that they had all been of one variety. No one, we imagine, who investigates the subject fully and impartially, can escape the conviction that the three existing breeds of pure Scotch cattle had all originally been of one type, had all sprung from one common source. Differing in minor points in accordance with the variances in the climate and other conditions under which they had been reared, they would still seem to have been so nearly alike in all the chief characteristics which distinguish races from each other, that they ought to be viewed as belonging to one large well-defined group or type. Even yet, after having passed through long ages of widely different treatment, they present such strong similarities as afford substantial proof of their reputed common origin and close affinity. Those marked distinctions which they have come to display are, with the exception of that striking peculiarity, the want of horns (which shall presently be dealt with), exactly such as might be calculated to arise from the variations in their respective conditions of life, more particularly from the divergencies in the mode of treatment to which their owners have subjected them for many generations, nay, even for centuries. The truth of this statement will receive verification when, in dealing with the characteristics of the polled Aberdeen or Angus breed, we come to compare the sleeky polls which have been reared on the highly cultivated arable farms of the cold, dry north-east, with the more shaggy hornless cattle which have been produced on the soft natural pastures of Galloway, where the rainfall is much greater, and the cold less intense. Then a glance at the distinctions between the small "skranky" native horned cattle of the bleak, stormy, northern heights, and the massive, handsome Highlanders that occupy the lower, softer, greener, and better sheltered regions of the west, supplies equally forcible testimony of a similar kind.

In the foregoing digression we have indicated very briefly the grounds upon which we assign to all varieties of true Scotch domestic cattle (some years ago grouped into three distinct breeds) one common origin in the aboriginal wild horned cattle of ancient Caledonia. We have now to trace the source and early history of the Aberdeen or Angus polled breed. It follows from what has been stated that we regard this beautiful race as a direct branch of the aboriginal horned cattle of Scotland thrown off by those sudden, "proper," "spontaneous," or "accidental" "organic changes" referred to in the preceding chapter. We go further, and say that the breed is indigenous to the very districts which still form its headquarters, the north-eastern counties of Scotland, with Forfar and Aberdeen as chief centres. There we believe it to have originated, and there it has been brought out as one of the most handsome and most valuable of living varieties of cattle.

It would seem that in the ancient horned domestic cattle of Scotland there had been a tendency to those "spontaneous variations" that result in the loss of horns. We have seen that throughout the country numerous hornless varieties have appeared from time to time, most of them in such localities and under such circumstances as preclude the idea of their all having sprung from one offshoot, and force the conclusion that each represented a fresh departure or distinct "sudden organic change." We have learned from Johnson and Pennant that about a century ago there were hornless cattle in the Isle of Skye and in the county of Sutherland. Of these all traces have been lost. Youatt has told us that about the middle of the eighteenth century there were "some" polled cattle in the old district of Galloway. These, it has been seen, have developed into an important and well-established breed bearing the name of its native district. A mass of evidence has made us aware that, late in the last century and early in the present, polled cattle were pretty well diffused over certain parts of the north-east corner of Scotland. From these have come in direct descent the famous breed whose history and characteristics we have set ourselves to trace.

As to the precise date or period at which those sudden organic changes which have given us the Aberdeen or Angus polled breed may have occurred, we are left without any ray of light. It has been lost in the mists which envelop the darkened agricultural era ending with the last century. From negative evidence we conclude that the loss of horns must have occurred more than a hundred years ago. Beyond that the subject rests mainly on conjecture.

A careful investigation of all known works and circum-

stances relating to the matter has led us to believe that,
towards the end of the last century and beginning of the
present, the higher parts of that section of the north-east
of Scotland comprising the counties of Forfar, Kincardine,
Aberdeen, and Banff had been occupied by a horned race
of cattle, and the lower districts partly, perhaps mainly,
by the same race, and in part also by a polled variety.
In arriving at that conclusion, we have to some extent
been influenced by circumstantial as well as by direct
evidence We have already noticed the perplexing absence of precise descriptions of cattle in the earlier works
relating to the agriculture of the north, as well as of other
parts of the country. In several of the earlier books
dealing with rural matters in the north-east of Scotland,
reference is made to the varieties of cattle which then
existed; but, as a rule, they are simply described as
having been large or small, as useful and docile, or as
wild but handsome. In none of these publications do
we find what could be called a complete and minute
sketch of the animals referred to. It is thus found that
the identification of some of the varieties spoken of by
writers whose works appeared towards the close of the
last century or the beginning of the present is a matter
of considerable difficulty.

The breed takes one of its sub-titles from the old district of Angus, now mainly comprised in the county of
Forfar. It is proved that there have been polled cattle
in that district for a very long period of time. In a
pamphlet issued in March 1882, Mr James C. Lyell,
Monifieth House, Forfarshire, says: "That a breed of
hornless cattle existed in Strathmore [a strath which
runs through Forfarshire] in very early times, is attempted
to be proved from one of the ancient sculptured stones of
Meigle, which is figured on Plate LXXVII. of the Spalding
Club's 'Sculptured Stones of Scotland.' This stone is now
in the old schoolhouse of Meigle, which has been set apart

as a museum for the preservation of these wonderful relics of prehistoric times. After examining it carefully, I am not satisfied that the two cattle depicted on it represent hornless animals. Judging from the engraving alone, I believed that the cattle represented were polls; but the artist has not adhered strictly to particulars in his drawing, as any one may see who compares it with the stone. In the same volume there are other representations of cattle, apparently polled, but I have not had an opportunity of comparing the drawings with the originals."

The same writer states that in an old MS. account-book belonging to Mr. G. B. Simpson, Broughty-Ferry, Dundee, commenced in 1683 by Mr Grahame of Balmuir, Kincaldrum, Dryborough, Duntrune, Powrie, and Meathie, the following among many other entries of cattle transactions occur: "Account of oxn bought June 9th, 1752.—To one humble oax from James Cramond, at 30 [pound Scots, value 1s. 8d. sterling]; to for 5 oxn at Monifith, at 34, 170; to 3 at Forfar, at 28, 84; to a branded oax, at 37; to a coy at Monifith, at 22; to ane oax at Methie, at 50; to ane oax at Methie, at 36." A little further on this entry is found: "June 14th, 1757—bought at Tealing roup, a two-year-old quach doded, at 26, 12; a yellow qugh, one-year-old, at 21, 6; a black D, one-year-old, at 17, 16; a yelow stot, one-year-old, 22, 6; a black quach calf, at 12, 8; a yelow stot calf, at 17, 6." Another entry in 1757 gives a list of the stock then on Balmuir: "10 oxen in the plew; 6 hors and 2 stags (staigs); 2 dodeds; 4 at calf-time; 4 three-year-olds; 2 year-old stots; 3 three-year-old quaes; 5 year-old quaes; 2 calf stots; a cow." Mr Lyell, who has evidently examined carefully Ochterlony's description of Angus in 1684-85, as well as other early records of rural matters in Angus, says "the humble ox from James Cramond is the first mention of a polled beast" he had discovered. He seems, however, to think it probable that the "excellent breeds" which, according to Ochterlony, were kept two hundred years ago by the "Earles of Strathmore, Southesk, Panmure, and Edzell, Pourie, Balnamoone," may have been "polled or dodded."

The first printed reference we have found to polled cattle in Angus occurs in the Old Statistical Account of the parish of Bendochy, near Coupar-Angus, and on the border of Forfarshire. The Rev. James Playfair, the writer of the account of this parish, dated 1797, says: "There are 1229 horned-cattle, of all ages and sexes, in the parish. I have no other name to them; but many of them are dodded, wanting horns." These two sentences are exceedingly interesting and suggestive. In early times, the word cattle included both the ox and the horse; and it would seem that, to distinguish the former from the latter, the terms "black cattle" and "horned cattle" had been commonly employed. It is evident, from Mr Playfair's remarks, that even so late as the end of last century, the term "horned cattle" had not been limited to its literal meaning, but had comprehended all varieties of the ox. There is little doubt that, had he not been of a more discriminating turn of mind than many early writers on agricultural matters, and in particular than most of his brethren who contributed to Sir John Sinclair's 'Statistical Account of Scotland,'—in fact, had he not been a skilful naturalist, as well as a minister of the Church, he would have left us without the simple but significant explanation that, although he had no other name but "horned cattle" to give the cattle of Bendochy, yet "many of them are dodded, wanting horns." In all probability, the loose application of such distinctions as *black* and *horned*, just indicated, is largely to blame for the puzzling ambiguity which many of the early writers have thrown around most of the varieties of cattle they pretended to describe. The statement of Mr Playfair, however, in conjunction with the quotations produced from Mr Lyell's pamphlet, would seem to be sufficient to justify the belief that, during the closing de-

cades of the eighteenth century, there had been throughout Angus a considerable proportion of polled cattle. This
idea is further supported by the following quotation from
the ' General View of the Agriculture of Angus,' published
in 1813 : " With regard to the permanent stock, they are
of various breeds, and differ very much from each other in
shape and quality. Little attention is paid to the selection
of the males or females by whom the breed is propagated ;
and no pains have been taken to elicit a breed distinguished
by any peculiar properties, either as a good milking or a
good fattening breed. A great proportion of the permanent stock are humlies—that is, they have no horns ; and
in this particular they seem allied to the Galloway breed."

Youatt's account of the origin of the polled cattle of
Angus is strangely contradictory. In his well-known
work on ' Cattle, their Breeds and Management,' published
about 1835, he says : " There have always been some polled
cattle in Angus ; the country-people call them humlies, or
dodded cattle. Their origin is so remote, that no account
of their introduction into this county can be obtained from
the oldest farmers or breeders. The attention of some
enterprising agriculturists appears to have first been directed to them about sixty years ago [that would be about
1775], and particularly on the eastern coast and on the
borders of Kincardineshire." Having described the characteristics of the breed, and noted in particular the operations of the late Mr Hugh Watson of Keillor, Youatt remarks
that the Angus cattle " are not quite equal to their ancestors, the Galloways, in quickness of feeding and fineness of
grain," and adds, that " in many places the Angus cattle
have gradually given way to the old occupiers of the land,
the Galloways." The inconsistency between these statements is very striking, and detracts greatly from the
value of Youatt's evidence. In support of the suggestion
which has sometimes been made, by others as well as
Youatt, that the Galloways had been the ancestors of

the polled cattle of Angus, there is absolutely no proof whatever.

About 1792, or soon after, some Galloway bulls were introduced into Forfarshire by Lord Panmure—the first importation of the kind of which we have any record —and although, as expressed by Mr Bowie, Mains of Kelly, the Galloway cross added to the "dodded ranks," it was not satisfactory in its results, and was consequently abandoned. It has been shown that, nearly half a century before Lord Panmure's introduction of Galloway bulls, there were polled cattle in Angus, and that, in 1797, "many" of the cattle in the parish of Bendochy, at the extreme corner of Angus, from Lord Panmure's estates, were "dodded, wanting horns." These, and the other considerations previously submitted, have impelled us to set aside Youatt's second statement as to the origin of the Angus doddies, and to accept the conclusion that they are, as already stated, indigenous to the district; and that the peculiarity of no horns having suddenly appeared at some remote period, has attained the fixity it now displays through long-sustained selection in breeding.

A variety of polled cattle has also existed in the county of Aberdeen from time immemorial. The breed, now scattered all over the county, formerly had its headquarters in the Buchan district, which originally embraced the lower parts between the river Don and the river Deveron. It is stated by Keith, in his 'Diocese of Aberdeen,' published in 1730, that the Thanedom of Buchan "is so called because abounding of old in pasture, paying its rents in cattle—for the word in Irish signifies *cow-tribute.*"[1] In all the early works dealing with the agriculture of Aberdeenshire, the cattle of Buchan are referred to as a distinct and useful breed; but in no book or record of any kind written before the present century have we

---

[1] By others the name Buchan is said to be derived from the Gaelic words "Bo," meaning an ox, and "caen," the head.

found it stated whether they were polled or horned. We however possess evidence which proves not only that very early in the present century a polled variety of cattle *prevailed* over the lower parts of Buchan, but also that, at different places in the county of Aberdeen, hornless cattle had been bred, even during the eighteenth century, and that too with some degree of care and skill. It cannot be doubted that the polled breed, which is well known to have been the prevailing breed in Buchan about the opening of the present century, was the direct continuation of those famous old Buchan cattle which are spoken of as a valuable "native" race in early works; and in view of the fact that the absence of horns was a dominant characteristic seventy or eighty years ago, we can hardly be wrong in concluding that, far back into the eighteenth century, if not indeed much earlier, there had been polled cattle in Buchan.

Dr Skene Keith, in his 'Agricultural Survey of Aberdeenshire,' published in 1811, states that this county then raised "a greater number and value of black cattle than perhaps any other in Scotland." He dwells at some length upon the circumstances connected with the earlier attempts to improve the native cattle of Aberdeenshire, and presents a table giving "a general view of the different breeds of black cattle in the county of Aberdeen," at the time he wrote. In this table four varieties are enumerated, as follows: (1.) Largest English or foreign breed; (2.) Largest Scotch or Fifeshire, mixed with native; (3.) Native and unmixed lowland or Aberdeenshire; and (4.) Native and unmixed or Highland breed. But while he thus classifies the different varieties, and also gives much interesting information as to their respective working, fattening, grazing, and milking properties, he produces a most imperfect representation of their general appearance. He tells us nothing either as to their form or colour (the term "black cattle," as already stated, was at one time applied to all domestic varieties of the ox), nor does he say whether any or all were horned or hornless. He submitted his "general view" of the breeds for correction to Mr George Williamson, farmer, St John's Wells, Fyvie, Aberdeenshire, who was then "the principal cattle-dealer in the north of Scotland," and who, with his two brothers, James and Robert, generally sold "about 8000 cattle yearly in the markets of England and of the south of Scotland, of which two-thirds are raised in this county." The Messrs Williamson approved of the table, and supplied Dr Keith with a great deal of information regarding the cattle trade. They stated that "they decidedly prefer the true native breed, unmixed, and raised by good keeping, to the mixture of the Falkland or Fifeshire breed with that of this county, and consider both these to be much superior to the English or to any foreign breeds. . . . They consider the *small* Highland cattle, which are generally bought by inferior dealers, as *too restless and impatient* for feeding well. They prefer the native low-country breed to the larger ones, as they are most easily maintained, more hardy in work, have flesh of the finest grain, and pay better in proportion to the goodness of their keep."

It should be noted that the testimony of the "Stately Williamsons" (as they were familiarly called) carries with it the very highest authority. Besides being largely engaged in cattle-dealing, they also farmed extensively. Dr Keith says: "They rent about 2000 Scotch acres of land, besides £500 of grass rent, within the county. They have at present [1810] about 200 acres of turnips employed in feeding as many black cattle and in rearing 400 cattle or winterers." Mr George Williamson in particular was a man of great worth and enterprise. Over his grave in the churchyard of Fyvie, Aberdeenshire, there is a monument bearing the following inscription: "George Williamson, late in St John's Wells, died 17th April 1823, aged 75, on whose remains this monument was erected by

the Aberdeenshire Agricultural Association, as a mark of
respect for his upright and honourable conduct in private
and public life, and in testimony of the great benefit derived by the county of Aberdeen from his meritorious
exertions as an eminent cattle-dealer for upwards of fifty
years." George Williamson had commenced dealing in
cattle about 1770. It thus becomes evident that long
before the advent of the present century, there had been
a distinct native breed in the lower parts of Aberdeenshire, possessed not only of such well-defined features as
to mark it out as a separate breed, but also of such excellent properties as that the most extensive and most experienced cattle-dealer and farmer of the day regarded it
as superior to all the other varieties which then existed
in the county. It would seem that the Williamsons had
taken special care to impress upon Dr Keith their "decided" preference for the native low country breed in its
purest form. It was the *true* native breed *unmixed*"—
the native low country breed—which they so unhesitat-
ingly placed above the others.

Youatt, in his work on cattle, brought out about 1835,
gives a great deal of information regarding the different
varieties of cattle then existing in Aberdeenshire. Like
Dr Keith, he divides them into four classes—namely,
"the native unmixed Highland" horned breed, "which
he found towards the interior and on the hills;" the
crosses between the native and Fifeshire and other races
(which came to be known as the Aberdeenshire horned
breed); another "variety consisting of all the pure breeds
from the north of England and the south of Scotland;"
and the "polled cattle of Buchan." Regarding the last,
he says: "Besides these [the other three classes mentioned
above] there is a breed of polled cattle, said by some to
be different from the Galloways, and to have existed from
time immemorial. Others, however, with greater reason,
consider them as the Galloways introduced about thirty

years ago, and somewhat changed by change of climate
and soil. They are of a larger size than the horned,
although not so handsome. Of late they have been much
improved by careful selection from the best of their own
stock, and are becoming more numerous. In some districts they are equal to or are superseding the horned
breed. They usually equal in weight the larger varieties
of the horned breed, but the quality of their meat is said
to be inferior. As they are, in a measure, occupying the
situation of the larger horned cattle, these, in their turn,
are intruding on the cattle of the hill country." Youatt
quotes from Mr R. Gray, who, writing in reference to the
Buchan cattle in the 'Quarterly Journal of Agriculture,'
says: "The best sort used to be polled, and some of them
that do not begin to have Ayrshire blood in them are so
still, and are of a dark or brown colour. The breed of
cattle in Buchan is peculiar to that part of the country."

Youatt would seem to have favoured the idea that the
polled cattle which he found existing in Buchan—*i.e.*, the
lower parts of Aberdeenshire—at the time he collected his
information—between 1832 and 1835—were not really
"native cattle," but "Galloways introduced about thirty
years ago." We have been unable to discover any evidence in support of this suggestion, and we possess such
strong testimony in opposition that we are compelled to
regard it as erroneous. Dr Keith has told us that in 1811
there were four distinct classes of cattle in the county—
namely, (1.) "English or foreign breeds;" (2.) "Scotch or
Fifeshire, mixed with native;" (3.) "Native and unmixed
lowland or Aberdeenshire;" (4.) "Native and unmixed or
Highland breed." Some twenty or twenty-four years later,
Youatt found the first, second, and fourth varieties still in
the county. The native unmixed Highland breed, he
says, existed "towards the interior and on the hills," but
he makes no mention of the native unmixed low country
breed. In its place in the lowlands, where it was left by

Dr Keith in 1811, Youatt finds "a breed of polled cattle;" and in our opinion the latter ought to be regarded as the direct continuation of the former. In other words, we think it is manifest that the "native low country breed" which Youatt found there some twenty or twenty-four years later, really belonged to the same race,—the one, in fact, being the direct lineal descendants of the other. If this were not the case, then we would be shut up to the belief that in the interval between the times when Keith and Youatt collected the information for their respective works, the "native low country breed" had entirely disappeared—an occurrence that we imagine could scarcely have happened. It is extremely improbable that a "native" race possessing such valuable properties as the Williamsons assigned to the "native low country breed" should be so utterly neglected and abused, as to drive it out of existence in the short period of twenty years. Of all the varieties in Aberdeenshire in 1811 it would appear to have been decidedly the best; and on that account we should rather expect it to have been preserved with even more than usual care. The Buchan humlies, spoken of by Youatt, form the only link through which its continuity could possibly be established; and to us it seems manifest that these Buchan humlies have really come in direct descent from the valuable native unmixed lowland breed so highly prized by George Williamson and his brothers.

In support of these conclusions we have still further evidence. Youatt, when collecting material for his work on cattle, applied to the late Duke of Gordon for information regarding the stock of cattle on and around his Grace's estates. At the desire of his Grace, the late Mr A. Macpherson, then factor on the Gordon estates in the Huntly district, sent to Youatt a communication on the subject. For some unknown reason, only a portion of the information supplied by Mr Macpherson was made use of; but through the kindness of his grandson, Mr Andrew Mac-

pherson, solicitor, Huntly, we are enabled to produce
the communication in full. Mr Macpherson entered the
farm of Gibston in 1803, and his letter to Youatt was
written from Huntly on 28th September 1832, when he
was sixty-three years of age. It proceeds as follows :—

" The county of Banff and the adjoining counties of Aberdeen and Moray may all be regarded as one district for the
present purpose. In the Buchan quarter of Aberdeenshire a
variety of the polled cattle is the principal breed; but over
all the rest of the district, that which is generally termed the
Aberdeenshire horned is the ancient, and is still the prepon-
derating stock. It is well known and appreciated by cattle-
dealers and graziers from the Moray Firth to Smithfield.
These two kinds have existed time out of mind in the district, and their origin is believed to be equally obscure with
that of the other animals, wild and tame, which abound in the
land. The Galloway breed of polled cattle was introduced
into the district about thirty years since, and has increased
so much that it now forms a large portion of the heavy stock
in our markets. Several other breeds were also brought in
of late years—such as the Ayrshire, and the Teeswater Short-
horned from England; but these are hardly observable in
mass, being so few in number. Crosses are numerous between the breeds mentioned; but these do not appear as distinct classes, being mostly joined to the parent stocks, as they
happen to resemble the one kind or the other in size, or the
article of horns. They possess, however, some of the qualities of both the stocks from which they are derived. A cross
between the Argyleshire, reckoned the largest of the real
Highlanders, and the heavy-horned, has been found valuable,
and encouraged. The horned Aberdeenshire vary greatly in
size, according to selection and keeping. In the fertile districts of the low country, abounding with summer pasture
and winter food, they reach at full growth from fifty to seventy
stone Dutch, and have been known to feed to the weight of
fifteen and sixteen hundredweight. In the hills and barren
parts they reach from twenty to thirty stone; and between
these extremes every variety of weight abounds, depending
on the circumstances stated. The polled cattle, being kept
chiefly in the low country, do not vary so much in size as the

horned. They generally equal the heavier classes of the horned in that respect; but it is not considered here that their quality is equal to that of the horned when brought to the shambles. All cattle have greatly improved within the last thirty or forty years, owing to the introduction of the turnip husbandry, sown grasses, and the general improvements in agriculture. The cattle of this district are well adapted for grazing and the dairy. They are pastured in the fields in summer, and fed with straw and turnips in winter; sometimes with steamed potatoes. Calves are fed with milk warm from the cow. That is the general practice; but they are sometimes allowed to suck, and in a few instances reared partly upon oil-cake.

" The present Duke of Gordon has at different times within the last thirty years brought the best selection of bulls and cows that could be found in Galloway into the district. The same also from Argyleshire, the Scottish isles, and the Teeswater from Yorkshire, from which great benefit has arisen, by their increase and mixture with the original stock and with each other; and his Grace's example has since been extensively followed by agriculturists and breeders of cattle."

We thus have evidence of a most trustworthy kind, that while undoubtedly the Galloway breed of polled cattle had been introduced into Aberdeenshire about the opening of the present century, and that while by the time Youatt had commenced to collect his information the progeny of this introduction had increased so much as to form "a large portion of the heavy stock in our markets," there had also been a distinct "variety of the polled cattle" forming "the principal breed" in the "Buchan quarter of Aberdeenshire," where it had "existed time out of mind." Mr Macpherson says the polled cattle were kept chiefly in the low country; and this, together with his other statements, supplies substantial confirmation not only of the idea that the famous "native low country breed" so highly commended by George Williamson, and the polled cattle which Youatt speaks of, were really the same variety, but also that the former, like the latter, were hornless.

Mr Ramsay, in his 'History of the Highland and Agricultural Society of Scotland,' published in 1879, gives an extract from a communication which he had received from Mr George Stodart, "lately farmer in Culter-Cullen, Foveran, now (January 1879) in his 97th year, and who made his first purchase of cattle in 1801." Mr Stodart, who died in June 1880, says :—

"There were at the beginning of the century both polled and horned cattle in Buchan, but the horned cattle were mostly in the Highlands of Aberdeenshire. The horned and polled were mixed in the low districts. The biggest market was Aikey Fair, and there was another market, Kepple Market, in New Machar. At Aikey Fair about one-half were polled and one-half horned, but they were all of the Aberdeenshire breed."

Mr George Barclay, now farmer at Stocherie, and his forefathers, bred Aberdeenshire cattle at Auchmill and Yonderton, King-Edward, for more than two hundred years, and a good many of their animals were polled. The late Mr John Marr, Cairnbrogie, Tarves, commenced to breed Buchan polled cattle early in the present century, probably about 1810, or soon after. His son, Mr W. S. Marr, Uppermill, one of the most extensive breeders of Shorthorns in Aberdeenshire, favoured the authors with a communication in reference to his father's herd. He says: "My father commenced to collect them before I remember—I would suppose about sixty-five years ago. They were not like the present polled. They had not the same points, being more round in the quarter, short-legged, thick, well-fleshed animals; most of them brown round the muzzle, and many of them with a brown stripe down the back. They were known as the Cairnbrogie breed. There were several public sales of young bulls and heifers at Cairnbrogie, when they realised good prices for these days. There were no Shorthorns in the district at that time. For the purpose of improving their stock, my father and the late Mr Hay, Shethin, then in the farm of Craigies, went to Galloway about 1823 [probably two or three years earlier] and bought the pick of that district. I do not remember the number they bought, but I think they would have had between 30 and 40. They were not kept long, as they did not retain condition with the same treatment as his own stock, and they were sold at a public sale along with some of his own breeding. I think Mr Hay did not keep his half of them long either."

Mr William Stronach, Ardmeallie, Huntly, who was an extensive breeder of cattle early in the century, states that in 1835 he purchased a Shorthorn bull to cross with his stock of cows, which " consisted generally of Buchan humel, the Aberdeen horned, or a mixture of these breeds."

We have already seen that Mr George Williamson, St John's Wells, Fyvie, had been an ardent admirer of the " native low country breed." We have expressed our opinion that these famous native cattle were not only the progenitors of the modern Buchan humlies, but were themselves also polled. At any rate, there is un-doubted testimony that Mr Williamson was a breeder of polled cattle. The late Mr M'Combie of Tillyfour stated that he obtained some of his earlier polled animals from St John's Wells. In his first catalogue, issued in 1850, an entry reads as follows : " Matilda, an Aberdeen cow, bred by the late Mr Williamson, St John's Wells."

Another of the foremost agriculturists of his day, the late Mr Robert Walker, Wester Fintray, was also a breeder of polled cattle ; and his herd would seem to have been continued by his son James, who succeeded him. Dr Skene Keith, writing in 1810, refers to Mr Robert Walker as an advanced farmer, and quotes the following as showing the success he had attained as a breeder and feeder of cattle—

viz., that he (Mr R. Walker) had "received £50 each for two bullocks reared upon his farm, and killed at seven years old; that he received £35 each for other two only four years old; and that he has frequently received £30 for young stots either sold to the cattle-dealer, or fed to the butcher." It is not stated that these were polled cattle, but it is proved beyond doubt that very early in the present century Mr Walker did breed polled cattle at Wester Fintray. It is stated in the 'Farmer's Magazine' for 1846 (vol. ii.), that Mr James Walker was then one of "the most successful breeders of black cattle in the north of Scotland, particularly the polled Aberdeenshire breed, for which he has acquired much and well-merited celebrity."

It would appear that although it had its headquarters in Buchan, the polled breed had even in the last century been reared in other parts of the county. Mr William Anderson, Wellhouse, Alford, in a communication dated April 13, 1881, says: "My father and uncle farmed land in the Vale of Alford in the end of the eighteenth century, and bred polled cattle. Sometimes the bulls were black and sometimes brindled, but they were always polled. My father would not have bred from a horned bull, and he always disliked horned cattle. He and my uncle took prizes for black polled cattle at the shows of the Vale of Alford Agricultural Society, formed soon after 1830." Mr Anderson also states that there were other breeders of polled cattle in the Alford district, such as Mr Reid, Greystone, father of the present tenant; Mr Taylor, Wellhouse, and others. Then through Mr James L. Douglass, banker, Ballater, and others, we learn that polled cattle had been bred very early in the present century in the upper districts of Aberdeenshire. Mr Douglass says: "As to the introduction of polled cattle into the Cromar district, I cannot assign a particular date. The late Rev. Mr Brown, minister of Coull, who died in the end of

1823 or beginning of 1824, had a small farm rented along with his glebe, and had a very excellent stock of cattle, chiefly of the polled breed ; also the late Mr Harry Lammond, of Pitmurchie, on his farm of Strathmore, previous to his death in 1829, had polled cattle for many years, always using a polled bull. The late Mr Robert Douglass, farmer, Culsh, had a polled bull in 1822, while his cows were horned, as almost all the cows in Cromar at that date were."

We have thus set forth as briefly as possible the main reasons which have induced us to regard the Aberdeen or Angus polled breed not only as a direct branch of the aboriginal cattle of Scotland, but also as indigenous to the very districts which still form its headquarters,—the north-eastern counties of Scotland, with Forfar and Aberdeen as chief centres. The improved breed is derived directly from the ancient polled cattle of Angus and Buchan—two varieties of the same type, known in the former as "Doddies," and in the latter as "Humlies." And we have endeavoured to show the great antiquity of the race in its hornless form in these two districts. We believe that originally the loss of horns had arisen from those spontaneous variations, or accidental or proper sudden organic changes, spoken of by Darwin, Smith, and Low, and referred to in the preceding chapter. Nothing has been discovered that would enable us to fix the precise date at which these changes had occurred. It has certainly not been within the past hundred years—probably not within the past two or three centuries.

CHAPTER IV.

IMPROVEMENT OF THE BREED.

Little inducement to improve cattle a hundred years ago—Beef at one
penny per pound—Rearing cattle for farm-work — Introduction of
Holderness and Fife breeds — Demand for beef — Working cattle
abandoned—Improvement of native races—Choice of polled variety as
beef cattle—Improvement of polled cattle in Angus—Operations of
Mr Hugh Watson, Lord Panmure, Earl of Southesk, Mr William
Fullerton, Messrs Mustard, Mr Bowie, and others—Improvement of
the breed in Kincardineshire—Operations of Mr Walker, Portlethen,
and others — Improvement in Aberdeenshire — The efforts of Mr
William M'Combie of Tillyfour, and others—Introduction of Shorthorns—The crossing craze—Improvement in Banff and Moray—The
Ballindalloch and other herds—Encouragement by Agricultural So-
cieties to improvers of polled cattle—The 'Polled Herd Book'—The
Polled Cattle Society.

IT would seem that in the north of Scotland little attention had been given to the improvement of cattle till after
the middle of the eighteenth century. Prior to that there
had been scarcely any inducement to bestow trouble or
expense in developing either the beef or the milk producing properties of cattle. During the Queen Anne
wars, subsequent to the union of England and Scotland
in 1707, the farmers of the south of Scotland began to
export their surplus cattle to England. That trade continued and increased considerably, but did not until long
after extend its benefits in any substantial form to the
counties in the north and north-east. It is stated that in

1762 the English supply of salt beef for the Navy had proved insufficient, owing to a visitation of cattle disease in England, and that the deficiency in that and some succeeding years had been made up from Scotland "at the average price of one penny per pound."

Mr G. Robertson, in his 'Rural Recollections,' remarks that in 1740 the largest ox in the county of Kincardine, weighing from 43 to 51 imperial stones, "could have been bought for 20s., or at most, 21s.;" and that by 1764 the same class of cattle, "as full fed as the county could make them," would have sold at from £3 to £4 each. It is thus seen that even later than the middle of last century the farmers of the north of Scotland had little or no encouragement to develop the beef-producing properties of their cattle.

Other circumstances, however, arose which resulted in a marked improvement of the cattle in the north-eastern counties. Throughout these counties, as in other parts of Scotland, a large part of the farm-work was formerly—in some districts even after the opening of the present century —accomplished by oxen. The native cattle of the northeast having originally been rather small for the heavier part of this work, the larger farmers obtained their ploughoxen from the south of Scotland, chiefly the Lothians. About the middle of last century the Lothian farmers began to give up cattle-rearing for the growing of wheat and barley. This, together with the general progress of the country following upon the Union and the protracted wars of the time, raised the price of cattle, and induced the farmers of the north-east to turn their attention to the rearing of their own plough-oxen. The importing of these oxen from the south became decidedly a losing arrangement ; and soon after the middle of last century, the more practical landlords, and larger and more enterprising farmers, commenced the systematic improvement of the native stock, with the view of rearing cattle sufficiently

large for tilling their land and for other field-work. The
native cattle were not only submitted to better treatment,
but were also crossed with bulls of larger breeds, some
being taken from England—notably of the Holderness
breed—some from Holland, and some from the south of
Scotland. Satisfactory results were not obtained until
bulls of the Fife or Falkland breed were introduced. This
breed (said to be descended mainly from some English
cows which Henry VII. sent as a dowry to Margaret, his
eldest daughter, who in 1502 was married to James IV.
of Scotland, then residing chiefly at Falkland Palace, in
Fifeshire) was large and handsome; and between bulls of
it and cows of the native breeds of the north-east of Scotland, excellent varieties, both of work and butcher cattle,
were reared.

At length, however, in the increasing prosperity of
the country, and the advancement of skilful farming,
the true function of the ox — the production of beef —
came to be recognised and developed. The demand
for beef grew rapidly; and therefore, by degrees, the ox
was withdrawn from the plough, and put instead into the
feeding-stall. It was then found that development of
bone and muscle was not so essential or so valuable a
property as a capacity to produce, at an early age, a heavy
carcass of beef of the highest quality. The production of
beef had in fact become the main object to be aimed at.
Bone and muscle were discounted, and the new ideal was
a maximum of beef with a minimum of bone, little offal,
and prime quality.

The farmers of the north-eastern counties abandoned the
rough big-boned varieties of cattle they had formerly found
suitable to their wants, and cultivated instead the smaller,
broader, and better fleshed sorts that were less useful in
earlier years when oxen had to do the work of horses.
Cattle were more liberally fed and more carefully housed,
and thus the north-east of Scotland rapidly became famous

for its beef-producing cattle—a distinction which in recent years it has pushed into still greater prominence.

In this new demand for beef-producing cattle the progenitors of the polled Aberdeen or Angus breed were not long in having their excellent fattening-properties duly recognised. We have seen that in Aberdeenshire the " native low country breed "—the ancestors of the Buchan humlies—had nearly a hundred years ago become quite famous among the leading cattle dealers and feeders for having "flesh of the finest grain," and for being better payers, " in proportion to the goodness of their keep," than any of their contemporary varieties. Then, from Youatt and others, we learn that in Angus the doddies had at an early date developed similar qualities—"their natural fitness for stall - feeding, and the rapidity with which they fattened." The discovery of these valuable properties in the native polled race naturally enough induced its owners, both in Angus and Aberdeen, not only to strive to maintain its purity, and develop still further its better qualities, but also to effect improvement in points where defects were apparent. We cannot fix the precise date when these systematic efforts to improve the breed within its own limits actually commenced, either in Angus or Aberdeen. We have good reason to believe that in both they had been begun some time before the advent of the present century.

It will be convenient, and in accordance with the order in the preceding chapter, to notice first the progress of the breed in Angus. The late Mr Hugh Watson, farmer, Keillor, Meigle, Forfarshire, if not the first, was certainly the most systematic and most successful early improver of the breed. Both his father and grandfather were ardent admirers of the Angus doddies. The late Mr William Fullerton, Mains of Ardestie, in a manuscript document (which has been kindly placed at our disposal by his son, Mr James Fullerton, Dundee), states that Mr Hugh Wat-

son's grandfather "had the breed for upwards of forty
years, which leads us back to 1735." We understand
that the Watson family is in possession of a letter from
the late Mr Henry Stephens, author of 'The Book of the
Farm,' from which it would seem that at a still earlier
date the great-grandfather of Mr Hugh Watson had for a
long period reared doddies on his farm of Cattie, in the
parish of Bendochy, near Cupar-Angus. Mr Hugh Watson was born on his father's farm of Bannantyne, of New-
tyle, in 1789, and became tenant of the neighbouring farm
of Keillor in 1808. It is stated that from his boyhood he
loved the Angus doddies, and he certainly lost no time in
devoting his energies to their improvement. When he
entered Keillor he received from his father six of his
"best and blackest cows, along with a bull, as a nucleus
for an Angus doddie herd." It is recorded, however, by
his son, Mr William Watson, now in the United States
of America, that he was not satisfied with the merits
of these, and that "he started in the same summer for
Trinity Muir Market, Brechin, and purchased the ten best
heifers and the best bull he could procure showing the
greatest characteristics of the breed." Mr William Watson says : "The heifers were black, brindled, and black
with brown muzzles and brown streak along their back.
The bull was black, and all black my father stuck to, thus
working the other colours out of fashion." Mr Fullerton
states that Mr Watson, in selecting these animals, had the
assistance of Mr Mustard—"likely Mr William Mustard,
Fithie, his brother, Mr James Mustard, not having been
tenant of Leuchland till 1811,"—and adds that the heifers
came from "near Farnell, which points to either the late
Mr Ruxton, tenant of Farnell, or to the late Mr David
Aymer, tenant of East Carcary, as their breeders. Both
these gentlemen were long keepers of this breed, and Mr
Aymer's stock had a peculiar style of their own. I purchased his two-year-old heifers in 1834. They were par-

D

ticularly good, had extraordinary coats of hair, and peculiarly large, hairy, well-set ears." With these sixteen
females and two bulls, Mr Hugh Watson commenced the
systematic improvement of the Angus doddies—a work
which he prosecuted with distinguished vigour and success
till near the close of his life in 1865. It will be more
convenient to notice in a subsequent chapter the leading
families tracing to Mr Watson's herd. Several of these
have become extinct in the female line, but eight still
survive, although some are not generally recognised as
Keillor tribes.

Mr Watson was eminently fitted for the important
work he took in hand. He was a man of surpassing in-
tellect, unlimited perseverance, and accurate judgment.
In many ways he would seem to have presented a striking resemblance to his great prototypes in the Shorthorn
world, the brothers Colling, who had commenced the improvement of Shorthorn cattle just twenty-eight years (in
1780) before the famous Keillor polled herd was founded.
It has often been remarked with truth that what the Collings were to the Shorthorns, Mr Hugh Watson was to the
polled Aberdeen or Angus breed. The late Mr William
M'Combie of Tillyfour, M.P.—the only man who could be
set up as a rival to Mr Watson—bears the most generous
testimony to his eminence. In his work on 'Cattle and
Cattle-Breeders,' Mr M'Combie says: "Among those who
have distinguished themselves as breeders of Aberdeen
and Angus polled cattle, the late Hugh Watson, Keillor,
deserves to be put in the front rank. No breeder of Aberdeen and Angus will grudge that well-merited honour
to his memory. We all look on him as the first great
improver, and no one will question his title to that distinction. There is no herd in the country which is not
indebted to Keillor blood."

Unfortunately, there is little known of Mr Watson's
operations as a breeder. In his wide circle of intimate

friends he included the late Mr John Booth, Mr Wetherell, Mr Anthony Maynard, Mr William Torr, and other noted breeders of Shorthorns; and there is good reason to believe that in many points connected with the building up of his herd of improved polled cattle, he was to some extent guided by the experience of these great patrons of the rival breed. Mr H. H. Dixon, in 'Field and Fern,' says Mr Watson "was purely catholic in his cattle tastes. Bracelet, Charity, and one or two more of the pure Booths, were the models he kept in his eye in building up his blacks; and even in a shire so strongly wedded to its own breed, he did not shrink from saying so." His motto would seem to have been, "Put the best to the best, regardless of affinity or blood." He bred from none but the choicest specimens at his command, and did not hesitate to follow the example of the Collings, the Booths, Thomas Bates, and other celebrated Shorthorn breeders, in mating animals closely related to each other. It is evident that he practised in-and-in breeding to a considerable extent. It is also clear that he aimed at building up particular lines or families, and that to some extent he bred each of these families within itself. He did not pursue persistently that intricate system of in-and-in breeding adopted by most of the noted early improvers of Shorthorns; but in this point he so far followed their example. Perhaps the truest description that could be given of his method of breeding is, that he bred from none but the best—those that came nearest to his ideal—and that he did not care whether these were closely related or not. He no doubt discovered that under his improved system of breeding, which may truly be called a system of "selection," he could raise better animals than could be found on Trinity Muir, or anywhere else in those days; and that of course led him to breed in closer relationship than he might otherwise have done. He may not have approved of in-and-in breeding in principle, but, like the earlier improvers of Shorthorns, he frequently put it into practice, with results that were eminently satisfactory.

Mr Watson would seem to have been a careful, liberal, and successful feeder, as well as a skilful breeder. A few years after starting his herd, he commenced the practice of allowing calves to suckle cows in the house, and found that it produced excellent results. This plan is described by himself as follows: "The cows intended for nursing generally calve early in the season, about the month of January or February, when a stranger calf is procured from some of the small tenants in the district who have dairies. This calf is suckled with the others by the same cow; and although the cow at first shows great dislike to the stranger, in a few days she receives it very quietly, care being taken that both are put to suck (one on each side) exactly at the same time by tying the calves' bands to the stall or the band of the cow, so as to keep each calf at its own side. They remain with the cow for fifteen or twenty minutes, by which time her milk is perfectly drawn away. As the calves advance in age they eat hay, sliced potatoes, porridge, and other food that they are inclined to take. By the 1st of May, or as soon as grass is ready, they are weaned and turned out from the byre, when two fresh calves are immediately put into their stalls and receive the same treatment, excepting that they are turned out at twelve o'clock, after they have got their suck, to eat grass, and are brought into the byre again in the evening, when the cows come in to be sucked. This set is ready to wean by the 1st of August, and a single calf is put into the feeding-pen and fattened for the butcher, the season being now too late for rearing. As these are fed off, the cows are let off milk, having each suckled *five calves*. It is necessary to have a very careful and steady person to attend to the suckling, which has to be done three times a-day—viz., early in the morning before the cows are turned out to grass, at mid-day, and in the

evening when the cows come into the byre for the night
and get a little cut grass, tares, or other green food. The
byre is arranged so that the cows have each a stall of
about 4 feet wide, with their heads to the wall; and on
the opposite wall the calves are tied up, two in a stall,
exactly behind the cow, so that there is little trouble in
putting them to the cows, and no chance of misplacing
them. The fat calves have in some seasons been sold at
£5 each, this being the scarcest time of the year for veal."

Mr Watson gave much attention to the preparing of
cattle for the show-yard, and early in his career he in this
respect achieved great success. His son, Mr William
Watson, says: "The list of awards to my father during
his lifetime for various descriptions of stock—in England,
Ireland, Scotland, and France—amounted to upwards of
five hundred." The first occasion on which he exhibited
polled cattle under the auspices of the Highland and
Agricultural Society of Scotland was at Perth in 1829.
His first prize pair of polled oxen at that show attracted
much attention by their size, symmetry, and quality.
One of these was a great beauty, and a choice butcher's
animal. He was exhibited at the Smithfield Show in
London the same year, and there too he was greatly admired. When slaughtered by a leading metropolitan
butcher (Mr Sparks, of High Street, Marylebone), his
carcass was found to be of very rare quality, the meat
being fine in the grain and well mixed; while his fat
weighed no less than 240 lb.—about 84 lb. more than
the fat of the famous "Durham Ox." Another remarkable animal shown at Perth in 1829 by Mr Hugh Watson
was a heifer, which, like the oxen, was bred by himself,
and which, at the request of the Highland Society, was
exhibited at the London Smithfield Show as a sample of
the excellence to which the Scotch polled breed might be
brought. There she was the admired of all admirers.
She was then 4½ years old, and her dead weight was esti-

mated at between 130 and 140 Dutch stones.   Before
being slaughtered, she, like the "Durham Ox," was
publicly exhibited for some time.   Her purchaser at
Smithfield paid £50 for her—a very handsome price for
more than half a century ago.   She was a round, low-set,
compact animal, the symmetry and evenness of her parts
having been wonderful.   The bone of her fore-leg, which
her breeder long kept in his possession, is said to have
been little thicker than that of a roe-deer.   At the time
she was killed, her brisket was barely 8 inches from the
ground, and her inside fat was found to be equal in weight
to one-fourth of her gross dead weight.   Another wonderful animal of Mr Hugh Watson's breeding, "Old Grannie,"
or the Prima Cow, No. 1 in the 'Polled Herd Book,' is
noticed in a subsequent chapter.   Mr H. H. Dixon, in
'Field and Fern,' says Mr Watson gave the Irish a taste
of the quality of his earlier polled celebrities.   "His four-
year-old Angus ox [out of Old Grannie] went over, and
was placed first for the Purcell Challenge Cup at Belfast,
and, yet, strange to say, died after all in the plough at the
Royal Home Farm, when he was rising eighteen.   Still
his fame was in all lands, as a traveller in India found
his portrait pasted up on a temple of Vishnu."

Besides Mr Watson, there were in Angus a good many
enterprising agriculturists, who at a very early date—some
even earlier than Mr Watson—devoted attention to the
breeding and improving of the native polled cattle.   Prominent among these were the late Lord Panmure ; the
late Sir James Carnegie ; Lord Southesk ; the late Messrs
Mustard, Leuchland and Fithie ; the late Mr Bowie, Mains
of Kelly, and his son, Mr Alexander Bowie, the present
tenant ; the late Mr William Fullerton, Mains of Ardestie ;
the late Mr Ruxton, Farnell ; the Hon. Charles Carnegie ;
Mr Ferguson, Kinnochtry ; Captain Carnegie of Craigo ;
Mr J. Lyell, Shielhill ; the late Mr Scott, Balwyllo ; Mr
Lyall, Carcary ; Colonel Dalgairns of Balgavies ; Mr

Aymer, East Carcary; Mr Leslie, The Thorn; Mr Archibald Whyte, Braedownie; Mr W. Whyte, Spott; the late Mr Lyell, Arrat; the late Mr Goodlet, Bolshan; the late Mr Pierson, The Guynd, &c. Of these Lord Southesk, Mr Alexander Bowie, Mr Ferguson, Mr Leslie, and Mr Whyte still possess herds, and their operations will be noticed afterwards.

Accounts will be found of two different herds at Kinnaird Castle—one of great antiquity, annihilated by rinderpest in 1865, and another founded about two years ago. There is good reason to believe that the property of the Carnegie family has long been a stronghold of the breed. Ochterlony, in his description of Angus in 1684, 1685, states that the Earl of Southesk owned the whole of the parishes of Kinnaird and Farnell, which contained "ane excellent breed of horses, cattle, and sheep;" and from other sources we gather that polled cattle had been bred extensively on the estates even before the commencement of the present century. The Hon. Charles Carnegie, brother of the present Earl of Southesk, has kindly furnished us with an account of the extinct Kinnaird herd, in which he states that it is impossible to trace the origin of that old stock, "which had probably gone on from generation to generation from a very remote period."

Mr Bowie, Mains of Kelly, owns the oldest herd now existing. It was commenced in 1809—the year after the foundation of the Keillor herd. What we shall have to say regarding it, more particularly in reference to the bulls produced in the herd, will fully establish its title to rank as one of the most useful agents in the improvement of the breed. Mr Ferguson, Kinnochtry, commenced to rear polled cattle in 1835, and has ever since been a devoted, intelligent, and successful breeder.

It is generally understood that the late Lord Panmure (born 1771, died 1852) did not himself establish a herd of polled cattle till about 1835. We have, however, good reason for believing that long before that time—in fact, prior to the opening of the present century—he had given close attention to the rearing of the native polled cattle, and had done much to encourage his tenants and others in improving the breed. Mr William Fullerton gives it as his opinion that few men did more for "the doddies" than Lord Panmure, and remarks: "He not only bred beasts himself which did good service, but, as President of the East Forfarshire Association, he fostered the breed. He stimulated his tenants to breed good doddies, and amongst others, Mr Bowie, Mains of Kelly, and his worthy father. I must confess he filliped me on to try my skill as a breeder." In another manuscript document in our possession, Mr Fullerton says: "In the early part of this century, Lord William Ramsay Maule of Panmure, seeing there were points in the doddies capable of being improved, tried the experiment of having so many Angus cows put to Galloway bulls. Procuring eight or ten of these bulls, he had them suitably located over his estates. The result of this crossing was such a failure, that all attempts to improve the old breed in this direction were abandoned. Lord Panmure after this disappointment set himself to form a Society for the purpose of advancing the agriculture of the district, and, in particular, for improving the old doddie breed. In this he was greatly aided by the other landlords of the east of Angus, more especially Mr Arklay of Dunninald. The movement culminated in the formation of the East Forfarshire Farming Association, Lord Panmure being chosen perpetual President, and Mr Arklay, Vice-President for the first year. No breed of cattle were awarded prizes but the breed of the county. The competition took place yearly on Trinity Muir in the latter end of July or first week of August. Members competing had to bring forward at least a pair of queys, and for every 100 acres and above, which they farmed, they were bound to bring forward another quey. In com-

peting in the class of stots, a pair had to be exhibited for
the first fifty acres farmed, and for every other fifty acres
the competitor was bound to bring forward another stot."
There is in existence, we believe, an oil-painting of three
cows exhibited under the auspices of the East Forfarshire Association, one being a "rigged" cow belonging to
the late Mr James Black, Barrelwell, and the winner of
the first prize on the first occasion on which the Society
offered prizes for cows.

It would seem that Lord Panmure had still been
anxious to try the effect of a fresh cross upon the Angus
cattle, for in 1838 or 1839 he commissioned his agent, Mr
Collier, Hatton, to select for him half-a-dozen of the best
polled Buchan heifers to be obtained. One of these
heifers, named Black Meg, and purchased from Mr Silver,
Netherley, Muchalls, on the Kincardineshire coast near
Aberdeen, became the dam of the celebrated bull Panmure 51, whose sire was a bull named Hector, bred by Mr
Hector, Fernyflatt, Kincardineshire. Lord Panmure held
a public sale in 1841, when Mr William Fullerton purchased the young bull Panmure 51. The dam of Panmure 51 passed into the hands of Mr Bowie, Mains of
Kelly, and to him she produced the cow Mary, dam
of Mary of Kelly 2nd 1192, progenitrix of Mr Bowie's
Martha tribe, to which his race of bulls called Major belong. Another animal of Lord Panmure's breeding was
the cow exhibited by Colonel Dalgairns of Balgavies, at
the show of the Highland Society at Dundee in 1843,
where she gained the first prize. At that show Mr Fullerton also headed the old bull class with Panmure 51,
and won the first prize for lots of three cows, in which
latter class he had strong competition from the Keillor,
Portlethen, Leuchland, and Wester Fintray herds. One
of Mr Fullerton's three cows was Dairymaid, bred by
Lord Panmure. It is interesting to note that descendants of Colonel Dalgairns's first-prize cow at Dundee

(bred by Lord Panmure) exist in Mr Scott's herd at Easter
Tulloch.

Mr William Fullerton's long connection with the polled
breed will be referred to later on. He was born in 1810,
began to breed polled cattle in 1833, and died in 1880.
His first important purchase was that of the famous cow
Black Meg 766, and from one of her daughters and the
celebrated bull Panmure 51, he produced Queen Mother
348, foundress of the meritorious Queen tribe. Mr Fullerton was a painstaking and intelligent breeder, and his
name will ever live as that of one of the most distinguished
improvers and most accurate judges of his favourite hornless breed. The two brothers, Messrs William Mustard,
Fithie, and James Mustard, Leuchland, both bred polled
cattle early in the present century. The latter was not
only one of the earliest, but also one of the most careful,
breeders of doddies ; and descendants of his stock made an
excellent appearance in other herds, notably in that of
Mr Lyell, Shielhill. Mr William Fullerton has recorded
with genuine humour some of his earlier contests with his
good neighbour Leuchland. In 1844 they had a trial of
strength with eight cows from each herd, the "stakes"
being an "Edinburgh dress-coat." Mr Fullerton won, and
we are informed that the coat was in due time delivered
at Ardovie. "Mr James Mustard," says Mr Fullerton,
"bred with greater care than almost any one I ever knew."
By the late Mr M'Combie of Tillyfour the system pursued at Leuchland is also very highly commended. Mr
Ruxton, Farnell, was another intelligent and systematic
breeder, paying close attention to the purity of his herd.
He at one time had a blue or light-coloured tribe, which
had been kept on the farm in a pure condition for many
years. A few were black, but the majority were blue.
They were called "droners," and Mr Fullerton tells us that
he "never saw a secondary droner blue or black." The
late Mr Scott, Balwyllo, built up and long maintained a

large and excellent herd, which will be found fully noticed later on.

The Howe o' Mearns, in Kincardineshire,—a continuation of the Vale of Strathmore,—has also had a share in the producing and improving of the polled Aberdeen or Angus breed. Formerly, polled cattle were more numerous amongst the farmers of Kincardineshire than now. Mr William Fullerton, who assisted in awarding the prizes at upwards of thirty shows in the county, states that he did not think that any time since 1833 there were, relatively speaking, more than one-fourth as many doddies in Mearns as in Angus, but adds that he had seen twenty-five polled cows in the "bught"—adjudicating ring—at Fettercairn which would have done honour to any county. Foremost amongst the improvers of the breed in Kincardineshire must be placed the late Mr Robert Walker, Portlethen Mains, near Aberdeen, who for more than half a century occupied a leading position, not only as a breeder of polled cattle, but also as an advanced agriculturist generally. He founded his herd in 1818, and continued it with much success till his death in 1874. He bred and owned many noted animals, including the show-yard heroes Fox Maule 305, and Banks of Dee 12. In one season the descendant of the latter bull gained no fewer than seven first prizes and one second. Referring to Mr Walker's success in the show-yard, Mr M'Combie, in 'Cattle and Cattle-Breeders,' says: "It would be endless to attempt to sum up his victories—local, national, and international,—they are spread over such a large surface." Among the others in Kincardineshire who took a leading part in the improvement of polled cattle were the late Mr Hector, Fernyflatt; his son-in-law, the late Mr Glennie, Fernyflatt; the late Sir Thomas and the late Sir Alexander Burnett, Barts. of Leys ; Colonel M'Inroy, The Burn; and the late Sir John Stuart Forbes, Bart. of Pitsligo, Fettercairn House, who gave substantial encouragement and assistance to Mr Ravenscroft in start-

ing the 'Polled Herd Book.' The principal existing herds
in Kincardineshire are those owned by Sir Thomas Gladstone, Bart. of Fasque; Mr Scott of Easter Tulloch; and
Mr George J. Walker, Portlethen Mains.

It has already been indicated that in Aberdeenshire, as
in Angus, the systematic improvement of the native polled
breed within its own limits would seem to have been carried on to some extent before the beginning of the present
century. It has also been seen that by 1810 the polled
cattle of Buchan had attained to the highest favour with
the leading cattle-dealers and cattle-breeders, who even
then preferred it in its pure "unmixed" state to all the
other varieties in the county. The superior beef-producing
properties of the native polled breed naturally induced
the leading agriculturists to draw to it more exclusively
as the demand for beef became greater; and thus it is
found that by 1820 a good many of the more prominent
farmers in the lower parts of Aberdeenshire had commenced the rearing of pure polled herds on an extensive
and systematic scale. Prominent among these were the
late Messrs Williamson, St John's Wells; the late Mr
Robert Walker, Wester Fintray; the late Mr Marr, Cairnbrogie; the late Mr Hay, Shethin; and the late Mr Stephen,
Conglass.

After this there came a peaceful intruder, which ultimately became so powerful as that for a time it threatened to entirely displace the native polled cattle. The
fame of the improved Shorthorns after Colling's great sale
in 1810 (when Comet reached 1000 guineas) spread rapidly
over the length and breadth of the land. About the end of
last century, Shorthorns had been introduced into Scotland
by Mr Robertson of Ladykirk, Berwickshire, and General
Simpson of Pitcorthie, Fifeshire. Mr Rennie of Phantassie
obtained cattle from Mr Robertson, and at the first shows
of the Highland Society at Edinburgh in 1822 and 1823
exhibited Shorthorn oxen, which, by their extraordinary

merit, excited great astonishment and admiration. In 1827, at a public sale of Shorthorns held at Phantassie, Captain Barclay of Ury, Kincardineshire, and Mr Alexander Hay, Shethin, attended, and both made purchases. Within the next few years their example was followed by Mr Cruickshank, Sittyton ; Mr Grant Duff of Eden ; Mr Longmore of Rettie, and others,—and from the herds of these gentlemen drafts of young Shorthorn bulls were dispersed either publicly or privately every year. The improved Shorthorn was found a very different stamp of an animal from the big, coarse, ungainly Holderness or Teeswater that, as we have seen, had been tried at an earlier period. The improved bulls, mated with native polled cows, produced better butcher cattle than had yet been known—animals remarkable alike for aptitude to fatten, wealth of flesh, constitution, and quality of beef. Crossing in this fashion therefore became almost a craze. Handsome profits were realised from it, and for a time it seemed as if farmers had been rendered oblivious to the risk of running out their reserve of pure polled cows, which were as necessary as the Shorthorn bulls for the raising of the class of cattle which had aroused this excitement, and which soon reached the highest prices in Smithfield market. And it was not only in Aberdeen that the craze for crossing had displayed itself. It also invaded Angus, and there induced many farmers, much to their own chagrin afterwards, to allow their excellent herds of pure-bred polled cattle to degenerate into stocks of ever-varying crosses.

It is fortunate, however, that in both the great strongholds of the polled Aberdeen or Angus breed there were a number of shrewd, far-seeing agriculturists who grasped the full significance of the new fashion in cattle-breeding. They recognised the danger which threatened the native polled cattle, and with commendable courage they determined to disregard the popular taste, and to maintain more jealously than ever the purity of the polled race. The men who had taken the lead in preserving the Angus doddies are mentioned in an earlier portion of this chapter.

In the county of Aberdeen, one man, the late Mr William M'Combie of Tillyfour, M.P., stands ahead of all others as the great deliverer of the polled race. He was among the first to discover its threatened extinction; and knowing full well its value to the country, he resolved to do what in him lay to protect it from the danger to which it had become exposed. It is doubtful, we think, whether any other single individual has ever done more to improve and popularise any breed of live stock than the late Mr M'Combie did to improve and make known his pet race of polled cattle. Taking up the good work so systematically commenced by Mr Hugh Watson, Mr William M'Combie carried it on with a skill and success that have few equals, and that will hand down his name to posterity as that of the chief improver of the polled Aberdeen or Angus breed. It has been said that what the Collings did for Shorthorns, Mr Hugh Watson did for the polled breed. It might be said with equal truth that what the Booths have been to the "red, white, and roan," Mr William M'Combie was to the "glossy blacks." Than that, higher credit could be paid to no breeder of live stock; and every one who has any acquaintance with the subject will admit that it is due to the memory of the late Laird of Tillyfour.

Mr M'Combie was born at Tillyfour in 1805, and died in the spring of 1880. His father, who owned the small estate of Tillyfour, was for many years one of the leading cattle-dealers in the north of Scotland; and young Mr M'Combie, before he had completed his "teens," also devoted himself to trading in cattle. About 1829 he became tenant of the farm of Tillyfour, and immediately after he gave up dealing in lean stock, and commenced the formation of a polled herd. It would seem that his

father, who of course had exceptional opportunities of
knowing the value of the breed as compared with others,
had held the native polled cattle in high favour.   Mr
William M'Combie, in replying to the toast of his health
at a banquet to which he was entertained in Aberdeen in
1862, said: " I was led by a father whose memory I revere,
to believe that our polled cattle were peculiarly suited to
our soil and climate, and that, if their properties were
rightly brought out, they would equal, if not surpass, any
other breed as to weight, symmetry, and quality of flesh.
I resolved that I would endeavour to improve our native
breed."   The Tillyfour herd dates from 1830, and was
finally dispersed in 1880, a few months after the death of
its worthy owner.   The material used and produced by
Mr M'Combie, as well as the system of breeding which he
pursued, will be so fully described afterwards, that a
few sentences will suffice here.   He started his herd with
cattle bred in the county, some on Tillyfour itself, and
some by the Messrs Williamson, St John's Wells, Fyvie;
Mr Walker, Wester Fintray, and others.   With these old
local strains he worked for some years, producing many
excellent animals, and gaining numerous prizes.   At Mr
William Fullerton's sale at Ardovie in 1844 he purchased
Queen Mother 348 as a yearling heifer for £12, 10s., and
from her he built up his celebrated Queen tribe, which
has probably done more than any other to spread and
enhance the good name of the breed.   It will be shown
in our account of the Tillyfour herd that Mr M'Combie
pursued close breeding to a considerable extent, and that
with much ingenuity he blended the material which ultimately produced such excellent results as the progress of
his herd displayed.

Mr M'Combie's success in the show-yard has few parallels in the history of farm-stock.   In the third edition of
his volume entitled 'Cattle and Cattle-Breeders,' no fewer
than seventeen pages are occupied by a mere record of

the premiums won by animals belonging to the herd prior
to 1875. Not content with a large share of Scotch and
English honours, he several times entered international
contests in France, and on all occasions returned with
new laurels and fresh fame for his favourite blacks. Probably the crowning victory of his life was achieved at
the great International Exhibition held at Paris in 1878.
On that occasion, in addition to several leading "class"
honours, he carried off, with a group of beautiful young
polled cattle, all bred at Tillyfour, not only the £100
prize for the best group of cattle bred by the exhibitor in
the Division foreign to France, but also the £100 prize
"for the best group of beef-producing animals bred by
the exhibitor." In fat stock as well as breeding shows,
Mr M'Combie has often proved invincible; and altogether,
it may safely enough be said that the high reputation
which the breed has deservedly gained beyond the bounds
of the British empire has to a very large extent been
fostered by the remarkable show-yard achievements of the
Tillyfour herd.

The show-yard career of "Black Prince," one of Mr
M'Combie's many fine polled oxen, deserves special mention. This animal, bred at Tillyfour, was exhibited at
the Birmingham and Smithfield Fat Stock Shows in 1867,
when four years old, and at both shows made almost a
clean sweep of the special honours. At Birmingham he
won the £15 and silver medal as the best in his class;
the Earl of Powis's silver cup, value £25, for the best
steer or ox bred and fed by the exhibitor; two special
prizes for the best Scot; the Hotel and Inn keepers' thirty-
guinea cup for the best animal in all the cattle classes;
and the gold medal or £20 for the best steer or ox in the
show. At Smithfield he won the first prize and silver
medal as the best in his class, and the £40 silver cup for
the best steer or ox in the show, along with the £20 gold
medal to his breeder. From Birmingham the ox was, by

the Queen's desire, forwarded to Windsor for her Majesty's inspection; and her Majesty was afterwards graciously pleased to accept from Mr M'Combie her Christmas baron of beef from the carcass of this fine animal, of which her Majesty had expressed great admiration. A year or two afterwards her Majesty visited Tillyfour, mainly for the purpose of inspecting Mr M'Combie's herd of celebrated polled cattle, and she was interested in finding, in Mr M'Combie's dining-room, the head of the beautiful animal she had seen at Windsor. Black Prince was sold by Mr Giblett to Messrs Lidstone & Scarlet, Bond Street, London, for £120, the head having been retained by Mr M'Combie, who had it stuffed and placed in a prominent position in his dining-room at Tillyfour.

The important work to which Mr M'Combie devoted himself so assiduously for nearly half a century has been helped forward in a very substantial manner by many other enterprising agriculturists in the county of Aberdeen, both landlords and tenant-farmers, who have also devoted much money, time, and attention to the improvement of the native polled cattle. The operations of most of these will be referred to when we come to notice extinct and existing herds. The following (in addition to those already named) deserve to be mentioned here, as having specially distinguished themselves as improvers of polled Aberdeen or Angus cattle—namely, Mr William M'Combie of Easter Skene; Colonel Fraser of Castle Fraser; Mr Harry Shaw, Bogfern; Mr James Reid, Greystone; Mr William Anderson, Wellhouse; the late Colonel Gordon of Fyvie; the late Mr Dingwall Fordyce of Brucklay, M.P.; Colonel Ferguson of Pitfour; the late Sir Alexander Bannerman, Bart. of Crimonmogate; the late Dr Robertson of Indego; the late Mrs M'Combie, East-Town; Mr Farquharson, East-Town; Mr Walker, Ardhuncart; Mr Walker, Westside of Brux; Mr Lumsden of Clova; Mr Farquharson of Haughton; the Marquis of Huntly; the

E

Earl of Aberdeen; Mr P. Davidson of Inchmarlo; Mr
Reid, Baads; the late Mr M'Combie, Cairnballoch; Mr
Hunter, Confunderland; Mr P. Cran, Old Morlich, &c.

The contiguous counties of Banff and Moray have in
no small degree contributed to the improvement of the
polled Aberdeen or Angus breed. In fact, the premier polled
herd of the present day—that belonging to Sir George
Macpherson Grant, Bart. of Ballindalloch, M.P.—has its
home on the borders of these two counties, near the
junction of the rivers Spey and Aven. The origin of
the Ballindalloch herd has been lost in the mists of antiquity. Of its early history nothing more definite is
known than that (as described by Mr M'Combie) it is
" perhaps the oldest in the north," and that it has been
"the talk of the country " for very many years. The
present Baronet is an enthusiastic and accomplished
breeder. For many years he has given close personal
attention to the management of his large and valuable
herd, and the success achieved by him has been so remarkable that we believe no one will dispute the title of the
Ballindalloch herd to the premier position, which, since
the dispersion of the Tillyfour herd in 1880, has been
generally assigned to it. The influence which the Ballindalloch herd has exercised in the improvement of other
stocks could hardly be overestimated. Sir George has
been specially successful in the rearing of bulls ; and these
have been eagerly sought after by breeders throughout
the country, in whose herds they have given undeniable
testimony of their choice breeding. In a word, the fame
of the Ballindalloch herd is equally great in the breeding
paddock, the show-yard, and the sale-ring ; and this is
probably the highest tribute that could be bestowed upon
any herd. The other leading improvers of polled cattle
in Banff and Moray have been the late Mr George Brown,
Westertown ; the late Mr Robert Walker, Montbletton ;
the late Mr Morison of Bognie ; the Earl of Fife ; Mr W.

J. Tayler of Glenbarry; the late Mr Alexander Paterson, Mulben; the late Mr Skinner, Drumin, and his son, Mr William M. Skinner; the late Mr Robertson, Burnside; and the late Mr John Collie, Ardgay. The late Mr George Brown's father bred polled cattle at Westertown more than half a century ago; and when Mr George Brown himself succeeded to the farm in 1853, he devoted his attention in a very special manner to the rearing of the breed. He procured the best material available, and devised a skilful and systematic plan of breeding which gave promise of grand results, but which was prematurely closed by his early and much-lamented death in 1874. Of the operations of Mr Brown and other breeders and improvers more anon.

'Improvers of polled cattle have received hearty encouragement in their noble work from the many influential agricultural societies which have existed in Scotland during the greater part of the present century. We have seen that at least one society in the old county of Angus —the East Forfarshire Farming Association—was started early in the century, mainly for the purpose of promoting the improvement of the native polled cattle. In the county of Aberdeen, where there are more than a score of similar societies, the improvement of the polled breed has in most cases been one of the chief objects kept in view. As early as 1812 "black humble" cattle were exhibited and won prizes at the show of the Garioch Farmers' Club, which was established in 1809, and still continues as active and useful as ever. At the second show of the Highland Society, held at Edinburgh in 1823, a second prize was won by a polled or "dodded" ox bred in Aberdeenshire; while at the Society's first provincial show, held at Perth in 1829, prizes were offered for polled cattle. On the latter occasion, as noted elsewhere, Mr Hugh Watson exhibited some of his famous Keillor doddies, both in the fat stock and breeding classes.

Ever since that time the Highland Society has given due attention to the polled breed of the north-east, and has more than once taken official notice of its peculiarly high merits. At the Perth show of the Highland Society in 1852, there would seem to have been an excellent display of polled Aberdeen or Angus stock, for in the portion of the official report of that show referring to these, we find the following sentences : "The Directors rejoice that this and preceding shows indicate a praiseworthy amount of effort and care on the part of breeders of polled stock, followed by a corresponding improvement in the stock. They cannot but regard it as the most valuable breed of Scotland, combining as it does in a great measure the constitution of the Highlander with the feeding properties of the Shorthorn." In 1834 the Highland Society appointed a Committee to consider and report as to the general arrangements for its live stock shows. The Committee gave special attention to the classification of " the particular classes of stock, or breeds as they are called, which the Society will recognise and encourage in their pure state by the offer of specific premiums ;" and recommended that the live stock department be divided into four sections—one for Shorthorns, one for West Highlanders, one for Ayrshires, and another for " the polled breeds of Galloway and the northern districts."

The Society adopted the recommendation, and acted upon it until 1848, when separate sections were arranged for the Galloways and the polled cattle of the north-eastern counties.

The starting of the 'Polled Herd Book' forms an important event in the history of Aberdeen or Angus cattle. The movement was taken up actively by Mr Edward Ravenscroft, who, after many years of difficult work, made heavier by an unfortunate mishap, succeeded in bringing out the first volume in 1862. The collection of the materials for the first volume had been commenced about

twenty years before that date, but in 1851 the whole of
the matter which had been obtained was destroyed in
the fire which in that year took place in the museum of
the Highland Society in Edinburgh. This was indeed a
great misfortune, and it seemed for a time as if the desired
object would have to be abandoned. In 1857, however,
Mr Ravenscroft, at the urgent request of some of the leading breeders, headed by Lord Southesk, recommenced the
work, and succeeded in completing the first volume by
1862. Although, as we shall have occasion to point out
afterwards, the volume contains many inaccuracies, its
publication was nevertheless an event of great importance
to the breeders of polled cattle. Mr Ravenscroft, in the
preface, says: "While regretting the apathy of some
breeders, and the opposition of others, during the progress of the work, I should be ungrateful did I not record
the valuable assistance I have received from the Earl
of Southesk; Sir John Stuart Forbes, Bart.; the Hon.
Charles Carnegie, M.P.; Mr Alexander Bowie, Mains of
Kelly; Mr Fullerton, Ardestie Mains; Mr Robert Walker,
Portlethen; and the late Mr Threshie, Dumfries. Without their aid I am afraid the work would never have seen
the light." Soon after the issue of the first volume the
polled herds in Angus were decimated by rinderpest;
and this, together with the apathy created among the
breeders of pure-bred stock by the mania for rearing
crosses, which succeeded the general introduction of Shorthorns into the north, resulted in long and unfortunate
delay in bringing out the second volume of the 'Herd
Book.'

On the occasion of the Highland show at Perth in
1871, a meeting of breeders of polled cattle was held, when
it was decided that the 'Herd Book' should be revived.
The copyright of the work had previously been obtained
by Mr Alexander Ramsay of Banff, and arrangements were
made whereby the work should be carried on jointly by

Mr Ramsay and Mr H. D. Adamson, late of Balquharn, Alford. The second volume was brought out in 1872, and since then four volumes have been issued. The third, fourth, and fifth volumes were produced under the sole charge of Mr Ramsay, and breeders of polled cattle are much indebted to him for the careful and efficient manner in which he executed the difficult and important work that devolved upon him. The sixth volume was published in 1881. It contains the names of 190 breeders, and the register of 1193 animals—855 cows and heifers, and 308 bulls. There have now been registered 1930 bulls, and 5054 cows and heifers, making in all 6984 animals. In the first four volumes Galloway cattle are registered along with the polled Aberdeen or Angus breed, but the Galloway Cattle Society acquired the copyright of the Galloway portion after the issue of the fourth volume. Since then the 'Herd Book' has been confined exclusively to the race to which it was from the outset mainly devoted. The following is the qualification for entry in vol. vii., which is in preparation—viz., "Either (1) that the sire and dam are both in the 'Herd Book;' or (2) that the sire, and the sires of the dam and of the grand-dam, be all entered in the 'Herd Book,' and that the grand-dam should come from a reputedly pure stock, provided that this rule shall not apply to the produce of cows whose produce has already been registered in the 'Herd Book.'"

Another important step in the history of improved polled Aberdeen or Angus cattle was the establishment of the Polled Cattle Society. The movement was promoted heartily by Sir George Macpherson Grant, Bart., M.P., and others; and at a meeting of breeders held at Perth in 1879—strangely enough, under the same auspices as the meeting held in 1871 to consider the revival of the 'Herd Book'—it was formally decided that the Society should be established. Accordingly, the Society was started in the autumn of that year. Her Majesty the

Queen became Patroness of the Society; the Marquis of Huntly was chosen as the first President, and Sir George Macpherson Grant and the late Mr William M'Combie of Tillyfour the first Vice-Presidents. On the death of Mr M'Combie in 1880, the late Earl of Airlie was appointed one of the Vice-Presidents. Mr Alexander Ramsay was appointed Secretary. The Society acquired the copyright of the 'Herd Book' from Mr Ramsay, and an Editing Committee was appointed to supervise the registering of animals. The chairmanship of the Editing Committee has been intrusted to the Hon. Charles Carnegie, whose extensive and accurate knowledge of all matters pertaining to the breed fits him peculiarly for this responsible work.

The objects of the Society are set forth as follows: (1.) To maintain unimpaired the purity of the breed of cattle hitherto known as polled Aberdeen or Angus cattle, and to promote the breeding of these cattle; (2.) To collect, verify, preserve, and publish the pedigrees of the said cattle, and other useful information relating to them; (3.) To further the above objects by continuing the issue of the publication called the 'Polled Herd Book;' (4.) To receive subscriptions and other payments in return for, or in consideration of, the issue of copies of the publications of the Society, and the entry in any such publication of the names and pedigrees of polled cattle; and (5.) To make by-laws for conducting the business and regulating the proceedings of the Society, and to enforce the same by fines or otherwise."

CHAPTER V.

CHARACTERISTICS OF THE BREED.

Early characteristics of the northern polls—Two varieties in Buchan—
The effect of early crosses with Shorthorns—The colour of the breed
—"Scurs"—Shapes, size, and symmetry—Increase in size—General
improvement in form, &c.—Comparison of polled and Shorthorns—
Full description of a typical polled animal—Comparison with Galloways—The breed's surpassing beef-properties—Excellent quality of
its beef — High value of polled crosses—Early maturing — Weights
and prices of polled oxen—Milking-properties—Wide and growing
reputation of the breed—Great increase in value.

THE reader will already have obtained glimpses of the
chief characteristics of the native polled cattle of Angus
and Aberdeen. Youatt's testimony to the early development of rapidly fattening-properties in the Angus doddies
has been quoted. We have also indicated the very high
character given by the Messrs Williamson, the chief
Aberdeenshire cattle-dealers and cattle-breeders of eighty
years ago, to the beef-producing and paying qualities of
the Buchan humlies as far back as 1810.

It would seem that formerly there were two types of
polled cattle in Buchan. In a communication addressed
to us, Mr William Forbes, Newark Brick-Work, Ellon,
whose grandfather was a farmer in Buchan, and bred
polled cattle, says : "The cattle in Buchan about half a
century ago and earlier might be said to have consisted
of horned and polled black cattle in about equal propor-

tions. The polled cattle were of two classes, one large
and another small. I knew the small kind well. They
were rather puny creatures, always thin in flesh, and very
badly used. They were pre-eminently the crofter's cow,
as they were able to live through the winter on the straw
of oats and bere, and water, if necessary. Of the larger
portion of the cattle, about one-half were jet black, excepting the udder, which was usually white, and often the
whole underline was white. They could not stand starva-
tion so well as the small polls, but with better treatment
they gave a heavier yield of milk. When creamed, however, their milk was thinner than that from the small
cows. A considerable portion of the cattle were large-
sized, well-fleshed brindled polls; and these were the
finest-looking animals in Buchan. When well fed, they
had a short glossy coat of hair; some were good milkers,
but some went to flesh and fat instead of milk. A few
were of a dull red colour, but they were not so high in
favour as the brindled cattle. The polled cattle were the
dairy stock. The butter they produced was very fine
in summer and autumn, but hard and white in winter.
The establishing of a beef trade with England, and the
introduction of Shorthorn bulls and turnip husbandry,
opened up a new era for Buchan. The native cattle
fattened well, and money was made by doing so. Shorthorn bulls were introduced, and put to all kinds of cows.
Often when a Shorthorn bull was mated with a small
polled cow, the produce was a black poll of the finest
character—immensely superior to either of the parents.
When a heifer of this stamp was again put to a good
Shorthorn bull, the result was quite as fine a black poll,
of still larger size. If the produce were also a heifer, and
mated with a pure Shorthorn bull, the produce was still
a poll, yet larger in size, but bluish-grey in colour. If a
heifer again, and put to a Shorthorn bull, the produce was
once more a grey poll, probably lighter in colour. When

this form of crossing was continued further, Shorthorn colours appeared, sometimes with scurs, but oftener with the regular short horns of the male parent. I observed this experiment tried in several cases, with exactly the same result. With the larger polls with white underlines, the horns and colour of the Shorthorn bull were earlier transmitted to the produce, generally at the second or third crosses. I therefore look upon the small polls without white spots as the pure original Buchan humlie."

Writing on similar points, Mr Alexander Lamb, farm-manager to Colonel Ferguson of Pitfour, Aberdeenshire, says: " As far back as I can remember—that is, forty years or so—there were two kinds of polled cattle in Buchan. Mr Hutchinson, Cairngall, near Longside, had from 12 to 16 cows I used to see always grazing in the same field. They were not the jet black the present race of polls are. They had a brownish tinge along the back, white udders, often a stripe of white along the underline, clean necks and heads, long bodies, rather sharp at the shoulders, deep at the flank, and square in the hind-quarters—as far as I can remember, not unlike the cow [Pride of Aberdeen 9th 3253] Mr Auld bought at the Tillyfour dispersion for 270 guineas. The other type of polled cows I remember was quite different from the one I have described. She was jet black, ewe-necked, sharp on the shoulders, rather broad on the loins, narrow behind, thin in the thighs, bent in the hind legs, with knees rubbing on each other when walking; and had a very large belly. Old men tell me that this kind of cow had excellent stock when crossed by the first Teeswater bulls that came to Buchan.

"These two types of polled cows I have described were to be met with all through Buchan. They were quite a contrast to each other in their movements. The former had a jaunty majestic gait when walking (what we call a 'swashy' appearance). The other went amb-

ling along with her nose quite near the ground. Both
types were famed for their milking qualities, and especially their fine-flavoured butter."

Mr James Smith, Burnshangie, writing of the polled
cattle formerly in Buchan, says: "On some of the larger
farms in this neighbourhood, the markings of the different
families or stocks would seem to have been very distinct
and preserved. They went by the names of the different
farms on which they were bred. Thus, the Strichen
breed were mostly brindled; while at Gowanfold, in
Rathen, there was a belted race—black animals with a
white belt round their waist. There was also a 'rigget'
race, or black with a white ridge along the back. The
most general sorts, however, were black, or black with a
little white below, and about the legs, a white udder being
regarded as the sign of a good milker. There was also
another very good sort, black with a brown back. The
cows—of course I am speaking of the better sorts—were
deep, wide, roomy animals,—a necessary feature; and
their milking-properties, which were good, were carefully
cultivated. I recollect well the Skillymarno polled stock.
They were black with white udder, and generally a white
spot in the face. Some of them came as a 'tocher' [mar-
riage dowry] with Skillymarno's daughter, on her marriage
to the tenant of the next farm to my father's. Here they
were several times crossed with good Shorthorn bulls;
but although they became blue in colour, no scurs were
ever seen upon them. I happened to mention this to one
of the Messrs Cruickshank of Sittyton, who remarked that
he could quite understand it, for they had obtained a
polled cow from the late Mr John Hutchinson of Monyruy; and after her progeny had been crossed for five generations with Shorthorn bulls, neither horns nor scurs
appeared. The nearest approach to the best types of our
old Buchan cows that I can recollect seeing is old 'Charlotte of Fyvie,' purchased by Lord Southesk at the disper-

sion sale at Fyvie in 1881. Mr Auld's 270-guinea cow [Pride of Aberdeen 9th 3253] is also a good deal of the same stamp."

Formerly, both in Angus and Aberdeen, the breed embraced a variety of colours as well as difference in size. Black, with some white spots on the underline, was the prevailing colour. Some were brindled — dark-red and black stripes alternately; others were red; others brown; and a few what Youatt called "silver-coloured yellow." But since systematic improvement was commenced in thorough earnest, all shades of colour excepting black have been at a discount,—indeed almost entirely "dishonoured." Now the cry is, "black and all black." It is not easy, however, to wholly obliterate features that have at any time been characteristic of a race of stock; and even in the "best regulated families" a "reversion" to one or other of these unpopular shades of colour still occasionally displays itself. A shade of brown is not rejected, and not a few of the best-looking and most highly priced animals of recent years have had some white about the underline, chiefly around the udder. Red or brindled, however, are wholly inadmissible; and when animals of these shades do appear, they are not bred from. In most herds one or two red calves have appeared, but a brindled calf is now rarely dropped. But while these colours are unpopular, it should be remembered that they do not denote impurity. They simply indicate that an ancient characteristic of the breed, which modern fancy has doomed to extinction, has in the mysterious workings of nature been able to temporarily reassert itself.

And here it may be well to draw a distinction between those occasional unwelcome cases of "harking back" to discounted colours, and another deviation from the rule which now and again appears in some strains in the form of "scurs." These "scurs" are small, rounded pieces of horn, without horn-cores, and attached loosely to the head.

We do not regard them as a recurrence of an original characteristic, but rather as denoting contact in comparatively recent times with some horned race. We have seen that both in Forfarshire and Aberdeenshire a race of horned cattle has from time immemorial—at least as far back as history and tradition carry us—existed alongside the ancestors of the improved polled breed, the former occupying the higher, and the latter the lower ground. We have no record of any systematic combination of the two races; but a hundred years ago, and even less, farmers saw no special advantage in keeping any breed absolutely pure from generation to generation. They had not then learned—what not a few personally interested in the subject have even yet to learn—the value of an *unstained* pedigree. It may therefore be concluded that the polled and horned varieties were in these days occasionally intermixed. Moreover, we have it on record that, towards the end of the last century and early in the present, the Buchan "humlies" were crossed with Ayrshires, and the horned breed of Fife and other races; and the Angus "doddies" with Ayrshires and other breeds. Youatt tells us, no doubt on Mr Hugh Watson's own authority, that the latter gentleman's famous Smithfield heifer, already referred to, "had a remote dash of Guernsey blood in her." In these circumstances, and in view of the known tendency of peculiarities in remote ancestors to display themselves from time to time, it is only natural that now and again an animal of the breed should appear with "scurs." They are scarcely ever seen on females. Some strains are more liable to them than others. In no family are they of frequent occurrence, and in some they have never once been observed. No effort should be spared to eradicate them from the breed. No animal showing the least sign of "scurs" should on any account be used for breeding purposes. If we had to choose between the two evils, we would much rather breed from a red animal than from one

with "scurs." The one feature is foreign to the breed; the
other simply not in accordance with modern fancy.

From the earliest accounts of the Angus and Aberdeen
polls, it would seem that they were even then noted for
symmetry of form, and that most of them were small in
size. They were generally so small, in fact, that oxen of
the breed were not considered suitable for the ordinary
light farm-work of a hundred years ago. It would seem
also that they have always been thick, low-set, round, very
compact, fine in the bone, with soft hair, mellow skin,
rich cover of flesh, fine head, hardy constitution, and great
aptitude to fatten, their beef being of the finest quality,
and beautifully mixed. The polled Aberdeen or Angus
cattle of to-day are just magnified animals of the same
type. Most of the good points they formerly possessed
have been still further developed, and brought to a higher
condition of usefulness; while some defects that characterised the breed a hundred years ago have been wholly or
partially removed. There has been a very great improvement in size during the present century. They are now
large cattle—scarcely inferior, indeed, in weight to any other
variety in the country. At a casual glance they seem
decidedly smaller than average Shorthorns; but on closer
examination, or on the "scales," the difference is generally
found to be much less than had at first sight been supposed, and often disappears altogether. As a rule, polled
animals are lower-set, or thicker and more compact, than
average Shorthorns—the latter being more "pointy," and
longer in the legs.

The ancient symmetry of the breed has been more than
maintained, and now in this respect it is surpassed by no
other breed in the British Isles, or perhaps anywhere else. A
really good northern poll leaves very little to be desired in
the symmetry of its parts. The improved race have wider
and better sprung ribs than their ancestors had, and are
also longer and better filled up from the hooks backwards,

as well as more richly fleshed, finer in the bone, of superior quality, and sweeter and more gay, especially about the head. Their general fattening-properties too, notably in regard to early maturity, have been very greatly improved. Some admirers of the breed, who have a distinct recollection of the animals that gained fame in show-yards twenty-five or thirty years ago, maintain that, in comparison with these, the show-yard animals of to-day exhibit little or no improvement. They admit that there has been great improvement in the "rank and file" of the breed, and that a much greater number of good specimens are seen in the show-yards now than formerly; but some of those celebrated animals that a quarter of a century ago enlisted their warm admiration, have never in their eyes been excelled. The same statements have been heard in regard to almost every breed of live stock in the country; but while in some instances they may be perfectly accurate, we believe that as a rule they are not so. We judge all things by comparison; and we believe that as we watch the progress of a breed that is being constantly improved, our standard of comparison becomes higher unconsciously. We cannot help believing, especially if full value were given to character or appearance of "breeding," that better animals of the polled Aberdeen or Angus breed have been shown within recent years than were to be seen a quarter of a century ago; and we are probably not far wrong in attributing the contrary impression, which has been mentioned, to the fact that those who hold that impression have not made full allowance for the higher standard of comparison which their long experience must almost of necessity have brought them to apply.

In general form a model polled animal differs considerably from a model Shorthorn. Both should be lengthy, deep, wide, even, proportionate, and cylindrical. The polled animal, however, should be more truly cylindrical in the body than the Shorthorn. Its points should be

more quickly rounded off; or, in other words, the frame
of the polled animal is not so fully drawn out to the
square as that of the Shorthorn. Critics have pointed out
in some of the best polled animals now or recently living,
a tendency to approach too nearly to the square type of
the Shorthorn.   In a beef-producing animal, a broad,
square frame can hardly be said to be a blemish; for if
it is thoroughly well covered all over, it will carry more
beef than a rounder frame. A compact, well-rounded
frame, however, has always been a leading characteristic
of the polled breed, and the main reason why a square
Shorthorn-looking frame is objected to in a polled animal
is, that such a form is foreign to the breed, and therefore
apt to arouse suspicions of impurity. The admirers of the
breed claim for it valuable natural properties not found to
an equal extent in any other breed ; and they fear that
should the breed lose its characteristically natural appearance, it may also lose its superiority in those valuable properties—" the genuine article should always bear
its trade-mark."   Careful improvers of the breed are
specially particular as to the hind-quarters. While they
aim at developing long, level, thick, deep quarters, they
also strive to retain the rounded appearance which was
originally one of the dominant characteristics of the
breed.

The head of the polled male should not be large, but
should be handsome and neatly set on. The muzzle
should be fine ; the nostrils wide ; the distance from the
nostrils to the eyes of only moderate length ; the eyes
mild, large, and expressive ; the poll high ; the ears of
fair size, lively, and well covered with hair ; the throat
clean, with no development of skin and flesh beneath the
jaws, which should not be heavy; the neck pretty long,
clean, and rising from the head to the shoulder-top, and
surmounted by a moderate "crest," which contributes to
masculine appearance—a desirable point in a bull. The

neck should pass neatly and evenly into the body, with full neck-vein. The shoulder-blades should lie well backwards, fitting neatly *into* the body, and not lying awkwardly *outside* it : they should show no undue prominence on the shoulder-top, on the points, or at the elbow. An upright shoulder in cattle is generally accompanied by a light waist—an important, and in all breeds a much too common, defect. The chest should be wide and deep, so as to give plenty of room for lung-development. The bosom should stand well forward between the fore-legs, and underneath should be well covered with flesh and fat. The crops should be full and level, with no falling off behind them ; the ribs well sprung, springing out barrel-like, and neatly joined to the crops and loins ; the back level and broad ; the loins broad and strong ; the hook-bones not too wide—narrower than in an average Shorthorn ; the quarters long, even, and rounded, with no hollow from the hooks to the tail ; the tail should come neatly out of the body, not too far up the back, and not higher at the root than the line of the back. A high tail-head was to some extent characteristic of the ancient polled breed, but it is one of the defects that are being gradually removed by the more scientific systems of breeding now pursued.

Some good polled cattle, too, have been found to show a development of soft worthless flesh and fat on the rounds behind ; but that defect, which is disliked very much, is also almost obliterated. The tail should hang straight down, close to the body all the way till it comes near to the level of the flank. On both sides of the tail the quarters should turn away in a rounded manner, swelling out downwards, and ultimately passing into thick deep thighs. The twist should be full, and the hind-legs set well apart, and not detached from the body until the level of the flank is reached. The flank should be full and soft, so that a good handful may be got out of it. The bottom line

should be as even as the top and side lines; and the bones
of the legs fine, flat, and clean, with plenty of muscle and
flesh above the knees on the fore-legs. The body should
stand neatly and gracefully on the legs; and when the
animal is stationary, the fore-legs should be perfectly
straight, and the hind-legs very slightly bent forwards
below the hock. All over the frame there should be
a rich and even coating of flesh. Even the hook-bones,
and other prominent parts, should be well covered; and
above all, there should be no patchiness—no hollows, and
no rolls of hard flesh, with spaces of soft useless fat between them, such as are always found in a patchy animal.
Except in rare cases, the skin is fairly thick, but soft and
pliable: it ought to be so free over the ribs, as that one
could fill one's hand of it. The hair is, as a rule, not
long, but fairly thick and soft; and in the best animals
shows two growths, or rather two lengths—one short and
thick, and the other longer and thinner. When walking, a
good animal of the breed presents a very compact, graceful,
and symmetrical appearance. Indeed it is fairly enough
claimed for the breed that in these and in some other
respects it has hardly any equals, and no superiors. The
above description refers more correctly to bulls than to
cows. The latter, of course, differ considerably in character. The head is much finer, the neck thinner and
cleaner, with no crest; the shoulder-top sharper; the bone
altogether finer; the skin not quite so thick; the udder
large, and milk-vessels large and well-defined.

In appearance, as well as in other characteristics, the
polled Aberdeen or Angus breed differs substantially from
the polled Galloway race. The former has lived under a dry
cold climate, and has been fed in the house during a large
part of the year. The latter has its home in a moist
climate, and has spent much more of its time in the open
fields. The differences between the two are just such as
might be expected from their different conditions of life.

The Galloway, as already noted, has a thicker skin and stronger coat of hair, and has altogether a slightly more shaggy appearance than the northern polled cattle, and does not mature quite so quickly.

It is claimed that the northern polls surpass all other races of cattle in the production of beef. On that point there is of course considerable difference of opinion; for at the present day, when the beef-producing properties of our other leading breeds, notably the Shorthorn and Hereford, have been developed to so high a degree, it could not be expected that with anything like unanimity any one breed would be accorded the premier position. Be that as it may, we think the polled Aberdeen or Angus breed may safely be said to be inferior to none as all-round beef-cattle, and superior to all others in some respects. The brilliant and unequalled position it has latterly taken, alike in the show-yard and market-place, sufficiently establishes its claim to that description. Its show-yard achievements will be fully noticed afterwards. Here it may be noted, that at the Paris Exhibition in 1878 it carried off every single honour for which it was entitled to compete, including the £100 prize for the best group of beef-producing cattle in the Exhibition; and that in British show-yards, both fat stock and breeding, it has attained to a leading position. In a strictly butcher's point of view, it has very seldom to yield to any other race of cattle.

The superiority over most other breeds, for the butcher's purpose, lies mainly in the excellent quality of beef, and in the high percentage of dead meat to live weight. As a rule, the beef of the northern polls is very well mixed, and contains a greater proportion of compact, finely grained flesh, and less soft, coarse fat, than most other kinds of beef. Inside, the carcass is usually well lined with fat of the finest quality; while in the density and quality of the carcass itself, the breed may fairly enough claim the premier position among all our leading breeds of cattle. Some place the small Devon breed alongside, if not even before it, in this respect; but with that exception, we do not think that any other breed in the British Isles will on an average yield so high a percentage of dead meat to live weight. In butchers' phraseology, it "dies" well and "cuts up" admirably. In all the leading fat-stock markets in the country the breed is held in high estimation, and, as a rule, commands the very highest prices—in fact, generally a higher price in comparison to its size and live weight than any of the other leading breeds. This is especially the case at the great Smithfield Christmas Market in London, where the plump compact polls from the north never fail to find a ready sale at the highest quotations.

The breed is specially adapted for crossing with Shorthorns. Indeed, perhaps the very best beef-producing animal that has as yet been reared is a cross between a Shorthorn bull and a polled cow. Throughout the north-east of Scotland that system of crossing is pursued very extensively. Nearly nine-tenths of the famous Aberdeenshire beeves, so highly prized in the London market, are crosses between these two breeds. The best system is to mate the polled cow and the Shorthorn bull; but the reverse system, which, owing to the scarcity of polled cows, is freely practised, also gives excellent results.

It is noticeable that, as a rule, those of these crosses that approach the most nearly to the Shorthorn type are, if anything, the largest in appearance, and attain the greatest live weight. It is equally well known, however, that those which most closely resemble the polled breed not only bring the highest price when fat, and yield a larger percentage of dead meat to live weight, but also command the greatest number of customers and the readiest sale. An influential cattle-salesman in England stated the other day, that for a black polled ox or heifer, or even a cow, he could find three buyers for one who would bid for an

animal of any other variety ; and that the longer he stood
" week after week behind cattle in the markets," his
estimate of black polled cattle as beef-producers became
greater and greater. At local fairs and sales of farm-
stock throughout the north-east of Scotland, lean black
polled one and two year old cattle generally bring from
£1 to £2 per head more than a corresponding class of roan
horned crosses. An Aberdeen butcher of long and extensive experience states, that he considers it safe to give
about 5s. more per cwt. for a well-fed polled animal than
for a similarly finished horned cross.

Among some not directly acquainted with the improved
Aberdeen or Angus cattle, an idea has prevailed that the
breed is slow in coming to maturity—that it grows slowly
and fattens slowly. Formerly that may have been the
case ; indeed there is no doubt that it was. Now, however, the breed has been so greatly improved in that respect
that it matures almost as early as any of the other leading
breeds. When well fed from their birth, good specimens
of the breed become ripe at the age of from twenty-four to
twenty-eight months ; and it is also worthy of note that
animals of the breed that are being fattened will retain the
levelness and quality of their flesh longer than those of
most other kinds. At the Smithfield Club Show in London in 1879, the highest increase in weight per day from
birth was shown by a two-year-and-nine-months-old steer
of the polled Aberdeen or Angus breed, shown by Sir
William Gordon Gordon Cumming, Bart. of Altyre, and
bred by Mr Grant, Advie. At the Smithfield Club Show in
London in 1880, the average daily increase in weight of the
six steers of the polled Aberdeen and Angus breed under
three years old was 1.78 lb., and that of the corresponding
class of Shorthorn steers, 1.79 lb. In 1881 Sir W. G. G.
Cumming won the Smithfield Champion Cup, and the cups
for the best steer or ox and best heifer or cow, with two
polled animals, each under three years old.

Since the rage for "young beef" became so strong as it now is, a great many polled cattle have been fed off when from twenty-four to thirty months old; and at that age good animals bring from £25 to £35, a few even exceeding the latter sum. In the London Christmas market, choice three-year-old black polled bullocks bring from £40 to £48, and even in some cases over £80. In some years the late Mr M'Combie of Tillyfour obtained an average of more than £50 a-head for his best lot in the Smithfield market, and he sometimes exceeded £44 a-head all over. Great weights have been reached by specially good animals. Mr M'Combie's celebrated ox Black Prince—the champion of 1867 already mentioned—came within a fraction of a ton in dead weight; while his prize ox at Poissy in 1857 weighed 2728 lb. at the age of 4 years and 4 months. A prize bull bred by Mr M'Combie, and the sire of one of the Tillyfour prize oxen at Poissy in 1862, was slaughtered at the age of two years, and his dead weight exceeded 14 cwt. The champion heifer Beauty, bred by Mr William Brown, Linkwood, Elgin, and the winner of many show-yard honours to Mr James Reid, Greystone, Mr John Cran, Kirkton, and others, was found to weigh, when slaughtered at the age of four years, more than 16 cwt. Two prize polled oxen bred by Mr Stephen, Conglass, weighed 16½ cwt. each in the carcass, and were sold at £80 and £75 respectively. The prices obtained in the London Christmas market afford a fair indication of the weights of the best class of polled bullocks when fully fattened. Some years ago, cattle intended for that great market were kept till three and a half or four years old—in certain cases even longer—and then 11, 12, and 13 cwt. (dead weight) were common weights. Now the majority average from thirty to thirty-four months, and at that age the dead weight generally ranges from 7 to 8 or 9 cwt. Some choice animals even exceed 10 cwt.; and the average of good well-finished thirty-month bullocks would be from

8 to 8½ cwt. Two-year-old polled bullocks, reared and fed in the ordinary way—that is to say, without any special forcing—usually bring, on an average, from £28 to £32 a-head.

Half a century ago the northern polled cattle were noted for their great milking-powers. Youatt mentions that the polled cows of Buchan, small as they then (1832-35) were, gave from 3 to 4 gallons — from 12 to 16 quarts—of milk per day, and sometimes even as much as 7 gallons, or 28 quarts. The improvers of the breed have as a rule aimed chiefly at developing beef-producing properties; and thus the cultivation of milking-powers has to some extent been neglected. As a rule, however, the northern polls give a good account of themselves in the dairy. Several tribes are excellent milkers, over 16 quarts per day being obtained from many cows; and we feel convinced that, with a little care on the part of breeders, the race might be brought into a prominent position among dairy cattle. The milk of the breed is noted for its quality, which is superior to that of the milk from several other breeds. The late Earl of Airlie, writing to the 'North British Agriculturist' on December 26, 1879, in reference to the milking-properties of the breed, says: "I have at present seventeen pure polled Angus milch-cows in my dairy. The greater number of these give from 12 to 14, and sometimes 16, Scotch pints for a considerable time after calving. The milk is admitted to be much richer than that of either the Shorthorn or the Ayrshire. As regards the length of time for which they will continue to give milk, my cow Belle of Airlie 1959, dam of Belus 749, as pure a polled animal as any in the 'Herd Book,' used to be milked all the year round. Last year when I was from home they left off milking her about a month before she calved, and she died of milk fever, induced, as I believe, by the circumstance that she had not been relieved of her superabundant milk. The cow, Miss Macpherson 1252, of the Erica tribe, which I purchased recently of Mr Adamson, is now giving 6 Scotch pints a day, more than nine and a half months after calving." Writing at a later date on the same point, the Earl of Airlie says: "The Scotch pint to which I referred is a measure of 12 gills, equal to 3 imperial pints, or 1½ imperial quarts. When I wrote on this subject I had some cows that (newly calved) gave 14 Scotch pints or 21 English quarts; and one cow, I think, 15 pints or 22½ English quarts. I have now some cows that are giving as much as 12 Scotch pints, or 18 English quarts, daily, though quite three months calved. The cows are milked three times a-day, which I believe to be the usual practice in Scotland. I do not know the weight, as the pint and quart are measures of capacity, so that of course the weight depends on the specific gravity of the milk. But it is admitted, I believe, that the milk of the polled Angus is richer in cream than that of either the Shorthorn or Ayrshire."

The northern polls have risen rapidly in public estimation within the past ten or fifteen years. Their reputation may now be said to be world wide. Animals of the breed have been exported to the Australian colonies, to the Continent of Europe, to South America, and to Canada and the United States. In the two latter countries an exceedingly keen demand has sprung up for them, and it is probable that within the past eighteen months more than 500 specimens of the breed have crossed the Atlantic. The cry from the United States is still for more polls, and it is probable that although every animal of the breed now in this country were sent across to them, the wants of our transatlantic cousins would still be unsatisfied.

This great expansion in the demand for the northern polls has of course brought forth a corresponding increase in their market value. About twelve months ago good polled cows, with ordinary pedigrees, would have sold at from 30 to 45 guineas; while females of the better bred and more distinguished families gave from 50 to 100 guineas on an average. Since then, prices have risen by at least 50 per cent, and still higher figures could be obtained for choice animals if their owners could be induced to part with them. The highest sum yet paid for one animal was that (270 guineas) given for Pride of Aberdeen 9th 3253, by Mr R. C. Auld, Bridgend, at the Tillyfour dispersion sale in 1880.

CHAPTER VI.

NOTES ON SOME EARLY POLLED CATTLE.

Inaccurate entries in vol. i. of 'Polled Herd Book'—Statement by the
late Mr Fullerton, Mains of Ardestie, on breeding of cow Black Meg
766, and bull Panmure 51—Communication from Dr Simpson, Marykirk, regarding sire of Panmure 51—Mr Collier, Hatton, on the breeding of Panmure 51—Errors in entries of Keillor cattle—Confusion as
to bulls Old Jock 1 and Grey-breasted Jock 2—Account of the Keillor
Jocks—The Keillor cows Favourite and Beauty—Supplementary information respecting the pedigrees of the bulls Monarch 44 and the
Tillyfour Victors.

HAVING traced the progress and improvement of the
polled breed, we might now proceed to notice the leading
herds. In order, however, to render the account of them in-
telligible, it is necessary to interpose some remarks regarding a few of the early celebrated polled cattle whose pedigrees
have been inaccurately or imperfectly recorded in vol. i. of
the 'Herd Book.' In stating the unquestionable fact that the
'Herd Book' entries of several of the animals that were most
employed to effect the early improvement of the breed are
in a state of confusion, we have not the slightest intention
of reflecting on the way in which Mr Ravenscroft per-
formed the duties of editor of vol. i. There is evidence
that he discharged his work with care, and that he put
himself to a good deal of trouble in endeavouring to secure
accuracy. We believe the errors have been caused in great
measure by the untoward circumstances that attended the

production of the first volume. The collection of materials for vol. i. was commenced in 1842. The whole of the documents were deposited for safety in the Museum of the Highland and Agricultural Society in Edinburgh, and when the fire took place in the buildings there in 1851, they were unfortunately all destroyed. The loss was irreparable. Mainly through the instrumentality of the Earl of Southesk the work was again begun in 1857, but it was not until 1862 that the first volume of the 'Herd Book' was actually published. In the interval, several of the finest polled herds in the country were attacked with rinderpest or pleuro-pneumonia. In some cases only a wreck of formerly magnificent herds remained after the devastation wrought by these fell diseases, and more than one of the fragments had been finally dispersed ere the first volume made its appearance. It must also be said that private notes of pedigrees were not systematically retained by many breeders; and Mr Ravenscroft has stated that "in some cases where assistance was naturally looked for, obstacles were thrown in the way of procuring information."

If in 1862 it was not easy to obtain reliable details regarding the breeding of several of the early registered polled cattle, we need scarcely remark that the task is now much more difficult of accomplishment. We are pleased to say, however, that after the most careful investigations, we have succeeded in procuring information which we think clears away several of the more glaring inaccuracies in vol. i. It is to be hoped that breeders may not long be without a revised edition of the first volume of the 'Herd Book,' with corrections made under the authority of the Polled Cattle Society. The interests of the breed demand that this should be undertaken without undue delay, and it is rendered more necessary by the fact that the first volume is out of print. We shall refer in the first place to—

The Cow Black Meg 766, and the Bull Panmure 51.

Hundreds of polled animals, many of them among the most famous of the breed, are descended from Mr Fullerton's cow Black Meg 766, and Lord Panmure's bull Panmure 51. The pedigrees of these two animals, as printed in vol. i. of the 'Herd Book,' are altogether misleading. Black Meg 766 has had placed before her name an asterisk, the sign adopted to distinguish the Galloway from the Aberdeen or Angus cattle, when the pedigrees of both breeds were recorded in the same 'Herd Book,' and Panmure 51 is said to have been out of Black Meg 766. These are two very serious inaccuracies. The name of the sire of Panmure is not given, and the whole antecedents of these two celebrated animals are, so far as the 'Herd Book' entries go, shrouded in complete mystery. Breeders of polled cattle are under a debt of gratitude to Mr Thomas F. Jamieson, Mains of Waterton, Ellon, for having conducted such investigations as have solved the difficulties which arose from the erroneous entries of these animals. Writing to us under date 9th February 1882, Mr Jamieson says: "When I occupied the post of Fordyce Lecturer at Marischal College, Aberdeen, I devoted some attention to the subject of polled cattle along with other matters, and I found that all the best blood of the Aberdeen and Angus doddies traced back to three fountain-heads—viz., 1st, Mr Fullerton's Black Meg; 2nd, the bull Panmure, from Brechin Castle; and 3rd, the Keillor Jocks. Unfortunately the first volume of the 'Herd Book' is a complete mass of confusion in regard to the pedigrees and history of these animals at least; and I therefore considered myself very fortunate in getting from Mr Fullerton himself authentic communications giving me all that he, the possessor of Black Meg and Panmure, knew about these animals." Mr Jamieson has kindly furnished us with the more important parts of Mr Fullerton's statements

addressed to him at various times in the years 1872 and
1873, and we feel privileged in being able to place them
before our readers. Mr Fullerton wrote from Mains of
Ardestie as follows:—

"I was fortunate at Ardovie in 1833 in starting to
breed doddies—as we then called the breed—from a few
cows of excellent milking-qualities. To no cow I then
had was I more beheld than to a cow called Black Meg.
She was a most wonderful beast this, and a great milker,
and steady all the year round, although in her latter years
she did fall off in this respect a good deal; but then I
suppose she was having calves up to nearly twenty years
of age. I shall never forget how her calves dwindled
down in size; but it mattered not after we got hold of
them—we had only to milk them well, and they all came
to have size enough. To describe this cow. She was low
on her legs, as otherwise, but of lengthy and heavy build,
on small bone. Her back was straight as a rash, and her
tail so well set on that you would never tire to stand
behind her and to look along her back. Then her hooks
were so level, wide enough and not too wide. Then her
ears and eyes full and sticking well out; then her beautiful
jaw and muzzle, with fine, good-natured expression of face,
were such, and when taken as a whole, why one could
stand and look at Meg and not weary for a whole hour, as
she chewed the cud! Then her hair—my eye, such hair!—
'we shall never see the like again;' of the best quality,
and on to her flanks you could almost hide your hand in
it. She had a streaked udder, had a knack of having
quey calves, and in the colour of their udders they stuck
to the old lady's pattern. My cow, Queen of Ardovie 29,
daughter of Black Meg, was very like her mother in some
points, but was a heavier and more stately cow. Princess
of Ardovie 831, daughter of the Queen, was also a magnificent cow. I sold her to the late Mr Watson, Keillor, for,
I think, 28 guineas—a big price in those days. She calved

the day she arrived at Keillor. Mr Watson afterwards
showed her in Ireland, where she beat all comers, and he
sold her for 60 guineas. Her calf was a quey she had at
Keillor, and I bought it at Mr Watson's sale in 1847 for
35 guineas. I had only one calf out of this quey (Princess
Daughter 832), when in 1859 pleuro-pneumonia got
amongst my herd of pure polled—I cannot tell how—and
between the 8th of January and 1st of June I had the
misfortune to bury about 100 head of as well-bred cattle
as ever were in any one's possession, reckoning that I had
one way or other met with a loss of £2000. I have twice
since commenced to breed the polled sort, and for a second
and third time have I been all but cleared out by that fell
disease, pleuro-pneumonia, and I am now frightened to
keep a 60-guinea beast, and am breeding from £25 cows
with a Shorthorn bull. I find these cows terrible eaters,
and often wish I had a few Black Megs, Queens, and
Princesses. The big brutes of cows I have, I am convinced, eat a third more food than ever I saw doddies
do; and I do not find we are so well served with milk,
and I feed higher than I ever fed the blacks, nor is the
milk of that rich quality my old favourites used to supply
me with. So much as to the milking-qualities of the
black polled breed, and the ready tendency to fatten and
also to milk well that all cows of the breed have as
well as their progeny, who are of good mellow handle, and
have plenty of good hair.

"The famous bull Panmure 51 was not bred by me at
all, but by the late Lord Panmure, from whom I bought
the bull when a year and a half old. He was out of a cow
called Black Meg, belonging to his lordship, not certainly
to me—and I never at any time said so. It is a misprint
altogether of Mr Ravenscroft, the editor of vol. i. of the
'Herd Book,' to confuse in the way he has done Black
Meg of Ardovie with Black Meg of Panmure. I do not
think at the time the late Lord Panmure bred this bull

that he had over three or four polled cows in all; and
certain I am of this—he had no Galloways. Therefore a
double mistake occurs by Mr Ravenscroft placing either
my Black Meg or his lordship's Black Meg amongst the
Galloway cows in the 'Herd Book.' As for me, I never
had a beast of the Galloway blood in my life; and at an
early period of the existence of the Eastern Forfarshire
Association (about the end of the last or beginning of the
present century), a trial to introduce the Galloway blood
into this county not succeeding at all well, the late Lord
Panmure, the then—and indeed he was the perpetual—
President of this Society, had ever afterwards an utter dislike to the Galloway breed, and, as is well known by many
in this county to this day, would not have tolerated the
existence of a beast of this breed in any moor, park, or
paddock on his wide domain. Therefore his Black Meg
was not a Galloway. But the bull Panmure is on canvas
in the Mechanics' Hall, Brechin, painted by the great J.
Phillip; also he is now before me and on canvas by the
same great man, and presented to me by the late Lord
Panmure; and let any judge look at these paintings, and
say if he sees the very slightest resemblance to the Galloway breed. Not he! No! Half a judge would even say
so. His elegant head and stately outline would at a glance
at once bring out such a remark as, 'There has been no
Galloway blood there—no, no!'

"Further, as to Black Meg of Ardovie 766, where did
she come from? I purchased this cow from an excellent
man now no more — Mr Thomas Fawns, cattle-dealer,
Brechin. He brought her from the north, and I always
understood that she was bred in Buchan, although I think
Mr Fawns got the cow off the estate of Mr Arbuthnot in
the Mearns. She cost scarce £15; yet in those days she
was looked upon as bought at rather a foolish price. For
all that, I know not of any other three five-pound notes I
ever laid out so profitably.

"The bull Panmure 51, again, and as to his dam. Neither was the price of this bull a bad investment. His price at eighteen months old was £17, 17s. While Black Meg of Ardovie was a great bearer of quey calves, this bull was a great getter of males. I saw him stand as winner of the third prize at Aberdeen with his two sons, Monarch 44, and the Colonel, both bred by me, standing beside their father—Monarch having the first and Colonel the second prize. Of course Panmure was by this time some eight or nine years old, and so wanted to some extent the outline and sprightliness of a three or even a five year old. Still, and to make allowance for the service he had rendered, there would have been but small mistake, if any, to have made his sons stand below him. I do not think I have ever seen such a dashing three-year-old as he was at Dundee in 1843.

"As to Black Meg of Panmure, dam of the bull Panmure, I think I only saw her once, and all I recollect of her is that she had a large streaked udder, and, if I am correct, was amazingly well ribbed; also a very strong cow. Who the bull Panmure's father was I am not certain."

These most valuable communications from Mr Fullerton still left one point uncertain—viz., the sire of Panmure 51. Mr Jamieson, in his indefatigable efforts to procure reliable information, accordingly prosecuted his inquiries further. He received from Dr Simpson of Marykirk, in Kincardineshire, the following interesting letter, which we have Mr Jamieson's permission to quote. The letter is dated September 30, 1873, and reads :—

"As soon as I thought the harvest would be finished, I went over to have an interview with David Fullerton, who was grieve to the late Lord Panmure at Brechin Castle, when the famous polled bull Panmure was calved. David states that he was out of the cow Black Meg; that his sire was a black bull very like the calf himself, from

the farm of Fernyflatt, parish of Kinneff, at that time
farmed by Robert Hector.   David mentions that during
the seventeen years he was grieve at Brechin Castle, there
were none of the Shorthorn cattle ever there.   Their dairy
cows were pure Ayrshires, and were always kept strictly
separate from the black polled cattle.   He also tells me
that Panmure was ultimately bought by Mr M'Combie of
Tillyfour, and remembers well that, previous to that purchase, the Forfarshire breeders always beat the Aberdeenshire ones, but after that, *vice versa.*"

We may explain that it was Mr Farquharson Taylor,
Wellhouse, Alford, who bought Panmure 51, after he had
gained the first prize at the Highland Society's show in
1843.

Steps were taken in 1876 to rectify the errors in these
pedigrees in the ' Herd Book.'   Mr Fullerton wrote a letter,
dated 20th October 1876, to the editor of the ' Herd Book,'
making a short declaration similar in substance to that
given in the foregoing; and breeders possessing vol. i. of
the ' Herd Book ' were requested to delete the asterisk pre-
fixed to the entry of Black Meg 766, as well as the words
signifying that she was the dam of Panmure 51.   As
regards the bull Panmure, it was ascertained from Mr
John Collier, Hatton, Arbroath, that he purchased his dam
in the year 1839 for Lord Panmure.   The purchase was
made from Mr Silver of Netherley, and " it was understood
that the cow was bred in Buchan."   The sire of Panmure
was certified by Mr Collier to have been a bull named
Hector, bred by Mr Hector, Fernyflatt.   This bull does not
seem to be entered in the ' Herd Book.'   It was decided
to regard Black Meg 766 as the cow that belonged to Mr
Fullerton, and that produced his Queen of Ardovie 29;
and to hold that the dam of Panmure 51, Black Meg,
belonging to Lord Panmure (of whom Mr Collier testified
that she had not a drop of Galloway blood in her), had
not been registered.

G

These very unfortunate inaccuracies have thus been corrected since the appearance of vol. iv. of the 'Herd Book,' but the facts are made still more clear by the publication of Mr Fullerton's and Dr Simpson's interesting correspondence with Mr Jamieson.

The Keillor Jocks.

Mr Hugh Watson's herd at Keillor was one of those that, in the period that elapsed between the inception and the actual publication of the first volume of the 'Herd Book,' had been scourged by pleuro-pneumonia, and had been finally dispersed. To the causes we have indicated as explanatory of the confusion that occurred in many of the entries in vol. i. has to be added, in the case of the Keillor herd, a defective system of nomenclature, most of Mr Watson's animals having been called by the same names. There was a series of Jocks, distinguished merely by the prefixes "Tarnty," "Black," "Old," "Grey - breasted," "Young," "Second," &c. Then the females went under the common names of "Grannies," "Favourites," or "Beauties." It sometimes happened, too, that these names were applied indiscriminately to different animals, and it would also seem that some at least of the Keillor entries were made from recollection without the aid of documents. Reference to such easily accessible authorities as show and sale catalogues would have prevented several inaccuracies that have occurred.

The chief errors in the Keillor pedigrees are those that have crept into the entries of the bulls Old Jock 1 and Grey-breasted Jock 2. The pedigree of Old Jock 1, as given in vol. i., is very meagre. It simply states that he was bred by Hugh Watson, Keillor, and was the sire of certain animals. A footnote mentions that he was "descended by sire and dam from the old stock of Keillor doddies, a herd which obtained celebrity so far back as

1800. Old Jock gained the Highland Society's first prize in
1844, and was sold for one hundred guineas." We shall
here only state that in 1844 the Highland Society gave
no prizes for polled breeding stock. The pedigree of
Grey-breasted Jock 2 is thus printed in vol. i.: "Calved,
1840. Bred by Hugh Watson, Keillor. Sire, Old Jock 1;
dam, Favourite 2." The footnote adds, "Grey-breasted
Jock obtained the Highland Society's first prize at Dundee
in 1843, and at Inverness in 1846, and was afterwards
sold to Mr Kirkaldy, near Ballinasloe, and exhibited by
him at Londonderry in 1847, where he carried off the first
prize of the Royal Dublin Society. In 1852, at thirteen
years old, he gained the sweepstakes over all the bulls in
the yard at the Highland Society's show at Perth."

One inaccuracy in this entry is as to the dam of Grey-
breasted Jock. The dam is said to have been Favourite 2.
In the pedigree of Favourite 2 her sire is given as Grey-
breasted Jock 2—an evident impossibility. Then the
footnote mentions that Grey-breasted Jock 2 gained the
first prize at the Highland Society's show at Dundee in
1843. According to the date of birth given in the 'Herd
Book,' Grey - breasted Jock would in 1843 have been
three years old, and if exhibited at Dundee must have
competed in the aged class. It is well known that the
first prize aged bull at Dundee in 1843 was Panmure 51.
It is next stated that Grey-breasted Jock was sold to Mr
Kirkaldy, near Ballinasloe, and gained for him the first
prize of the Royal Dublin Society at the show at Londonderry in 1847. The Royal Agricultural Society of Ireland
held a show at Londonderry in 1847, but the first-prize
bull was not exhibited by Mr Kirkaldy, and was not
Grey-breasted Jock. The first prize bull, shown by Mr
Watson, was an animal (erroneously entered in the catalogue under the name of Strathmore) "calved in March
1842; bred by the exhibitor." It will strike most people
as singular that if Grey-breasted Jock was sold to Mr Kirk-

aldy in Ireland in 1847, he should have again turned up in
Mr Watson's possession in 1852, and gained the sweepstakes at the Perth show of the Highland Society that
year.

In the foregoing analysis of the recorded pedigrees and
statements in the 'Herd Book' as to Old Jock 1 and
Grey-breasted Jock 2, we have hinted at several obvious
contradictions. We have made minute inquiries into the
facts, and have compared the entries in vol. i. with—
(1) published letters from Mr William Watson, son of Mr
Hugh Watson; (2) letters addressed to the authors, in
response to applications for information, by Mr Thomas
Ferguson, Kinnochtry, Coupar-Angus, a contemporary of
Mr Hugh Watson, and well acquainted with his stock; (3)
Mr Hugh Watson's sale catalogue at Auchtertyre in 1853;
(4) catalogues of the early shows of the Royal Agricultural
Society of Ireland; (5) extracts furnished to us by the
recorder of the Highland Society, Mr Thomas Duncan, of
the original entries of the Keillor bulls exhibited at the
shows of the Highland Society; and (6) the private catalogue of the Tillyfour herd, dated 1850. We annex a
summary of the information gleaned from the evidence of
these authorities. It has been deemed advisable, so as to
make the statement as clear as possible, to give all that
we have been able to ascertain regarding the whole of the
bulls known as Jocks that were at Keillor, and to arrange
them in chronological order :—

(1.) The first Jock used at Keillor was the bull TARNTY
JOCK, calved in 1806, and purchased by Mr Hugh Watson at the Trinity Muir market, Brechin, in 1808. He is
not entered in the 'Herd Book.'

(2.) The SECOND JOCK was after Tarnty Jock, and out of
one of the cows which Hugh Watson received from his
father, William Watson, in 1808. This bull is not entered
in the 'Herd Book.'

(3.) The third Jock, named BLACK JOCK, was after Jock

No. 2 in this list, and out of a sister of his own. This appears to have been the bull that gained for Mr Watson the first prize at the Highland Society's show at Perth in 1829. He is not registered in the 'Herd Book.'

(4.) The fourth Jock was GREY-BREASTED JOCK (No. 2 of 'Herd Book'). He was calved in 1839. His sire was Black Jock (No. 3 in this list), and his dam was a cow closely inbred to himself, and not entered in the 'Herd Book.' Grey-breasted Jock, of whom Mr William Watson and Mr Ferguson have a distinct recollection, gained the first prize at one of the shows of the Highland Society: it is uncertain which. In 1843 he was exhibited at the show of the Royal Agricultural Society of Ireland, at Belfast, in the catalogue of which he is entered as " Jock, four years and six months old." He there gained the first premium of forty sovereigns and the medal. After the Belfast show he was sold to Mr G. D. H. Kirkaldy, Hearnesbrook, Eyrecourt, near Ballinasloe, and never returned to Scotland. He is described by Mr William Watson as having been " of immense length, short on his leg, elegant in his gait, and masculine-looking: he was grand and massive all over, as well as a most kindly feeder."

(5.) The fifth Jock was OLD JOCK (No. 1 of the 'Herd Book'). This bull was bred by Hugh Watson, in 1842. He was got by Grey-breasted Jock (No. 2 of the 'Herd Book'), and was out of Old Favourite,—the dam of Favourite 2, and also of Angus 45. Old Favourite was lot one of Mr Watson's sale in 1848, when she was bought by Mr Bowie, Mains of Kelly. In Mr M'Combie's private catalogue, dated 1850, Angus 45 is stated to have had for dam " No. 1 at Mr Watson's sale." Old Jock gained the first prize as a yearling at the Highland Society's show at Dundee in 1843, and the first prize in the aged class at the Highland Society's show at Inverness in 1846. The only information given in the entry of the bull at the latter show was, that he was " aged four years and six months,

and was bred by the exhibitor." He was also the bull
exhibited by Mr Watson at the show of the Royal Agricultural Society of Ireland at Londonderry in 1847, when
he gained the first prize. The name under which he was
entered at that show was Strathmore; and the confusion
of names is still further increased by it being said in the
catalogue that he was after Old Jock—this designation
having apparently been applied to the various Keillor bulls
in the order of seniority. The age of Old Jock is placed
beyond dispute by the entries in the show-catalogues.
Thus he wins the first prize as a yearling at the Highland Society's show at Dundee in 1843; at the Highland
Society's show at Inverness in 1846 he is entered as "aged
four years and six months;" at the Royal Irish Society's
show at Londonderry in 1847 he is described as having
been "calved in March 1842,"—these three separate entries
strictly corresponding on the point of age.

Old Jock also gained the sweepstakes for bulls at the
Perth Highland show in 1852, when he was about eleven
years old, although he is entered in the catalogue as fourteen years and four months old. A somewhat noteworthy
reference to Old Jock was made in the report of the 'Perth-
shire Advertiser' on the show at Perth in 1852. The report was evidently from the pen of a gentleman who had
acted as a judge at the Londonderry show in 1847, and
went on to say: "In the class of old bulls, Mr Watson
showed his celebrated bull, Jock, for the sweepstakes; he
being disqualified for competing for the premium, having
obtained the Society's first prize at Inverness in 1846.
This bull is confessedly the best animal of the polled
breed ever exhibited in a showyard. Four years ago, at
the meeting of the Irish Agricultural Society at Londonderry, we assisted in judging Jock with his competing
brethren. He was not only the best bull in his own class,
but he stood second for Mr Purcell's 100-guinea cup for
the best animal in the showyard; and it was our opin-

ion then, as it is now, that Jock should have stood first.
Being second, however, in such circumstances, was high
merit, there being thirty-two Shorthorn bulls, many of
them first-class, independent of all the other breeding
animals in the showyard." A striking confirmation of the
accuracy of the remarks we have made about Old Jock is
furnished by the catalogue of Mr Watson's sale at Auchtertyre, in 1853. Nearly all the cows and heifers at that sale
are stated to have been after Old Jock,—thus proving,
apart from other evidence, that it was this bull that
was used by Mr Watson from 1843 to 1852. Mr Dixon,
in 'Field and Fern,' says Old Jock was one of Mr Hugh
Watson's favourite bulls. He was, observes Mr Dixon,
"the most stylish of the lot, and showed, as his owner
never scrupled to say, much of the Shorthorn superiority
in hair and touch." Mr Ferguson says: "Old Jock was
the best polled bull I ever saw; and he never looked better
than when he was taken in at 180 guineas at the Keillor
sale in 1848, at which Mr Wetherell officiated as auctioneer,
using the sand-glass." Mr William Watson says: "My
father used to think Old Jock the best bull he ever bred;
and, as a sire, he has never been surpassed in the annals
of polled stock. He was a grand grazier, iron in constitution, and of superlative quality."

(6.) The sixth Jock was BLACK JOCK (No. 3 of the
'Herd Book'). This bull, calved in 1848, was after Old
Jock 1, and out of Old Grannie 1. He was purchased
by Mr Ferguson, Kinnochtry, when three months old, for
seventeen guineas, and was used in his herd.

(7.) The seventh Jock was YOUNG JOCK (No. 4 of the
'Herd Book'), calved in May 1849: he was also after Old
Jock 1, and Mr Ferguson says he was out of Octavia 331.
He gained the first prize at the Highland Society show at
Perth in 1852, at which he was entered as "3 years and
4 months old." Young Jock was acquired by Mr Ferguson,
Kinnochtry, in whose herd he was afterwards used.

It is, we think, clearly established by the foregoing, that in vol. i. of the 'Herd Book,' the identity of Grey-breasted Jock 2 and Old Jock 1 has been confounded. It appears evident that Grey-breasted Jock 2, who was the senior and not the junior, as would be gathered from the 'Herd Book' entries, never returned to Scotland after his appearance at Belfast in 1843, and that he was succeeded as stock sire at Keillor by his son Old Jock 1, whose fame excelled that of Grey-breasted Jock, and who continued in service in Mr Watson's herd until 1853 or 1854. It follows from this, that most of the animals credited in the 'Herd Book' to Grey-breasted Jock 2 were really got by Old Jock 1. We will only mention a few of the more celebrated—viz., Black Jock 3, Young Jock 4, Strathmore 5, Angus 45, &c. The most important link in this chain of evidence is perhaps the fact that Grey-breasted Jock was sold to Mr Kirkaldy of Hearnesbrook in 1843, and remained in Ireland. It should also be added that Mr William Watson and Mr Ferguson agree in stating that Old Jock 1 was the bull exhibited at Dundee in 1843, Inverness in 1846, and Perth in 1852.

The Keillor Favourites and Beauties.

From our remarks as to the Keillor Jocks, it will be seen that there were two cows belonging to Mr Watson named Favourite. Old Favourite (the dam of Old Jock 1, of Angus 45, and of Favourite 2) was not entered in the 'Herd Book.' She was a famous show cow, and was sold at Mr Watson's sale in 1848 to Mr Bowie, Mains of Kelly, for 40 guineas. Mr Ferguson, Kinnochtry, bought her daughter, Favourite 2.

There has been a great deal of confusion regarding the cows at Keillor called Beauty. Three, at least, of the Keillor cows were named Beauty. One of these, Beauty of Buchan 5, passed into the possession of Mr Ferguson,

Kinnochtry.   Another was Beauty (not registered), best
known as the dam of Emily 332, from whom springs the
famous Ballindalloch Ericas.   In the volumes of the 'Herd
Book' published prior to 1879, Emily was said to have been
out of Beauty 96, bred by Sir James Carnegie.   In the
notes supplied to us by the Honourable Charles Carnegie
on the Kinnaird herd, this inaccuracy is fully dealt with.
Emily 332 was bought by the Earl of Southesk for £37
at Mr Watson's sale in September 1853.   She was lot 20
of the sale, and her pedigree was printed in the catalogue
as follows—"Angus, heifer: by Old Jock, dam Beauty—
the dam of Sir T. Burnett's famous bull."   We are informed by Mr Ferguson, Kinnochtry, that this Beauty,
bred at Keillor, the dam of Emily 332, became the property
of Sir Alex. Burnett, and that Mr Hugh Watson bought
her and her yearling bull, The Baronet 339, back from
Crathes in 1856.   Another Beauty bred at Keillor was
Beauty of Tillyfour 2nd 1180, after Young Jock 4, and
out of Favourite 2.   She was a very good cow, with a
large lump on one of her fore legs, and was bought by
Mr M'Combie of Tillyfour at the Keillor sale in 1860 for
£64.   At Tillyfour she produced Ruth 1169 and Jilt 973.

At the Keillor sale in 1860, Mr M'Combie also bought
the daughter of Beauty of Tillyfour 2nd, named Miss Watson 987, for £34 or £37.   Miss Watson, who was sold at
the Tillyfour sale in 1867 to Mr M'Combie of Easter
Skene, is erroneously entered in vol. ii. of the 'Herd
Book' as out of Beauty of Buchan 5.   The error is repeated in the pedigree of Miss M'Combie of Fyvie 1519,
a daughter of Miss Watson, and purchased by the late
Colonel Gordon at the Tillyfour sale in 1867 for 61
guineas.   It also occurs in the pedigrees of the bulls
Derby 377, Disraeli 401, Reform 408, and Taurus 410—
all of whom were descended from Beauty of Tillyfour 2nd
1180, and through her from the Keillor Favourites, and not
from Beauty of Buchan 5, whose dam was Old Grannie 1.

Monarch 44 and the Tillyfour Victors.

The pedigrees of the bull Monarch 44 and the three Victors—Victor 46, Victor 2nd 47, and Victor 3rd 193—who figure prominently in the records of the early Tillyfour cattle, have been imperfectly registered in vol. i. of the 'Herd Book.' We are enabled to supplement the information given in the 'Herd Book' from the private catalogue of the Tillyfour herd, dated 1st January 1850, for the use of which we are indebted to Mr R. C. Auld, Mr M'Combie's nephew. Monarch 44, calved 1843, and bred by Mr Fullerton, Ardovie, was after Panmure 51, and out of Julia 671. These facts are stated in the 'Herd Book.' Of Julia 671, however, no particulars are given in the 'Herd Book' entry, except that she was bred by Mr Fullerton. She was got by Panmure 51, and was out of Susanna, whose dam was Black Meg 766, and sire Captain 97. Mr Fullerton remarked that Susanna did Black Meg no discredit. The three Victors were full brothers, all bred by Mr M'Combie, after Monarch 44, and out of Jean Ann 206. Victor 46 was calved in 1846, Victor 2nd 47 in 1848, and Victor 3rd 193 in 1850.

We are aware of other incorrect entries in vol. i.; but as they are not of so vital a character as the foregoing, we shall endeavour to rectify them as we refer to the various herds in which the animals were produced or principally used.

CHAPTER VII.

EXTINCT HERDS.

(1) The Keillor herd : Old Grannie 1—Her remarkable career, and list of her calves—The Kinnochtry Princesses, Baronesses, and Emilys—Mr Watson's cows Old Favourite and Favourite 2—The Kinnochtry Favourites—Beauty of Tillyfour 2nd 1180—the Wellhouse Ruths and Ballindalloch Jilts—Mr Watson's Beauty and the Ballindalloch Ericas—Lord Southesk's Dora 333—Mr Harry Shaw's Jane of Bogfern 540—The Portlethen Pansys—List of families descended from Keillor cows—Famous bulls bred at Keillor.—(2) The Ardovie and Ardestie herds : Black Meg 766—Panmure 51—The Tillyfour Queen tribe—Families tracing to Ardovie stock—Earl o' Buchan 57—Mr Fullerton's losses by pleuro-pneumonia.—(3) The Tillyfour herd : Cows owned by Mr M'Combie in 1850—Queen Mother 348, and her illustrious offspring—Mr M'Combie's system of breeding—Table showing descendants of Queen Mother 348 —The Pride of Aberdeen family—Remarks on famous animals at Tilly-four—Mr M'Combie's unparalleled success in the show-yard—His public sales.

THE history of the origin, building up, and composition of extinct herds has an important bearing not only upon the leading existing herds, but likewise upon the position which the breed generally has come to occupy. We shall therefore present some details relating to those herds that, although now dispersed, have in the greatest measure con-tributed to the improvement of the breed.

Keillor.

As already noticed, Mr Hugh Watson, Keillor, Forfar-shire, was the first to establish a regular herd of polled cattle. His operations are described in Chapter IV., and therefore a short sketch will suffice here.

Perhaps the most notable animal bred by Mr Watson was Old Grannie, or the Prima Cow, No. 1 of the 'Herd Book.' She was calved in 1824, and died on 1st July 1859, at the age of thirty-five years and six months. Mr Watson's object in keeping her till she died of old age was to ascertain how long an animal of the breed with a fine constitution could be profitably kept, and to what age it would live in its natural state. Old Grannie was the dam of 25 calves, 11 of which were registered in the 'Herd Book.' She gave up breeding in her twenty-ninth year, and yielded no milk after nursing the calf of the previous year. She was exhibited at the Highland Society's show at Aberdeen in 1858, when her owner was awarded the Society's medal as the exhibitor of so remarkable an animal. The cattleman (James Thomson), who had attended her all her lifetime, and had been in the service of Mr Watson for forty-two years, was presented with a medal and premium of 100 francs by the "Société Protection des Animaux Justice et Compassion Hygiène de Paris," through their secretary, M. Dutrone. A photograph of the old cow, taken two days before she died, was, at the request of His Royal Highness the Prince Consort, placed in the collection of cattle photographs at Balmoral in October 1859. Of this photograph an engraving appears in vol. i. of the 'Herd Book,' from which these facts are extracted. The following are the names of the calves of Old Grannie, whose pedigrees are recorded in the 'Herd Book': Bulls, Strathmore 5, calved 1851; Old Windsor 115, sire Black Jock 3; First Memus 129, sire Black Jock 3; Hugh 130, calved 1852, sire Old Jock 1; The Baron 134, sire Black Jock 3. Cows: Hope 3, sire Grey-breasted Jock 2; Lady Clara 4, sire Grey-breasted Jock 2; Beauty of Buchan 5, sire Grey-breasted Jock 2; Young Favourite 61, sire Grey-breasted Jock 2; Edinburgh 64, sire Grey-

breasted Jock 2; Keillor 231, calved 1852, sire Old Jock 1.
It is probable that the date of calving of some of these is
inaccurately stated, and we may note that while the last-
named is given in the list of her produce as one of the
calves of Old Grannie, the dam is not specifically stated
in the entry of Keillor 231. The blood of Old Grannie 1
circulates in the male line in many existing tribes of
cattle, and she has also several living female descendants.
In 1839, Mr Ferguson, Kinnochtry, obtained from Mr
Watson two of Old Grannie's daughters—Young Favourite
61 and Edinburgh 64—and they are now worthily represented by the Kinnochtry Princesses, Baronesses, and
Emilys, to whom reference is made in other portions of
the work. Another daughter of Old Grannie, Lady Clara
4, was bought by Mr M'Combie of Tillyfour, from whom
her daughter Mariana 622 passed into the possession of
Mr M'Combie of Easter Skene.

We are glad to say there are still numerous descendants
of the Keillor cows Old Favourite (who has not been
registered in the 'Herd Book'), and her daughter Favourite
2, respecting the identity of whom there has been some
confusion which it is impossible to completely unravel.
Favourite 2 was bought by Mr Ferguson, Kinnochtry; and
Old Favourite was sold to Mr Bowie in 1848, but she left
no female produce at Mains of Kelly, although she was the
dam of Mr Bowie's bull Earl Spencer 2nd 25. Old Favourite, we may here recall, was the dam of Old Jock 1 and Angus
45. From Favourite 2, Mr Ferguson's Favourite family is
directly descended. Octavia 331 was bought by the Earl
of Southesk at Mr Watson's sale at Auchtertyre in 1853
for £44, being entered in the catalogue as after Old Jock
and out of Old Favourite. Octavia is without female
representative, but her blood is still preserved by the
stock descended from her in the male line, particularly
in the Kinnochtry, Mountblairy, and Montbletton herds.
Beauty of Tillyfour 2nd 1180, out of Favourite 2, and after

Young Jock 4, was purchased by Mr M'Combie of Tillyfour at the Keillor dispersion sale in 1860 for £64. In
Mr M'Combie's possession, she, as already noted, bred in
1863 Jilt 973, and in 1865 Ruth of Tillyfour 1169, both
after Black Prince of Tillyfour 366. We need say nothing
here about the descendants of these animals, further than
to remark that with the Kinnochtry Favourites, the Ballindalloch Jilts, the Wellhouse Ruths, and the Aboyne
Madges, Mr Watson's grand strain of Favourite blood is
in no danger of extinction. The Favourite tribe is further
represented by the offspring of Miss Watson 987, purchased at Keillor in 1860 by Mr M'Combie of Tillyfour.

The Keillor blood is also maintained in the female line
by the Ballindalloch Ericas. Emily 332, bred at Keillor,
and out of one of Mr Watson's cows called Beauty, was
bought by the Earl of Southesk at the Auchtertyre sale in
1853 for 39 guineas, Octavia and Emily having been the
two highest-priced animals at the sale. Emily's daughter,
Erica 843, by Cup-Bearer 59, was acquired from Lord Southesk by Sir George Macpherson Grant, Bart. of Ballindalloch, M.P., and with her he founded his well-known
Erica tribe.

A very superior cow called Dora 333, bred by Mr Watson, was bought by the Earl of Southesk. She founded
a valuable tribe, now extinct in the female line, but still
potent in the male line, through the bulls Druid 225,
Damascus 495, Don Fernando 514, Delaware 457, and
Draco 338, used at Kinnaird, Rothiemay, Tillyfour, Easter
Skene, and Ardhuncart respectively.

Mr Harry Shaw, Bogfern, obtained two heifers from
Mr Watson. From one of them, Jane of Bogfern 540,
by Grey-breasted Jock 2, there are some descendants, the
most noted perhaps being Lord Fife's fine cow Corriemulzie 1701.

From another Keillor cow, named Panmure 278, the
Portlethen Pansy family springs.

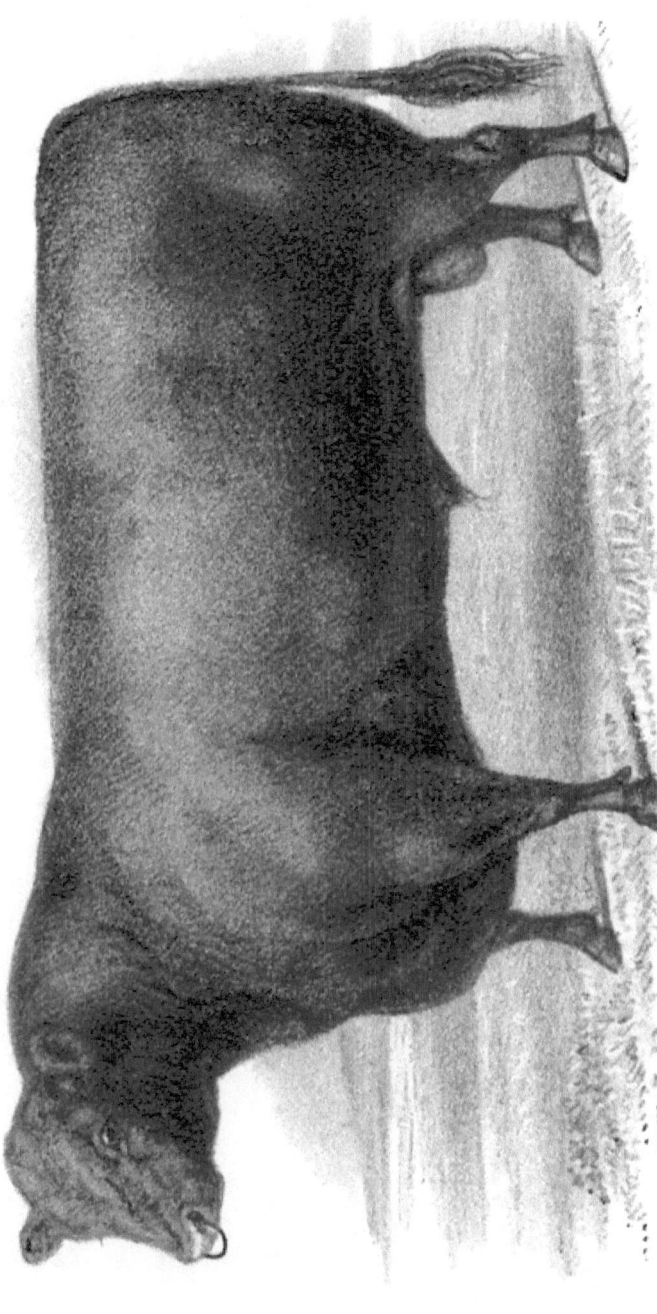

From Life by A.M°Cauci

Hanhart imp.

JUSTICE (1462) at 4 YEARS OLD.

Winner of 1st Prize at Highland Society's Shows at Perth 1879 & 1st at Stirling 1881.

The Property of Snr George Macpherson Grant, Bart, of Ballindalloch

The following shows at a glance the leading Keillor strains of which female representatives exist, as well as those that are extinct in the female line:—

KEILLOR FAMILIES.

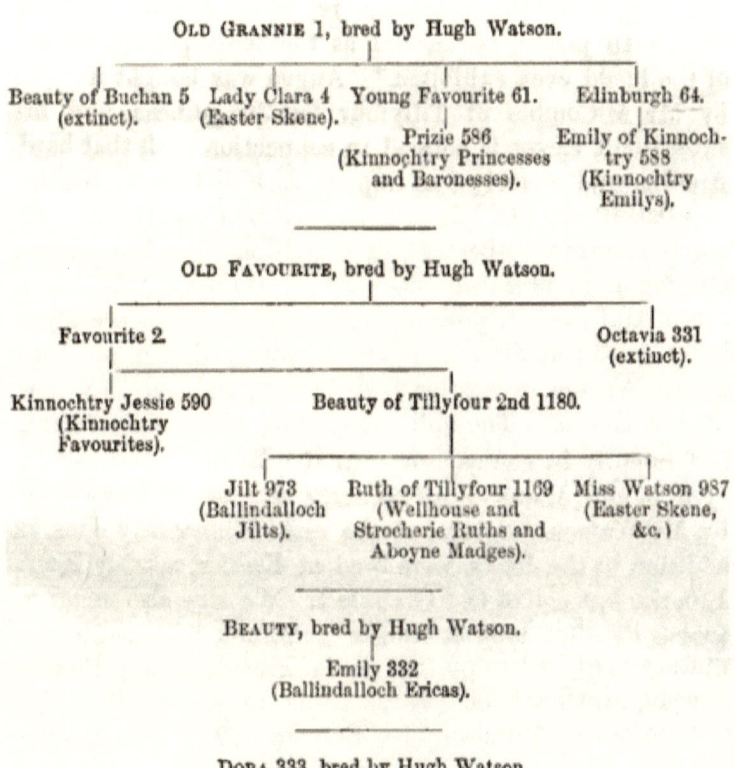

OLD GRANNIE 1, bred by Hugh Watson.

Beauty of Buchan 5 (extinct).   Lady Clara 4 (Easter Skene).   Young Favourite 61.   Edinburgh 64.

Prizie 586 (Kinnochtry Princesses and Baronesses).   Emily of Kinnochtry 588 (Kinnochtry Emilys).

OLD FAVOURITE, bred by Hugh Watson.

Favourite 2.   Octavia 331 (extinct).

Kinnochtry Jessie 590 (Kinnochtry Favourites).   Beauty of Tillyfour 2nd 1180.

Jilt 973 (Ballindalloch Jilts).   Ruth of Tillyfour 1169 (Wellhouse and Strocherie Ruths and Aboyne Madges).   Miss Watson 987 (Easter Skene, &c.)

BEAUTY, bred by Hugh Watson.

Emily 332 (Ballindalloch Ericas).

DORA 333, bred by Hugh Watson (extinct).

JANE OF BOGFERN 540, bred by Hugh Watson (Collithie, Gavenwood, Burnshangie, &c.)

PANMURE 278, bred by Hugh Watson (Portlethen Pansys).

There is scarcely a herd of polled cattle in which the blood of the Keillor bulls is not present. For information regarding the Keillor Jocks we would refer our readers to the chapter immediately preceding. Another celebrated bull bred by Mr Watson was Angus 45, after Old Jock 1, and out of Old Favourite. He was the first prize two-year-old at the Highland Society's show in 1848, and the judges on that occasion reported of him "that he may with justice be classed as the most perfect animal of the breed ever exhibited." Angus was bought in 1846 by Mr M'Combie of Tillyfour for 36 guineas, and his subsequent career is noticed in connection with that herd. Another and scarcely less impressive bull bred at Keillor was Pat 29, after Old Jock 1, and out of Favourite 2. He was the sire of Cup-Bearer 59 and Hanton 228, whose names are found in numerous pedigrees. Marquis 212, also a son of Old Jock 1, proved a most useful sire in the Portlethen herd; as did also Fyvie 13, who, although not bred by Mr Watson, was after Old Jock 1, and out of a cow bred at Keillor. The bull Craigo 260, whose name figures prominently in connection with the Ballindalloch, Montbletton, and Mains of Advie herds, was out of a cow bred by Mr Watson. Several of the early Kinnochtry sires, in addition to the Jocks, were bred at Keillor, notably Hugh 130, the last calf of Old Grannie 1. We may also mention, among the sires bred at Keillor, Strathmore 5 (used in the Crathes herd), Adam 39 (the sire of President 205), Protection 49, Maynooth 58 (whose name appears in Balwyllo pedigrees), Old Windsor 115, Emperor 128, First Memus 582, The Baron 134, Wattie 135, Deeside 168, &c.

Mr Watson sold large drafts in 1848 and 1853; and in 1860, after a most successful and distinguished career, the Keillor herd was dispersed. Times were bad then, and the herd was not in good order, having shortly before passed through a heavy ordeal of pleuro-pneumonia. The prices were accordingly comparatively low. It has, how-

ever, been sufficiently well established that the Keillor
doddies, the dispersion of which occurred under these
adverse circumstances, exerted a most powerful influence
on the improvement of other herds; and happily there is
no likelihood of those interested in polled cattle overlook-
ing or underestimating the services of Mr Watson, continued without intermission for more than half a century,
in developing the merits and spreading the reputation of
the breed.

Ardovie and Ardestie.

Mr William Fullerton, who farmed at Ardovie, and
latterly at Ardestie, commenced to breed polled cattle in
1833, his first important purchase being the cow Black
Meg 766. The famous bull Panmure 51 was added to the
herd in 1841. For particulars respecting the breeding
and appearance of Black Meg 766 and Panmure 51, whose
descendants are now held in high favour, we would refer
our readers to the exhaustive statements respecting them
contained in the preceding chapter. In a letter written
in 1876 to Mr Bowie, Mains of Kelly, with a perusal of
which that gentleman has favoured us, Mr Fullerton
remarks: "When I purchased the bull Panmure 51, late
in September or early in October 1841, he was a year and
six months old, so he was three years old off in 1843 when
he gained the first prize in the class of aged bulls at the
Highland Society's show at Dundee. He cost me £17, 17s.,
a price which a calf would not likely have brought." Panmure became one of the most impressive bulls in the history of the breed. In vol. i. of the 'Herd Book' there
are eleven of his calves registered, but that is only a small
number of his produce. The calves got by Panmure, whose
pedigrees are printed in vol. i., are: bulls—Richmond 6,
calved in 1844, and who passed into the possession of
Mr Ruxton, Farnell; Earl Spencer 24, calved in 1844, and
well known in connection with the Mains of Kelly herd;

H

and Monarch 44, calved in 1843, bought by Mr Ruxton, and
sold by him to Mr Arklay, Bowhill, Brechin, from whom
he was acquired by Mr M'Combie of Tillyfour : cows—
Princess 47, calved in 1843, the dam of the celebrated
Balwyllo sire President 205 ; Lady Panmure 59, who belonged to Mr Ferguson when in Ashmore ; Eliza 65, who
also belonged to Mr Ferguson ; Jean Ann 206, calved in
1844, from whom Mr M'Combie's Victors were bred ;
Miss Taylor 230, calved in 1853 ; Queen Mother 348,
calved in 1843 (out of Queen of Ardovie 29), the foundress of the renowned Queen tribe ; Queen of Scots 72,
and Eppy 73, bred by Mr M'Combie of Easter Skene ;
Queen of Kinnochtry 572, belonging to Mr Ferguson; and
Princess Daughter 832, who was bred by Mr Hugh Watson.

As we have said, there is not the slightest doubt that Panmure left many more calves than those that have found
a place in the ' Herd Book.' In 1843 he was sold to Mr
Farquharson Taylor, Wellhouse, Alford, and was used extensively, and with splendid results, in his herd, and also
in the herds of many others in the Vale of Alford. Of his
numerous progeny in Aberdeenshire, however, there is little
record further than that contained in the pedigrees of the
animals purchased at Mr Fullerton's sale. This sale was
held in 1844, and the event may be truly described as a
starting-point in the annals of the breed. We treat at
length, elsewhere, of the principal descendants of Mr Fullerton's Queen Mother 348. Mr M'Combie has placed it
on record that—" It is to Mr Fullerton I owe my success
as a breeder. I shall always look up to him as the founder
of my stock. From the cow Queen [Queen Mother], bought
by me from Mr Fullerton, has sprung a race of females that
have driven competition before them in Scotland, England,
and France.

Although it is chiefly in the descendants of Black Meg
766, the dam of Queen of Ardovie 29, who produced Queen
Mother 348, that Mr Fullerton's fame as a breeder is pre-

served, these were by no means the only animals of celebrity bred by him. Susan of Balwyllo 422, and Isabella of Balwyllo 423, who established tribes at Balwyllo, were bred by Mr Fullerton, as were also Lively 256, the foundress of the Portlethen family of that name ; Flora 70, the foundress of a family of Floras at The Thorn ; Guinea Pig 120, who went to Mains of Kelly, and from whom Mr Bowie's Gainsborough bulls are descended; Ardestie 1183, the progenitrix of the Mains of Kelly Ardesties ; and others of lesser note.

Isabella of Balwyllo 423, Susan of Balwyllo 422, and Lively 256, bred by Mr Fullerton, were after the bull Earl o' Buchan 57, first prize winner in the aged class at the Highland Society's show at Glasgow in 1850. We are able, by reference to the letter from Mr Fullerton to Mr Bowie, already alluded to, to furnish a few interesting particulars regarding Earl o' Buchan 57. Mr Fullerton says : " I bought a bull from the late Mr Cooper, Hillbrae, Buchan, and I fearlessly called this bull Earl o' Buchan. I found out the bull in this way. His mother was a great big cow, with splendid back and hooks, and plenty of hair; she had a 'snod' rather short head, and had a tap hanging down over her forehead. If you could have found a fault, she was thin on her thighs, but on the whole a wonderful cow, and of great substance. I saw the cow and her calf in the showyard at the Highland Society's meeting at Aberdeen in 1846. The cow, I think, calved in the yard, and it was fancying the calf that made me buy the cow. It was lying covered up with grass at its mother's head, and I only saw its head at first sight. Its face was all glazed like, as you have seen a calf's face when the mother is like to drown it with milk. I made the man take the grass off the calf and set it on its feet. It pleased me much. Mr Cooper would not sell, he said; but by the help of Mr Paterson, Mulben, Mr M'Combie, and others, I at length bought cow and calf. I won at Glasgow with the bull.

It is a mistake to say the mark of the blistering was then on his side. He did not take pleuro when my beasts died. I suppose I saved him by keeping him in an end of the straw-barn."

The last observation as to Earl o' Buchan recalls the disastrous fate of Mr Fullerton's fine herd, which is one of the most melancholy incidents in the records of the breed. Here is Mr Fullerton's own pathetic statement: "My herd was swept off by pleuro in 1859, when in five months I buried 100 head of, I believe, the best herd of polled cattle in Scotland at the time. I reckoned my loss was not under £2000; but had this [1876] been the date of my loss, the figure would have to be raised a little. How my beasts caught the disease, I could never say. I had more polled cattle than my farm would keep, and I had animals on several other farms, both on grass and turnips, which had, I suppose, brought home the fell disease. I had again got a considerable length to recoup my old position, but three times my herd—of nearly thirty at one time, and twenty head or thereby at other two times—was carried away." But for the sales made by Mr Fullerton in 1843 and 1844, it is possible that his choice cattle would now be without representatives. Thanks, however, chiefly to Mr M'Combie of Tillyfour, no families of polled stock are more numerous or more valued than the descendants of those cultivated forty years ago by Mr Fullerton at Ardovie and Ardestie.

Tillyfour.

In other portions of the work, we refer to the position and proceedings of Mr M'Combie of Tillyfour, as a breeder of polled cattle. Here we shall endeavour to furnish a sketch of the material of which his herd was composed, his system of breeding, and notes on some of the more remarkable animals reared at Tillyfour. The Tillyfour herd dates from 1830, Mr M'Combie having about that time succeeded his father in the farm. We do not think it is possible to convey a more accurate description of the stock with which Mr M'Combie first acquired his fame as a breeder, than by quoting from the private catalogue of his herd, dated 1st January 1850. In a short prefatory note to the catalogue, Mr M'Combie says most truly, that " he had directed his earnest attention to the improvement of the Aberdeen or Angus polled breed, with respect to size, symmetry, fineness of bone, strength of constitution, and disposition to accumulate fat, sparing no expense in obtaining the finest animals from the purest stocks." The following is a list of the cows that were in the Tillyfour herd in 1850: 1, Young Charlotte 103, bred by Colonel Dalgairns of Balgavies, sire Black Hugh 316, dam Charlotte ; 2, Lady Ann of Balgavies 102, bred by Colonel Dalgairns of Balgavies, sire Black Hugh 316, dam Lady Ann ; 3, Jean Ann 206, bred by Mr Fullerton, Mains of Ardovie, sire Panmure 51, dam Queen of Ardovie 29 ; 4, Princess, bred by Mr Fullerton, sire Panmure 51, dam a pure Angus cow ; 5, Lady Scott, bred by Mr Scott, Balwyllo, sire Albert, dam belonging to Mr Scott ; 6, Cleopatra, bred by Mr Scott, Balwyllo, sire Albert, dam belonging to Mr Scott ; 7, Balwyllo, bred by Mr Scott, Balwyllo, got by the first prize two-year-old bull at the Eastern Forfarshire Society's show in 1843, dam May Rose ; 8, Queen Mother 348, bred by Mr Fullerton, Ardovie, sire Panmure 51, dam Queen of Ardovie 29 ; 9, Victoria, bred by Mr Watson, Keillor, sire Second Jock (Old Jock 1), dam belonging to Mr Watson ; 10, Clara, bred by Mr Watson, Keillor, sire Second Jock (Old Jock 1), dam belonging to Mr Watson ; 11, Violet, bred by Mr Watson, Keillor, sire First Jock (Grey-breasted Jock 2), dam a pure Angus cow ; 12, Matchless, bred to the owner, sire Panmure 51, dam Matilda ; 13, Duchess, bred by Colonel Fraser of Castle Fraser ; 14, Matilda, bred by the late Mr William-

son, St John's Wells ; 15, Diana, bred by the owner, sire
Monarch 44, dam Georgiua; 16, Mary, bred by Mr
Wilson, Netherton of Clatt; 17, Jenny Lind 27, bred
by Mr Pirie, Colithie ; 18, Georgina, bred by the owner;
19, Amelia, breeder unknown; 20, Susan, bred by Mr
David Watt, Kintocher, sire Rory; 21, Lola Montes 208,
sire Monarch 44, dam Queen Mother 348; 22, Young
Jean Ann 144, sire Monarch 44, dam Jean Ann 206 ;
23, May Rose, bred by the owner, sire first prize bull at
Eastern Forfarshire Agricultural Association's show, dam
Balwyllo; 24, Fair Maid, bred by the owner, sire Monarch
44, dam Lady Scott ; 25, Sophia, bred by the owner, sire
Monarch 44, dam Georgina; 26, Young Mary, sire Monarch 44, dam Mary; 27, Annabella, bred by the late Mr
Walker, Wester Fintray. The bulls in the Tillyfour herd
in 1850 were Victor 46, bred by Mr M'Combie, sire Monarch 44, dam Jean Ann 206; Angus 45, bred by Mr
Watson, Keillor, sire Second Jock (Old Jock 1), dam No.
1 at Mr Watson's sale (Old Favourite) ; and Victor 2nd
47, bred by Mr M'Combie, sire Monarch 44, dam Jean
Ann 206.   The bulls referred to, as most intimately connected with the herd at the time, were Panmure 51, and
his son Monarch 44. In order to provide sufficient information to enable the reader to identify the cows and
bulls in the Tillyfour herd in 1850, we have filled in the
' Herd Book' numbers where possible.   We have also
in most cases omitted Mr M'Combie's description of the
variety to which the animals belonged.   His practice apparently was to refer to animals bred in Forfarshire as
"Angus;" to those bred in Aberdeenshire, and uncon-
nected with the Forfarshire stock, as "Aberdeen;" and to
those bred by himself in which the "Angus" and "Aberdeen" blood was mingled, as "Aberdeen and Angus."
    The strain with which Mr M'Combie's name is most
closely identified is that of the Ardovie Queens, and to
the members of this tribe we shall now particularly

allude. The notes in a former chapter on famous polled
cattle, and our remarks on the herd of Mr Fullerton, Ardovie, convey details, so far as known, as to the breeding
and characters of Black Meg 766, and her daughter, Queen
of Ardovie 29, whose sire was Captain 97, bred by Mr
Sim, Panlathie. Mr M'Combie was present at the Ardovie sale in 1844, and purchased a yearling heifer out of
Queen of Ardovie 29, that he afterwards called Queen
Mother 348, the name having been suggested by the con-
troversy then raging in reference to the Spanish marriages.
Queen Mother was after the celebrated bull, Panmure 51,
and the price paid for her was only £12, 10s. The cow
proved somewhat obstinate as a breeder. Mr Dixon, in
'Field and Fern,' says: "As she turned from her few
first services, she was put for a penalty to draw wood, and
did all the ridging-up of thirty acres of turnips as well."
It was not till 1847 that she had her first calf. Queen
Mother gained numerous prizes at the national and local
shows, being, when thirteen years old, the second prize
cow in a very strong class at the Highland Society's meeting at Inverness in 1856. She was then sold to Mr Bowie,
Mains of Kelly, and died on 20th August 1858, apparently
from old age.

The 'Herd Book' records four calves out of Queen
Mother—Lola Montes 208, Bloomer 201, Windsor 202,
and Victoria of Kelly 345. The first three were bred by
Mr M'Combie, and the last was bred by Mr Bowie after
he obtained the cow in 1856. In Mr M'Combie's book,
'Cattle and Cattle-Breeders,' he enunciates opinions as to
breeding which it will be useful to quote here. "In-and-
in breeding," he says, "may be pursued for a time, until
the type is developed; but to continue for any length of
time to breed in-and-in is not only against my experience,
but, I believe, against nature." In the breeding of these
three daughters of Queen Mother, the principle on which
Mr M'Combie proceeded is illustrated. He desired to

"develop the type," and for that purpose resorted to the
mating of animals very closely related. He put Queen
Mother to Monarch 44, bred by Mr Fullerton, and acquired by Mr M'Combie shortly after the Ardovie sale in
1844. Queen Mother, as we have already mentioned, was
after Panmure 51, and Monarch was not only a son of
Panmure, but also out of Julia 671, a daughter of Panmure. Moreover, Julia was out of Susanna, a daughter
of Captain 97 and Black Meg 766. From this mating
of Queen Mother and Monarch came, in 1847, the heifer
calf Lola Montes 208, while another mating of Queen
Mother and Monarch resulted, in 1849, in the production
of Bloomer 201. Mr M'Combie then slightly varied his
system, only, however, in the direction of still greater
concentration of blood. Queen Mother was, in 1849,
put to Victor 46. Victor was a son of Monarch 44,
and out of Jean Ann 206, a full sister of Queen Mother
348. Thus Queen Mother, Monarch, and Jean Ann were
all by Panmure. Those acquainted with such matters
will recognise that, by these alliances, the blood of Panmure was nearly as much concentrated in the Tillyfour herd as was that of Favourite 252 in the early
Shorthorn pedigrees of Charles and Robert Colling.
There was certainly no degeneracy in the produce of
this very close cross between Victor and Queen Mother,
for the cow Windsor 202, who resulted from it, was one
of the most handsome as well as one of the best breeding
animals at Tillyfour. Notwithstanding her excellence,
however, Mr M'Combie evidently thought he had gone
far enough in the direction of in-breeding.

In fact, it would appear as if he had considered that he
had gone too far, because, instead of, as might have been
expected, following up the use of Monarch and Victor on
the closely bred Panmure cows with a slightly diluted
out-cross, he next introduced into his herd a bull that, so
far as the 'Herd Book' shows, had no connection with

his own stock. This was the celebrated Angus 45, bred by Mr Watson, Keillor, after Old Jock 1, and out of Old Favourite. In taking this step, Mr M'Combie proved, what was frequently manifested in his career as a breeder, that he was not influenced by jealousy of any rival. When he discovered a really good and pure-bred animal, he did not care, provided it suited his purpose, in whose herd it had been produced, but bought it if he happened to be in want of it. Mr M'Combie had already "developed the type" of his Queen tribe, and had proved its excellence by its capacity to produce within itself such stock as Lola Montes, Bloomer, and Windsor. He could therefore afford to disregard any suggestions that he was in danger of compromising his reputation as a breeder by going to Keillor for a stock sire. Angus joined the Tillyfour herd in 1848, having been bought at Mr Watson's sale that year for the comparatively small sum of £36. In our notice of the Keillor herd we quote the opinion of the judges at the Highland Society's show at Edinburgh in 1848 as to the merits of Angus, who there won the first prize, Mr M'Combie's Victor being second. Angus was used for a considerable time at Tillyfour, but it is a singular fact that only three calves after him, and out of cows descended from Queen Mother, are entered in the 'Herd Book.' These were—Charlotte 203, out of Lola Montes; The Belle 205, out of Bloomer; and Beauty of Morlich 2072, out of Windsor 202. It is from Lola Montes's calf Charlotte that the most valued branch of the Queen tribe has sprung. Charlotte, who was considered one of the best cows bred at Tillyfour, had a most distinguished show-yard career, on which we will only remark here that her winnings included first prizes at the Highland Society's show, and at the Paris Exhibition in 1856.

Angus was succeeded at Tillyfour in 1854 by Hanton 228, purchased from his breeder, Mr Bowie, Mains of Kelly, for £105, after he had gained the first prize of

the Highland Society at Berwick.   Hanton was got by Pat
29, bred by Mr Watson, Keillor (a son of Old Jock 1 and
Favourite 2), and out of Lizzie 227, whose sire, Spencer's
Son 154, was a grandson of Panmure 51.   Mr M'Combie
in using him, therefore, was able, at the same time that he
continued the blood of Angus 45, to infuse more of the
Panmure blood among his stock.   Hanton got a great
many excellent calves, and he was used with especial
success on the Angus 45 cows, the most noteworthy produce being Charlotte's three daughters—the invincible
Pride of Aberdeen 581, Empress of France 578, and
Daisy of Tillyfour 1165.

   It is very instructive and interesting to observe Mr
M'Combie's next step in breeding.   Hanton gave a
diluted reinfusion of Panmure blood, and so satisfied
does Mr M'Combie seem to have been with the result,
that he altered in practice the principle he had laid down—
that in-and-in breeding should be abandoned after the
type is developed.   We have stated that the cow Windsor
202 was the closest of the in-bred daughters of Queen
Mother.   Mr M'Combie bred from her in 1856 the
splendid bull Windsor 221, after Hanton 228.   He was
not then in need of a stock sire, Hanton being still in
use, so Windsor 221 was sold to Mr Brown, Westertown.
In 1858 the cow Windsor 202 calved, to Hanton,
Rob Roy Macgregor 267, and this full brother of Windsor
221 was the animal Mr M'Combie selected to succeed
Hanton.   It will have been gathered from our remarks
that Rob Roy Macgregor had not the violent Angus 45
cross.   He was used in the herd with much success, and
was followed by his son Black Prince of Tillyfour 366,
who was out of Maid of Orleans 580 (a daughter of
Bloomer 201 and Hanton), and also without the Angus
45 cross.   We believe Black Prince of Tillyfour to have
been one of the most impressive bulls bred by Mr
M'Combie.   By the successive use of Hanton, his son,
Rob Roy Macgregor and Roy Roy Macgregor's son, Black

Prince of Tillyfour, Mr M'Combie had again gone as far in the direction of line breeding as his opinions on the subject would permit him; and he then thought it advisable to have some more fresh blood.

Mr M'Combie's next choice of a sire was in every respect most judicious. He attended the Kinnaird sale in 1861, and purchased the bull calf Don Fernando 514, bred by the Earl of Southesk. Don Fernando was a son of Windsor 221, of Mr M'Combie's own breeding, and his dam, Dulcinea 334, was out of the Keillor cow Dora 333, her sire Cup-Bearer 59, going back to the Keillor and Ardovie blood, so skilfully blended at Mains of Kelly. As a successor to Don Fernando, Mr M'Combie bought President 4th 368, bred by Mr Leslie, The Thorn. His show-yard achievements alone—he having been first prize yearling and two-year-old at Highland Society's shows— would have entitled him to a place at Tillyfour, but in addition to that, his breeding was very fine. An analysis of his pedigree discloses a strong infusion of Panmure and Ardovie blood, mixed with Keillor strains. Bright 454, after Black Prince of Tillyfour 366, and out of Mr Collie's Normahal, was next used. In Mr M'Combie's subsequent selection of sires there was not perhaps quite so much method displayed, although most of the bulls were more or less intimately connected with the Panmure and Queen sorts. It should be borne in mind that it was in 1868 that Mr M'Combie was chosen to represent his native county in Parliament, and during the time he occupied a seat in the Legislature of the country—from 1868 to 1876, when he retired—he was necessarily unable to exercise so much personal supervision as formerly over the management of his herd.

It will be convenient and useful to introduce here a table showing the principal descendants of Queen Mother 348, discontinuing the list with the names of animals that have formed families, and noting the lines that are without living female representatives :—

QUEEN MOTHER 348, calved 1843, sire Panmure 51, dam Queen of Ardovie 29, by Captain 97, g.d. Black Meg 706.

- **Bloomer 201, by Monarch 44.**
  - Windsor 262, by Victor 46.
    - Victoria of Kelly 345, by Cup-Bearer 59.
    - Beauty of Mortlich 2972, by Angus 45.
  - Alice 234 (extinct).
    - Maid of Orleans 580, by Hanton 228 (extinct).
    - The Belle 205, by Angus 45.
      - Fancy of Tillyfour 1195, by Hanton 228.
      - Lovely of Tillyfour 1166, by Rob Roy Macgregor 267.

- **Lola Montes 296, by Monarch 44.**
  - Favourite 1257, by Hanton 228.
    - Matilda of Yonderton 1712, by Hanton 228.
    - Duchess of Westertown 927, by Rob Roy Macgregor 267.
  - Margaret 579, by Hanton 228 (extinct).
    - Daisy of Tillyfour 1165, by Hanton 228.
      - Rosy, by President 4th 368.
      - Vine of Tillyfour 1167, by Black Prince of Tillyfour 366.

- **Charlotte 203, by Angus 45.**
  - Empress of France 578, by Hanton 228.
    - Pride of Aberdeen 581, by Hanton 228.
      - Dandy of Drumin 949, by Rob Roy Macgregor 267.
  - Crinoline 204, by Victor 3rd 193.
    - Eugene of Tillyfour 3257, by President 4th 368.
    - Chaff 855, by Black Prince of Tillyfour 366.

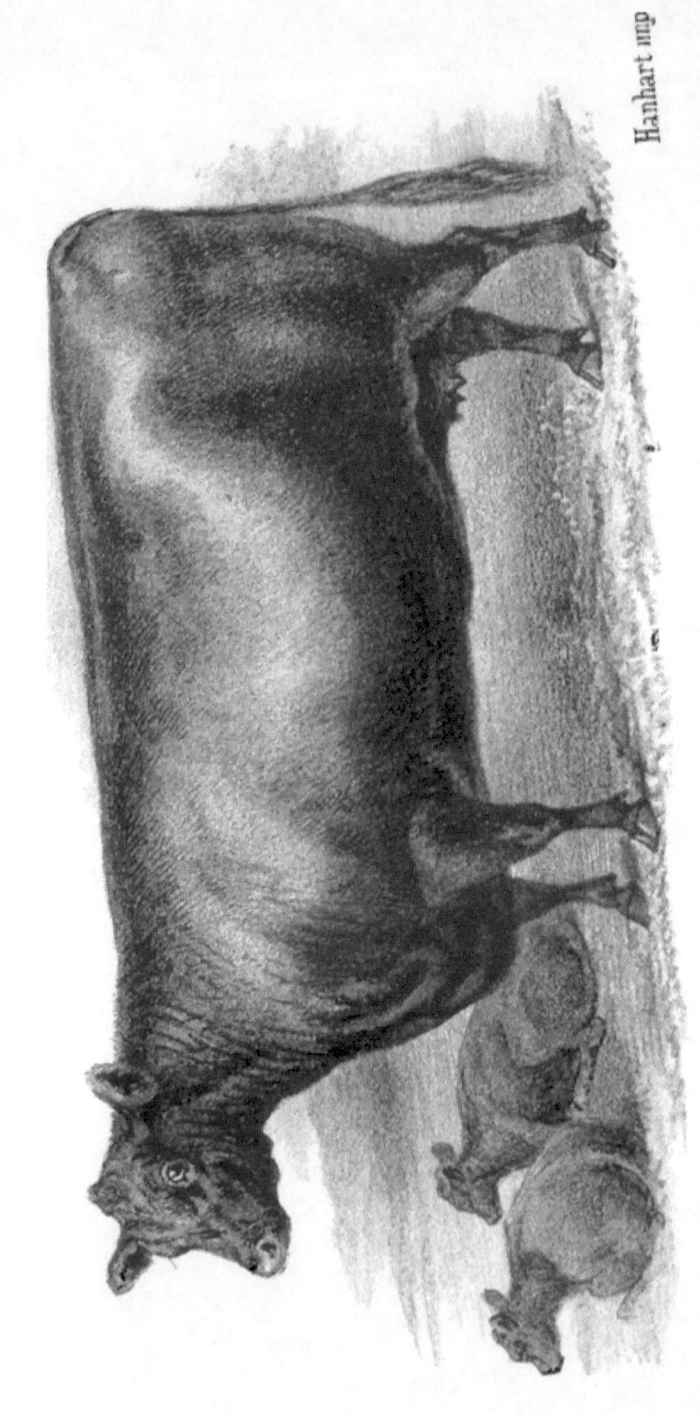

Of the descendants of Queen Mother, Charlotte 203, and her daughter Pride of Aberdeen 581, were the most illustrious. After the preceding remarks we need say nothing here regarding the celebrity of the animals embraced in their pedigrees. Nor is it necessary at present to enlarge on their individual merit. Sufficient proof of their excellence is found in the fact, that these two cows were considered about the best of any breed exhibited at two great international shows—Charlotte at Paris in 1857, and Pride of Aberdeen at Battersea in 1862. Mr M'Combie paid special attention to the development of the branch of the Queen tribe founded by Pride of Aberdeen. She bred exceedingly well, and the family of polled cattle in which occur the names of Mr M'Combie's favourite cows, Pride of Aberdeen, Charlotte, and Queen Mother, is held in very high esteem by breeders.

It ought to be noticed that at Mr Fullerton's sale in 1844, Mr M'Combie purchased Jean Ann 206, a full sister of Queen Mother. From her he bred his three Victor bulls, as also Young Jean Ann 144, who was the dam of the Highland Society's first prize cow Fair Maid of Perth 313, by Angus 45. The strain is now extinct in the female line.

Hitherto we have confined our remarks on the Tillyfour herd to the members of the Queen tribe bred there. Although that was the family to the rearing of which Mr M'Combie devoted his chief attention, he also owned and bred several famous animals of other strains. Among these we may mention Beauty of Tillyfour 2nd 1180 bred at Keillor, and of Mr Watson's Favourite tribe. Besides several good bulls, Beauty 2nd bred Miss Watson 987 by President 3rd 246; Jilt 973 by Black Prince of Tillyfour 366; and Ruth of Tillyfour 1169 also by Black Prince of Tillyfour. We need not at present dwell on the distinguished descendants of this branch of the Keillor Favourite tribe. Of other celebrated animals owned or bred by Mr M'Combie, a few may be noticed as follows: Rauiston 352, the foundress of the Drumin Beauty and the Mulben Caroline families; Young Jenny Lind 207, the foundress of the Mains of Kelly Jennets; Kate 12, foundress of the Kinnaird Kathleens; Young Charlotte 103, foundress of the Montbletton Charlottes; Bess 1181, foundress of the Indego Graces; Bracelet 1010, by Black Prince of Tillyfour 366, foundress of the Melville Bracelets; Mayflower of Montbletton 614, foundress of the Montbletton Mayflowers; Mr Collie's prize cow Mayflower 314; Normahal 726, and Zara 1228, from whom sprung the Ardgay Zaras; Nightingale 262, foundress of the Portlethen Nightingales; Heiress of Balwyllo 461, from whom descends the Balwyllo Isabellas now at Montbletton; Lady Clara 4, and Mariana 622, from whom sprung the Easter Skene Lady Claras; Young Lady Ann 307, foundress of the Westertown Lady Anns; Matchless 390, representing the very old herd of Mr Williamson, St John's Wells, from whom Mr Brown, Westertown, bred the dam of President of Westertown 354, &c. Some years before his death, Mr M'Combie added to his herd from Mulben and Aboyne a good many descendants of Pride of Aberdeen. He also bought members of the Sybil and Halt families from Baads, and these became very distinguished in his hands. Purchases were further made at Rothiemay, Easter Tulloch, Melville, and elsewhere.

It affords us pleasure to be able to give a few remarks descriptive of some of the most famous of the Tillyfour cattle. These we have been favoured with by Mr William Joss, now residing at Blairshinnoch, near Banff, and who had charge of the Tillyfour herd in its palmy days, from 1857 to 1868. Mr Joss's remarks are so interesting, and his sketch is so graphic, that we take the liberty of presenting his statement in his own words: " I am somewhat at a loss what to write about the polled cattle, as, after a lapse of twenty-four years, it is no wonder although their

characteristics are fading from my memory. I have tried
to bring them in view again, and shall begin my description with the bull Hanton 228. He was a bull of great
constitution. As an evidence of this, I may state that after
his return from the Paris Exhibition in 1856, where he
got foot-and-mouth disease, he lay for a week in an old
smithy not able to rise, but he ate three cakes of oilcake
a day (each cake generally weighs 7 lb.), and a feed of
bruised oats, and during that time he took on three inches
in girth. He got boots made, was shipped to Inverness,
and took the first prize. Hanton was very lengthy, and
handled like a glove. The only thing bad about him was
his head, on which were loose scurs, which made the head
look a little square. He was serviceable to the end, and
had the use of himself, although of great weight — he
usually scaled a ton. When in condition, he was as play-
ful when seven years old as a yearling, but with strangers
he got crusty. No wonder he did so, considering the ex-
posure to which he was subjected at shows, travelling by
sea and land. He had also to be thrown now and again
to have his feet dressed, as they never recovered the disease. As everybody was poking and punching at him, he
was always ready for 'war' if he thought any one was
meddling too much with him. He had a great fondness
for travelling in the cattle-van, and ran into it whenever he
saw the door let down. He was a very sure stock-getter,
and taking him altogether, few better have appeared.
Standard-Bearer 229 (the first prize bull at the Highland
Society's show at Aberdeen in 1858) was of another type
—low standing and smaller in size, but very sweet. He
had immense fore-end, but was not proportionable in the
hind-quarters. He was not a good breeder; and I knew
of only one calf by him when at Tillyfour, out of a small
dairy cow; but I believe he had some after he went to
Carron on Speyside. As I have said, this bull had an
extra fore-end, for I well remember tying him in his stall

at Aberdeen in 1858, with his head out to the alley, and
the people remarking that I was making the most of him.
Among other bulls I particularly remember when I was
at Tillyfour, were Don Fernando 514, Lord Clyde 249,
President 4th 368, Bright 454, Champion 459, Rob Roy
Macgregor 267, and Black Prince of Tillyfour 366. As to
the last two, I think they were kept on for stock—not so
much for the merits they had, but because they were good
useful bulls, with good pedigrees. During the time they
were stock bulls at Tillyfour, I think the number of cows
was heavy, and they were never fed for show-yard
purposes, consequently they were very useful in serving,
and had good crops of calves. Turning to the cows at
Tillyfour, I may first mention Charlotte 203. Like her
fellow-traveller Hanton 228, she possessed an excellent
constitution, as was proved by her coming through all the
diseases that the bovine race is heir to—foot-and-mouth,
pleuro, &c. &c. She was all over a sweet-looking, level,
nice-touching cow, with fine temper; and when in her
summer dress, the letters E. U. I.—burnt into her neck
when she gained the first prize at Paris in 1856, and
which came in in white hair—looked like a medal round
her neck. I consider Charlotte the best cow of the breed
I ever saw. It made no difference lean or fat, she was
always level-looking, without patchiness of any kind
about her. She was an excellent breeder to the last, and
generally had better heifers than bulls. Bloomer 201 was
larger than Charlotte, but not so level and sweet, nor so
fine in the bone. She was an excellent worker in any
kind of harness, worked her ten hours the time of the
turnip laying down, and brought up twin calves. This
was to get her to keep to her service, and keep her down
in condition.

"Writing about that brings it to my mind that Daisy
1165 and Fancy 1195, who both came to be Highland
Society first-prize cows, when two years old were not

like to keep to their service, and were fed on barley
straw and water the most of a summer season, and
yet maintained condition rarely met with. I mention
this to show the good constitution of the race. Crinoline
204, out of Charlotte, was a sweet cow, and had white
legs, but was not quite so robust as some of the others.
Lola Montes 208 was an old cow before I saw her, and
was losing her shapes with a rheumatic leg. The cow
Windsor 202, like Bloomer, was a worker, and threw some
excellent stock. Pride of Aberdeen 581 was a very small
calf, and was not thought much of when a calf, until she
was weaned, as her mother, Charlotte, was not a great
milker. I had always a favour for the calf. One day
when Mr M'Combie and I were looking over her, he made
some not very favourable observation about her, and I said
I should not wonder although she were *the Pride of Aberdeen*, which she was, at the summer show. Hence the
name and origin of this distinguished tribe. As she grew,
she turned the nearest to perfection in animal I ever saw,
but, like her mother, never was a great milker. She was
a good breeder of heifers, and a fine feeder, which was one
of the principal things I had to look to at that time.
Many of the rougher cows in the herd were far better
milkers, and some of these rough cows produced grand
bullocks. One cow, Lady Agnes, a big, rough, large-
quartered beast, was the mother of the celebrated ox,
Black Prince. Fair Maid of Perth 313, Kate of Aberdeen,
two Mayflowers, Nightingale 262, Beauty of Tillyfour 2nd
1180, and Jenny Lind, all run in my mind as first-class
cows. The Belle 205 was an instance of a free-martin
breeding, as she was a twin with a bull. She was a sweet
cow, and came out of the pleuro."

It has sometimes been remarked that Mr M'Combie's
fame as a breeder rests chiefly on the fact that he was able
to send out a wonderful lot of females, and that he had
but little success as a breeder of bulls. This observation

is not well-founded. It is quite true that the bulls bred
by Mr M'Combie did not figure so prominently in the
show-yard as the females reared at Tillyfour. That was
perhaps due mainly to the fact that the male animals were
too valuable to force for showing purposes. Any one who
wishes to estimate accurately the merit of the Tillyfour
bulls, should look at the accounts of the Westertown, Kinnaird, Ballindalloch, Mains of Kelly, Easter Skene,
Drumin, Rothiemay, Castle Fraser, Montbletton, Kinnochtry, Tullochallum, and numerous other herds. A
few of the bulls bred at Tillyfour may be noted. First
there were the three Victors; then Windsor 221; Alford
231; Young Panmure 232; Napoleon 257; Rob Roy
Macgregor 267; Black Jock of Tillyfour 365; Black
Prince of Tillyfour 366; Sir James 369; Derby 377;
Defiance 397; Marshal 399; Garibaldi of Haughton 707;
Hero 400; Disraeli 401; Trojan 402; Reform 408;
Squire 436; Bright 454; Champion 459; Scotsman
474; Remarkable 482; Major of Tillyfour 509; Clova
517; Black Prince of Clova 518; Tam o' Shanter 491;
Shah 680, &c.

We shall not attempt to enumerate the prizes won by
Mr M'Combie in the show-yard, which, from the first
premium won at Alford in 1832 to the crowning victory
at Paris in 1878, furnishes a record of success without
precedent in the annals of stock-breeding. A remarkable
feature connected with Mr M'Combie's show cattle was that
nearly all his prize animals were of the Queen tribe. If
there were few of this tribe in the champion group at
Paris, the reason is not far to seek. Mr M'Combie, as we
already mentioned, was unable so carefully to supervise
the management of his herd when he was in Parliament as
when he could devote his whole attention to it. But for
this, we feel satisfied he would not have allowed so many
of his best animals to be sold in 1874. Had not this sale
taken place, it might not have been necessary for him to

have included representatives of other families than his own in the group which won the highest honours that have yet been bestowed on the polled breed.

Mr M'Combie held numerous sales of breeding cattle. The first of these took place in 1850, and the dispersion sale was in 1880. Altogether about 350 breeding animals were sold publicly from the Tillyfour herd for upwards of £14,000. The influence of the herd has been widespread. There is not a breeder who has not profited by the lifelong exertions of Mr M'Combie towards the improvement of the breed.

CHAPTER VIII.

EXTINCT HERDS—CONTINUED.

(1) The Westertown herd: Families reared by Mr Brown—Sires used full of Panmure 51 and Queen blood—Mr Brown's method of breeding—Loss by pleuro-pneumonia—Revival of the herd—Its success in the show-yard.—(2) The Kinnaird herd: Its antiquity—Description of the early polled cattle at Kinnaird—Cows in the herd in 1840—Remarks on tribes cultivated at Kinnaird—Old Lady Anne 743—The Floras, Formosas, and Fannys—The Sarah and Beauty tribes extinct in female line—The Earl of Southesk and his herd—His important purchases—Dora 333, Kate 12, and Kathleen 339—Cup-Bearer 59, and his show-yard victories—Pride of Angus 176—Octavia 331—Emily 332, and her daughter Erica—The bull Windsor 221—Notes on the cattle bred at Kinnaird—The fatal rinderpest, and extinction of the herd.—(3) The Ardgay herd: The Zara tribe—Fair Maid of Perth 313, and Mayflower 314—The Honourable Charles Carnegie's recollections of the Ardgay stock.

Westertown.

At Westertown, Fochabers, a herd of polled cattle was owned by the late Mr George Brown's father about half a century ago, and animals exhibited from it gained prizes at the early shows of the Morayshire Farmers' Club. In 1853 Mr John Brown gave up to his son, Mr George Brown, the entire management of the farm. The Westertown herd may thus, for all practical purposes, be said to date from that year. When the herd was dispersed in 1874, it consisted of five families. These were the Roses, tracing from Marion 308 (calved in 1855, by the Tillyfour bull Uncle Tom 90), bred by Mr James Fraser, Lhanbryde, Elgin; the Victorias, tracing from Victoria of Auchinbo 127, bred by Mr Gordon, Auchinbo, who for many years owned polled cattle; the Lady Anns, tracing from Young Lady Ann 307, bred by Mr M'Combie of Tillyfour, calved in 1850, by Victor 46, and out of Lady Ann of Balgavies 102, bred by Colonel Dalgairns of Balgavies; and the Duchesses, tracing from Duchess of Westertown 927, bred by Mr M'Combie of Tillyfour, calved in 1860, and bought as a calf in 1860 for 19 guineas. Duchess was got by Rob Roy Macgregor 267, a son of Windsor 202, of the Queen tribe, and out of Favourite 1237, also of the Queen tribe, and, like Windsor 202, after Hanton 228. The remaining family was the Violet, from Clara 89, bred by Mr Brown. Among other cows in the herd, but extinct in the female line for many years prior to 1874, were Paris Kate 309, calved in 1850, bred by Mr Bowie, and purchased in 1857 at West Scryne for £41; and Matchless 390, calved in 1849, bred at Tillyfour, after Monarch 44, and descended from the St John's Wells herd.

The first sire of importance used by Mr George Brown was Victor 46, calved in 1846, bred by Mr M'Combie of Tillyfour, after Monarch 44, a son of Panmure 51, and out of Jean Ann 206, a daughter of Panmure 51. Then followed Uncle Tom 90, another bull bred at Tillyfour, but whose pedigree is not recorded. Next came Earl Spencer 3rd 26, from Mains of Kelly, a great-grandson of Panmure 51. In 1856 Mr Brown bought a bull calf from Mr M'Combie, which proved the most valuable and potent animal introduced to the herd. The bull was Windsor 221, calved in 1856, after Hanton 228, and out of Windsor 202, who was a daughter of Victor 46 and Queen Mother 384, being thus very closely bred from the Panmure and Queen blood. Windsor was sold in 1858 to the Earl of Southesk, and his doings at Kinnaird and in the show-yard are fully noticed in connection with that herd. On the

sale of Windsor 221, King Charles 236, bred by Lord Southesk, and descended on the dam's side from a daughter of
Monarch 44, was transferred to Westertown. The chief
sires afterwards used were all bred at Westertown. They
were Prince Albert 237, calved in 1858, a son of Windsor
221 and Maid of Moray 310; President 354, calved in
1859, a son of Windsor 221 and Elizabeth 391, by Victor
46, Elizabeth being of the St John's Wells Matchless strain ;
Captain 468, calved in 1863, a son of President 354, and
Rose 3rd 925 by Prince Albert 237 ; Success 469, calved
in 1865, a son of Captain 468 and Duchess 927 by Rob
Roy Macgregor; March 355, calved in 1867, a son of Success 469 and Lady Ann 926 by Prince Albert 237 ; Baron
Settrington 356, calved in 1869, a son of Duchess 927 and
March 355; and Duke of Perth 357, calved in 1870, a
son of March 355 and Rose 3rd 925.   It will thus be
seen that all the sires used by Mr Brown (with the exception of Uncle Tom 90, of whose breeding there is no
record) had flowing in their veins a plenteous stream of
the blood of Panmure 51 and the Ardovie Queens.

Mr Brown was perhaps, of all breeders of polled
cattle, the most systematic. There was no haphazard in
his mode of breeding. He fixed upon a certain strain of
blood and a certain type of cattle, and he laboured to
realise a distinct aim with such skill and method as had
been displayed by the Messrs Booth and Mr Bates in
breeding Shorthorns. His cattle were bred from close
affinities, but the dangers of excessive in-breeding were
guarded against by keeping a large number of stock bulls.
As the result of Mr Brown's rare tact and judgment, a
thoroughly characteristic herd was built up. His animals
possessed a uniformity of type and style that was quite
unmistakable. In the show-yard the herd had reached
high eminence for several years previous to 1860, when it
sustained a serious reverse. At the Highland Society's
show at Dumfries that year, Mr Brown exhibited three

animals. They all won prizes, but the victory was dearly bought. The cattle caught pleuro-pneumonia at Dumfries, and communicated it to the rest of the herd, which, before the plague was stayed, was reduced to seven animals. Mr Brown courageously, and with renewed energy and determination, resumed breeding with this remnant of a previously splendid herd. Showing was abstained from until 1868, when the bull March retrieved the laurels of the herd; and until Mr Brown's death in 1874, show-yard honours again fell thick and fast. The new herd had thus been actually in existence for only about fourteen years, a period too brief for the maturing of Mr Brown's plans. Had his life been spared a few years longer, it was confidently expected that Mr Brown would have made Westertown the scene of as wonderful achievements in cattle-breeding as Warlaby or Kirklevington. But this was not to be. Mr Brown's death in 1874 abruptly terminated a career that was full of promise. At the dispersion of his herd in 1874 the animals fell into good hands. They enriched many already valuable stocks, and specimens of the Westertown families still exist in considerable numbers. It is to be regretted, however, that no one has attempted to complete the half-finished work commenced so systematically and successfully by Mr Brown.

Kinnaird.

The Honourable Charles Carnegie has kindly favoured us with a long and most interesting communication regarding the first herd of polled cattle at Kinnaird Castle. This herd occupied such a prominent position, and animals bred in it have so largely contributed to the improvement of herds into which they were introduced, that information regarding it is of much importance. The extinction of the herd by rinderpest in 1865 was a calamity to the polled breed.

It is, Mr Carnegie says, impossible to trace the origin of
the Kinnaird stock, which has probably gone on from
generation to generation from a very remote period.　At
the time of the minority of the late Sir James Carnegie of Southesk, which lasted from 1805 till 1821, the
home farm of Kinnaird was farmed by his mother, Lady
Carnegie, and then all the cattle were polled Angus—
indeed, probably there was no other breed in the district.　Lady Carnegie frequently spoke to the Honourable
Charles Carnegie about her cattle and their splendid
milking-qualities, also of her system of rearing calves.
This system consisted in feeding the calf with a mixture
of skimmed milk and boiled turnips—her secret of getting the calves to take to it kindly being to put some of
the boiled turnips into the very first milk that was given
to the calf, as, if the calf had ever tasted pure milk, it
would have been very difficult to induce it to drink the
mixture.

As far as known to Mr Carnegie, no stock but polled
Angus was at Kinnaird until about 1834, when one or two
Ayrshire cows and an Ayrshire bull were got.　The best
of the Angus cows were then sent to the bulls in the
neighbourhood, there being polled stock at that time at
every one of the adjacent farms.　The use of the Ayrshire
bull was discontinued in 1840, though some of the Ayrshire cows continued to be kept till 1849; and Mr Carnegie remembers some most excellent stock got by the
polled bull from these remaining Ayrshires.　They were
generally black and polled, and some of them might easily
have been taken for pure Angus.

At the time of Mr Carnegie's first personal recollection of the Kinnaird herd, there were about seven pure
Angus cows, besides the cows belonging to the servants,
all of which were polled.　The prevailing colour of the
Kinnaird herd, as of all the cattle in the county, wa
black; but there was hardly a herd which had not a

brindled cow in it, and, in many, a dun or a grey. Those
of the latter colour were called "droners," and were supposed to have a strain of Dutch blood in them, by descent
from some cows brought over by a Dutch company that
attempted to reclaim the basin of Montrose. Mr Carnegie remembers, especially, grey cows belonging to the
late Mr Lyall, Old Montrose; the late Mr Ruxton, Farnell; and the late Mr Mustard, Leuchland. The Kinnaird herd in 1840 had no grey cows, but the brindled
cow Brandy is one of Mr Carnegie's earliest recollections.
She was a very great favourite of the late Sir James
Carnegie, who used to say that she was the handsomest
Angus cow in the byre, except Lady Anne. She was of a
regular brindled colour, red striped with black, and had
very large hairy ears. A daughter of hers was pure red,
but not being a good milker, was not retained. There are
no traceable descendants of this cow. In 1840 there were
the following polled cows in the byre at Kinnaird: Old
Lady Anne 743, of whom more afterwards; Lucy 670
(misnamed "of Craigo" in the 'Herd Book,' she having
nothing to do with that place), bought as a calf from the
late Mr Lyall, Old Montrose, then at Carcary; Brandy,
the brindled cow mentioned above; Charlotte, Margaret,
Jane, and Mary. Jane died in 1840, and the other ones,
without 'Herd Book' numbers, have left no traceable
descendants. The cattleman, however, had a dun-coloured
cow called Beauty. She was the dam of Beauty 96, also
of a dark-dun colour, and of a black cow entered in the
'Herd Book' as Angus 95.

The only addition made to the herd by Sir James, except
the descendants of the above, was in 1846, when the cow
Sarah 140 was bought from the late Mr Lyall, Old Montrose.
The bulls used were Colin 35, calved in 1840, after the
Old Montrose bull Wattie 135, and out of Lucy 670. As
a yearling, he beat the celebrated Panmure 51 at the local
show; but the style of keeping he afterwards got was not

likely to make a show-yard animal of him, and he was unsuccessful at the Highland Society's show at Dundee in
1843.   Colin was succeeded by his son, Southesk 34, from
Old Bell 98; and just before Sir James Carnegie's death in
1849, a young bull was purchased from Mr Ruxton, Farnell.   This bull was a son of Adam 39, and his name
appears in some pedigrees.   He was used only for those
cows that were too closely bred to Southesk, as he turned
out to have scurs, being the only beast with scurs Mr
Carnegie ever saw at Kinnaird in the late Sir James's
lifetime, except a cow bought for one season for milk.

At the time of Sir James Carnegie's death, the following
pure animals were in the herd : of the Lady Anne tribe—
Old Bell 98, Smutella 329, Lady Anne 97 (miscalled in
'Herd Book' " of Craigo "), Nelly, Bell of Kinnaird 328,
Fanny of Kinnaird 330, Meg 708, and Violet 327, the last
four being heifers; of the Sarah tribe — Sarah 140, and
her daughter, Mary of Kinnaird 326 ; of the Beauty
tribe—Mona 325, and a sister of hers not entered in
'Herd Book;' the cow Angus 95, of the same tribe, belonged to the park-keeper.

The oldest and most important tribe in the herd was
the Lady Anne tribe.   The cow Old Lady Anne 743 was
a very old cow at the time of Mr Carnegie's earliest recollections, and she must have been calved about 1820.   She
was said to have been a prize-taker in her time.   Mr
Carnegie believes Old Lady Anne to be the oldest cow
recorded in vol. i. of the 'Herd Book.'   Old Lady Anne
and all her descendants, even to the present time, have
been most excellent milkers.   They had the especial
property of continuing to give a large quantity of milk till
close on the time that they were due to calve, and, if
allowed, they would continue to milk on till their calving.
The old cattleman used to say that he believed that, from
one year's end to the other, Old Lady Anne and her
descendants gave more milk than any of the Ayrshires,

though they might not give so much just after calving.
All the members of the tribe at Kinnaird were also very
docile.   This family is now represented by three strains :
one through Flora of Portlethen 244, one through Formosa
186 (inadvertently entered in vol. i. of 'Herd Book'
among bulls)—both descendants of Fanny of Kinnaird 330
—and one through Lavender 1007, a grand-daughter of
Lady Anne 97.

The Sarah 140 tribe is extinct, except in the male line,
the bulls Kinnaird 224 and Mariner 148 of that tribe
having, however, left a good many noteworthy animals.

The Beauty 96 tribe is probably extinct, as the Erica
family is descended from another Beauty, as must also be
the son of Beauty 96, given in some pedigrees.   Beauty
96 had only one calf, and that a heifer, Mona 325.

Sir James Carnegie died in 1849, and was succeeded by
his son Sir James, now Earl of Southesk.   No addition
was made to the herd till 1851, in which year were purchased the bull Balnamoon 36 from the late David
Carnegie Arbuthnott, and the heifers Charlotte (not
entered in 'Herd Book') and Dora 333 from Mr Ruxton,
Farnell.   These heifers were both bred by Mr Watson,
Keillor, and the latter was the foundress of what was
generally considered the best family in the Kinnaird herd.
So little, however, were fancy stock prized in those days,
that Dora was (being supposed a doubtful breeder) bought
for £19, 5s.   She gained many prizes, and Lord Southesk
was offered 100 guineas for her at the great show at Paris,
where she took the second prize.   In 1852 was bought
from the Crathes herd Kate 12, together with her heifer
calf, Kathleen 339, by Strathmore 5.   Kate 12 was bred
by the late Mr M'Combie of Tillyfour.   A more important purchase, however, took place at the Highland Society's
show at Perth that same year—namely, that of the bull
Cup-Bearer 59, from Mr Bowie, Mains of Kelly.   Cup-
Bearer was then two years old, and had won the first

prizes at the Highland Society and local shows. He
proved a most valuable acquisition to the herd—leaving
a great number of good stock ; and it is curious to note
that Mr Carnegie is aware of only one calf out of the very
large number that he got that had any trace of scurs.
The portrait of Cup-Bearer is in vol. i. of the ' Herd
Book,' and a representation of his head is on the binding
of that volume. The price paid for this magnificent bull
was £60.

In 1853, Pride of Angus 176, the first-prize two-year-
old heifer at the Royal Northern Society's show, was
bought for £100 from the late Robert Scott of Balwyllo.
In the same autumn, at the Auchtertyre sale of the late
Mr Watson, Keillor, the cow Octavia 331, and the yearling heifer Emily 332, were added to the herd. The former was a prize heifer, and was entered in the catalogue
as by Old Jock 1, dam Old Favourite. She turned out,
however, not to be in calf, and was put to Cup-Bearer 59.
The issue was Odin 153, who was sold to Mr Morison of
Bognie, and whose name appears in so many of the
Bognie and Montbletton pedigrees. The heifer Emily
332 is entered in the same catalogue as by Old Jock
1, dam Beauty, "the dam of Sir T. Burnett's famous
bull." There was, as already stated, some confusion regarding the various Beauties in the ' Herd Book,' and Mr
Carnegie believes that there are three, if not more, separate animals of that name, all bred by Mr Watson, Keillor,
and probably all nearly related. None of these had
anything to do with Beauty 96, who was, as mentioned
before, of a totally different strain of blood. Mr Ferguson, Kinnochtry, informs us that Beauty, the dam of
Emily 332, was sold by Mr Watson to Sir Alexander
Burnett. Mr Watson bought her and her yearling bull,
The Baronet 339, back from Sir Alexander in 1856. Emily
332 became noted as the dam of Erica 843, whose blood
is now so well known. She was a cow of fair but not

very large size, with a most perfect head, and splendid quality. She was, however, always a little dipped in the back, which prevented her from taking high honours in the show-yard. She was a most valuable dairy cow, and besides breeding Erica 843, had several other fine calves, two of them having gone to Denmark.

The next addition was made in 1857, by the purchase of the cow Caroline of Kinnaird 562, and the heifer Thetis 568, from Mr Bowie, Mains of Kelly. The former was rather an unfortunate cow, as her calves generally died. She was, however, the dam of Columbia and Clarissa, both Highland Society prize-winners. The prices were between £60 and £70 for Caroline, and over £30 for Thetis. In 1858, Lord Southesk bought the heifer Princess Philomel 269, from the late Mr Walker, Portlethen. The price was 37 guineas, as it was thought doubtful if she was in calf. She was a very fine cow, and through her daughter, Perdita 848, by Druid 225, is ancestress of the celebrated Palmerston 374. In the winter of the same year, Lord Southesk bought from the late Mr Brown, Westertown, the cow Irene 311, and the bull Windsor 221. The price of the cow was £50, and that of the bull was £150 in money and the bull-calf King Charles 236 (by Druid 225, out of Kathleen 339), whose name appears in many pedigrees. Windsor was a very fine bull, with grand fore-end and back, and he left a great many good stock, both at Westertown and Kinnaird.

In 1859, at the sale of the late Mr Scott's (of Balwyllo) cattle, the following were bought: Balwyllo Queen 445, price about 50 guineas ; Topsy 447, price over 40 guineas ; and the heifer Rosebud 460, price about 70 guineas. At the same sale the Honourable Charles Carnegie bought Keepsake 427 and Charlotte of Balwyllo 470 ; but as he relinquished his then intention of taking a farm, these animals were added to the Kinnaird herd. Balwyllo Queen 445 was a very fine cow. She took prizes both at the Highland

Society and local shows, and was the dam of Jupiter 471
and Quadroona, both winners of first prizes at the Highland Society's shows. In 1861, Empress of France 578
was bought from Mr M'Combie of Tillyfour for 60 guineas.
She was a full sister of the famous Pride of Aberdeen 581,
whom she greatly resembled, except that she was rather
dipped in the back. She was, when purchased, in calf to
Lord Clyde 249, and the produce was Julius Cæsar, the
third-prize bull at Battersea as a yearling, and second at
the Highland Society as a two-year-old. The next addition, and the last before the fatal rinderpest, was in 1863,
when the cows Heather Bell 717 and Gem 719 were
bought for 60 guineas and 40 guineas respectively at the
dispersion of the Balwyllo herd.

During the years between 1849 and 1865 many excellent animals were bred in the herd. It is of course unnecessary to mention every animal, but some of the most
noteworthy were as follows : In 1851 was calved Ada 338,
by a bull bred at Leuchland, and out of Dora 333. Ada
had not a calf till she was over four years old, and was one
of the largest cows of the breed Mr Carnegie ever saw. She
was honourably mentioned at the Paris show in 1856. In
1852 and 1853 were calved Flavia 376, Flora of Portlethen 244, Barbara 337, and Lavinia 336, all by Balnamoon, and of the Lady Anne tribe ; and Dulcinea 334,
by Cup-Bearer 59, out of Dora 333. The first three all
took prizes as heifers at the local shows, and Barbara 337
was a very excellent type of the Angus cow, a splendid
milker, and a very steady breeder. Flavia 376 and Flora
244, though not so large, were both very neat ; and the
late Mr Walker, Portlethen, informed Mr Carnegie that
Flora brought up three calves at one time. Dulcinea 334
was, however, "the pick of the basket," and was one of
the best cows of the breed. She was not shown as a
heifer, being a late calf, but as a cow she was first at the
Royal Agricultural Society's show at Chester. She was

twice third at the Highland Society's shows, and won
many local prizes. She did not milk well her first two
years, but developed into a good enough milker, rearing
twin-calves one year.

In 1854, Dora 333 produced Druid 225, and Mary of
Kinnaird 326 Mariner 148; and the same year Octavia
331 produced Odin 153,—all by Cup-Bearer 59. Odin 153
was sold to Mr Morison of Bognie, and was the ancestor of
many of the best stock in that part of the country. His
son, The Earl 291, won the first prize at the Highland
Show for the late Mr Walker, Montbletton, and he seems
to have thoroughly made his mark. Mariner 148 was
sold to Mr Lyell of Sheilhill, and was the father of Tom
Pipes 301 and Prospero 302, both Highland Society first-
prize winners. Druid 225 was, however, the most distinguished of the three. Owing to his being a late calf,
and his having been obliged to be fired in one of his legs,
he was not formidable as a yearling; but as a two-year-old
there have probably been few finer specimens of the breed.
He combined large size with fine quality and a most excellent temper; and, admirable as is his portrait by Gourlay
Steele, it hardly does justice to the perfection of his quarters. He carried everything before him as a two and three
year old, and was only beaten when four years old for the
Dutrone prize at Aberdeen, at the somewhat memorable
show of 1858; and at Battersea in 1862, when eight years
old, he was placed second to Prospero 302, the reason
alleged by the judges being that the younger bull would
be the more serviceable animal. Druid 225, however, with
all his show-yard excellences, had a grave defect—he was
not a very useful bull. The stock that he did get were all
very good, but there were very few of them. Through his
sons, King Charles 236 and Raven 270, and his daughters,
Perdita 848, the granddam of Palmerston 374, and Thalia
1233, the dam of Theodore 393, his blood flows in the
veins of many of the best beasts in the country. The

same year was also calved Poppy, by Cup-Bearer 59, out of Pride of Angus 176. She was second as one of a pair at the Royal Northern as a yearling; first as a two-year-old; second at the Highland Society's show at Inverness as a two-year-old; and won first prizes at the Angus Agricultural Society's shows at both ages. She was sold to Mr Collie, Ardgay, for about £60, and he changed her name to Empress 312. She had only one calf, a bull. Kitty, by Cup-Bearer 59, out of Kate 12, was shown with her in the pair that took the first prize as yearlings at the Angus show, and second at the Royal Northern. Kitty was sold to Lord Cawdor.

In 1855, in the whole herd there were only two heifer calves. One of these, Oriana 378, by Cup-Bearer 59, out of Octavia 331, was a very late calf. She, however, won the first prizes at the Royal Agricultural Society's show at Chester as a heifer, and at Warwick as a cow; also two first prizes at local shows as a cow. She was one of the neatest animals in the herd, though not big. She was sold to the late Mr Goodlet, Bolshan, in 1861, for 40 guineas. She left very good stock; but it was almost all kept at Kinnaird, and was exterminated by rinderpest. Her blood is, however, to be found in some pedigrees, through her son Orestes 273. The bull calves in 1855 were a good lot, but few of them appear in modern pedigrees. Mark, afterwards called Kinnaird 224, by Cup-Bearer 59, out of Mary of Kinnaird 326, a hand-reared calf, was bought by the late Mr Collie, Ardgay, and became a celebrated bull. He was first at the Highland Society's show at Glasgow as a two-year-old, and carried all before him at local shows. He was a very heavy bull, which was somewhat remarkable, as his mother was a very small cow—in fact, the smallest cow in the herd. He had a grand fore-end, but wanted a little at the top of the tail. His name appears in many pedigrees, and his stock were uniformly good. A good young bull,

Dictator, by Cup-Bearer 59, out of Dora 333, was sold to
Mr Sproat, Borness, in Kirkcudbrightshire; and Epicure
114, by Cup-Bearer 59, from Emily 332, went to Sir J. S.
Forbes of Fettercairn.   The bull Fortitude 28, by Balnamoon 36, was also calved in 1855.   On the last day of
1855 was calved The Admiral 227, by Cup-Bearer 59, out
of Ada 338.   This was a very good young bull, but he was
of course too old for showing.   He was taken into the
herd, but was not a very useful sire.   Fusilier 226, by
Cup-Bearer 59, out of Fanny of Kinnaird 330, a very neat
little bull, calved in 1856, was also kept, and got some
very good stock, though nothing celebrated came from
him.   In this same year, 1856, Emily 332 had a bull calf
named Erebus, that was sold to go to Denmark.   There
were only four heifers this year, one of whom, Blossom of
Kinnaird 565, by Cup-Bearer 59, from Barbara 337, was a
prize-winner at local shows; and another, Dahlia 569, by
Druid 225, out of Dulcinea 334, who, although rather a
poor yearling, developed into a fine young cow, but died
of quarter-ill whilst nursing her first calf.   This was
the only death from that complaint that happened in the
herd.   It is curious that it should have attacked a grown-
up animal—one, moreover, in not very high condition.

The year 1857 was more of a heifer year than the two
previous ones had been.   Deodora 1232, by Captain Cook
143, from Dulcinea 334, was a day or two too old to show.
She, however, distinguished herself as a breeder—Delaware
457, Damascus 495, and Sultan 477 being all from her.
The two former were by Windsor 221, and were sold
to Mr M'Combie, Easter Skene, and Mr Tayler of Glenbarry respectively.   The 'Herd Book' records many prize-
winners got by them.   Sultan 477, by Prince of Wales 453,
was bred by the late Mr Paterson, Mulben, to whom
Deodora 1232 was sold.   He seems to have got some good
stock at Mulben.   Mr Tayler informed Mr Carnegie that
he parted with Damascus 495 only on account of his

K

bad temper. This is somewhat remarkable, as Deodora
1232 was, with perhaps the exception of her half-sister
Dahlia 569, the tamest cow at Kinnaird. She and her
sister would either of them come from a long distance
if called, and would follow like a pet dog any one they
knew. Florence of Kinnaird 1274, by Druid 225, out of
Flavia 376, of the old Kinnaird stock, was a very taking
heifer. She won a prize at the Royal Agricultural show,
and some prizes at local shows. She was sold to Lady
Dunmore, and lived for many years at Dunmore as a pet,
though by no means a useless one, as she, like the rest of
her kind, was a fine dairy cow. Dolores 1285, by Cup-
Bearer 59, out of Dora 333, was a rather late calf, but
was shown as a two-year-old, and at the local shows
stood second to her more celebrated neighbour Erica 843.
Dolores 1285 proved a very good breeder, and she and
most of her stock were retained at Kinnaird, unfortunately to perish with the rest of the herd. She had one
bull calf, Draco 338, by Windsor 221. Mr Walker, Ardhuncart, Mossat, bought him as a calf, and he did most
excellent service in his herd.

Last but not least of the heifers of 1857 must be mentioned Erica 843, by Cup-Bearer 59, out of Emily 332.
Not being either an early or a very strong calf, Erica 843
was not shown as a yearling. In the autumn of 1858,
the late Mr Collie, Ardgay, paid a visit to Kinnaird, and
was so much struck by her beauty, that he begged Lord
Southesk to make her up for the shows next year. This
was done, and at the local show she was first, and very
much admired. Unfortunately, however, at the Highland
Society's show she was, from certain reasons, out of condition, and consequently looking at her worst, her fault, a
slight tendency to slackness in the back, showing very
prominently—so much so, that the judges put her out
before either of her companions Dolores 1285 and Florence 1274. That Erica would have been beaten on her

merits at that show is, however, quite certain, as her successful rival was the celebrated Pride of Aberdeen 581, probably the best heifer of the breed yet seen. She would, however, if in good condition, have probably been second. In 1861, as a cow, Erica 843 was placed third at the Highland Society; but one of those before her was disqualified, so that she was actually second. She was also first at the local show. In that year she was sold to Sir George Macpherson Grant for 50 guineas, the highest price at the Kinnaird sale. It is needless to remark here on the many excellent animals that now trace descent from this valuable cow. Erica 843 herself was not a very large cow, but was almost bigger than what is called "a big little one." She stood on very short legs, and had a lovely, feminine head, and splendid quality. Lord Southesk remarked, that after the sale he much regretted he had sold her, but that now he was glad, as otherwise her race might have been also extinguished.

The only bull calf of any note in 1857 was Raven 270, by Druid 225, out of Rebecca 340. Raven 270 was used in the herd, and got one or two good animals. He was a fair but not first-class bull, and won the first prize at the local show as a yearling, beating the bull Young Panmure 232, who subsequently beat him at the Highland Society's show, where Raven was not placed.

In 1858 the calves altogether were not equal to those of 1857. Of the heifers, Dorothea and Olympia 1300 were perhaps the best. They were both by Fusilier 226—one from Dora 333, and the other from Octavia 331. Dorothea, who had a little more white than was desirable, won the first prize at the Royal Agricultural Society at Warwick as a yearling. She was subsequently sent out to Canada along with a young bull, Orlando, by Raven 270, out of Octavia 331, as a present to the late Sir George Simpson. Whether they left any stock there or not is not known to us. Formosa 186, by Captain Kidd 184, out of

Flavia 376, the ancestress of the numerous Floras and
Fancys of East Tulloch, was also calved in 1858, but was
never exhibited. The most noteworthy of the bull calves
of 1858 was King Charles 236, by Druid 225, out of
Kathleen 339. As a calf he went to the late Mr Brown,
Westertown, as part payment for the bull Windsor 221.
Mr Brown afterwards sold him to Sir George Macpherson Grant. At Ballindalloch he seems to have done good
service, as many first-class animals, both there and at
Advie, have his name in their pedigree. King Charles
236, when seen at the Highland Society's show in Edinburgh in 1859, was a bull of immense size, girthing more
than the Shorthorn bulls of the same age. He also had a
very good head, and fine quality. He was, however, not
quite a true-made bull, and Mr Carnegie was somewhat
disappointed with him, as, when a calf, he promised
to be very superior. A good bull calf by Cup-Bearer
59, out of Emily 332, called Ethelred 272, was sold to Sir
J. S. Forbes; but we are not aware if he has left any living
descendants.

In 1859 the most prominent bull calf was Black Douglas
311, by the Balwyllo bull President 3rd 246, out of the
cow Barbara 337, of the old Kinnaird stock. The late Mr
Collie, Ardgay, took a very great fancy to this calf, and
offered 80 guineas for him, which, as Windsor 221 had
lately been added to the herd, and consequently two in-
fusions of fresh blood were not wanted, was accepted.
Black Douglas 311 never quite fulfilled the promise of his
youth. He had from the first a complete aversion to oil-
cake; and though he got some good stock at Ardgay,
he did not turn out the wonder Mr Collie expected when
he bought him. Another bull calf of the same year was
Domino, a rather late calf, by Raven 270, out of Dora 333.
He had small scurs, and was sold to Mr Morison of Bognie.
As the pedigrees in the Bognie herd were not well kept, it is
impossible to say if there is any of his stock left; but from

his breeding he ought—bar the blemish before mentioned—
to have been a valuable bull.   The best heifer of the year
was Kalliope 1234, by Raven 270, out of Kathleen 339.
She grew into a cow of very fine quality, but was never
better than local-show form.   She proved a very good
breeder, the two bulls Commodore 490 and Cavalier 411,
and the heifer Clio, all by Windsor 221, being far above
average, the heifer especially having carried all before her
both as a yearling and two-year-old ; and the bulls having
left good stock, Commodore 490 in the Castle Fraser herd,
and Cavalier 411, first with Colonel M'Inroy at The Burn,
and afterwards at Easter Tulloch.   A very perfectly shaped
heifer calved late that year was Iris 844, by Windsor 221,
out of Irene 311.   She was sold to Sir George Macpherson
Grant at the same time as Erica, but unfortunately she
died in calving.

The year 1860 was a good year for heifers.   Ophelia, by
Windsor 221, out of Oriana 378, was calved a day or two
too soon to show; but she was probably the best of the
lot, and was intended to have been the show cow in 1866,
along with Esmeralda, a daughter of Druid 225, and Emily
332, who was calved in October or November the same
year.   These two beautiful cows were very good specimens of the get of their celebrated sires.   Mr Carnegie
says Ophelia was a large-framed, upstanding, Juno-like
cow, perfectly level in her flesh, and a fair toucher; while
Esmeralda was more of the Venus type, with fine head,
deep brisket, small bone, and splendid quality.   She was,
however, not quite so evenly fleshed as Ophelia.   It is
melancholy to think that two such animals have left no
descendants to perpetuate their excellence.   Ophelia succumbed to the rinderpest.   Esmeralda, after a desperate
battle with the disease, recovered, but proved useless as a
breeder.   Due to calve in the month of March 1866, she
retained her calf till about October 1867, when she calved
a dried-up object, about the size and appearance of an over-

roasted hare. This remarkable specimen is now in the
museum of Dr Mathews Duncan. If, however, Ophelia
and Esmeralda could not be shown as heifers on account
of their ages, there were others who could. Columbia, by
Windsor 221, out of Caroline 562, won the first prize at
the Highland Society as a yearling; also, along with Bella-
donna, by Windsor, out of Barbara 337, the first prize at
the local show. Columbia was next year third as a heifer
at Battersea, and not being a breeder, was sent to the
Smithfield show, where she won the first prize. There
were two other very beautiful heifers, calved rather late
in 1860, both by Druid 225,—one Kassandra, from Kathleen 330; and the other Perdita 848, from Princess Philomel 269. Both these were sold at the sale in 1861. Kassandra was bought by the late Mr Paterson, Mulben, in
whose possession Mr Carnegie saw her in 1866, a very
handsome cow. She has left no recorded descendants.
Perdita 848 was sold to the late Mr Walker, Portlethen,
and seems to have done well with him, as the celebrated
Palmerston 374 was a descendant of hers. Of the bulls
calved in 1860, Delaware 457 has been mentioned already.
The only other noteworthy one was Diodorus, the third-
prize two-year-old at the Battersea show. He was by
Windsor 221, out of Dora 333, and was afterwards sold to
go to Denmark.

In 1861 was calved Rosetta, by Druid 225, out of Rosebud 460, the first prize yearling at Battersea, and second
two-year-old at the Highland Show; and Quadroona, by
Windsor 221, out of Balwyllo Queen 445, the first-prize
Highland Society's two-year-old heifer. The latter was
fed, being no breeder, and won first prizes at Birmingham
and Smithfield shows. Thalia 1233, by Druid 225, out of
Thetis 568, was also a nice heifer, but was spoiled by having a calf when little more than a year old. Thalia 1233
was the mother of the Easter Tulloch bull, Theodore 393, by
Jupiter 471. Of the bull calves of that year, Damascus

495, and Draco 338, have been already noticed. The two most promising calves were, however, considered to be Don Fernando 514, by Windsor 221, out of Dulcinea 334, and Julius Cæsar, by Lord Clyde 249, out of Empress of France 578. The former was sold as a calf to the late Mr M'Combie of Tillyfour. He was the sire of Hero 400, from whom many good things are descended. Mr Carnegie was much pleased with the stock from him at Mr M'Combie's sale in 1867. He was, it is believed, foundered in his legs, otherwise he might have been a show bull. Julius Cæsar was retained in the herd. He was third as a yearling at Battersea, and second at the Highland Society's show the following year, and was a bull of great substance and considerable merit, though by no means a perfect animal. His stock, however, were so good, that it was a matter of regret that he was not kept longer in the herd. King Henry 390, by Windsor 221, out of Kathleen 339, was also sold as a calf in 1861. He was a May calf; and Mr Scott, Easter Tulloch, got him for fourteen and a half guineas. Mr Carnegie never saw him after the sale, but has heard that he turned out very well. He certainly has left very worthy descendants.

In 1862 the heifers were again to the front—Clio, by Windsor 221, out of Kalliope 1234, and Clarissa, by a young bull, Don Roderick, a son of Dulcinea, out of Caroline 562, carrying all before them, at the Highland Society and local shows, both as one and two year olds. Clio was exposed for sale in 1865, but was bought in. She was afterwards slaughtered,—some of the other cattle in the same building with her being supposed to have rinderpest. Clarissa was sold at the same sale to Mr Goodlet, at the reserve price of 40 guineas. She, however, died of rinderpest in his possession. The most promising bull calf of 1862 was one by Druid 225, out of Barbara 337. He was sold to Mr Holmes, Mataura Plains, New Zealand, and named Southesk 2nd. Mr Carnegie has rea-

son to believe it to be probable that it was a descendant
of this bull that found its way to the Sandwich Islands,
where it is said to have done much to improve the breed
of cattle. In November 1862 was calved the bull Jupiter
471, by Windsor 221, out of Balwyllo Queen 445. This
excellent bull recovered from the rinderpest, and took the
first prize at Dundee, and afterwards at the Highland
Show. He was then sold to Mr Paterson, Mulben, in
whose possession he got a great many stock. He was a
bull of large size and good substance; but, like other
Balwyllo animals, was a trifle rough in the hair—not
enough, however, to be a very grave defect.

Of the calves of 1863, 1864, and 1865, it is almost needless to write. There were many of them that were as
good as any of those before them; but the record almost
invariably is, " died of rinderpest." The bulls Commodore
490 and Cavalier 411, calved respectively in 1863 and
1864, have been noted; as has also been Theodore 393,
calved in 1865. There was, however, a calf—Gustavus,
by Wellington, a young Balwyllo bull, out of Gem 719,
calved in 1864, of whom Mr Carnegie has heard it said
that he improved the stock of a whole glen.

In 1865 the rinderpest came, and practically annihilated
the Kinnaird herd. Of the nature of this disease, it is
not within the scope of this volume to deal. It is sufficient to say that it seems to yield to no treatment, and
that female animals who have recovered from it seem
never to be of any use as breeders. In the case of the
Kinnaird herd, the recoveries were only five—viz., the
bull Jupiter 471, and the cows Dulcinea 334, Esmeralda,
Heather Bell 717, and Balwyllo Queen 445. Dulcinea
334 had one calf, a bull called Don Sebastian, by Jupiter
471. This animal, the sire of Southesk of Kelly 465,
promised to be a very fine one; but was afterwards
obliged to be slaughtered, owing to an internal tumour
which probably was congenital. Heather Bell 717 had a

deformed calf. Balwyllo Queen 445 cast calf, and none of them ever bred again. Esmeralda, as before mentioned, calved a dried-up fœtus more than a year after time. The only pure-bred cows left were Rhoda 566, and Bella, belonging to two of the servants. These animals never had the rinderpest. From the first came Bolshan 420, and from the latter Southesk of Kelly. Bella is not entered in the 'Herd Book,' but was by Raven 270, out of Bell of Kinnaird 328. Lord Southesk also bought a heifer by Windsor 221, out of Gem 719, with whom he got the first prize as a yearling at the show at Dundee. She was afterwards sold to Lord Airlie.

Ardgay.

Mr John Collie, Ardgay, Forres, had a fine herd of polled cattle, which was dispersed in 1866. In founding the herd, Mr Collie, who was a very good judge, picked up in the locality a number of animals which, although of short recorded ancestry, were of more than ordinary individual merit. Blinkbonny 315, one of these, was the dam of Marion 308, the foundress of the Westertown Rose family. Another was Dorrit 316, calved in 1850, bred by the trustees of Mr Howitt, Rothiemay; and it is in connection with the descendants of this cow that the fame of the Ardgay herd is chiefly perpetuated. Dorrit, when in the possession of Mr Charles Kay, Earnside, bred in 1855 Hinda 322, whose sire is not recorded. In 1857, in Mr Collie's possession, Hinda was put to Lord Southesk's bull Kinnaird 224 (a son of Cup-Bearer 59), and the produce was Normahal 726. Normahal was again put to Kinnaird, and in 1860 gave birth to Zara 1228—the second-prize two-year-old heifer at Battersea in 1862. Zara was bought by Mr M'Combie of Tillyfour, to whom she bred, among others, the heifers Kate of Aberdeen, by Black Prince of Tillyfour 366, and Matilda of Tillyfour 1175,

by Bright 454. Of Kate of Aberdeen (not entered in
the 'Herd Book') Mr Dixon says, "She was certainly the
best calf of any breed we have ever looked over." Kate
was the first-prize yearling and two-year-old at the Highland Society's shows in 1864 and 1865. It is, however,
through the descendants of Matilda and her daughter
Pride of Alford 1778, first-prize yearling at Kelso in 1872,
that the tribe is now best known. Mr M'Combie also
purchased Normahal, who was the dam of the famous
Bright 454; while from Zara was bred the bulls Champion 459 and Scotsman 474. Another animal bred by Mr
Collie from the cattle obtained in the locality was Marius
564, the first-prize yearling bull of the Highland Society
at Inverness in 1865, afterwards passing into the possession of the late Mr Robertson, Burnside. Mr Collie
also owned Fair Maid of Perth 313, of the Queen tribe,
purchased at Tillyfour in 1857 for £86. She was the first-
prize cow at the National show at Edinburgh in 1859.
He won with Mayflower 314, bred at Mulben, the first
prize for cows at the Highland Society's show at Perth in
1861. The famous Balwyllo cow, Keepsake 427, was at
Ardgay for some years, as were also several other cows
from Kinnaird and Balwyllo. The chief sires in the herd
were Black Douglas 311 and Kinnaird 224—both bred by
Lord Southesk, and the latter the second-prize two-year-
old at Glasgow in 1857—and Arthur of Balwyllo 478.

The Honourable Charles Carnegie, who in November 1857
went to Mr Collie as a pupil, has supplied us with a few
notes regarding the Ardgay herd. When Mr Carnegie
went to Mr Collie's, he found there the following polled
stock—viz., Fair Maid of Perth 313, Empress 312—bought
from the Earl of Southesk for 60 guineas—Blinkbonny
315, Cordelia 320, Dorrit 316, Hinda 322, Nannie 321,
Duchess 317, Mayflower 314, and some heifer calves.
Fair Maid of Perth, afterwards in succession second
and first at the Highland Society's shows, was a grand

cow. Her fault was, that she was a little too prominent
over the hooks. She was a difficult animal to prepare
for the show-yard, as she had a tremendous appetite
and gave a lot of milk. Empress 312, who had a bull
calf—Prince Imperial 223—never bred again, and the calf
proved useless. Blinkbonny was a very well-topped cow,
but wanted in underline, and had a plain head. Cordelia
never bred anything worth noticing, though herself not deficient in second-rate merit. Dorrit was a very neat, sweet
little cow, and far superior to her daughter Hinda, who was
commonplace in appearance. Hinda, however, always bred
well. Dorrit's heifer calf Alice was a prize-taker, but being
a free-martin, never bred. One of Hinda's calves was Lala
Rookh 730, whose name appears in many pedigrees, and
who herself was a very good heifer. Nannie and Duchess
were both of a good, useful sort, and the latter was the
granddam of Mr M'Combie's celebrated ox Black Prince.
Mayflower turned out a beautiful cow. She was second
and first at the Highland Society's shows, though it is
believed that in the latter case she failed to qualify, not
being in calf. Mayflower ended her show-yard career at
the Smithfield show, where she won the first prize for Mr
M'Combie, who bought her along with several others a
few years later. During the time that Mr Collie continued
to keep polled stock, he bred several animals of note.
Normahal 726 and Zara 1228, descendants of Hinda, were
both very good. The former was a very taking heifer;
and though she did not grow very large as a cow, she
looked extremely well when Mr Carnegie saw her and bid
for her at Mr M'Combie's sale in 1867. Zara, who won
the second prize at Battersea, was also a very handsome
heifer, and, as previously noticed, could boast of being
the ancestress of many prize-takers.

CHAPTER IX.

EXTINCT HERDS—CONCLUDED.

(1) The Balwyllo herd : Its characteristics—The Princess, Isabella, Victoria, Keepsake, Annie Laurie, Emily, and other families.—(2) The Mulben herd : Origin and progress—Sires used by Mr Paterson.—(3) The Castle Fraser herd : Position in show-yard—Breeding of bulls used—Sale in 1870.—(4) The Aboyne Castle herd : The Marquis of Huntly's services to the breed, and their recognition—Sketch of animals composing the herd—Madge of Portlethen 1217.—(5) The Duff House herd : Notes regarding chief animals—Their wonderful success in exhibition.—(6) The Balquharn herd : Mr Adamson's aim in breeding—Dispersion in 1881 the best public sale of polled cattle that has ever been held.—(7) Other herds : Fyvie Castle, Tullochallum, Brucklay, Fernyflatt, Bognie, Indego, Garline, &c.

Balwyllo.

AMONG the early Forfarshire herds, that at Balwyllo occupied a high place, and its blood still circulates in many famous stocks. We are indebted to the Honourable Charles Carnegie for the following account of the herd: The late Mr Robert Scott of Balwyllo, who died somewhere about 1846 (I am not sure of the precise date), had a herd of polled cattle that was well known in my boyhood. After his death the herd was carried on by his son, also Robert Scott, who took a great interest in it, and was very successful in the show-yard. After his early death his mother continued to manage the farm of which, in 1863, she herself took the lease. At this date the whole of the stock was brought to the hammer, but Mrs Scott bought one or two very good animals. They, however fell victims to the rinderpest, and since then no pure stock has been kept at Balwyllo. Previous to the final dispersion in 1863, the trustees had a large draft-sale on the termination of the lease of the farm of Powis, on the Southesk estate, and it is to the descendants of the animals sold at these sales that we must now look for the blood of this fine herd.

The characteristics of the herd in my memory were great size and fleshiness, and very early maturity, which made the Balwyllo yearlings always very hard to beat in the show-yard. There was, however, a slight tendency to coarseness in the bone, or unlevelness of flesh, as they grew up, and a slight roughness of hair, especially in the males, which detracted from the general sweetness in appearance of many of the mature animals.

I will note in detail, as far as my memory serves me, some of the most remarkable animals, taking them, for convenience' sake, in families :—

The Princess Family.—This family—descended from Princess 47—must not be confounded with the Kinnochtry family of the same name, although, curiously enough, there is a descent in the male line of the latter family from the former. The foundress of the family, Princess 47, was bred by the late Mr Ruxton, Farnell, and was got by the celebrated Panmure 51. Princess herself was a considerable prize-taker, and I have always heard her spoken of as a very handsome cow, and free from the defects I have mentioned as sometimes to be seen in the Balwyllo cattle. From Princess 47 were bred three bulls, all of whom were used in the herd, one being Stanley 52, by Joseph 53, a Balwyllo-bred bull, and the other, President 205, by the Keillor-bred Adam 39. I have no recollection of Stanley, but I have seen President 205, though I have no further memory of him than that he was handsome. He was a very successful prize-taker, as will be seen from the record

of his prizes in vol. i. of the 'Herd Book.' The third bull
from Princess, Noble 245, was a pretty good bull, though
inferior to his brother. He was, however, decidedly hard
in the hair. Princess 47 has two recorded daughters—
viz., Bracelet 50, by Joseph 53, and Maggie of Balwyllo
433, by Maynooth 58. The former, Bracelet, was a prize-
taker, but I have no personal recollection of her. I remember, however, a very pretty daughter of hers, Bracelet
2nd 455, by Stanley 2nd 198; who was sold at the sale at
Powis in 1859. The other daughter of Princess—viz.,
Maggie of Balwyllo 433—I remember well. She was
rather smaller than many of the rest of the stock, but she
was neat, and what I call "ladylike." Her stock were all
good. Her son, Tom 310, by Windsor 221, was a very
fine bull, and was second at the Highland Society's show
at Perth in 1861 as a yearling, besides taking first prizes
at local shows. He was bought at the Balwyllo sale in
1863 by Mrs Scott for 40 guineas, and died of rinderpest. Maggie of Balwyllo's three daughters were Balwyllo
Queen 445, by Rob Roy 56; Princess Balwyllo 459, also
by Rob Roy; and Heather Bell 717, by President 3rd 246.
Of these the second was sold to Mr Lyell, Shielhill, as a
yearling, and a very nice one she was. The other two
were both bought by the Earl of Southesk. These
two sisters were not unlike, both being very favourable specimens of the herd. Balwyllo Queen 445 took
many prizes both at the Highland Society and local shows,
and was the dam of Jupiter 471, and Quadroona, both
by Windsor 221, and both Highland Society first-prize
winners. Balwyllo Queen was also the dam of Bessie
Bell of Balwyllo 710, by Rob Roy, a very nice cow, sold to
Mr Collie, Ardgay, along with her bull calf, Arthur of
Balwyllo 478, at the 1863 sale, for 40 guineas and
25 guineas respectively. Neither Balwyllo Queen nor
Heather Bell bred after the rinderpest, except the latter,
who, as already stated, had one deformed calf. I much

fear that this most valuable strain of blood is now absolutely extinct, except through the male line.

The Isabella Family.—The cow Isabella of Balwyllo 423,
bred by Mr Fullerton, Ardestie, after Earl o' Buchan 57,
was, at the time I first saw her, a somewhat aged cow.
She was, however, of good shapes and quality, fine in the
bone, and with a good head. At the time of the sale in
1863 she was over fourteen years old, and was bought by
Mrs Scott for eighteen guineas. She was a regular breeder,
and eight of her calves were recorded in the 'Herd Book.'
One of these, Rob Roy 56, by Prince Edward 55, was used
a great deal in the herd, and got very good stock. He
himself, though large and fleshy, had rather rough hard
hair, and a very big belly, which somewhat disfigured him.
Another son of Isabella, President 3rd 246, by President
2nd 54, was a far finer animal. He was a bull of very true
shape, and large, but his hair was not so good as it might
have been. He was a noted prize-taker, but was, except
once at a local show, always second to Windsor 221. He
was sold at the Powis sale in 1859, to Mr Watson of
Keillor, for, I think, 40 guineas. He got good stock
both at Balwyllo and Keillor, and many of the best of the
present race of cattle have his blood in their veins. Of
two other sons of Isabella, Raglan of Balwyllo 247, by
Stanley 2nd 198, and Robert the Bruce 309, by Noble 245,
I have no recollection. Four heifers are entered in the
'Herd Book' as daughters of Isabella. Balwyllo Nightingale 439, who was sold at the Powis sale to Mr Glennie,
Fernyflatt, was a very sweet beast, though not so big as
most of the family; but Heiress of Balwyllo 461 and Peerless 711, both by Noble 245, were magnificent heifers, and
both of them were first-prize yearlings at the Highland
Society. The former was sold at the Powis sale to Mr
M'Combie of Tillyfour for over 70 guineas, and she
afterwards passed into the possession of the late Mr
Walker, Montbletton; and I am glad to say that this fine

strain of blood is in no danger of being lost, there being
several descendants of this heifer worthy of their ancestry. Peerless 711 was to my mind the finer heifer of
the two, but was not so fortunate. In 1862 she had a
calf, Eglantine, by Sir William Wallace 308. She was a
very nice one, and was bought by Mr M'Combie of Tillyfour for 45 guineas, but I do not know what became
of her. She had twin-calves in 1863 (bull and heifer),
and being a doubtful breeder, was sold to me for £30 at
the sale. She proved not to be in calf, but afterwards
bred one calf. She was slaughtered at the rinderpest
time, and her calf died. There was a calf of Isabella's,
called Rosabella, sold to Mr Goodlet, Bolshan, at the
sale, for 22 guineas. She, I believe, also died of rinderpest. Another daughter of Isabella's is given in the
'Herd Book'—viz., Lucy of Balwyllo 830. She is only
mentioned there as the dam of a bull, Napoleon of Balwyllo 113, and I know nothing of her or him.

The Victoria Family.—Of this family the foundress,
Victoria 45, a prize heifer, seems to have been of an old
Balwyllo strain. She was got by Joseph 53, out of Tibbie
of Balwyllo 46, both of whom have no record except that
they were Balwyllo-bred. Victoria 45 was the dam of
Prince Edward 55, by President 205, a bull that was
much used in the herd, and of Victoria 2nd 428, also by
President 205. Victoria 2nd, who took prizes both as a
heifer and cow, was a large, fleshy, handsome animal, but
decidedly patchy. There are three daughters of hers entered—viz., Princess Royal 444, by Cup-Bearer 59 ; Topsy
447, by President 2nd 54 ; and Eugenie 458, by Rob Roy
56. Princess Royal 444 was not much to look at, but was
a most wonderful breeder. She was a good deal smaller
than most of the Balwyllo cattle, and had a little white on
her hind-legs and tail. Her first two calves were Lord
Clyde 249 and The Doctor 307, both by Rob Roy 56, and
both winners of first prizes at the Highland Society as

yearlings. The former was sold to Mr M'Combie of Tillyfour at the Powis sale for 81 guineas, and his name appears
in many good pedigrees. The latter was used in the Balwyllo herd. Princess Royal's next calf was Alice Maud 724,
by Black Prince of Balwyllo 248. She grew into a very
large, fleshy cow, a little wanting perhaps in beauty, but
of grand substance. She was sold for 63 guineas at
the sale in 1863, to Mr Walker, Portlethen, and has left a
numerous progeny. A yearling bull, Wellington of Balwyllo, who does not appear to have been entered in the
'Herd Book,' was sold to the late Mr Erskine, Wemyss,
for 40 guineas; and the bull calf Balwyllo Eclipse 781, by
Sir William Wallace 308, was bought for 23 guineas by
Mr Cran, Morlich, and his name appears in almost every
pedigree in that flourishing herd. Princess Royal 444
herself was lame at the sale, and was bought by me for
20 guineas. She and her heifer Helena, an animal of
great beauty, died of rinderpest, but her calf Princess
Louisa, by Legislator 489, survived, and was sold at the
Arratsmill sale in 1868 to Mr Paxton, Broomknowe, for
£35. A yearling named Lorelei, and a calf, Laura, were
sold at the same sale to Lord Clinton and Mr Lindsay,
Duninald, respectively, but I am not aware that they have
left any descendants. Topsy 447, Victoria 2nd's second
daughter, was a large beefy animal, but though a prize-
taker, was decidedly deficient in style, her head being
rather clumsily set on. She was bought at the Powis
sale for Lord Southesk, who, however, sold her at the
Kinnaird sale in 1861 for about half the money he gave
for her. Eugenie 458, the third daughter, was a large but
somewhat rough cow. She was bought at the sale in 1863
by Sir Thomas Gladstone; and though there is some doubt
in the matter, owing to the pedigrees not having been
accurately kept, I have every reason to believe that she
was either the dam or granddam of Eugenie of Fasque
3910, and she has left goodly descendants.

L

The Keepsake Family.—Keepsake 427 was bred at Balwyllo. She was got by President 205, dam Mapsie 76,
who seems to have been of old Balwyllo blood, and to
have been also the dam of the bull President 2nd 54.
Keepsake was the broadest-backed cow for her height I
ever saw. This at first made her look a little out of proportion, but she was (though perhaps wanting a little in
sweetness, and a trifle hard in the hair) a cow that you
always came back to, and her history shows that good
judges were not blind to her merits. Being lot 1 of the
Powis sale, she was sold very cheaply to me for 21 guineas.
I then transferred her to the Earl of Southesk, having,
as has already been explained, decided not to form a herd
at that time. She was sold at the Kinnaird sale two years
afterwards to Mr Collie, Ardgay, for 30 guineas. He afterwards sold her to Mr M'Combie of Tillyfour for £40, and
in her seventeenth year she was sold in 1868 to Sir George
Macpherson Grant for 27 guineas, with a bull calf at her
foot. With Keepsake's numerous descendants since she
left Balwyllo, I need say nothing here. At Balwyllo she
had three daughters—Trial 228, by President 205, of
whom I know nothing; Edith 2nd 464, by Rob Roy 56,
sold at the Powis sale as a yearling; and Ruby 713, by
Noble 245, a large but somewhat rough cow, sold at the
sale in 1863 to Mr Walker, Portlethen, for 22 guineas. A
son of Ruby 713, named Rudolph, by The Doctor 307,
was sold to Sir T. Gladstone for 24 guineas. He was a
fair animal, and probably some of the Fasque stock are
descended from him.

The Annie Laurie Family.—Annie Laurie 424, by
President 205, out of Jessamine 66, seems to have been
of the old Balwyllo strain, and I have some recollection
of seeing her as a good useful sort of an old cow. There
is one bull entered as out of her—viz., Prince of Devon
315. She is also entered as the mother of three daughters.
Rosa of Balwyllo 438, by President 2nd 54, was an enor-

mous heifer, but grew into a very patchy cow. Alice of
Balwyllo 463, by Rob Roy 56, was sold as a yearling at the
Powis sale; and Pearl 714, by Rob Roy 56, was bought
by Mrs Scott for 25 guineas at the Balwyllo sale. Pearl
was pretty good, and was a great milker. A daughter of
Pearl's, Clematis, by Sir William Wallace 303, was sold
to the Duke of Buccleuch for 49 guineas, being the highest-priced yearling at the sale. I did not myself think
her the best, and she had scurs.

The Emily of Balwyllo Family.—Emily of Balwyllo
421, by the Ardestie-bred Richmond 6, from old Balwyllo
blood, produced the bull West Australian 204, by President 205. This bull was taken to Ireland by Lord
Lurgan. Emily of Balwyllo had also two heifers—Young
Emily 425, by President 205, and Lady Jane 440, by
President 2nd 54. The former never, that I knew, threw
any first-rate stock, but the latter was a prize-winner as
a heifer, and though patchy behind, was from the hooks
forward a most magnificent cow. Lady Jane had one
daughter, Rosebud 460, by Rob Roy 56, who much resembled her dam, though rather worse in front and better
behind. Rosebud 460 was bought by the Earl of Southesk
at the Powis sale for about 70 guineas; but though she had
several calves, I do not think she has any living descendants. Lady Jane had two bull calves entered in the
' Herd Book,'—viz., Sir William Wallace 308, by President
3rd 246, and Pioneer 326, by Noble 245. The latter bull
was in the possession of Mr Whyte, Spott.

Other Families.—At the time of the dispersion sale in
1863, there were several good animals of other families,
but none that I recollect as calling for special notice, except perhaps the very neat cow Gem 719, bought by
the Earl of Southesk for 40 guineas, and her pretty
daughter Angelica, bought by Sir George Macpherson
Grant. There were also the old Kinnaird-bred cow Ada
338, her daughter Adela 849, and Hortensia; also a very

nice cow, Celardine, by Diodorus (son of Windsor 221 and
Dora 333) out of a daughter of Princess Philomel 269.
This heifer was bought by the Duke of Buccleuch for
32 guineas.

Mulben.

The late Mr Alexander Paterson became tenant of the
farm of Mulben, near Keith, in 1839, and shortly afterwards began to collect a herd of polled cattle. The herd
was maintained until his death in 1875. His first purchase was at Mr Thurburn's sale at Drum, Keith, in 1842.
He then bought a calf out of a cow bred in Buchan. This
calf was the dam of Madge 161, the foundress of the
Mulben Mayflower or Queen Mary family. Other acquisitions were made from time to time, but we shall
notice only those that have left living descendants. At
Mr Bowie's sale at West Scryne in April 1857, the cow
Lady Ann, entered in the 'Herd Book' as Raniston
352, was bought for £37. Raniston was bred by
Mr M'Combie of Tillyfour, and was descended from
the old herd of the Earl of Aberdeen at Haddo
House. From her sprang the Caroline family at Mulben.
In September 1857, at the dispersion of Mr Patrick
Davidson's herd at Inchmarlo, there was secured the cow
Jean of Inchmarlo 522. She was after a bull bred at
Portlethen, and had gained the first prize as one of a
pair at Aberdeen. The price was £34, 15s.; and Mr
Paterson also bought her dam Calder, after a bull bred at
Tillyfour. From Jean of Inchmarlo 522 the Ellen family
at Mulben were descended. From the Castle Fraser dis-
persion in 1870 came Fred's 2nd Darling 1045, of the
Ballindalloch Sybil family, for 37 guineas. At the
Tillyfour sale in 1871 a very fortunate purchase was
made in the heifer calf of Pride of Aberdeen 5th 1174,
after Jim Crow 4th 352, for 29 guineas. The animal,
of the Pride of Aberdeen family, was named Pride

of Mulben 1919, and the sale of her and her offspring formed the chief feature of the Mulben dispersion in 1876.

Among the sires used at Mulben were Malcolm of Bodiechell 269, second - prize bull at the Highland Society's show at Perth in 1861; Prince of Wales 453, bred at Westertown, got by a son of the Queen bull Windsor 221, and first-prize winner at the Highland Society's show at Stirling in 1874; Jupiter 471, bred by the Earl of Southesk, another son of Windsor 221, and first at Glasgow in 1867; Arthur 478, bred at Balwyllo; Sultan 477, a grandson of Windsor 221, and of the Kinnaird Dora family; Maccallum-More 722, by a son and out of a daughter of Windsor 221; Lochiel 723, after a son of Windsor; and Elgin 724 and Scotland 725, both sons of Maccallum-More 722. The principal points about these sires were their close relationship to the Queen bull Windsor 221, and their success in the show-yard. When the Mulben herd was dispersed in 1876, many of the animals were obtained by well-known breeders. Sir George Macpherson Grant bought Pride of Mulben 1919 for 91 guineas. The other members of the Pride family were bought by Mr M'Combie of Tillyfour, and Mr Adamson, Balquharn, at high prices. The Earl of Strathmore made his first purchases at this sale, and among the other buyers were the Earl of Fife, the Earl of Aberdeen, Sir W. G. Gordon Cumming, Bart. of Altyre; Mr Argo, Cairdseat; Mr M'Combie of Easter Skene; Mr Bruce, Collithie; Mr Wilken, Waterside, &c.

Castle Fraser.

At the Highland Society's show at Glasgow in 1867 Colonel Fraser of Castle Fraser was first for cows with Mina 1009; at Aberdeen in 1868 he was first with Lily 1114; and at Edinburgh in 1869 he was second with Sybil 974, who was, next year at Dumfries, awarded the

first prize. These salient facts illustrate the remarkable
show-yard career of the Castle Fraser herd, but they do not
exhaust the record of its winnings. At Dumfries, for
example, Colonel Fraser owned, in addition to the first-
prize cow, the second-prize two-year-old bull, the second-
prize one-year-old bull, and the second and third prize
two-year-old heifers. The rapid progress of this herd was
due to the discrimination and fine judgment exercised in
the selection of sires, to careful management, and liberal
and skilful preparation. In short, this appears to have
been a herd that was mainly built up by the use of highly
bred sires, the pedigrees of the females having been of a
plain description. The first notable sire used was Black
Jock of Tillyfour 365, calved in 1860, bred by Mr M'Combie of Tillyfour. He was after Hanton 228, and out of
Empress of France 578, who, being a daughter of Hanton
and Charlotte 203, was a full sister to the invincible Pride
of Aberdeen 581. The close breeding should be noted.
Charlotte's dam, Lola Montes 208, was closely bred from
Panmure 51, and Black Jock himself was a son of Hanton,
and out of a daughter by Hanton. Such a concentration
of similar blood was bound to result in the production of
an impressive animal, and the use of Black Jock in the
herd was wonderfully successful, for, put to the short
pedigreed dams, the produce was the first prize-cows at
Glasgow and Aberdeen. Then followed Priam 467, bred
at Mains of Kelly of Mr Bowie's Jennet tribe, his dam
having been bred at Tillyfour, and also after Hanton 228;
and Commodore 490, bred at Kinnaird, after Windsor
221. Next came Prince Charlie 487, calved in 1866,
bred by Mr Brown, Westertown, got by Success 467, a
grandson of Windsor 221, and out of Duchess 1st 930, by
which cross more of the finest Queen blood was obtained.
After him was used Reform 408, bred at Easter Skene,
got by that very finely bred bull Black Prince of Tillyfour 366, and out of Beauty of Tillyfour 2nd 1180, of the

Keillor Favourite family. Jamie 367, a son of Reform, followed. At the time of the dispersion of the herd in 1870, the sire in use was Cup-Bearer of Ballindalloch 451, bred by Sir George Macpherson Grant. He was a son of the first Erica 843 and Trojan 402, who was by Black Prince of Tillyfour 366, and out of Charlotte 203. Every one of the bulls used at Castle Fraser were thus, it will be seen, very well-bred, and were all nearly related.

The show-yard reputation of the herd collected a large company at its dispersion in 1870. The sale was one of considerable importance, for the foundations of four herds —those of the Marquis of Huntly, the Earl of Fife, the Earl of Aberdeen, and Mr Fordyce of Brucklay—were laid by purchases made on the occasion. Sir George Macpherson Grant acquired for 63 guineas the cow Sybil 974, who was afterwards exhibited by him, as she had been before by Colonel Fraser, with much success. She founded a family at Ballindalloch. Her twin daughters Fred's Darling 1055 and Fred's 2nd Darling 1045 each established a tribe at Mountblairy and Mulben; and Mr Dingwall Fordyce obtained Blanche 1117, who bred Bella Mary 1503 —who afterwards became the first-prize cow at the International show at Paris in 1878. Mina 1009 and Lily 1114 also established families, the members of which continue to be held in favour.

Aboyne Castle.

The interest displayed in the polled breed by the Marquis of Huntly was suitably recognised by his lordship's appointment as first President of the Polled Cattle Society. Lord Huntly commenced to breed polled cattle at Aboyne Castle in 1870. In that year he purchased at the Castle Fraser dispersion the two-year-old heifer Lively 1164, who had won prizes at the Highland Society's and Royal Northern Society's shows as a yearling and two-year-old. She was the highest priced animal at Colonel Fraser's sale, costing 67 guineas, and the price was justified by the excellent breeding qualities which she developed. At Tillyfour in 1871 was purchased Dora 1282 of the Daisy branch of the Queen tribe. She also proved a good investment, and besides breeding well, gained the first prize of the Highland Society at Glasgow in 1874. Her most notable produce were the bull Dragon 1178 used for some time in the Tillyfour herd; and the heifers Dorinda 2575 and Dewdrop 2581. In 1872 three animals were bought from the late Mr George Brown, Westertown. They were the bull Pluto 602 of the Victoria family, and the heifers Duchess 3rd 943 and Duchess 4th 944 of the Duchess branch of the Queen tribe. The sum paid for the three was 200 guineas. At Portlethen in March 1873, a pair of two-year-old heifers were acquired for 150 guineas: they were Cherry Blossom 901 and Flower Girl 895, the former of the Queen tribe, and the latter of the Kinnaird Fanny tribe. From Westertown, the same year, came Duchess 7th 1197 of the Duchess family, and Rose of Aboyne 1596 of the Rose family, the price of the pair having been 120 guineas. At Mr Walker's sale at Portlethen in 1873 two cows were bought, and at Drumin that year Gem 1595 of the Pride family and Beauty of Drumin 939 of Mr Skinner's Beauty family were bought for 131 guineas. At Mr Walker's dispersion at Balquharn, in 1874, was secured Madge of Portlethen 1217 of the Tillyfour Ruth family, full of Keillor blood. She herself won the first prize at the International show at Kilburn, and her son Monarch 1182 was a first-prize Highland Society winner, and gained the cup presented by Her Majesty the Queen at the Tarland show. Madge and five of her family carried off the prize awarded to the best group of polled cattle at the Royal Northern show in 1878. From Mr Ferguson, Kinnochtry, the Princess cows, Princess of Aboyne 1st 2572 and Princess

2nd 2570, were obtained for 120 guineas. The bull Duke of Perth 357 was secured at the Westertown dispersion in 1874. At Mr Hannay's sale at Corskie in 1877 the bull Warrior 1291, of the Rothiemay Victoria strain, was purchased for 155 guineas. He was the first-prize yearling at the Highland Society's show, and his dam sold for 111 guineas and his sire Young Viscount 736 for 225 guineas. Several animals were bought at the Indego, Auchlossan, Melville, Glamis, and Rothiemay sales. In 1878, at Tillyfour, Pride of Mulben 2nd 2359 was bought for 91 guineas and Vine 9th 3256 for 72 guineas; and at the Tillyfour dispersion in 1880, Charmer 3rd 3251 of the Queen tribe was obtained for 150 guineas.

The herd was thus based on the very best obtainable material, and was collected at an expense of about £2000. Showing was rarely resorted to, the object having been to keep a class of regular and useful breeding animals. A number of first-rate bulls were bred in the herd, and several of these were sold to the Marquis's tenautry on favourable terms. In this way, as well as others, the herd exerted a most beneficial influence. When specimens from the herd were exhibited they obtained high honours at the national and local shows. Thus Lord Huntly had the rare fortune of gaining the Highland Society's first prizes for aged bulls and cows at Glasgow in 1875, with Duke of Perth and Dora. Monarch was also a first-prize bull at the Highland Society, and his dam Madge, as already mentioned, was the first-prize cow at Kilburn in 1879. The chief distinction of the herd, and one that perhaps afforded its owner more satisfaction than any other, was the rearing of the Madge family. Madge proved a first-rate breeder, and her offspring were uniformly good. A large draft was sold from the herd in 1879, when 37 head averaged over £44; and in 1881 the herd was dispersed, the average for 32 head being over £50. The total proceeds of these two public sales was over £3200.

At the 1879 sale, Mr M'Combie of Tillyfour bought a good many animals, chiefly representatives of the various branches of the Queen tribe. Lord Tweedmouth also made several important purchases. At the sale in 1881, old Madge 1217 fell to the bid of Mr Smith, Powrie, for 100 guineas. Charmer 3rd 3251 was taken by Mr Wilken, Waterside, for the Honourable J. H. Pope, the Canadian Minister of Agriculture, for 100 guineas. Mr Burdett-Coutts bought Cowslip 2nd 3004 for 100 guineas, and Mr Greenfield of Beechwood secured Vine 9th 3256 for 115 guineas.

Duff House.

Few herds of polled cattle have had a more distinguished career than that which belonged to the Earl of Fife at Duff House, near Banff. For several years it occupied a leading position in the national and local show-yards, and during its short existence was instrumental in effecting considerable improvement among the live stock of the country. The bulk of the herd was taken over at valuation by Mr Hannay, Gavenwood; and as we shall have occasion to give an account of the polled cattle at Gavenwood, it is unnecessary here to enter minutely into the breeding and history of Lord Fife's stock. It is desirable, however, to indicate briefly the materials of which the Duff House herd was composed, and to record a few of its principal performances in the show-yard. Lord Fife founded his herd by the purchase, at Colonel Fraser's sale at Castle Fraser in 1870, of the cow Fanny of Corskie 1014 by Priam 467, for 53 guineas, and the bull-calf, Lord Ornoch 445 out of Fanny 1014 and after Jamie of Easter Skene 367, for 40 guineas. At the Easter Skene draft sale the same year was bought Beauty of Easter Skene 996, a member of the Keillor Favourite tribe, for 35 guineas. At Mr Tayler's sale at Rothiemay in 1872 was purchased Linnet 1706 of the Drumin Lucy family, for 23 guineas,

and the very fine heifer, Heather Blossom 1189 of the
Rothiemay Victoria family, for 30 guineas. In 1872 there
was also acquired at Sir George Macpherson Grant's sale
the valuable Erica cow, Erica 4th 1697, for 60 guineas.
From Mr Skinner's sale at Drumin in 1873 came Patience
of Corskie 1932 of the Drumin Rose family, for 40 guineas,
and Cowslip 1709 of the Drumin Lucy sort, for 30 guineas.
The cow Corskie 23rd B. 1062 was added at the Bognie
dispersion in 1874, for 37 guineas, and Major of Bognie
444 came from the same place at a similar price. The
splendid Pride heifer, Lilias of Tillyfour 1795, out of Pride
of Aberdeen 5th 1174, was a purchase at Mr M'Combie's
sale in 1874, for 46 guineas. No other animal was added
to the herd from public sales. In addition, however, to
the acquisitions made to the herd publicly, its numbers
and value were enhanced by private treaty. In fact, a
feature in the collection of this famous herd was the
additions made to it privately. We shall mention only
the more important of these transactions. Palmerston 374,
after winning the first prize in the aged class at the Highland Society's Dumfries show in 1870, was bought from
Mr Walker, Portlethen, and proved a useful and successful
stock sire.

A great many animals were bought in the Alford and
Tarland districts from Mr Shaw, Bogfern; Mr Hunter,
Confunderland; Mr Farquharson, East-Town, and Mr
Strachan, Wester Fowlis. Among these may be named
the fine cow Corriemulzie 1701, descended from the Keillor
herd, the second-prize cow at Stirling in 1873. From
Mr Walker, Montbletton; Mr Morrison, Auchlin, and
Mr Barclay, Yonderton, a large number of purchases were
made. The animals got from the Montbletton herd were
exceedingly fortunate. They included Jinny 1017, the
dam of Innes 1934, the first-prize cow at the Highland
Society's show at Aberdeen in 1876; Blackbird of Corskie
1704, the dam of the first-prize cow at Perth in 1879; and

others of note. In 1873 a very important addition was
made. In that year a bull-calf was bought from Mr Duff,
Hillockhead, Glass. The bull was called Young Viscount
736, and his fame has travelled wherever the polled breed
is known. A specimen of the Ballindalloch Erica family,
he was shown as a yearling at the Highland Society's
show at Inverness in 1874, as a two-year-old at Glasgow
in 1875, and in the aged class at Aberdeen in 1876, and on
each occasion he gained the first prize. He subsequently
gained the challenge cup and the M'Combie prize at the
Royal Northern at Aberdeen, and having been sold to Sir
George Macpherson Grant for 225 guineas, won for him the
first and champion prizes at the International show at Kilburn in 1879. He was used in the Duff House, Gavenwood,
and Ballindalloch herds with excellent results. In 1874,
at the Inverness show of the Highland Society, the bull
Gainsborough 596, who had won the first prize there, was
acquired from Mr Bowie, Mains of Kelly. The second-
prize bull at this show, John Bright 642, bred at Bognie,
was also used in the herd.

With such fine material, and under able management,
the Duff House herd came rapidly to the front. From
1872 to 1877 it supplied many of the Highland Society's
prize-winners. The greatest success was achieved in 1876
at the National Society's meeting at Aberdeen, where there
was an unusually grand display of polled cattle. Lord
Fife was then first for aged bulls with Young Viscount
736; first for two-year-old bulls with St Clair 1160; very
highly commended for the yearling bull Gladiolus 1161;
first for cows with Innes 1934; fourth for cows with Patience 1932; very highly commended with Blackbird 1704;
commended with Crocus 1400; and second for two-year-
old heifers with Maria 2nd 3015. As we have said, the
herd was valued over to Mr Hannay, Gavenwood, and
a notice of its subsequent progress will be found under
the heading "Existing Herds."

Balquharn.

Mr Henry D. Adamson, who went to the north of
Scotland to learn farming under Mr M'Combie of Tillyfour, naturally had his attention early directed to the
merits of the polled breed. During the time he occupied
the farm of Balquharn, near Alford, he always kept a few
polled animals, but the herd with which he ultimately
became associated was not actually started until 1876,
when he made an important purchase at Lord Airlie's sale
at Cortachy, Kirriemuir. From that year till 1881 he
paid great attention to the collection of his choice herd.
Mr Adamson's main aim appears to have been to gather
together some of the best specimens of the Pride of Aberdeen family in order to demonstrate that, for usefulness
and showing capabilities, it had lost none of its early
celebrity. In consequence of the owner's ill-health, the
herd was unexpectedly thrown into the market in 1881
when it realised the highest average price ever obtained
at a public sale of polled cattle—£56, 4s. 8d., for 36 head.
Mr Adamson's purchase at Cortachy, to which reference
has been made, was the Pride cow Regina 1179, out of
Pride of Aberdeen 3rd 1168 and after Jim Crow 3rd 350.
The price was 70 guineas. Pride of Mulben 3rd 3249,
after Elgin 724 and out of Pride of Mulben 1919, was
bought at the Tillyfour sale in 1878 for 100 guineas. At
the same sale Pride of Aberdeen 7th 1777, out of Pride
of Aberdeen 581 and after Derby 377, was acquired for
50 guineas. From Mr M'Combie was also obtained less
noteworthy members of the Pride tribe; and also the cow
Sybil 2nd of Tillyfour 3526 of the Baads Sybil family, a
member of the Tillyfour prize group at Paris, and a
first prize cow of the Highland Society. At the Tullochallum dispersion in 1877, the Erica cow Miss Macpherson
1252 was added for 90 guineas, but was subsequently sold
privately to the Earl of Airlie. Another Erica cow added

was Ermin 3532, bred at Burnside. The Kinnochtry
Favourites, the Rothiemay Georginas and Miss Morrisons,
and the Ardgay Zaras, were also represented in the herd.
Some of the Tillyfour sires were used, as also the Erica
bull Cluny 1283, but the chief sire was bred in the herd.
This was Knight of the Shire 1699, out of the Pride cow
Pride of Mulben 3rd 3249, and after the Queen bull
Dragon 1178. To Mr Adamson Knight of the Shire won
the first prizes as a yearling at the Royal English Society's
show at Carlisle, and at the Highland Society's show
at Kelso in 1880. He was also the first prize two-
year-old at Stirling in 1881. Other famous animals bred
in the herd were Pride of Aberdeen 18th 4321, out of
Regina 1179 and after Dragon 1179; Pride of Aberdeen
24th 4327, out of Pride of Mulben 3rd 3249 and after
Cluny 1283; Sybil 4th 4326, out of Sybil 2nd 3526 and
after Cluny 1283. At the dispersion of Mr Adamson's
herd in April 1881 Lord Tweedmouth purchased Pride of
Mulben 3rd 3249, for 225 guineas; Lord Southesk, Sybil
2nd 3526, for 180 guineas; Mr Auld, Bridgend, and
Mr Anderson, Wellhouse, Knight of the Shire 1699, for
165 guineas; Lord Tweedmouth, Pride of Aberdeen 18th
4321, for 160 guineas; Her Majesty the Queen, Pride of
Aberdeen 24th 4327, for 125 guineas; Lord Strathmore,
Sybil 4th 4326, for 110 guineas; and Mr Grant, Auchorachan, Regina 1179, for 105 guineas.

Other Herds.

Fyvie Castle.—The foundation of the herd at Fyvie
Castle was laid by the late Colonel Gordon in 1848 by the
purchase of a cow from Mr G. G. Robinson, Corskie,
Banff (who bred polled cattle prior to 1830), and two
heifers from Mr Watson, Keillor. These are now extinct
in the female line; but a son of one of the Keillor heifers,
named Fyvie 13, sold to Mr Walker, Portlethen, still keeps

up the strain on the male side. Purchases were early made
from Mr Malcolm, Bodiechell, who bred from the old
stock of Mr Walker, Wester Fintray, and from Mr
Farquharson Taylor, Wellhouse. From the former came
the ancestress of the Flower family, the cow being after a
son of the celebrated Keillor bull Angus 45, and from
the latter the Wellhouse family, tracing to a cow by
Panmure 51. The first bull used in the herd was Malcolm
of Bodiechell 269, twice second in the aged class at
Highland Society's shows. Other useful sires were introduced; and the milking-qualities of the breed being carefully developed, much good, far beyond the immediate
district, was done by stock from Fyvie. One of the most
famous animals bred in the herd was Sir Maurice 1319, of
the Flower family, well known in the Rothiemay herd.
The Fyvie herd was dispersed in 1881, when 32 head
averaged £30, 7s. 4d. The Earl of Southesk bought two
superior milking-cows of the Flower family at 89 and 88
guineas each.

Tullochallum.—Mr Gordon, Tullochallum, started a
herd of pure-bred cattle about 1867, by purchasing a
bull and five heifers from Mr Skinner, Drumin. The
bull was Drumin 744, after the Pride sire Hero 400, and
out of Ruby 951, of Mr Skinner's Beauty family. The
next bull used was Major of Tillyfour 509, of the Pride
family, being out of Pride of Aberdeen 581, and a half-
brother of Hero 400. Then came Knight of Aven 775,
of the Queen tribe, followed by Scotia 789, both bred at
Drumin; Prince Albert 2nd 745, a prize bull out of Kate
of Baads 1947, and Lord Provost 1304, bred by Mr
Hannay. Among the females added were Fancy of
Tillyfour 2nd 1799, of the Pride family, whose twin-
daughters were sold privately to Sir William G. Gordon
Cumming; Miss Macpherson 1252, of the Erica family,
out of Erica 3rd 1249, from Mr Duff, Hillockhead; a

Sybil from Ballindalloch; a Duchess and a Rose from Westertown, &c. The herd was dispersed in 1877, when 32 head averaged £34. The highest-priced animal was Miss Macpherson 1252, sold to Mr Adamson, Balquharn, for 90 guineas. From the Tullochallum herd were sent out some splendid commercial cattle, and it supplied Mr M'Combie of Tillyfour with a noted prize-ox at the Smithfield and Birmingham shows.

Brucklay.—The Brucklay herd that belonged to the late Mr Dingwall Fordyce was established in 1870, by the purchase at Castle Fraser of Blanche 1117, from whom was bred Bella Mary 1503, who gained for Mr George Bruce the first prize for cows at the International show at Paris in 1878. Tillyfour, Portlethen, Fyvie, Westertown, Rothiemay, Easter Tulloch, and Drumin furnished the other female additions to the herd. The chief sires used were M'Combie 430, bred at Tillyfour, after Bright 454, and out of Miss M'Combie 1118; and Knight of Aven 775, bred at Drumin, both of the Queen tribe. The herd was dispersed in 1876, when 38 head averaged £31.

Indego.—The late Dr Robertson of Hopewell had a herd of polled cattle at Indego, Tarland—animals from which were successfully exhibited at the shows of the Royal Northern Agricultural Society. The females in the herd were descended from the Tillyfour, Bogfern, and Haddo House herds. The best family, perhaps, was that tracing to Bess 1181, a daughter of Mr M'Combie's Rob Roy Macgregor 267. Bulls belonging to Mr Farquharson, at the adjoining farm of East-Town, were used, and at the time of the dispersion the stock sire was Sir William 705, after President 4th 368. This bull won the challenge cup at the Royal Northern show at Aberdeen in 1873, and was used in the Baads herd.

Bognie.—Mr Morison of Bognie was most energetic in

stimulating improvement in stock-breeding. He was a breeder of Shorthorns as well as of polled cattle; and of the "red, white, and roan," he purchased specimens from Mr Bates of Kirklevington. His chief attention was, however, devoted to the native polled breed, and he kept herds at Bognie and Montblairy. The Bognie herd was dispersed in 1874, on Mr Morison's death. Here also the records had been imperfectly kept. The herd was composed of members of four families: the Hawkhalls, which had been at Bognie for over thirty years; the Beautys, which had been there for over twenty years; the Corskies, descended from Mr G. G. Robinson's stock; and the Miss Carnegies, descended from a heifer bought at Captain Carnegie's sale at Craigo. The bull Odin 153, bred by the Earl of Southesk, after Cup-Bearer 59, and out of Octavia 331, of the Keillor Favourite tribe, gave a decided stamp to the herd, which was continued by the use of a succession of his descendants. Innocent 502, of the Portlethen Ida family, was used, as was also Major 444, bred at Castle Fraser. At the dispersion, the chief purchasers were the Earl of Fife; Mr Grant, Methlick; Mr Macgregor, Kincraig; and Mr Adamson, Balquharn.

Fernyflatt.—Fernyflatt was long a famous name in connection with polled cattle. It was there that Mr Hector bred the bull Hector, sire of the celebrated Panmure 51. Mr Glennie succeeded Mr Hector in the farm, and on the dispersion of the herd in 1876, on the death of the former, it was possible to point to the existence of a polled herd at Fernyflatt for forty years. Pedigrees had not been carefully kept, but the purity of the stock was undoubted. Females had been introduced from Balwyllo, Crathes, and Portlethen, and the best herds of the district had supplied sires. The first animal in the catalogue was Princess of Easter Tulloch 1026, from Mr Ferguson's Prizie 586. She was bought by Mr Ferguson, Ballunie. The

other cattle sold cheaply, the reward of Mr Hector's and
Mr Glennie's long-continued efforts being lost by the fact
that the herd records had been neglected.

Garline.—At Garline, Ballindalloch, Mr J. F. M'Gregor
bred polled cattle, and he had the good fortune to secure,
before the merits of the family were so widely recognised
as now, a specimen of the Ballindalloch Ericas. This was
Ella 1205, bred by Sir George Macpherson Grant, after
Kildonan 405, and out of Erica 843, the foundress of this
noted strain. At the dispersion of his small herd in 1874,
Sir George Macpherson Grant bought one of the Ericas,
Emma of Garline 1733. The other two, Ella 1205 and
Editha 1737, were acquired by Mr Robertson, then at
Burnside.

Of other extinct polled herds simple mention must
suffice. Mr Lyell owned a very fine herd at Shielhill, descended from the stock of Mr Mustard, Leuchland. From
it came the bulls Prospero 301 and Tom Pipes 302 (both
after the Kinnaird sire Mariner 148), who won high honours at the Highland Society's show at Perth in 1861,
and at the International show at Battersea in 1863.
Herds were also maintained by Mr Patrick Davidson at
Inchmarlo, at the dispersion of which, in 1857, Mr Paterson, Mulben, secured the foundress of one of his tribes; by
Sir A. Burnett, at Crathes, in which there was a large
infusion of Keillor blood—Mr Hugh Watson's Strathmore
5 having been used; by the Hon. Charles Carnegie at
Arratsmill, dispersed in 1868, after a struggle with
cattle-disease; by Captain Carnegie at Craigo, from whom
Sir George Macpherson Grant and Mr Walker, Montbletton, obtained some valuable animals at the sale in
1856; by the late Earl of Aberdeen, at Haddo House,
dispersed in 1861; by Mr Greig, at Middlethird, Strichen,

dispersed in 1875 ; at Wemyss, dispersed in 1864; by Mr
J. W. Barclay, M.P., at Auchlossan, where a large and
useful herd, much indebted to Westertown blood, was
dispersed in 1874; at Biallid, Kingussie, where Mr Gwyer
had a good herd, dispersed in 1879; at Bolshan, where
Mr Goodlet had a herd, mainly built up on material
obtained at Kinnaird, &c.

CHAPTER X.

EXISTING SCOTCH HERDS.

THE ROYAL HERD AT ABERGELDIE MAINS—Her Majesty the Queen and
the breed—ABERLOUR MAINS—ALTYRE—ARDHUNCART—AUCHORA-
CHAN—BAADS—A remarkable show-yard herd—The Sybils and Halts
—Prince Albert of Baads 1336 the first-prize Highland Society bull in
1879 and 1880—BALLINDALLOCH—The premier herd of the time—Its
antiquity—"The talk of the country" since Mr M'Combie's earliest
recollections—Sir John Macpherson Grant's purchases at Tillyfour in
1850—Improvement of the herd under Sir George Macpherson Grant
—Forty-two first prizes, and twenty-four special prizes, cups, and
medals, gained in 1879 and 1880—Sir George's principal purchases—
The sires used—Trojan 402, a son of the Paris cow Charlotte 203, and
half-brother of Pride of Aberdeen 581—His influence on the herd—
Juryman 404, Judge 1150, and Justice 1462—Young Viscount 736, the
champion bull of his day—Families cultivated at Ballindalloch—The
Ericas, the Jilts, the Sybils, the Nosegays, the Coquettes, the Lady
Fannys, and the Prides—Public and private sales—BALLINTOMB—
BALLUNIE—BALQUHAIN MAINS—BENHOLM CASTLE—BLAIRSHINNOCH
—BRIDGEND—Mr Auld's experience in connection with the Tillyfour
herd—Famous animals at Bridgend bred by Mr M'Combie—Pride of
Aberdeen 9th 3253 the highest-price cow of the breed—Knight of the
Shire 1699—Mr Auld's aim to collect as many branches of Mr M'Com-
bie's Queen tribe as are obtainable—BURNSHANGIE.

WE shall now furnish, with as much completeness as the
limits of our space will permit, a description of the existing herds of polled cattle in Scotland. In order to make
reference as easy as possible, we have, in alluding to the
herds, adopted the alphabetical arrangement.

Abergeldie Mains.

Her Majesty the Queen commenced a herd at Abergeldie Mains about a year ago. Her Majesty had previously manifested her interest in the breed by visiting Tillyfour and inspecting Mr M'Combie's fine herd. More recently, the Queen was graciously pleased to present a splendid challenge cup for the best animal of the polled breed exhibited at the shows of the Cromar, Upper Dee, and Donside Agricultural Association, at Tarland. This valued trophy was awarded to polled animals bred in the district embraced by the Association, and it has greatly stimulated careful cattle-breeding among the members. Her Majesty also honoured the Polled Cattle Society by becoming its Patroness. The royal herd was collected under the superintendence of Dr Profeit, and the first purchases were made from Mr Walker, Westside; Mr Lumsden of Clova; Mr Walker, Ardhuncart; Mr Strachan, Wester Fowlis, &c. At the Balquharn sale in 1881, the fine heifer Pride of Aberdeen 24th 4327, out of Lord Tweedmouth's 225 guineas cow Pride of Mulben 3rd 3249, was bought for 125 guineas. The Abergeldie herd was first represented in the show-yard at the meeting of the Royal Northern Agricultural Society at Aberdeen last year, when the first prize was gained for pairs of cows with Blossom 2nd 3951 and Mary 2nd 3952, bred by Mr Walker, Westside of Brux, and the fourth prize for yearling heifers with Pride of Aberdeen 24th 4327.

Aberlour Mains.

The late Mr Robertson, father of Mr William Robertson, Aberlour Mains, established a herd at Burnside, Ballindalloch, about forty years ago, bringing with him some polled cows from Dandaleith. Bulls were obtained from Ballindalloch, Tillyfour, Westertown, Ardgay, Bognie, and

Drumin. The herd took a high place at the shows of the
Spey, Aven, and Fiddichside Farmers' Club, instituted in
1856, two of Mr Robertson's prize heifers at these shows
going to Drumin, where one of them, Princess 950, founded
a valuable family. In later years much of the Erica blood
was infused by the use of males of that strain, and at the
Garline sale in 1874, Mr William Robertson acquired two
Erica females, Ella 1205 and Editha 1737. Apart from
these Ericas, the most valuable family in the Burnside
herd was the Honestys, a branch of the Drumin Lucy
family. These were remarkable milkers, old Honesty
1690 having yielded as much milk as any other two cows
in the herd. On leaving Burnside for Aberlour Mains,
Mr William Robertson sold the bulk of his herd in
May 1880, when 31 animals averaged £28, 7s. 8d., 16
cows making an average of £32, 7s. A new herd was
begun at Aberlour Mains. The herd, of which the nucleus
was descendants of the Ericas bought at Garline, and
Honestys bred at Drumin, now comprises Georgina 3893,
descended from the late Mr Robertson's cow Princess 950,
sold in 1862 to Mr Skinner; Delilah 3894, bred at Inver-
allan, of the Drumin Lucy family, and her three-year-old
daughter Rose of Aberlour 4845, by the Erica bull Egbert
1443; Honesty 3rd 3754, Helena of Aberlour 4849, Hon-
nesty 6th 4848, and Hetty 4844, these four of the Honesty
branch of the Lucy family; Jewel 1413, of the Jilt family;
Edma Erica 3759, of the Erica family; Heatherbells, of
Drumin blood; Young Favourite 3rd 3533, of Kinnochtry blood; and Duchess of Burnside 3762, descended
from Old Grannie 1. Several other good families are
represented, and the younger stock are after the Erica
bull Whig 1867; Souter Johnny 1615, bred at Drumin;
Moraystown 1439, a son of Adrian 2nd 622 and Forget-
me-not 1685; and the Erica bull Egbert 1443. One of the
sires now in use is Paris 1473, the first-prize two-year-old
at the Paris Exhibition. In collecting his new herd, Mr

Robertson has given much attention to the milking-properties of the breed; and his experience is that, by very little
extra trouble, it is possible, without sacrificing the merits of
the breed in beef-production, to rear animals that will yield
a copious supply of milk of choice quality. Mr Robertson
has made some important private sales. The Erica cow
Ella was sold to Mr Stevenson, Blairshinnoch, for 100
guineas; the Erica cows Editha 1737 and Elf 3751 went
to Mr Wallis, Bradley Hall, at long prices; the Erica cow
Esther 4843 was bought for Mr Stephenson, Newcastle-on-
Tyne; Honesty 4th 3757 was sold for exportation, as were
also three Erica females. Mr Stewart, Auchindellan, secured an Erica heifer, and the Erica bull Whig 1867 was
sold to Major Smith, Minmore, for 100 guineas.

Altyre.

Sir William G. Gordon Cumming, Bart. of Altyre, and
his factor Mr Robert Walker, have done much in recent
years to popularise the polled breed. On several occasions
animals from Altyre have won cups for Scotch cattle at
the Smithfield Fat Stock shows; and, as noticed elsewhere,
Sir William had the unique honour of gaining, not only
the Scotch cup, but also the champion cups for heifers and
oxen, and the "blue ribbon" of the show, with polled animals at London last year. The breeding herd at Altyre
has not hitherto appeared much in public competitions,
but it is of high merit, and contains a great deal of good
blood. The herd has been in existence since 1874. At
the Westertown dispersion, specimens of Mr Brown's Rose
and Victoria families were acquired. At Mulben, in 1875,
some of Mr Paterson's Mayflowers were introduced. The
heifer Oakleaf 1836, by Bon Accord 446, was bought at
Rothiemay that year for 54 guineas. In the summer of
1876, 60 guineas were paid to Mr Ferguson for Princess of
Altyre 3126, of the Kinnochtry Princess family. From

Mr Gordon, Tullochallum, Pride of the Findhorn 3243, and Pride of Altyre 3244, were bought privately. They were twin daughters of Fancy of Tillyfour 2nd 1799, a granddaughter of Pride of Aberdeen 581, and were after Talisman 640. Of the Daisy branch of the Queen tribe, representatives were obtained from Mr Mackessack, Earnside, for whom the cow Dido 3257, and Flora of Earnside 2113, had been secured at Tillyfour in 1871. The Kinnochtry Favourite heifer, Favourite of Altyre 3127, was bought from Mr Ferguson. Banshee 2981, by Jester 472, was also added to the herd. The sires used have been Senator 863, bred at Ballindalloch, out of the splendid cow Sybil 974; Black Watch 1242, bred by Viscount Macduff, after Gainsborough 596, and out of Lilias of Tillyfour 1795, of the Pride tribe; and Dustman 1667, bred at Aboyne, after Warrior 1291, and out of Dandelion 2569, of the Duchess branch of the Queen tribe. The herd thus comprises members of the following families: Pride, Daisy, Princess, Favourite, Westertown Rose, Mulben Mayflower, &c. Surplus females are sold privately, and the bull calves are in demand at the public sales.

Ardhuncart.

When Mr Walker's father entered the farm of Ardhuncart, Kildrummy, in 1811, he commenced breeding what was at that time considered pure Aberdeenshire cattle. About the years 1826 and 1840 he obtained fresh strains of polled blood from Wester Fintray, through Mr Ross, Oldtown, Tarland. Stock from the Crathes and Mains of Kelly herds were also introduced. That splendidly bred bull, Draco 338, after the Queen sire Windsor 221, and out of the Dora cow Dolores 1285, was bought at Kinnaird in 1861, and improved the herd very much. Cows and bulls were obtained from Tillyfour, Clova, Archballoch, and Reekie in Alford. The herd has never

been pampered or fed for show purposes, but has always
been kept in good breeding condition, and has stood high
in the prize-lists at the local shows.   The cows are all
good milkers, some of them yielding very heavily at the
pail.

Auchorachan.

This herd, belonging to Mr George Smith Grant, was
founded in 1875 by the purchase from Mr Skinner,
Drumin, of the heifer Bella 3136, representing the Catherine family.   Bella's first calf, Bella 2d 3551, got by the
Pride bull Thane 1243, is still in the herd.   She has had
other four heifer calves, all in the herd, except Barbara
4754, calved in 1880, who was sold in December 1881 to
Mr Wilken, Waterside, for 60 guineas.   They are a fine
breeding family, splendid milkers, and large - framed.
Another purchase from the Drumin herd was Mavis 2211,
of the Lucy family, bought at Mr Skinner's sale in 1876
for £48.   She only left one calf, Lady Lucy 3552, who
was the dam of Linnet 4751, calved in 1880, still in the
herd. This family has produced good milkers and breeders.
The next animal purchased was Christian 2nd 3549, at the
Easter Tulloch sale in 1876.   Bought at 22 guineas, she
has turned out a very profitable investment.   She is after
the Erica bull Emperor 396, and her dam is by Cavalier
411.   She has bred three heifers and two bulls.   The
heifers are all retained, being of a fine milking and easily
kept strain.   The bulls were sold privately, and left
superior stock.   Nosegay 2155, bred by Sir George Macpherson Grant, was added to the herd in 1876; and
although then fifteen years old, she bred a calf every year
until 1881, when, proving barren, she went to the butcher.
Unfortunately, her produce consisted of three bull calves
and only one heifer.   The heifer, calved in 1879, got by
Victory 1364, bred by Mr Melville Cartwright, is still in
the herd, and has proved an excellent milker.   She is a

big lengthy cow, with fine hair and quality, and has a
heifer calf at foot, after the stock bull Viscount Duff 1365.
The cow and calf are among the most valuable and best-
looking animals in the herd. Silvia 3073, of the Sybil
family, bred by Sir George Macpherson Grant, and purchased at Mr Gordon's sale in 1877, was the next addition. She has bred bulls which have been sold at good
prices, one this year bringing 40 guineas at the Aberdeen
joint sale.

In 1877 was purchased from Mr Duff, Hillockhead,
Glass, the heifer Erica 8th 3550, and the bull Viscount Duff 1365, bred by Lord Fife. For the two a
high price was paid. Erica 8th—herself, as her name im-
plies, an Erica—was sent to the fine Erica bull Elcho 595,
and produced in December 1878 a heifer calf, Erica 10th
3957. In October 1880, Lord Southesk, who was then
laying the foundation of a herd, wishing to get back some
of his old Erica family, went to Auchorachan and bought
from Mr Grant the cow Erica 8th, at the handsome price
of 100 guineas. Erica 10th is still in the herd, and, like
her dam, promises to be a first-rate milker. She had a
bull calf last year, which was retained, and this year she
has a fine heifer calf, after Cupid 2nd 1925. At the Marquess of Huntly's sale in 1879, the cow Bellona 2579 was
bought. She belongs to the Drumin Beauty family, and
is a cow of good substance and superior milking-qualities.
She has had two bull calves, which were sold privately,
and this year she had a fine heifer calf by Viscount Duff
1365. At the same sale was bought Guitar 4749 of the
Pride family. She has improved considerably, and has a
bull calf after Viscount Duff. From Mr Robertson, Burnside, was acquired the cow Honesty 1690, bred by Mr
Skinner, Drumin, of the Lucy family. She had a bull
calf, and is one of the best milkers in the herd. At Mr
Adamson's sale at Aberdeen in 1881, Mr Grant bought for
105 guineas the cow Regina 1179, a granddaughter of

Pride of Aberdeen 581, and noticed elsewhere as the dam of some capital stock. In calf when Mr Grant bought her, she produced in May 1881 a heifer by the Pride bull Knight of the Shire 1699. This calf is one of the purest-bred Prides living, and promises to become an animal of great merit. This year Regina had a bull calf, after Young Viscount 736. The stock bull is Viscount Duff 1365, grandson of the well-known Heather Blossom 1703, and after Young Viscount 736. The herd is in excellent breeding condition, in no way pampered, forcing for show-yard purposes having been avoided. With scarcely an exception, each cow has a calf every year. Auchorachan is situated about 900 feet above sea-level, and the thriving state of the herd shows that the polled cattle will do well where other breeds of a less hardy constitution could not thrive.

Baads.

In recent years no herd of polled cattle has had a more distinguished show-yard record than that of Mr George Reid, Baads, Peterculter. It supplied the first-prize cows at the Highland Society's and Royal Northern Society's shows in 1877, 1878, and 1880; the first-prize aged bull at these shows in 1880; the winners of the Challenge cups at Aberdeen in 1877, 1879, and 1880; the winners of the M'Combie prize at Aberdeen in 1879 and 1880; the first-prize heifer and the second-prize cow at the Paris Exhibition in 1878; and the first-prize bull and the first and second prize cows at the Royal English show at Carlisle in 1880. These animals were not all exhibited by Mr Reid, but they were either bred by him or descended from his stock, and, moreover, they were all of two strains of blood. This brief statement affords the most striking proof it is possible to give of the excellent material of which the Baads herd is composed. It is now nearly twenty-eight years ago since polled cattle were introduced

to Baads, and the first of the family, of which most of the
prize cattle we have referred to were members, was obtained about twenty-five years ago. At that time Mr
Reid's brother William purchased a polled heifer from the
late Marquess of Huntly at Aboyne Castle. This animal
came to Baads, and her calves being of rare merit, were
retained for breeding. No pedigrees were kept then, and
the first animal connected with the herd whose name is
mentioned in the 'Herd Book' was Maggie, bred at Baads,
who produced in 1870 the heifer Fancy of Baads 1948.
Fancy was after the famous show-bull President 4th 368,
who, after being used for some time at Tillyfour, was in
service for two years at Baads, and was the first bull that
in an especial manner left his mark on the herd. We
have already, in connection with the Tillyfour herd, said
something about his breeding. We may here note that
he was after the Balwyllo bull President 3rd 246, of the
Isabella family, and out of Flower of Strathmore 479.
Flower of Strathmore was got by Cup-Bearer 59, and on
the dam's side traced to Mr Fullerton's Flora 70, stated in
the 'Herd Book' (where the pedigree is imperfectly given)
to have been directly descended from Queen of Ardovie 29
and Panmure 51.

In 1873 and 1874, Fancy 1948, to the bull Sir William 705 (also got by President 4th 368, bred by Mr
M'Combie, Upper Farmton, and winner of the first prize
and Challenge Cup at the Royal Northern show in
1873), produced two heifer calves which have become
famous. They were Sybil 1st of Tillyfour 3524, and Isla
1965. Sybil 1st, when one year old, was exhibited by Mr
Reid at the Inverness show of the Highland Society in
1874, and gained the first prize. Along with another
heifer of Mr Reid's, Halt 3525, who won the second prize,
she was purchased by Mr M'Combie of Tillyfour for £100.
She next appeared in 1877 at Edinburgh, and gained the
first prize for cows—a similar honour falling to her at

Aberdeen that year, where she also gained the Challenge Cup. She was the second-prize cow at Paris in 1878. Mr M'Combie bred from her Sybil 2nd of Tillyfour 3526, who was second-prize yearling heifer at Edinburgh in 1877, first at Aberdeen that year, a member of the Paris group, and, passing into the possession of Mr Adamson, Balquharn, gained the first prize as a cow at Kelso, Carlisle, and Aberdeen in 1880, as well as the Challenge Cup and the M'Combie prize at the Royal Northern show. In Mr Adamson's possession she produced, among other calves, the heifer Sybil 4th 4326, who carried the first prize as a yearling to Lord Strathmore at the Highland Society's show in 1881. Sybil 1st was sold to the Earl of Airlie for 110 guineas, and Sybil 2nd to Lord Southesk for 180 guineas. At the Tillyfour and Balquharn sales, six animals of Mr Reid's Sybil family were sold at an average of about £100 each. The sort is now represented at Kinnaird, Cortachy, Glamis, Haddo House, and Guisachan. Isla, the other calf of Fancy 1948, was retained by Mr Reid. She gained the first prizes as a cow at the Highland Society and Royal Northern shows in 1878, and second at Carlisle in 1880, while she and three of her daughters made the very pretty group that won the first prize at Aberdeen in 1881. Isla has bred extremely well, her calves inheriting their dam's true form, substance, and quality. Another early purchase by Mr Reid was the heifer Matilda from Mr Dunn, Nether Ennenter, Leochel. In 1862 this animal to President 4th produced Kate of Baads 1947. Kate's calf in 1872 was Prince Albert 2nd 745, a first-prize bull at Aberdeen, and second at the Highland Society's shows. In 1873 she bred Halt 3525, who, after winning the second prize as a yearling heifer at the Highland Society's show in 1874, was, as already remarked, sold to Mr M'Combie of Tillyfour, in whose possession she bred Halt 2nd 3527, who was the first-prize heifer at Paris in 1878, and a member of the Tillyfour champion group, which thus con-

tained two animals tracing from the Baads stock. Kate's
calf in 1877 to the Ballindalloch bull Bachelor 690, at
Easter Skene, was Prince Albert of Baads 1336, one of
the best polled bulls ever bred. Prince Albert of Baads
was bought by Mr Anderson, Daugh, and won the first
prizes as a two-year-old at the Royal Northern and Highland Society's shows, and the first prizes in the aged class
at the Royal Northern, Highland, and Royal English
shows, gaining in 1879, when only two years old, the
Challenge Cup and M'Combie prizes at Aberdeen. Mr
Reid has a few other strains, among them one from Mains
of Kelly; but it has been with the descendants of Fancy
1948 and Kate 1947 that his fame as a breeder has been
earned. He keeps about a score of cows and heifers, and
is very particular in his selection of stock sires, which
have come from Tillyfour, Westertown, East-Town, Jessie-
field, Kinnochtry, Mains of Advie, &c.

Ballindalloch.

It will be admitted that the premier herd of polled
cattle at the present time is that belonging to Sir
George Macpherson Grant of Ballindalloch, Bart., M.P.
The herd is of very old standing, but it is not exactly
known when it was founded. The following extract from
Mr M'Combie's 'Cattle and Cattle-Breeders' sufficiently
proves that an excellent herd existed at Ballindalloch
long before there was any public record of the breed.
"Perhaps," says Mr M'Combie (whose recollections would
have gone back at least to 1820), "the Ballindalloch herd
of polled cattle is the oldest in the north. It has been
the talk of the country since my earliest recollection, and
was then superior to all other stock." In this opinion Mr
M'Combie is corroborated by all who take an interest in
these matters.

We find from the catalogue of the Tillyfour sale in 1850

that the late Sir John Macpherson Grant, father of Sir George
Macpherson Grant, bought two animals of some celebrity
—viz., Matchless, whose dam was bred by Mr Williamson,
St John's Wells, for £30, and Victor 2nd 47 for £20. Sir
John displayed much interest in the herd, and these pur- ·
chases show that he was even then infusing into it some
of the best blood obtainable at the time. It was not, however, until the present Baronet and owner came to reside
on his property in 1861, that the improvement of the herd
received that decided attention which made it take the
leading position in the country which it soon afterwards
did. As a proof of how greatly the herd has been improved in recent years, it may be mentioned that, while
in 1861 only four first and two second prizes were gained
at the county and district shows with representatives of
the original stock, the number of prizes gained by the
herd in 1879 and 1880 was as follows: 42 first prizes,
4 special money-prizes, 13 cups and 7 medals, besides 18
second prizes.

The first animal purchased by Sir George Macpherson Grant was Erica 843, acquired at the Earl of
Southesk's sale at Kinnaird in October 1861 for 50
guineas. For notes on the personal appearance of this
most celebrated cow, and her performances before she left
Kinnaird, we would refer our readers to the account of
that herd. Jilt 973, another remarkably good breeding-
cow, was purchased from the late Mr M'Combie of Tillyfour in 1867 for 70 guineas. She was the second-prize
two-year-old heifer at the show of the Royal English Agricultural Society at Newcastle, and also second at the
Highland Society's show at Stirling in 1865. Another
good addition was Sybil 974, purchased at the Castle
Fraser dispersion in 1871 for 63 guineas. She gained
almost every prize she could compete for, including first
as a cow in 1870 at the Dumfries show of the Highland
Society. Of the Pride family, valuable additions have

been made in Kindness of Ballindalloch 1412, bought
at Drumin in 1873, and that grand cow Pride of Mulben
1919, purchased at Mulben in 1876 at 91 guineas, the
highest price that had been paid up to that time for a
· female of the breed at a public sale. Other additions have
been made as follows, the whole having either been prize-
takers themselves or the dams of prize stock : Rose 3rd
925, purchased at Westertown in 1874; Maid of Orleans
2nd 1177, bought at Tillyfour in 1874; Nymph 972, who
came from Tillyfour in 1864; Madge 2nd 4180, bought at
Aboyne in 1879; Kate Duff 1837, bought at Rothiemay
in 1881 for 155 guineas; and Blackbird 3rd 3766, bought
at Gavenwood, &c.

The closest attention has without intermission been bestowed on the selection of sires, in the belief that as to
a great extent "like begets like," the stock sire should be
of the very best breeding, combined with the best shapes
that can be obtained, and in no case without good form in
every point.   Craigo 260, got by a Balwyllo bull, and out
of a cow bred at Keillor, was followed by King Charles
236, bred at Southesk, and got by the celebrated Druid
225, dam Kathleen 339.   The next sire introduced was an
animal of exceptional excellence.   This was Trojan 402,
purchased at Tillyfour in 1865 for 50 guineas.   Out of
the Paris cow Charlotte 203, he was after Black Prince of
Tillyfour 366.   An analysis of his pedigree shows no
fewer than twelve terminations in Panmure 51.   A half-
brother of Pride of Aberdeen 581, being out of the same
dam, he had by his sire Black Prince of Tillyfour 366 (out
of Maid of Orleans 580 and after Rob Roy Macgregor
267) more of the Queen and Panmure blood than even his
celebrated sister.   In fact there have been few, if any,
better bred specimens of the Queen tribe.   Trojan was
also individually of very superior character.   He won the
first prize as a yearling at the Newcastle show of the
Royal Agricultural Society of England, the second prize

of the Royal Northern Society, and the third prize of the Highland Society at Stirling in 1864; while in 1865 he was first at the Morayshire show at Elgin. A private catalogue of the Ballindalloch herd states that Trojan "did more good to the Ballindalloch herd perhaps than any other bull that has been in it. He was undoubtedly the first bull that gave the females the characteristics by which they came to the top a few years after his advent, and brought out fully the special features that make the Ballindalloch style so popular with the public."

Trojan was succeeded by the Montbletton bull Victor 493, who left some good animals. Other sires used were the champion bull Juryman 404, bred in the herd—sire Bright 454, dam Jilt 973; the first-prize bull Scotsman 474, bred at Tillyfour, out of Zara 1228 after Jim Crow 3rd 350; the Erica bull Elchies 563—dam Eisa 977, sire Juryman; the Erica bull Elcho 595—dam Erica 843, sire Juryman; Judge 1150, who won the gold medal at Paris in 1878 —dam Jilt 973, sire Scotsman. Of these sires, the most valued in the herd may be said to have been Trojan, Victor, Elchies, Elcho, Juryman, and Judge. The stock of the first four were characterised by sweetness, fineness of bone, excellent heads, for which the herd is famed; splendid quality, and grand ribs to carry plenty of flesh on the valuable roasting parts. The stock of the Jilt bulls have had rather more size combined with the other good qualities. One of the sires now in use is the renowned Erica bull Young Viscount 736, bought at the Montcoffer sale for 225 guineas, the highest price ever paid for a male of the breed. He has won every prize he can compete for, and being closely allied to the Ballindalloch cattle has proved a most excellent stud bull. Another sire at present in use is Justice 1462—dam Jilt 973, sire Elcho 595. This animal is distinguished alike by the highest individual excellence and the finest possible breeding. He was the first-prize yearling, second-prize two-year-old, and first-

N

prize aged bull at Highland Society's shows. The Pride
bull Petrarch 1258, out of Pride of Mulben 1919 and after
Hero 861, has also been used lately. It will thus be seen
that the three predominant strains introduced on the male
side have been the Erica, Jilt, and Queen. Many of the
sires used having also been bred in the herd, line-breeding
has been pursued to a certain extent, although it has not
been carried to an extreme point.

Distinguished success has been achieved in the building
up of families at Ballindalloch. The place of honour in
this respect must be accorded to the Ericas, of Keillor
origin. Of Erica's calves, eight have been registered, four
of each sex. These are Eisa 977, by Trojan 402; Erica 2nd
1284, by Chieftain 318; Enchantress 981, by Trojan 402;
Ella 1205, by Kildonan 405; Guardsman 658, by Windsor 221; Cup-Bearer 451, by Trojan; Exciseman 473, by
Victor 403; and Elcho 595, by Juryman 404. Erica continued to breed till September 1873, when she died at the
age of sixteen years. Eisa 977 won the second prize as a
cow at the Highland Society's show at Dumfries in 1870,
when she was placed next to Sybil 974. Next year, at
Perth, she gained the first prize, and is remembered as
a remarkably sweet, ladylike, evenly balanced cow. Indeed it is doubtful whether, for genuine feminine character,
quality, and symmetry, a finer specimen of the breed has
been seen since. Eisa's daughters, Eva 984 and Echo
2976, have also been prominent Highland Society winners,
and have bred remarkably well. Enchantress 981 was the
first prize as a two-year-old and second as a cow at the
Highland Society's shows in 1871 and 1872, and has left
a numerous and excellent progeny. Of the other two Erica
females out of the foundress of the tribe, one was sold.
Erica 3rd 1249, out of Erica 2nd 1284, went to Mr Duff,
Hillockhead. Among her descendants we may note the
splendid bull Young Viscount 736, first at Highland Soci-

ety's shows in the yearling, two-year-old, and aged classes, the champion at Kilburn, not to speak of numerous other honours; Erica 4th 1697, sold to Lord Airlie for 101 guineas; Miss Macpherson 1252, a grand milker, who also went to Cortachy; St Clair 1160, first-prize yearling and two-year-old at Highland Society's shows; Essence 4547, bought by Lord Southesk from Mr Hannay for 100 guineas, and winner of the second prize as a yearling at the Highland Society's show in 1881. Ella 1205, the fourth daughter of Erica, was bought by Mr Macgregor, Garline, and her offspring are also deservedly appreciated. The Erica bull Elcho 595 has the reputation of being one of the best heifer-getters of the breed, and left many excellent calves in several herds.

Space will not permit us to enumerate the whole of the famous members of this fashionable family, but enough has been said to explain how it has come to be justly regarded as one of the choicest strains of polled cattle. At the Aberdeen show of the Highland Society in 1876, an Erica was first in the class of aged bulls; another first in the class of two-year-old bulls; and another second in the class of cows. The Jilt family has been more distinguished for the production of bulls. Like the Erica sort, it is based on Keillor blood, Jilt 973 having been out of Beauty of Tillyfour 2nd 1180, bred at Keillor, and after the Queen bull Black Prince of Tillyfour 366, who, as already observed, was the sire of Trojan, so closely associated with the improvement of the herd. When Jilt was sold at the Tillyfour sale in 1867, she was in calf to Bright 454, another son of Black Prince of Tillyfour 366, and the produce was Juryman 404, first-prize two-year-old and first-prize aged bull at the Highland Society's shows. From Jilt was also bred Judge, the first-prize bull at Paris in 1878, and Justice, another first-prize Highland Society bull. All these animals have, as we

remarked, been used in the herd. Among the more noted
female produce of Jilt may be mentioned Jewel 1413,
Jewess 1916, and Juno 3374.

The Sybil tribe, although it has also bred well, has scarcely come so prominently to the front, the cows Siren 1915
and Sprite 3796 being perhaps its most noteworthy female
members. The older families at Ballindalloch have also
bred extremely well. That tracing from Miss Burgess
1198, bred in 1861 by Mr Burgess, Slack of Ballindalloch,
can count among its members Bertha 980, the first-prize
cow of the Highland Society at Stirling in 1873; Bachelor
690, the winner of two third prizes at Highland Society's
shows, and one of the most successful sires of recent years;
Birthday 3373, who gained the second prize at Paris, and
the first prize as a two-year-old at the Highland Society's
show at Perth in 1879; and Maid of Aven 2995, the first-
prize cow at the Highland Society's show at Stirling in
1881. The Lady Fanny and Coquette families have also
yielded some fine stock, and the Nosegay family is famous
for superior milking qualities. These three families trace
to the original stock at Ballindalloch. The Pride cows,
more recently introduced to the herd, have bred admirably.
Kindness of Ballindalloch 1412, is one of the best cows of
the family she represents, and is dam of some superior
stock, while from Pride of Mulben 1919 has sprung a few
of the highest priced animals of the breed.

Besides a large number of private sales, there have been
three public auctions at Ballindalloch. At the sale in
1872 the average for 19 head was £35, 18s. 5d., highest
price, £63; in 1876 the average for 21 head was £47, 15s.,
highest price, £84; and in 1879 the average for 37 head
was £24, 12s., highest price, £52, 10s. The last sale comprised few members of the choicer strains in the herd, and
was more of the nature of a weeding-out sale than the
others. We understand that since the autumn of 1881
to May 1882 twenty-three animals were sold privately for

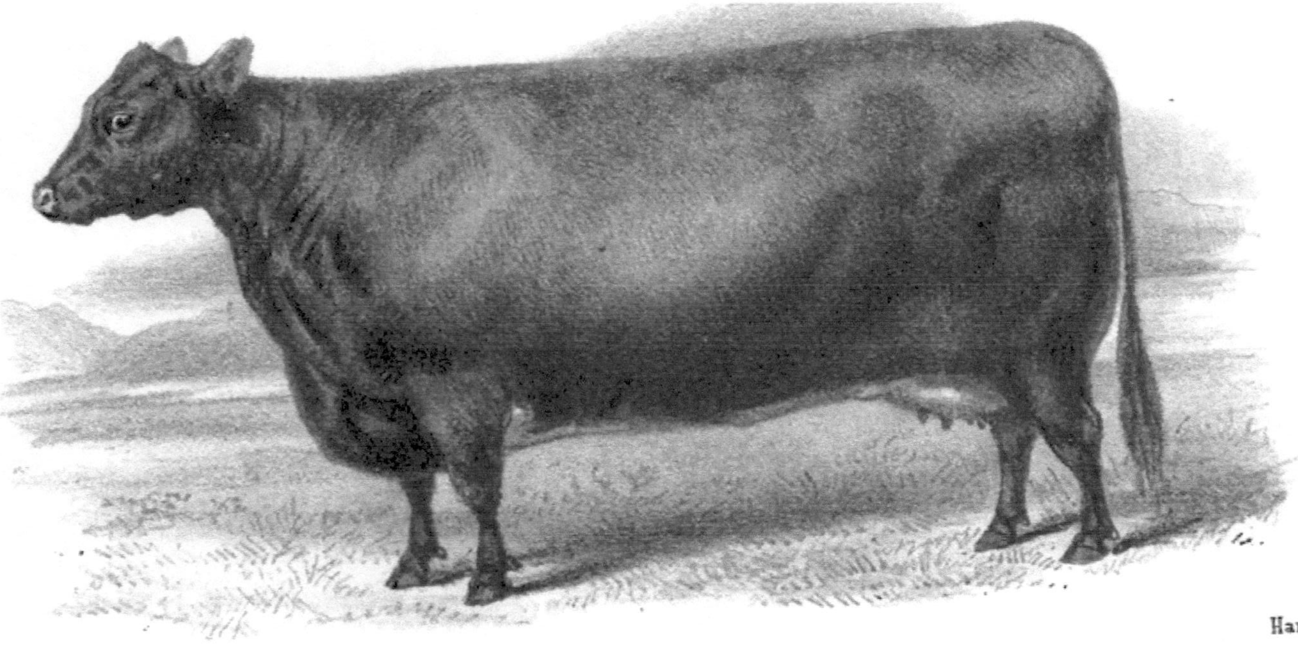

Hanhart imp

£1874, an average of over £81. Twelve of these were
bulls, and they averaged over £50.

In order to fully appreciate the excellence of the Ballindalloch herd, one has to see the animals gathered together
at their picturesque home, the Warlaby of the polled breed.
It is a treat that no admirer of cattle will ever forget to
inspect this large herd and trace the family character
running through every group. Polled breeders are proud
of Ballindalloch, and hope that the herd there may long
occupy the pre-eminent position to which the exertions of
Sir George Macpherson Grant and his ancestors have
brought it. When we obtained our information regarding
the herd in May 1882, it was composed of over one hundred
animals, with several cows still to calve. There were 32
Ericas, 24 females and 8 males; 14 Prides, 10 females
and 4 males; 9 Jilts, 6 females and 3 males; 1 Sybil; 2
Miss Burgesses; 16 Lady Fannys; 3 Nosegays; 5 Westertown Roses; 2 Montbletton Mayflowers; 5 Rothiemay
Georginas; with members of other families.

Ballintomb.

Captain Mann, Ballintomb, Grantown, owns a large herd
which was commenced in 1875 by the purchase of the
cows Corskie 31st B. 1278, bred at Bognie, and Bell of
Biallid 2099, bred at Burnside, with her heifer calf Baby
2316, and the bull Brux 947, bred by Mr Walker, Westside of Brux, Aberdeenshire. There have been added
since—Queen Mary 8th 3457, and Queen Mary 13th 3458
of the Mulben Mayflower family; Tabby 3077 from Tullochallum, with two crosses by Queen sires; Ada 3591,
also from Tullochallum, but of Easter Tulloch blood;
Madame Loftus 2231, grand-daughter of the Pride cow
Regina 1179, bought at the Rothiemay sale in 1878 for 59
guineas; Daphne 2992, of the Rothiemay Miss Morrison
family, bought at Ballindalloch in 1879; Coquette 9th

4271, also acquired at Ballindalloch; Fancy 4396 of the
Westertown Victoria family, from Earnside; Algina 2nd
3961, from Auchorachan; Pride of Aberdeen 27th 4928,
purchased at the Balquharn dispersion for 66 guineas;
Dandelion 2569, of the Duchess branch of the Queen tribe,
bought at Aboyne in 1881 for 59 guineas; Emma 1733, of
the Erica family; and Rose of Biallid 3842, of the Westertown Rose family. As stock sire Brux was succeeded
by Kaiser 1253, a very well-bred bull, after the Erica sire
Elchies 563, and out of the Pride cow Kindness of Ballindalloch 1412. The sire now in use is Jingo 1558, after
Sir Maurice 1319 and out of the Pride cow Madame
Loftus 2231. The herd numbers about 60 head, and contains representatives of the Erica, Pride, Duchess, Rose,
Coquette, Miss Morrison, and other families. Some bull
calves have been sold to America. The stock bulls, and a
few of the females, have been exhibited and have taken
good places at the county shows of Inverness, Moray, and
Nairn. Kaiser was also highly commended at the Highland Society's show at Stirling in 1881. The herd has
been carefully collected, and, as will be seen, is fairly representative of some of the best families.

Ballunie.

Mr James Ferguson, Ballunie, brother of Mr Thomas
Ferguson, Kinnochtry, has a small but very choice herd.
It was founded in 1876 by the purchase of Dido 3054 by
Juryman 404, of the Daisy branch of the Queen tribe, at
Lord Airlie's sale at Cortachy. This cow has left some
nice calves. From Kinnochtry was acquired one of the
Favourite tribe. At Mr Hannay's sale at Corskie in 1877
was bought Heather Blossom 3rd 3396, of the Rothiemay
Victoria family, after the 225-guineas bull Young Viscount
736 and out of the 111-guineas cow Heather Blossom 1703.
She had one calf, Heather Blossom of Ballunie 2nd 4883,

got by Shah 680, and died after calving in 1880. Emily
6th 3299, of the Kinnochtry Emily branch of the Keillor
Old Grannie tribe, was bought from Mr Thomas Ferguson.
The bulls used were the celebrated Pride sire Shah 680,
and the Princess sire Prince of the Realm 1695 at Kin-
nochtry. In 1880, Lictor 1698, bred at Aboyne, after
Warrior 1291 and out of Letty 2373, of the Castle Fraser
Lively family, was used.

Balquhain Mains.

Mr George Bean, on entering the farm of Balquhain
Mains in 1874, began to collect a herd of polled cattle.
He bought a cow and two two-year-old heifers at the sale
at Dandaleith in May of that year, and a two-year-old
heifer from Mr Bean, Netherthird—viz., Priscilla, a grand-
daughter of Lord Southesk's cow Perdita 848. In August
1875 Mr Bean purchased Newton 1387, second-prize bull
at the Strathbogie Farmers' Club show in 1875, and in
October of that year he bought the bull Tollo 1547 from
Mr Morrison, Tollo. From Mr Scott, Easter Tulloch, the
cow Crathes 4th was bought in 1876, and the same year
were added Lovinia 2nd 1924, from Mulben and Breeze
1841, from Mr Bean, Newton. In 1877, Rosavilla by
Maccallum-More 722, bred by Mr Paterson, Mulben, was
secured. The chief animals added since have been: Rose
of Boghead 1437, from Mr M'Knight, Boghead; Ella of
Tillyfour 1800, from Mr Turnbull, Smithston; Victoria 8th
3615, of the Victoria branch of the Queen tribe, from Mr
Farquharson, East-town; Meg o' the Mill 1480, from Mr
Hannay, Gavenwood; Nightingale 4th 3617, of Easter
Tulloch blood, from Mr Strachan, Inverebrie; Mary of
Westside 2033 and Faithful 879, the latter of the Kinnaird
Fanny tribe, at the Aberdeen Joint Sale in 1877; Abbess
3rd 3616, of Easter Tulloch blood, from Mr Turnbull, Smith-
ston; Catherine 2nd 2210, of Drumin blood, from Mr

Allsopp, Inverurie; Blooming Heather 3d 3572, of the
Rothiemay Victoria family, from Mr Tayler of Glenbarry;
Bloomer of Cardenston 2004 and Elizabeth of Morlich
2083, the latter of the Windsor branch of the Queen tribe,
at the Aberdeen joint sale in 1878 ; Brunette 2278, of the
Ballindalloch Miss Burgess family ; Orange Blossom 1489,
of the Rothiemay Georgina family, from Mr Bruce, Keig ;
Ida of Haddo 2559, of the Portlethen Ida family, from the
Earl of Aberdeen; Dandy 1075, of the Drumin Lucy
family and winner of the first prize as a heifer at the
Highland Society's show in 1871, from Captain Beedie,
Pitgair; Young Grizzle 1807, of the Easter Skene Grizzle
family, from Mr M'Combie of Easter Skene; Lizzie of
Morlich 4954, of the Windsor branch of the Queen tribe,
and Isabella of Morlich 3rd, from Mr Cran, Morlich; and
Godiva 2568, of the Pride tribe, at the Balquharn dispersion.
The sires used have been Tollo 1547, already referred to ;
Serapis 998, sire Hercules 687 dam Grizzle 995, bred at
Easter Skene, winner of the first prize at the Highland
Society as a two-year-old, and of numerous local prizes ;
Lowther 1388, bred at East-town, of the Victoria branch
of the Queen tribe; Abbot, after Hero 861 and out of
Abbess 3rd 3616 ; Maharajah 1893, Heather Bred Lad, and
Viceroy 2nd, the last four bred by Mr Bean. The sire now
in use is Leotard, bred by Mr Bean, descended from Old
Grannie 1. The herd numbers about twenty head, and
comprises specimens of the Mains of Kelly Victorias, Kin-
naird Fannys, Bognie Miss Carnegies, Kinnochtry Favourites, Drumin Catherines, East-town Patricias, &c.

A large number of sales have been made from the herd.
Bulls have been sold privately and at the Aberdeen joint
sales, at from fifteen to forty-five guineas. In November
1880, Mr Stephenson, Sandyford Villa, Newcastle-on-Tyne,
purchased Blooming Heather 2nd 3572, Lady Lizzie 4953,
and Lizzie of Morlich 4954 ; in March 1881 he purchased
Rose of Boghead 1437, Rose 5th 4958, Abbess 3rd 3616,

Abbess 5th 4956, and Faithful 3rd 4957; and in January 1882 he purchased Brunette 3rd, out of Brunette 2278, and Miss Carnegie, out of Miss Carnegie 4th 4090. Rosebery out of Rose of Boghead 1437 was sold to go to Wales; Abbot 2nd out of Abbess 3rd 3616 was sold to Mr S. Beattie, to go to America; Victoria Seraphina out of Victoria 8th 3615, Milkmaid 4766, Milkmaid 3rd, and Miss Mary out of Mary 2033, were sold to Mr Wilken, Waterside—the two first to go to America. Milkmaid 3rd went to New Zealand; Isabella of Morlich and Emerald were sold to Messrs Galbraith Brothers, Janesville, Wisconsin, America; and Viceroy 3rd was sold to Mr Thomson, America.

The herd has taken a fair position in the show-yard, although no animals are forced for exhibition. They have been shown mostly at the Inverurie, Insch, and Turriff shows, the bull Serapis having, besides prizes at the Highland Society's shows, won numerous local honours.

Benholm Castle.

Mr William Smith's herd was commenced at Stone o' Morphie, Montrose, in 1876. Mr Smith bought, at Lord Airlie's sale at Cortachy that year, the cow Bessie 1442, at £52, 10s. She was then in calf to Belus 749. The calf was a bull. Bessie has had other four bull-calves, and all the five have been prize-takers. Having missed calf in 1880, Bessie was sold fat. The same year Mr Smith purchased Rose of Guynd 2nd 2599, at £38, 17s., from Mr Bowie, Mains of Kelly. She was in calf to Gainsborough 3rd 598; and the calf was Gay Lass 3511, sold to the Earl of Airlie, when one year old, for £60. Mr Smith also sold the dam, with heifer-calf one month old, to Lord Airlie, at £50. The calf was Griselda 3877, sold at Lord Airlie's sale for £73, 10s.—the highest price realised at the sale. The same year there was bought from Mr Scott, Easter

Tulloch, the cow Nightingale 1742, with bull-calf at foot,
for £33, 12s. Barmaid 2207 was bought from Mr Walker,
Portlethen, and has proved a good breeder. Lively of
Powrie 3729 was purchased from Mr Scott, Easter Tulloch;
and a few other cows were added. The first stock-bull Mr
Smith had was Timour 3rd 1287, bought from Captain Grant
of Ecclesgreig, for £36. He was a good bargain—most of
his stock having been prize-winners—and he was sold fat
for £36. Northesk 1577, after Timour 3rd and out of Bessie
1442, was also used. Animals from the herd have been
exhibited only at the county shows of Kincardine and
Forfar, and they have been very fortunate—a good many
prizes having been gained.

Blairshinnoch.

The foundation of this herd was laid by Mr Stevenson
in 1867, when he was tenant of the home-farm of Careston,
Forfarshire—then the property of the Earl of Fife. The
herd at present consists of thirty females and three bulls.
The former are composed of representatives of the Crinoline branch of the Queen tribe,—tracing from Eugenie of
Tillyfour 3237 by President 4th 368, and out of Crinoline
204, bred at Tillyfour; Lady Jeans of Glenbarry tracing
from Nell of Careston 3430 by Damascus 495, and Queen
of Rothiemay 3425 by Napoleon 257, both bred by Mr
Tayler of Glenbarry; Rothiemay Georginas from Kate of
Careston 3434 by Damascus 495, bred by Mr Tayler;
Rothiemay Victorias, from Tibby of Rothiemay 3419 by
Napoleon 257, bred by Mr Tayler; and Sabrinas of Arratsmill, from Sabrina 3439, bred by the Hon. Charles
Carnegie. In addition to these there are two Montbletton
Mayflowers—Minette 4705 and Coronet 4548; a Maud
of Tullochallum; a Tillyfour Daisy, out of Vine 9th 3256,
sold at Aboyne for 115 guineas; the Erica cow Ella 1205,
and Juliet of Easter Skene 3808. The present stock sire

is Edgar Erica 1693, out of Ella 1205 and after the Erica bull Editor 1460. The other bulls used have been Nubian 1294—a son of Gainsborough 596—Blairshinnoch 1307, Bon Accord 446, Colonel of Careston 1305, and Clansman of Careston 1306.

Bridgend.

Mr R. C. Auld, nephew of the late Mr M'Combie of Tillyfour, had the advantage of studying the principles of cattle-breeding under the direction of his uncle. Latterly he was closely associated with Mr M'Combie in the management of the Tillyfour herd, and aided him in strengthening it after the sale in 1874, when too large an inroad was made on the stock. Mr Auld was engaged in the selection and preparation of the celebrated champion group at Paris in 1878; and was thus able to materially assist in the greatest victory ever achieved by the Tillyfour herd, and by the polled breed. On the death of his uncle, Mr Auld became tenant of the farm of Bridgend, on the Lynturk property of Mr M'Combie of Easter Skene. Bridgend lies a mile north-west of Tillyfour, and was farmed from a very early date by the late Mr M'Combie. Mr M'Combie soon discovered its value as a breeding and feeding ground; and it is noteworthy that many of the most famous of the Tillyfour breeding and fat stock were raised on it. It was here, under John Benzie's care, that the famous ox Black Prince was reared. Mr M'Combie's earliest sales were conducted at Bridgend, the first having occurred more than thirty years ago. Mr Auld took over the stock on Bridgend at valuation, among them being some pedigree polls. To these he determined at once to add some of the best blood obtainable of the tribes so long associated with his uncle's name. We believe the late Mr M'Combie left power to Mr Auld to retain one half of the Tillyfour herd as it

stood at his death, but at the desire of Mr M'Combie's
trustees, an arrangement was made by which the whole
herd was submitted to public competition. The sale of
the Tillyfour herd took place, as recorded elsewhere,
in August 1880, and several selections were made by Mr
Auld—viz., Pride of Aberdeen 9th 3253, Duchess 3rd 943,
and Pride of Aberdeen 20th, out of Gitana 2578. The
most notable of these was, of course, Pride of Aberdeen
9th, for whom Mr Auld gave 270 guineas, the highest
price ever paid either publicly or privately for a polled
animal. The herd at Bridgend has since been steadily increased, and it has now at its head the unrivalled Pride
bull Knight of the Shire 1699, disposed of at the Balquharn dispersion to Mr Auld and Mr Anderson, Wellhouse, for 165 guineas. The chief object aimed at by
Mr Auld in forming his herd, was to collect as many representatives as possible of the earlier branches of Mr
M'Combie's Queen tribe. There was more difficulty in
doing this than would at first sight appear, but Mr Auld
has already succeeded in obtaining more representatives
of Mr M'Combie's early branches than he himself ever
possessed at one time.

We note some of the more prominent animals at Bridgend. The place of honour is occupied by Pride of Aberdeen 9th 3253. This fine cow was one of the prize group
at the Paris Exhibition in 1878, being the only member
of Mr M'Combie's fashionable Pride family represented
in it. She belongs to the most valuable branch of the
Pride tribe, and is a grand-daughter of Pride of Aberdeen
581. She was early marked out as an animal that would
probably become a grand breeder; and she has not belied
that promise. At the Tillyfour sale, her two sons Heir
of Glory 1746 and Heir of Paris 1917 were much admired,
and it was doubtless these proofs of her remarkable breeding properties, combined with her personal merit and
high breeding, that induced Mr Auld to determine on

From Life by A McCauci

Hanhart imp.

"KNIGHT OF THE SHIRE" (1699) at 3 YEARS OLD.
The Property of R C Auld of Bridgend Aberdeenshire.

buying her, whatever the price might be. Since she went
to Bridgend, she has become a heifer breeder, and has had
two female calves, that of 1882 being a very beautiful
animal, after Knight of the Shire. Pride of Aberdeen 9th
was got by Sir Garnet 684, who was also sire of the champion cow Sybil 2nd of Tillyfour 3526, and was half
brother on the dam's side to Gaily 1793, the only cow
comprised in the Paris group. Mr Auld also owns Pride
of Aberdeen 10th 3250, got by Sir Garnet 684, and out of
that splendid breeding cow Pride of Aberdeen 5th 1174.
Four bulls have been bred from Pride 10th, one of them,
Knight of St Patrick, the first polled animal bred by Mr
Auld, having been selected by Messrs Gudgell and Simpson as stock sire of their very fine herd in Kansas, U.S.
He was sold for 120 guineas, and is an animal of rare
quality and style.

The other branches of the Queen tribe represented
at Bridgend are the Daisies, Duchesses, Charmers,
Windsors, Charlottes, Crinolines, and Rosys. There are
three Daisies in the herd. One of them is the cow,
Vine 10th 3288, by the Daisy bull Dragon 1178, sire of
Knight of the Shire 1699, and out of Vine 8th 3252 by
Sir Garnet 684. She had gone from Tillyfour to Moresdale Hall, thence to Storrs, and, having again been brought
to the North of Scotland by Mr Wilken, was acquired
from him by Mr Auld. The other Daisies are the heifer
Vampire Queen and the bull Wedgewood, bred by Lord
Tweedmouth. The Duchesses, so well known at Westertown, are represented by Duchess 3rd 943 and her son
and daughter. Duchess 3rd is a very closely bred cow,
and an analysis of her pedigree shows a most wonderful
concentration of Queen and Panmure blood together, with
a slight dilution of the old Matchless strain through her
dam's sire, President 354, thus preserving the St John's
Wells blood. The Crinoline family is represented by
Favourite of Blairshinnoch 3239, grand-daughter of Crin-

oline 204, and her bull calf. The Rosys trace from Rosy,
by President 4th 368, sold at the Tillyfour sale in 1871
to Mr Ross, Annesley. Rosy was a daughter of Charlotte
203, and her grand-daughter Rosy Queen is now at Bridgend. The Windsor family is represented by Nugget of
Morlich 2079, and a heifer and bull. We need say nothing here regarding this branch, the foundress of which,
Windsor 202, is so frequently referred to in these pages.
The Sylph branch has four specimens headed by Blooming
Queen, after Heir of Glory. The pedigree embraces the
names of those very fine cows—Bloomer 201 and The
Belle 205. There is a heifer calf of the Dandy branch,
tracing through Dandy of Drumin 949, and Empress of
France 578, to Charlotte 203. In addition to these de-
scendants of Mr M'Combie's Queen Mother, there are members of the Kinnaird Fanny, Mains of Kelly Jennet
(which, as elsewhere noticed, goes back to Mr M'Combie's
Jenny Lind 27), and several other families. As already
stated, the stock-bull is Knight of the Shire 1699, after
Dragon 1178 and out of Pride 3rd of Mulben 3249. He
was the first-prize two-year-old at the Highland Society's
show last year, and also won those coveted honours—the
Challenge Cup and the M'Combie prize—at the Royal
Northern at Aberdeen. We understand that an offer of
300 guineas has been refused for him.

From the Bridgend herd a large number of animals
have been disposed of to go abroad. The Queen cow
Matilda 3270 went to the Hon. Mr Pope, Canada; Dandy
2nd 3266 to Mr G. W. Henry, Kansas; Pride 20th to the
Hon. M. H. Cochrane, Canada; and Knight of St Patrick
to Messrs Gudgell & Simpson, Kansas. Very high prices
were paid for these.

Burnshangie.

A small select herd has been kept at Burnshangie,
Strichen, for the past twelve years. It was founded by

Mr Smith by the purchase of some animals in the Alford district. One of these, Black Bess of Burnshangie 1943, and several of her progeny, still remain in the herd. This family is of Keillor extraction, the granddam of Black Bess having been bred at Keillor; and as the bull Fyvie 737, descended from Mr Watson's stock, was used as stock-bull for seven years, the herd is largely impregnated with Keillor blood. The animals have never been forced for show-yard competition, the best females having been used as dairy cows. The herd has nevertheless taken a good position at the Buchan Society's shows. Black Bess 1943 was first as a two-year-old, and her daughters Stumpie 2297 and Stumpie 2nd 3150 were first as one-year-olds; and the one first and the other second as two-year-olds— Stumpie having been second last year as a cow. Another family in the herd—the Rompies—has produced several prize-winners, amongst them Rompie 3rd 4145, first as a yearling and two-year-old at Mintlaw. Her elder sister Rompie 2298 was second as a yearling and two-year-old, and first as a cow. She is now in good breeding form in the herd of Mr Skinner, Drumin. The stock-bull used last season was Lord Maurice 1881, bred by Mr Tayler of Glenbarry, after Sir Maurice 1319 and out of the Georgina cow Kate Darling 3573.

CHAPTER XI.

EXISTING SCOTCH HERDS—CONTINUED.

CAIRDSEAT—CLINTERTY—COLLITHIE—Mr Pirie's early herd—Mr Bruce's
herd—CONGLASS—Celebrated breeders in the Garioch forty years ago
—Mr Stephen's champions at fat stock shows—CORTACHY—Lord
Airlie's purchases at Mr M'Combie's sale in 1874—The magnificent
heifer Pavilion 3772—Three animals acquired at Tillyfour in 1878 at
an average of £93—The Ballindalloch bulls Juryman 404 and Elcho
595 used—Lord Airlie's efforts to develop the milking qualities of the
breed—DRUMFERGUE—Established thirty-five years ago, but records
lost—DRUMIN—Mr Skinner's Lucys and Beautys—Marshal 399, gave
the herd its characteristic of size—Mr Skinner's success in the show-
yard—EARNSIDE—EAST TOWN—The herd commenced prior to 1822—
Longevity of the Patricia family—EASTER SKENE—Mr M'Combie lays
its foundation forty-two years ago—Another testimony to the impressiveness of Panmure 51—Show-yard victories with his descendants—
—Over 300 prizes won by the herd—EASTER TULLOCH—The largest
herd in existence—Superiority of the blood contained in it—FASQUE
—A noteworthy breeding cow, Eugenie 3910—FINTRAY—GAVENWOOD
—Mr Hannay's efforts towards the improvement of the breed—The
Highland Society first-prize winners, Young Viscount 736, Innes 1934,
and Blackbird of Corskie 2nd 3024—Large and successful sales—
GLAMIS—An excellent herd of six years' standing.

Cairdseat.

Mr Argo's herd at Cairdseat was founded by the purchase in 1874, at Mr M'Combie's sale at Alford, of Sophia
1978, by Derby 377. Her daughter Snowflake 4049, by
Ballot of Wellhouse 634, and her granddaughter Sunshine
2nd 4383, by Wellhouse 1311, are now in the herd. Caroline 3rd 3581, by the Erica bull Emperor 396, came from

Easter Tulloch in 1876, and is still in the herd, with her heifer calf Chloe. Fred's 5th Darling 2363, of the Ballindalloch Sybil family, was bought at the Mulben dispersion in 1876, and is now represented by Fred's Fancy 4384 and Sybil's Darling 3rd. Sybil's Darling 4050, out of Fred's 5th Darling, was sold to Mr Wilken, Waterside, for £100, and her daughter went to the Ontario Experimental Farm. Kora 3582, descended from the Campfield herd; Lark of Tillychetly 3790, descended from Old Grannie 1, with her heifer calf; Kate of Campfield 2177, with two granddaughters; Inky 4381, from the Johnston herd; Rene 4607, of the Kinnaird Rebecca family from Easter Tulloch; Dnieper 4609, of the Rothiemay Georgina family from Cortachy; Keepsake 6th, out of Keepsake 3559; Lamina, out of Lizzie of Fyvie 2nd 4683, of the Fyvie Flower family,—are the other females in the herd, representing, as will be observed, some valued strains of blood. The stock-bulls used have been Ballot of Wellhouse 634, bred by Mr Anderson, Wellhouse; Etonian 1658, bred at Ballindalloch, out of that very fine Erica cow Eva 984, and after the Erica bull Elcho 595; and Standard 1829, bred by Lord Tweedmouth, after the Charmer bull Chamberlain 1570, and out of Rosebud 3rd 3339 of the Drumin Rose family. Etonian was first-prize yearling, and second in the two-year-old and aged classes, at the shows of the Royal Northern Society. The females are never fed for showing, but are kept in good breeding condition. Mr Argo has been very fortunate as regards the bulls used in his herd, and Standard, the present stock-sire, promises to turn out the best he has had. At the last Aberdeen sale Mr Argo received an average of about £41 for his bull calves.

Clinterty.

Mr George Reid of Little Clinterty, son of Mr Reid, Baads, commenced a herd at Smiddyhill, Tarland, in 1872,

by the purchase of a cow named Livy 2nd from Mr Bowie,
Mains of Kelly, and the bull Prince Albert 2nd 745, by Sir
William 705, dam Kate of Baads 1947, from Mr Reid,
Baads. Several other fine animals were added, but pleuro-
pneumonia broke out, and they nearly all succumbed to it.
After coming to Clinterty in 1876, Mr Reid determined to
make a fresh start, but again he was cleared out by pleuro
in 1878. The present is therefore the third herd begun by
Mr Reid. The bull Duke of Edinburgh 979 had been
added from Baads, and the chief purchases since have been
—Waterside Queen 2nd, of the Kinnaird Fanny family,
bought at Mr Wilken's sale in 1878; Hope 3895, of the
Drumin Lucy family, and Flossy 5027, of the Westertown
Victoria family, at Mr Robertson's sale at Burnside in
1880; Craigellachie 3882, by Warrior 1291, at Lord
Airlie's sale; Bella of Baads 4375, Spott of Baads 4378,
and Clara of Baads 5025, from Baads. In February 1881,
Black Prince of Greystone 1850 was bought from Mr
Reid, Greystone. He was a most promising bull, and a
first-rate stock getter, but unfortunately he died of splenic
apoplexy in July of the same year. In October 1881,
Lord Chancellor 1782, after Sir Maurice 1319, and out of
Crocus 2nd 3765, of the Balwyllo Isabella family, was acquired at the Rothiemay sale, and is coming on well. The
number in the herd at present is thirteen, representing
chiefly the Lucys of Drumin, the Westertown Victorias, and
the Livies of Mains of Kelly, &c. The only animal sold
from the herd was Prince Albert 2nd, who went to Mr
Gordon, Tullochallum. He gained a number of prizes,
including first at the Royal Northern, and second at the
Highland Society. Duke of Edinburgh was a prize-winner
at Tarland.

Collithie.

The farm of Collithie is a somewhat celebrated place in
the annals of polled cattle. The present tenant, Mr James

Bruce, has in his possession an oil-painting of the cows
Jenny Lind 27, and Old Jenny Lind 34, the former the
first-prize yearling at the Highland Society's show in
1847. These animals were bred by Mr J. Pirie, Collithie,
and were very much admired by the late Mr M'Combie,
who purchased Jenny Lind at a high price, and she became one of the matrons of the Tillyfour herd. Mr Bruce
started a herd of polled cattle in 1875, when he purchased
eight heifers, bred by Mr Morrison, Knockiemill, Turriff.
We need not enumerate them, as seven of them were sold
shortly afterwards. The animal retained was Fairy Queen
3063, after Elector 2nd 734, and descended from the old
stock at Mains of Hatton. This cow has proved remarkably useful. The other purchases were as follows: Pearl
3103, bred by Mr Scott of Easter Tulloch, after Prince of
Wales 2nd 3941; Sybil 2nd 1141, bred by Mr Shaw, Bogfern, and descended from Jane of Bogfern 540, bred at
Keillor; Charlotte of Bogfern 1257, bred by Mr Shaw;
Lucy of Morlich 2086, bred by Mr Cran, Morlich; Elizabeth 2083, bred by Mr Cran, of the Windsor branch of the
Queen tribe; Queen Mary 4th 921, bred by Mr Paterson,
of the Mulben Mayflower family; Ida 8th 2594, bred at
Drumin, of the Portlethen Ida family; and Julia of
Shevado 3029, bred by Mr Dingwall Fordyce, of the
Portlethen Julia family. These cows were all purchased
in 1876. In 1877, Fashion 982, of the Ballindalloch Lady
Fanny family, was bought from Mr Bruce, Burnside,
Fochabers, and Princess Dagmar 2nd 3021, of the Matilda
branch of the Queen tribe, from Mr Hannay, Gavenwood.
The sires used have been: Harry 3rd 661, bred at Bog-
fern, and descended from the Keillor herd; Hero of Mul-
ben 861, bred by Mr Paterson, of the Mulben Mayflower
family; Khedive of Ballindalloch 1153, bred by Sir
George Macpherson Grant, of the Pride family, and after the
Erica bull Elchies 563; Keillor 2nd, after Keillor 1370, and
out of Kate 3rd of Easter Tulloch 3562; and Lord Dun-

dreary 1495, bred at Tillyfour, of the Kinnaird Rebecca family. The herd numbers about thirty females, representing the families we have mentioned. In 1877, a heifer, Rosebud, was sold to Mr Henry Haynes, Drayton Basset, Tamworth; in 1878, Queen of Fernyflatt 2nd 2424, and Alicia 3980, were sold to Mr Anderson, Boghead of Cobairdy; in 1878, four cows and four heifers were sold to Mr Brown, Linkwood; in 1880, Ida 9th 3670, Julia of Collithie 3671, and Vine 4507, were sold to Mr Mackenzie of Portmore, at £33 each; in 1881, Lulu 4526, Pauline 3672, Princess Dagmar 5th 4526, and Fair Lady 4525, were sold to Mr Wilken, Waterside, at about £40 each, for exportation to the Hon. J. H. Pope, Canada; in 1881, Mr Wilken bought Pearl of Springbank, dam Pearl 3013, for Mr J. F. Foote, New Jersey, and Fair Flower 4726 for Hon. J. H. Pope; Princess Dagmar 6th 4827, sold to Mr Wilken a short time previously, also going to Hon. J. H. Pope. As to the longevity of the breed, Mr Bruce mentions that two years ago an old cow died at Collithie that in her seventeenth year produced twin calves for the fifth time in succession. The cow was kept solely for rearing calves, and they always did well, with the exception of those of the last year, when she was thoroughly exhausted. Latterly, however, the calves were more difficult to bring up and worse to feed.

Conglass.

Mr Stephen, Conglass, informs us that the Aberdeenshire breed of cattle has been on that farm beyond his recollection. Upwards of forty years ago his father had several of them, yellow as well as black, and some with horns, but he always bred from a polled bull, and the horns gradually disappeared. The late Mr James Walker, Wester Fintray; Mr Morrison, Balhaggardy; Mr James Collie, Middleton of Fintray; and Mr Stephen's father, were the principal prize-winners at the local shows at that time. Mr Stephen bought a bull from Mr M'Combie of Tillyfour in 1849, and he had bulls from him frequently afterwards. He purchased the bull Malcolm of Bodiechell 269, who gained the second prize in the class of aged bulls at the Highland Society's show in 1858. Malcolm was an animal of excellent quality and great substance, and was the sire of the ox bred by Mr Stephen which gained the Challenge Cup at the Royal Northern show in 1864, when three years old. Malcolm 2nd, got by Malcolm and from the Missie family at Conglass, was the best bull for getting first-class stock Mr Stephen ever bred. He was the sire of two oxen, one of which gained the second prize, when four years old, at Birmingham, and first at Smithfield in 1868; the other ox, in 1869, gained the first prizes both at Birmingham and London, being also awarded at Birmingham the first prize as the best ox in the Scotch classes, as well as the extra prize offered by Mr Ratcliffe. These oxen fetched 80 and 75 guineas respectively, and each carcass weighed 16½ cwt. Mr Stephen unfortunately sent Malcolm 2nd to the butcher before he knew his value. Heifers got by him also turned out first-class animals. At Christmas in 1871 Mr Stephen again exhibited at Birmingham an ox four years old, whose dam was by Malcolm 2nd, and he also gained the first prize. He caught foot-and-mouth disease at Birmingham, and did not stand up well at London; so Mr Stephen had to be content with a second prize there. The show-yard success of the Conglass cattle at Christmas closed for several years; the cows slipped calf, and the bulk of the animals were disposed of to the butcher. The line of the Missie family was, however, preserved, and was represented at the Smithfield Club show last year. The polled ox with which Mr M'Combie of Tillyfour gained the first prize at Poissy in 1862, and the following year at Smithfield, was bred at Conglass, and was, Mr Stephen informs us, heavier than the renowned ox Black Prince.

Cortachy.

The late Earl of Airlie commenced the breeding of polled cattle more than twenty years ago, but it was not until about 1865 that he began to devote special attention to the formation of a herd that rapidly came to the front. Among the early purchases were Delia 1533, New Year's Day 1124, and Jessica 2nd 3231, from Mr Whyte, Spott. Victoria of Kelly 345 was acquired from Mr Bowie, Mains of Kelly, and additions were also made from the Portlethen, Aldbar, Spott, The Thorn, Easter Tulloch, The Burn, and other herds. At the sale held by the late Mr M'Combie of Tillyfour at Alford in 1874, Lord Airlie secured four of the best-bred cows and heifers disposed of on that occasion. They were—Regina 1179, of the Pride family, purchased for 40 guineas; Sylph 2nd 1787, of the Queen tribe; Salvia 1781, of the Zara tribe, who cost 60 guineas; and Diana 1782, of the Daisy branch of the Queen tribe, who cost 76 guineas, being the highest price paid at the sale. Miss Macpherson 1252, of the Erica tribe, who had been bought at Tullochallum for 90 guineas, was secured by Lord Airlie at a very long price. At Tullochallum, in 1877, Lord Airlie purchased the heifer Dwina 3081, of the Rothiemay Georgina family, for 60 guineas. In the same year, at Mr Hannay's sale at Corskie, was purchased Erica 4th 1697 for 101 guineas, and some others of lesser note. At the Montcoffer sale in 1878, Lord Airlie paid 46 guineas for the calf Pavilion 3772. She turned out a magnificent heifer, and it was a great misfortune that she died when under three years old. A few good animals were bought at Rothiemay in 1878, but the most important purchases were made at Tillyfour in 1880. At that sale three animals were acquired at an average of over £93 each. They were— Pride of Aberdeen 5th 1174, at 135 guineas; Sybil 1st of Tillyfour 3524, at 110 guineas; and the calf Pride of

Aberdeen 23rd, at 35 guineas. Pride of Aberdeen 5th was the only daughter of the original Pride offered at the sale, and although in her thirteenth year, she looked fresh and useful. She had bred some of the finest members of this fashionable family produced in recent years, among them Mr Ferguson's national prize bull Shah, Mr Hannay's Lilias of Tillyfour, and Sir George Macpherson Grant's Pride of Mulben. Sybil 1st, who was bred at Baads, won, among other honours, the first prize as a cow at the Highland Society's show in 1877, and the first prize and Challenge Cup for the best animal of the breed at Aberdeen the same year. Her daughter, Sybil 2nd, after a very distinguished career, was sold to Lord Southesk for 180 guineas. Among other animals added at various times we may note Pride of Tarland 3148, Fair Lady 2159, Frances of Airlie 3050, Constance 4196, Nosegay 4th 2974, Lady Regula 4200, &c.

In the selection of sires, equal discretion has been displayed. Bolshan 420, bred by Lord Southesk, a local prize-winner, after Jupiter 471, a son of Windsor 221, and out of Rhoda 566, a daughter of Cup-Bearer 59, was followed by the national prize bull Juryman 404, of the Ballindalloch Jilt tribe. Belus 749, a son of Juryman, and bred in the herd, was next used. Potentate 1199, bred at Kinnochtry, after Shah 680, and out of Princess 3rd 1771, of Mr Ferguson's Princess tribe, proved a very useful stock sire. Logie the Laird 6th 1623, from Mr Bowie's herd, after Gainsborough 3rd 598, and from the same Lizzy family as produced the renowned Hanton 228, was secured at a long figure. Pontiff 1497, a son of Potentate, and descended from the Keillor herd, and Prince Chase 1454 of the Zara tribe, got by Challenger 1260, were also in service. The sires more recently used have been the Erica bull Elcho 595, the Pride bull Provost 1259, and the Erica bull Erison 1624—the two first-named bred at Ballindalloch, and the last bred in the herd.

It was expected that by the end of this year's calving season the herd would number about 105 head. The principal families represented are the Pride of Aberdeen, Erica, Sybil, Delia, Jessica, &c.

Among the show-yard honours won by the Cortachy herd were two second prizes at the Highland Society in 1879, with Pontiff 1497 and Pavilion 3772 ; two first prizes at the Highland Society's show in 1880, with the heifers Pavilion 3772 and Miranda 4204 ; a first and a second prize at Carlisle, with Ericson 1624 and Pavilion ; and the first prize for two-year-old heifers at the Highland Society in 1881, with Miranda, descended from Colonel M'Inroy's old stock at The Burn. A large number of prizes have also been gained at local shows.

Two public sales have been held. At the sale in 1876, 26 head averaged over £35 ; and at the sale in 1880, 43 head averaged over £30. At the sale in 1876, the Pride cow Regina was bought by Mr Adamson, Balquharn, for 70 guineas. At Mr Adamson's sale in 1881, Regina fetched 105 guineas, and her daughters Pride of Aberdeen 18th 4321, and Pride of Aberdeen 25th 4331, 160 guineas and 50 guineas respectively—Regina and her two calves thus averaging £110.

A feature of the Cortachy herd is its superior milking-qualities. Lord Airlie was careful to select animals of noted milking strains, and he was able to produce records which somewhat surprised those who disparaged the milking properties of the breed. To his lordship's efforts in this direction reference is made elsewhere.

Drumfergue.

The 'Herd Book' entries of the cattle belonging to Mr William Wilson at Drumfergue, Gartly, scarcely do justice to the breeding of the animals composing the herd. It was founded by the late Mr James Smith, Drumfergue,

about thirty-five years ago, by the purchase of a cow and
a bull from the Rev. Mr Rainy, Corse of Monellie, a famous
breeder, although he registered few of his stock. Mr
Smith, on two or three occasions, also bought animals
from the late Mr M'Combie of Tillyfour. One of the animals procured from Tillyfour was, we are informed, a cow
which gained a prize at the Paris Exhibition in 1856.
This occurred before the 'Herd Book' was published, and
therefore it is impossible to give names. Although the
herd has been kept pure since its commencement, and very
long prices were paid by the late Mr Smith for sires from
the best breeders in the country, Mr Wilson, on entering
the farm, was unable to trace the pedigrees further back
than to cows by Moonraker 591 and Ranger 590, both
bred by Mr Tayler of Glenbarry, the former after Elector
427, and descended from the Crathes herd, and the latter
after Bon Accord 446, and tracing from the Castle Fraser
herd. The sire in use at present is Fitzjohn 1687, bred
by Sir William Forbes, Bart., after Gainsborough 4th 1425,
and of the Mains of Kelly Lucy family. The bulls previously used by Mr Wilson were Lord Hamilton 1716, of
the Windsor branch of the Queen tribe, and Simon 1205,
a son of Palmerston 374. These bulls were all of good
breeding, and left stock of superior quality, and easily
fattened. The herd numbers about 30. Most of them
are descended from the old Drumfergue stock, the chief
addition having been Annie 2nd of Morlich 4257, representing the Windsor branch of the Queen tribe.

Drumin.

The Drumin herd was founded about 1856 by the late
Mr James Skinner, father of the present owner, Mr W.
M. Skinner. Mr Skinner then purchased three heifers
from Morayshire, the pedigrees of which were never obtained. From them spring three families, of which the

first recorded members are Fortune 945, Grace 946, and
Eliza 960. In 1862 there were bought from Mr Bowie,
Mains of Kelly, the heifers Young Lucy 947 and Young
Raniston 948. As these are the animals that established
the families that have mainly raised the reputation of the
herd, it is desirable to furnish a brief analysis of their
pedigrees. Young Lucy 947 was after Young Panmure
232, bred by Mr M'Combie of Tillyfour, the first-prize aged
bull at Dumfries Highland Society show in 1860.   He
was got by Hanton 228, and out of Crinoline 204, one of
the closest-bred Queen cows at Tillyfour, a daughter of
the celebrated Charlotte 203. Young Lucy's dam, Lucy
of Portlethen 287, was after Fyvie 13, a son of the Keillor
bull Old Jock 1.   Lucy of Portlethen 287 was out of the
same cow as Raglan 208, who was in the prize-list at the
Paris Exhibition in 1856, when Mr Walker, Portlethen, his
breeder, refused an offer of £230 from the Emperor Napoleon.   Young Raniston 948 was after Alford 231, a son of
Hanton 228 and the Queen cow Fair Maid of Perth 313,
a first-prize winner at the Royal English and Highland
Societies' shows. From these two heifers, acquired from
Mr Bowie, are descended the Lucy and the Beauty fami-
lies.   In 1862, two heifers were purchased from the late
Mr Robertson, Burnside. One of these died, but the other,
Princess of Burnside 950, has left a good family. At the
Tillyfour sale in 1867, the cow Dandy 949 was bought.
Her breeding was very fashionable, she being out of Empress
of France 578, a full sister of Pride of Aberdeen 581, and
after Rob Roy Macgregor 267, a full brother of the famous
Kinnaird bull Windsor 202.   At the same sale in 1867,
the heifer Pride 957, after President 4th 368, and out of
Pride of Aberdeen 3rd 1168, was acquired. The chief
females added since were Moonlight 1479, of the Rothiemay Georgina family, dam of those excellent bulls Sir
Roger 702 and Sir Wilfred 1157, both Highland Society
prize-winners; Rompie 2298, from Burnside, full of Queen

blood on the sire's side; Gondola 3275, a Pride heifer from
Aboyne; with other good representatives of the Tillyfour
Pride and the Mains of Kelly Victoria families.

In the selection of sires much judgment has been shown.
In 1862, the bull Defiance 397 was introduced from Tillyfour. He was got by Rob Roy Macgregor 267, and out
of the Queen cow Charlotte. It is to this bull and the
heifers from Mains of Kelly that the stock at Drumin
chiefly owes its character. Defiance was followed, in 1864,
by Marshal 399, and in 1865 by Hero 400, both from Tillyfour, and of the Queen tribe. Marshal was by Black
Prince of Tillyfour 366, a son of Rob Roy Macgregor, and
out of Fancy of Tillyfour 1195, a daughter of The Belle
205; while Hero was out of Pride of Aberdeen 581, and
after Don Fernando 514, a son of Windsor 221 and the
Kinnaird Dora cow Dulcinea 334. Marshal was a grand
bull of great substance, and the characteristic of size which
still follows the Drumin stock was inherited from him.
In 1868, Disraeli 401, from Tillyfour, was added; in 1870,
Clansman 398, a first-prize Highland Society bull; in
1873, Talisman 640, both from Rothiemay; and in 1875,
Adrian 2nd 622, bred by Sir Thomas Gladstone. The
other bulls used have mostly been bred in the herd—viz.,
Byron 639, an excellent stock getter; Comet 1410, second-
prize two-year-old at the Highland Society; Cupid 1411;
and Scottish Knight 1776. The bulls lately in use have
been Express 1821, of the Erica family, from Ballindalloch;
and Viscount Duff 1365, bred by the Earl of Fife, after
Young Viscount 736, and out of Heroine 3016, of the
Rothiemay Victoria family. The strong infusion of
Queen blood in animals already largely partaking of
that element is quite a feature in the rearing of this
very fine herd.

As will be gathered from the foregoing, the bulls used
at Drumin have distinguished themselves at exhibitions,
and females have also met with much success at the

local and county shows, while several national honours
have been won. At Aberdeen, in 1868, Mr Skinner was
first for two-year-old heifers; at Edinburgh, in 1869, third
with Beauty 959; at Dumfries, in 1870, first and third
for yearling heifers with Heather Bell 962 and Catherine
961, and third for cows with Beauty 959; at Inverness,
in 1874, third for two-year-old heifers with Sweetheart
1689; at Aberdeen, in 1876, first for heifer calves with
Gaiety 2219; at Edinburgh, in 1877, first for yearling
heifers with Sunshine 2nd 3333, who was also first as a
two-year-old at Dumfries in 1878, second as a cow at
Perth in 1879, third at Carlisle and fourth at Kelso in
1880, and fourth at Dumfries in 1881. The Lucys and
Beautys are the favourite families in the herd. Some fine
stock are also descended from the Heather Bell family,
notably the group of Patiences at Gavenwood. Pavilion
3772, a member of this family, was one of the most perfect heifers of the breed ever seen.

Mr Skinner has held two public sales. The sale in
1873 was the best of the kind held up to that date. Cows
averaged £43, 13s., two-year-old heifers £44, 10s., yearling
heifers £34, 13s., heifer calves £26, 17s., bull calves £27.
At the sale in 1876, cows averaged £49, 10s. 6d., two-year-
old heifers £45, 10s., one-year-old heifers £35, 19s. 3d.,
bull calves £36, 2s. 4d., heifer calves £24, 3s. Mr Skinner
had a very fair share of the American trade last spring.
The herd was never in better condition than at present,
and comprises about 50 head, old and young.

Earnside.

This herd, belonging to Mr James Mackessack, was
founded about twenty-six years ago by purchases from
Mr Robertson, Burnside, Ballindalloch. These early
animals were not registered, but they are still represented. Mr Mackessack, in 1871, bought from Mr Paterson,

Mulben, Queen Mary of Mulben 1043, of the Mayflower family, after Jupiter 471. She was a prize yearling at the Banff and Aberdeen shows, and from her descends an excellent race, the cow having had twin calves four years consecutively. She is still in the herd, and although thirteen years old, is breeding regularly, and retains fine style and great substance. Another good sort traces from Florence 3142, bought from Mr Brown, Westertown, after President of Westertown 354, and representing Mr Brown's Victoria family. At the Tillyfour sale in 1871, Mr Paterson, Mulben, bought for Mr Mackessack the cow Dido of Tillyfour 3257, with heifer calf by Cup-Bearer of Ballindalloch 451 (subsequently named Flora of Earnside 2113). The price was 45 guineas, and the family from which these animals were descended was the Daisy branch of the Queen tribe. Flora, 2113, was imperfectly entered in vol. iii. of the 'Herd Book.' At the Westertown dispersion in 1874, Mr Mackessack secured Lady Ann 926 for 39 guineas; Barbara 2nd 989, after Alaster 2nd 462, and out of Barbara of Easter Skene 808, came from the Easter Skene herd. Fanny 1061, of the Rothiemay Miss Morrison family, and after Damascus 495, was bought at Mr Tayler's sale in 1872 for 47 guineas. At Mr Hannay's sale in 1878, Crocus 1400, of the Montbletton or Balwyllo Isabella family, was acquired for 50 guineas. A specimen of the Leochel Lass family at Haughton was bought at a high price. The animals we have mentioned comprise most of the additions made in the female line. The sires used in the herd have been obtained from Burnside, Ballindalloch, Drumin, and Aboyne Castle. Among them were the Jilt bull Jester 472, and the Drumin bull Scotia 789, the former fourth, and the latter second at Highland Society's shows. The herd usually numbers about thirty head, and has taken a creditable position at the Moray and Nairn county shows, notwithstanding that the animals have not been forced for exhibition.

East Town.

Mr James Farquharson's herd at East Town, Tarland, was established prior to 1822. No 'Herd Book' being then in existence, pedigrees were not kept. The oldest strain now represented is that tracing through Patricia 1606, calved in 1856, and bred by Mrs M'Combie at East Town, to Jess, also bred there. Jess, Patricia, and Beauty 1608, all of this family, bred until they were about twenty years of age, and they were a robust, useful lot of cattle. Among the bulls used in the herd were Banks of Don, bred by Mr Walker, Ardhuncart, the sire of Patricia; a bull from Mr Bowie, Mains of Kelly; Duke, bred by Mr Paterson, Mulben; Commodore 490, bred by the Earl of Southesk, after the splendid Queen sire Windsor 221, and out of Kalliope 1234; Prince of East Town 435, bred at Tillyfour; Lord Kelly 511, bred by Mr Bowie, Mains of Kelly, got by Victor of Kelly 353; Wallace of Tillyfour 683, bred by Mr M'Combie after Clova 517, and out of Ruth 1169; Baron Settrington 356, bred at Westertown, after March 355, and out of Duchess of Westertown 927 (he was twice first at Highland Society's shows); Osman 1531, and Haddo 2nd 1532, sons of Archbishop 787, bred by the Earl of Aberdeen; and Heir-Apparent 1263, bred at Tillyfour after Gainsborough 3rd 598, and out of Pride of Aberdeen 10th 3250. The last named is the present stock sire. Among the cows added to the herd were Mary 4th 1260, bred by Mr Bowie, Mains of Kelly; Victoria 4th 908, bred at Mains of Kelly, a prize heifer of the Victoria branch of the Queen tribe; and Lady Forbes 1993, bred by General Forbes of Inverernan, out of Sylph 1774, of the Queen tribe. The chief families in the herd are the Patricias, the Victorias, and the Lady Forbes's. Braes o' Mar 715, bred at East Town, descended from Patricia, was the sire of the well-known prize-winner Sir Maurice 1319. Sales have been made to various Scotch breeders, and some animals from the herd have gone to England. Stock from East Town are not exhibited except at the local show at -Tarland, where they always occupy a good position.

Easter Skene.

Mr M'Combie of Easter Skene has, like his cousin of Tillyfour, devoted much attention to the improvement of the polled breed. The foundation of his herd may be said to have been laid in 1840 at Lynturk, where Mr M'Combie kept a number of polled cows of the native breed. Close attention to breeding was given some years later. The circumstance which caused this greater care to be bestowed was the superiority of the stock produced in the herd by the noted bull Panmure 51. As previously stated, Panmure was bought, after his victory at Dundee in 1843, by Mr Farquharson Taylor, Wellhouse, and he was used by Mr M'Combie at Lynturk, as well as by several other breeders in the Vale of Alford. In vol. i. of the 'Herd Book,' Mr M'Combie registered two calves by Panmure—Queen of Scots 72 and Eppy 73. These have been erroneously entered in the 'Herd Book' as having been after Panmure of Wellhouse 119. They were really got by Panmure 51. For several years the herd at Easter Skene was almost exclusively composed of the descendants of these cows by Panmure 51, and there was no lack of testimonies to their excellence. At the Aberdeen show in 1853, Queen of Scots headed a strong class of twelve, beating Lord Southesk's famous Dora; while at the same show, Mr M'Combie was first for bulls with Roderick Dhu 89, also bred by himself. Mr M'Combie obtained some blood in the female line from Mr Farquharson Taylor, notably the dam of Alaster 256, whose sire was Hanton 228. Alaster 2nd 462, a son of Alaster 256, on one occasion at Aberdeen defeated the celebrated Portlethen bull Fox Maule 305 ;

while his grandsire Caledonian 2nd 409 was the first-
prize two-year-old at the Aberdeen show of the Highland
Society in 1868,—the son of Caledonian Second, Taurus
410, having been first-prize yearling at the Highland
Society's show at Perth in 1871. Numerous proofs could
be adduced of the remarkable power of these early Easter
Skene cattle to transmit their merit to their offspring.

Mr M'Combie very properly attributes the excellence
of his herd mainly to the Panmure blood. Feeling con-
fident that he could get nothing better, he has clung to
it tenaciously, and the female additions to the herd have
been few, although also very choice. Among them may
be mentioned Mariana 622, of the best Keillor blood, her
sire having been Old Jock 1, and her dam Lady Clara 4,
a daughter of Old Grannie 1. Marjory 809 and Lark 1000
—the latter a prize heifer at the Royal Northern Society's
shows—were bred from this strain. Miss Fraser 985 was
introduced from the herd of Colonel Fraser of Castle
Fraser. She was a prize-winner herself, and was dam
of Queen Mary 990, one of the best cows ever bred in
the herd, she having been the second-prize two-year-old
at the Highland Society's show at Inverness in 1865, and
first as a cow at Dundee in 1867. An unnamed cow that
came from Mulben also proved a valuable addition to the
herd. In 1867, to the bull Reform 408 she produced
Grizzle 995, the foundress of a family that has distinguished itself alike in the breeding and fat stock
classes of the local and national shows. This family is
now most largely represented in the herd, and its members
are almost invariably of unusual merit. At Tillyfour in
1867 was purchased a somewhat famous animal. This
was Miss Watson 987, who had accompanied her dam,
Beauty of Tillyfour 2nd 1180, to Tillyfour from the
Keillor sale in 1860. Miss Watson was after President
3rd 246, and her dam, we may note, is inaccurately stated
in the 'Herd Book' to have been Beauty of Buchan 5.

The cow was a half-sister to those renowned animals Jilt 973 and Ruth 1169, all of whom are of the Keillor favourite tribe. Two females—Prudence 1809 and Black Bess 1811—were acquired from Mr Skinner, Drumin, and more recently additions have been made from Gavenwood and Tillyfour. The early sires used were bred at Easter Skene. In 1861 Delaware 457, of the Dora family, and after Windsor 221, was bought from the Earl of Southesk; Reform 408, after Black Prince of Tillyfour 366, and out of Beauty of Tillyfour 2nd 1180, came from Tillyfour, as did also Moudiewart 680, after Jim Crow 3rd 350, and out of the Queen cow Charmer 1172. Bachelor 690, bred by Sir George Macpherson Grant, after Juryman 404, and out of Bertha 980—both Highland Society first-prize winners—was used in the herd for only two seasons, but he left a large number of remarkably good stock. Among other sires used was Paris 1473, bred at Tillyfour, out of Matilda 1175, of the Zara tribe, and after Valiant 663. Paris was the first-prize bull at the Paris exhibition, and was one of the Tillyfour Champion group. His sire Valiant was bred at Easter Skene, and it is worthy of note that the Easter Skene herd produced the sire of two of that celebrated group—Paris and Witch of Endor 3528. Mr M'Combie considers Paris to have been one of the best stock bulls that was ever at Easter Skene. His sire Paris 3rd was winner of the first prize as best yearling at the Highland Society and Royal Northern shows in 1881, and was sold for 150 guineas to the Hon. M. H. Cochrane, Compton, Canada. Another son of Paris and Black-amore, bred at Ballindalloch, after Judge 1150, and out of Edina 2987, of the Erica tribe, are at present being used as stock sires.

Three drafts have been sold—one in 1871 at an average of about £31, one in 1874 at an average of £24, and one in 1880 at an average of £27. The herd now numbers of registered animals 13 cows, 6 heifers, and 2 bulls, in addition to calves. Mr M'Combie has in his possession over 300 prize tickets won by animals from his herd at the local and national shows—a sufficient and striking testimony to the merit of the Easter Skene stock.

Easter Tulloch.

Mr James Scott of Easter Tulloch, Stonehaven, owns perhaps the largest herd of polled cattle in existence. It numbered at one time about 200 head, and notwithstanding numerous sales, it is still of very imposing dimensions. Not only are the cattle at Easter Tulloch numerous, but they are exceedingly well bred. Mr Scott has himself brought out several good animals, and in the hands of other breeders, who practise a more liberal system of feeding, stock reared from his herd have taken very high positions. Mr Scott himself keeps his herd in very lean condition, but when his animals are generously treated "blood tells." About 1866, some sixteen females and bulls were purchased from Mr T. Ferguson, Kinnochtry. The purchases from Kinnochtry and their descendants form the bulk of the herd. Among the animals acquired from Mr Ferguson we may note Princess of Kinnochtry 914, of the Keillor Favourite tribe, and foundress of Mr Ferguson's well-known Princess family; Princess of Easter Tulloch 1026, a daughter of Princess of Kinnochtry, Duchess of Easter Tulloch 1028, also a descendant of the Keillor cow Favourite 2, through Prizie 586; Levitz 1034, a descendant of Lord Panmure's first-prize cow at the Highland Society's show at Dundee in 1843; Mary of Easter Tulloch 1035, descended from a dam by Panmure 51; Kate of Easter Tulloch 1036, of the same strain as Levitz 1034; Agnes of Easter Tulloch 1966, of the Kinnochtry Emily family, tracing to Old Grannie 1. At the Kinnaird sale in 1865 Mr Scott purchased the cow Formosa 186 (erroneously entered among bulls in

vol. i. of the 'Herd Book'). She was a grand-daughter
of Fanny of Kinnaird 330, and proved a very valuable
addition to the herd. Reubena 1033, by Jupiter 471, out
of Rebecca 340, a daughter of Bell of Kinnaird 328, was
also acquired from Lord Southesk. Bamba 1200, bred by
Mr Walker, Portlethen, after Duke of Wellington 1200,
and representing one of the oldest Portlethen strains with
the cross of Porty 50, was also added, and has founded an
excellent family of Mayflowers, of which the most
distinguished specimen was Witch of Endor 3528, a member of Mr M'Combie's champion Paris group in 1878, and
sold at the Tillyfour dispersion in 1880 for 151 guineas. A
good sort traces to a cow bred by Mr Robert Scott, Upper
Tulloch. It is known as the Blue Bell family, and from it
Mr Scott bred Bluebeard 648, the first-prize two-year-old
bull at the Highland Society's show in 1874, and one of
the best two-year-olds seen in recent years. He unfortunately succumbed to an attack of foot and mouth disease
when three years old. From Mr Strachan, Wester Fowlis,
was obtained the foundress of another family, and a race
of Ashentillys spring from an unregistered cow Agnes, bred
at Easter Tulloch. Among the bulls used were Cavalier
411, bred at Kinnaird after Windsor 221, and out of
Kalliope 1234; King Henry 390, also bred at Kinnaird,
got by Windsor 221, and from Kalliope's dam, Kathleen of
Kinnaird 339; Colonel of East Tulloch 391, bred at The
Thorn after President 3rd 246, and the winner of second
prize as a yearling at the Highland Society's show in 1863;
Tamarlane 392, bred by Mr Scott, after Colonel of East
Tulloch, and out of Blue Bell of East Tulloch 1027. Tamarlane gained several local prizes, and was second at the
Highland Society's show at Edinburgh in 1869, when Prince
of Wales 2nd 394, bred and exhibited by Mr Scott, was
the first-prize yearling. Theodore 393, the sire of Prince
of Wales 2nd 394 (bred at Kinnaird after Jupiter 471, and
out of Thalia 1233), was also used in the herd; as was

Ralph 395, the third-prize yearling at Dumfries in 1870,
and Emperor of East Tulloch 396, bred by Sir George
Macpherson Grant, and out of the Erica cow Eisa 977.
Most of the sires subsequently used have been bred in the
herd.

Fasque.

Sir Thomas Gladstone, Bart., founded a herd in 1863.
The first animals bought were the yearling bull Rudolph
and the cow Eugene 458, from Balwyllo; Rudolph was out
of Ruby 713, a daughter of Keepsake 427, and Eugene
was after Rob Roy 56, and out of Victoria 428, a well-
known prize cow.   Of the heifers added from time to time
two were from Portlethen, two from The Thorn, four from
Haddo House, and one from Easter Skene.   The sires
bought for use in the herd were Adrian 439, from Portlethen; Harry 440, from Easter Tulloch; Serapis 998, from
Easter Skene; Diamond 1862, from Aboyne Castle; and
Donald Roger 1719, from Greenmyre, Old Meldrum.
Adrian 2d 622, Milton 621, and Negro 1398, bulls bred
at Fasque, have also been successful stock-getters.   Negro,
Diamond, and Donald Roger have been most recently or
are at present in use.   Adrian was sold to Sir George Macpherson Grant; Adrian 2d, to Mr Skinner, Drumin; and
Serapis, to Mr Bean, Balquharn.   Bull-calves have been
sold to Lord Clinton, Colonel M'Inroy, and others, at good
prices.   There are usually about a dozen pedigree cows at
Fasque.   Of those at present there are Eugenie 3910,
grand-daughter of the Balwyllo cow, and seven of her
descendants: Mayflower 4809, Mary of Haddo 3676,
and Alice of Haddo 3676, from the Earl of Aberdeen's herd; Negress 2d 2514, bred by Mr Adamson,
Balquharn; and Phenice 2512, of an old Fasque strain.
A noteworthy circumstance connected with the herd is
the remarkable breeding career of Eugenie 3910.   She is
now thirteen years old, and has had thirteen calves, all

of which came to maturity, and is still in breeding condition. Her stock have been very successful in the showyard. All of them have taken the highest honours when exhibited at local shows; and Adrian 2d out of Eugenie, and after Adrian, was second as a two-year-old at the Highland Society's show, and again second in the aged class when the property of Mr Skinner, Drumin. Emilie 2513, his full sister, was first at the Highland Society as a one-year-old. Eurydice 2515, after Harry, and out of Eugenie, was third at the Highland Society as a yearling. Adrian, bought at Portlethen when a calf, carried the first prizes at all the local shows, second at the Highland Society's show as a two-year-old, and first in the aged class when three years old at the Highland Society's show at Kelso in 1872. Serapis, bought at Easter Skene when a calf, was first at all the local shows, and first at the Highland Society's show at Edinburgh in 1877 as a two-year-old.

Fintray.

Sir William Forbes, Bart., of Craigievar and Fintray, commenced a herd a few years ago. He has made some very judicious purchases of animals, characterized by good blood and superior individual qualities, and the herd will doubtless at no distant date take a prominent position among the stocks in the country. The first additions were from the old established herd at Westside of Brux. Madge 7th 4223 was added from Mulben. The Baads cow Maid of Culter 1964, a daughter of Kate of Baads 1947, was acquired, and her offspring ought to be valuable, for she is a full sister of Halt 3525, and a half-sister on the dam's side of the renowned Prince Albert of Baads 1336. Tifty of Fyvie 7th 4686, of the Fyvie Flower family, was bought for 63 guineas at the Fyvie dispersion; Lucy of Kelly 7th 3502 came from Mr Bowie's herd; and Flower of the Nile 4579, of the Ballindalloch Lady Fanny sort, was acquired at the Rothiemay sale last year. The chief stock sire was Saracen 1689, out of the Champion cow Sybil 2d 3526, and after the Queen bull Dragon 1178. After being used several seasons in the herd, Saracen was sold at a high price to the Earl of Southesk.

Gavenwood.

Mr Hannay, Gavenwood, near Banff, factor for the Earl of Fife, has been closely associated with the improvement of the polled breed during the last twelve years. Under his active and judicious superintendence, the celebrated Duff House herd was collected and brought to the eminent position which it shortly came to occupy. The late Earl of Fife having limited the extent of his home farm, a portion of the herd was acquired by Mr Hannay; and from a similar cause, the remainder of the herd, then owned by the present Earl of Fife, was also a few years later taken over by Mr Hannay. In a former chapter we furnished an account of the Duff House herd, and it is therefore unnecessary in this place to repeat the information given regarding the materials on which the herd was based, and its leading achievements. It will be observed that the Duff House herd comprised specimens of most of the principal tribes of the breed, and several of the most famous animals produced in recent years. For convenience we shall date the separate existence of the Gavenwood herd from 1876, as in that year Mr Hannay himself first appeared prominently as an exhibitor, winning, at the Aberdeen show of the Highland Society, the first prizes for yearling bulls and two-year-old heifers. Among the more renowned animals then or subsequently in Mr Hannay's possession, a few may be noted. Young Viscount 736, of the Erica tribe, and first-prize bull in the yearling two-year-old and aged classes at Highland Society's shows, imparted character to the herd, and was used in it for several years with great success. Innes 1934, the first-prize cow of the Highland Society in 1876, was also in the herd, as well as her dam, Jinny 1017. Another fine cow was Lilias of Tillyfour 1795, a grand-daughter of Pride of Aberdeen 581, and dam of three splendid bulls—Challenger 1260, used in the herd; Black Watch 1242, who went to Altyre; and Proud Viscount 1264, used in the herd, and sold to go to America. There were several of the fashionable Erica tribe, such as Erica 6th 3023, a prize-winner at Highland Society's shows; Erica 7th 3019; Erica 4th 1697, sold to the Earl of Airlie for 101 guineas; and dam of the prize bull St Clair 1160, sold to Mr Melville Cartwright of Melville for 81 guineas; Essence 4547, sold to Lord Southesk for 100 guineas, and winner of the second prize of the Highland Society as a yearling heifer in 1881; Era 3833, a frequent local prize-winner, and others. In fact, away from Ballindalloch there was no finer collection of Ericas in the country than at Gavenwood. Heather Blossom 1703, of the Rothiemay Victoria family, was herself a very fine cow, and bred some beautiful calves, among them the twins Heather Blossom 2d 3395, and Heather Blossom 3d 3396, sold to Mr Ferguson, Kinnochtey, and Mr Ferguson, Ballunie; Warrior 1291, the first-prize yearling bull at the national show in 1877, and who was sold to the Marquis of Huntly for 155 guineas; Heroine 3016, a prize cow, and dam of Young Hero 1837, used at Montbletton, a national prize bull, and Viscount Duff 1365, used at Auchorachan, both sons of Young Viscount 736. Heather Blossom was sold to Mr Pearson of Johnston for 111 guineas. Patience of Corskie 1932, of the Drumin Rose family, gained many prizes, and was dam of that magnificent heifer Pavilion 3772, who carried for Lord Airlie the first prizes of the Highland Society as a yearling and two-year-old, as well as the first prize of the Royal Agricultural Society of England at Carlisle in 1880. The Montbletton Mayflower family has been

cultivated with much success by Mr Hannay, particularly
the branch springing from Blackbird of Corskie 1704, a
daughter of Mr Walker's Lady Ida 1021. Blackbird 1704
was sold in 1881 to Mr Cartwright of Melville for 66
guineas. Her daughter Blackbird 2d 3204, gained the
first prize of the Highland Society for cows in 1879.
Blackbird 3rd 3766 was acquired by Sir George Macpherson Grant for 71 guineas, and Blackbird 4th 3769 went to
Lord Strathmore. Black Standard 1541, after St. Clair
1160, and out of Blackbird 1704, was used in the Auchlin
and Waterside of Forbes herds. Last year Blackbird 2nd
3024 had twin calves, Benefit 5015, and Benefit 2nd 5016,
by Challenger 1260. Corriemulzie 2nd 3415, out of Lady
Ida 1021, gained no fewer than twelve prizes, among them
several challenge cups, at the county show, and second
prize as a two-year-old at the Highland Society in 1879.
Another calf of Lady Ida's was Violet of Montbletton 1399,
who bred His Excellency 1271, the stock bull at Skene,
and was sold in 1878 to Lord Strathmore for 80 guineas.
Idyll 4541, out of Lady Ida 1021, and after Young Viscount
736, was the third prize as a yearling heifer at the Highland Society's show in 1880. Zingra 2471, the first-prize
two-year-old heifer at the Highland Society's show in
1876, was sold to Mr M'Combie of Tillyfour for 81 guineas.
Corriemulzie 1701, bred at Bogfern, and descended from
the Keillor stock, was twice second in the cow class at
Highland Society's shows. Crocus 2nd 3765, after Young
Viscount 736, and from the Balwyllo Isabella family, was
sold to Mr Tayler of Glenbarry for 82 guineas. Jemel
1413, of the Ballindalloch Jilt family, won several prizes,
and was sold to Mr Walker, Montbletton, for 58 guineas.
Good animals were also bred from the Westertown
Duchess branch of the Queen tribe; Mr Barclay's Matilda
branch of the Queen tribe, the Ballindalloch Sybil tribe;
the Zara family; the Castle Fraser Blanche family; the
Rothiemay Georgina family, etc. From the last named

came Sir Wilfred 1160, bred at Rothiemay, who won the first prize as a yearling at the Highland Society in 1876, and the second as a two-year-old, and was sold to Lord Strathmore for 100 guineas.

We have incidentally referred to the chief sires used in the herd. Young Viscount 736 was followed by Challenger 1260, of the Pride tribe. This animal was used with the best results for several years. Owing to the date of calving he could not compete as a yearling or two-year-old. His photograph appears in volume v. of the 'Herd Book.' A lengthy bull of great style and levelness, he had splendid front and rare quality. Mr Hannay refused 200 guineas for him when he was one year old. Proud Viscount 1264, out of the same dam (Lilias of Tillyfour), and after Young Viscount, was also used. These animals suited admirably with the produce of the two first-prize Highland Society bulls Palmerston 374, and Gainsborough 596.

Three public sales were held, and they were among the most notable events of the kind in the annals of the breed. At the sale in 1877, 68 animals brought £3046—average £44, 15s. 10d., highest price £162, 15s. ; at the sale in 1878, 38 animals realized £1874, 5s.—average £49, 6s. 5d., highest price £236, 5s. ; and at the sale of 1881, 46 animals realized £1555, 1s.—average £33, 16s. 1d., highest price £74, 11s. Numerous sales have been made privately, many of the animals going to Canada, the United States, and South America. Stock from Gavenwood are also spread all over Scotland and England.

Writing on February 6th 1882, Mr Hannay supplied us with the list of the animals then in his herd. Of the May-flower family there were seven specimens comprising— Blackbird 2nd 3024, her yearling heifer Blue Ribbon 4554, her twin heifer calf Benefit 5015, her half-sister Blackbird 5th 4557, Corriemulzie 2nd 3415, Idyll 4541, and the yearling bull Sir Idris. There were five Ericas — Erica 6th 3023, her heifer calf Esperanza,

Easter 4540, her heifer calf Estella   , and Erar 3833.
Four were of the Fyvie Flower family—viz., Waldine 4563,
Lady Mar 3917, etc.; two Rothiemay Victorias, Heroine
3016, and her bull calf Hesperus   ; six Rothiemay
Georginas, Caledonia 4550, Kelvine 5017, Aivrin 4551,
Oslin 4552, Orange Leaf 1839, and Orellana; five Prides,
Pride of Aberdeen 16th 3302, Lilias of Tillyfour 1795,
Pride of Aberdeen 26th 4560, Prætoria and the bull Chal-
lenger 1260; four Drumin Roses, Patience of Corskie 1932,
Patience 2nd 3768, Patria 4549, and Patroness 4561; four
Westertown Roses, Rosy Dream 4545, Rosareyne, and two
others; five Tillyfour Ruths, Ruth 2nd 1783, Ruth of
Yonderton 2237, Ruth 3rd 4432; Rhuna, and the bull calf
Rutherglen; two Matildas of the Queen tribe, Midnight
4670, and Meteor; besides a Zara, a Lady Fanny, an
Advie Rose, and about half a dozen others. A large num-
ber of these have since been sold privately, many of them
having gone to England and America.

Glamis.

The Earl of Strathmore commenced a herd at Glamis in
1876. At the Mulben sale that year there were purchased
Ellen 2nd 2358, Queen Mary 5th 2360, and Queen Mary
12th 3514. At the Ballindalloch and Drumin joint sale
the same year, there were bought Beauty of Garline 1247,
and Sweetheart 2nd 2218. The bull Neptune 1152 was
purchased from Sir George Macpherson Grant before the
sale. In 1877 two cows were bought from Mr Leslie,
The Thorn, viz., Farnell 3rd 3247, and Flora Macdonald
2nd 3513; and the same season Fred's 6th Darling 3404;
Cowslip 2nd 3004, Frenzy 2nd 3378, and the bull Sir
Wilfrid 1157 were bought at Mr Hannay's sale at Corskie.
In 1878 there was a further purchase from Mr Hannay,
viz., Violet of Montbletton 1399, and Blackbird of Corskie
4th 3769. In that year there were also added from Mr

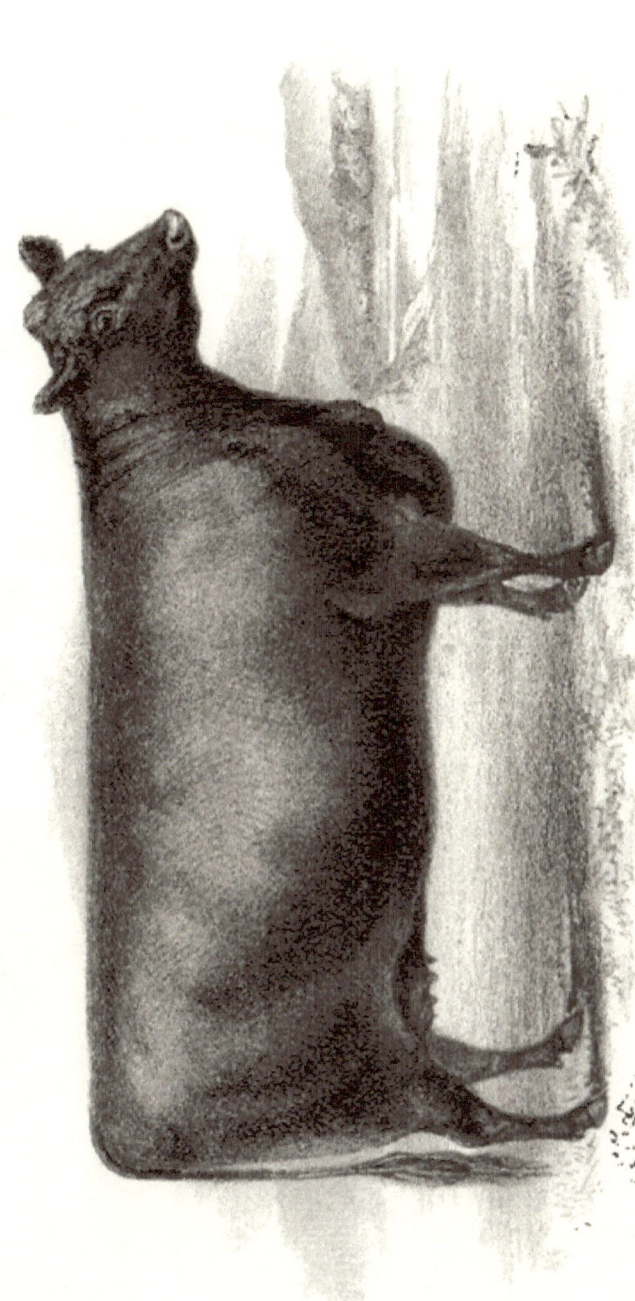

on Stone by AM.Cauci.   Hanhart imp

"SYBIL 4ᵗʰ(4326) at 2 YEARS OLD.
First Prize at the Highland Society's Show, at Stirling 1881.
The Property of the Earl of Strathmore, Glamis Castle Forfarshire.

Skinner, Drumin, the cow Sweetheart 1689, and from
Ballindalloch the Erica bull Elcho 595. In 1879 there
was purchased from Mr Grant, Advie Mains, the cow
Blanche of Advie 3588, and Evelyn of Advie, now Echo
of Glamis 4119 ; at the Ballindalloch sale Julia 4250, and
at Melville sale Mina 5th 3844, and at the Aboyne sale
Duchess 4th 944. In 1880 there was bought at the Tillyfour sale the calf Fairy 8th 4802, the pride bull Knight of
the Legion 1494, and Bismarck 2nd 1860. At Mr Adamson's sale in 1881 Edith 4th 3320, Pride of Aberdeen 25th
4331, and Sybil 4th 4326 were added, and from Mr Reid,
Baads, there was secured Isla 2nd 3999 ; from the Aboyne
sale Medusa 2577 ; from Sir W. G. Gordon Cumming,
Pride of the Findhorn 3243, and Barbelle 4299 ; from Mr
Smith, Stone o' Morphie. The sires used have been the
Keepsake bull Neptune 1152, the Georgina bull Sir Wilfrid 1157, the Erica bull Elcho 595, the Pride bull Knight
of the Legion 1494, and the Rothiemay Miss Morrison
bull Bismarck 2nd 1860.

The herd now consists of the following cows :—Beauty
1st of Glamis 3314, Blanche of Advie 3588, Echo of
Glamis 4119, Sweetheart 1689, Violet 1399, Barbelle 4299,
Sweetheart of Glamis 4266, Edith 4th 3320, Isla 2nd
3999, Medusa 2577, Pride of the Findhorn 2243; two-year-
old heifers Sweetheart 1st of Glamis 4806, Fairy 8th 4802,
Pride of Aberdeen 25th 4331, Corskie 6th, Mayfly Beauty
3rd 4801, Blackbird of Glamis 4805, Victoria of Glamis
4804, and Sybil 4th 4326. There are also eight one-year-
old heifers mostly got by Elcho and a number of heifer
calves. The families represented thus comprise—Prides,
Montbletton Mayflowers, Drumin Lucys, Baads Sybils,
Mulben Ellens, Kinnaird Fannys, Advie Roses, Aboyne
Madges, etc.

A joint sale with Lord Airlie was held at Glamis in
1880, when 22 head averaged £35, 18s. In April 1881
Beauty of Glamis 3515 was sold for £120, three one-year-

old heifers at £40 each, and a bull calf from Cowslip by
Elcho at £40, all to Hon. M. H. Cochrane for shipment to
Canada, and later in the year Mr Beattie purchased from
Mr Cochrane Mina Julia and Cowslip at 80 guineas each.
The bull Elcho was sold to Lord Airlie for £84.

Among the prizes won by the Glamis herd we may note
the following :—First at Kilburn for one-year-old bulls,
with Bombastes 1548; third at the Highland Society's
show at Perth for one-year-old heifers with Queen Mary
1st 3312; fourth for two-year-old bulls at Kelso and
Carlisle with Bombastes; third for one-year-old bulls at
Kelso with Ensign 1656; first for one-year-old heifers at
Stirling with Sybil 4th 4326; and second for one-year-old
bulls with Bismarck 2nd. The herd, it will be seen, has
been gathered together from the best sources, and under
Mr Ralston's care it has already acquired a high reputation,
the selections have been judiciously made, and the home
management doing full justice to the fine material collected.

CHAPTER XII.

GLENCORRIE—GREYSTONE—High prices for animals to New Zealand and America—GUISACHAN—A fashionable herd in the far north—Splendid collection of Queens—Charmer 2nd 1797, Dewdrop 2581, Heir of Glory 1746, Witch of Endor 3528, Pride of Mulben 3rd 3249, Pride of Aberdeen 18th 4321—HADDO HOUSE—HATTON CASTLE—Mr Garden Duff's good fortune with the Queens and Sybils—HAUGHTON—The Leochel Lass family—HILL OF SKILMAFILLY—HILLOCKHEAD—Erica 3rd 1249 and Young Viscount 736—JOHNSTON—Destruction of the herd by Pleuro-Pneumonia—KINNAIRD—The Earl of Southesk, after trying the "White Faces," returns to his first love—Ericas, Fannys, and Sybils—KINCRAIG—The breed in a trying climate—KINNOCHTRY —Mr Ferguson' spurchases from Keillor—The Princesses, Baronesses, Emilys, and Favourites—Sires used at Kinnochtry—In-breeding on the Keillor stock—Important sales to Scotch, Irish, and American breeders—The Kinnochtry herd in the show-yard—MAINS OF ADVIE— Success with Ballindalloch blood—The Advie Roses—Elcho 595, and Juryman 404—Mr Grant's system of breeding.

Glencorrie.

MR PETRIE began a herd at Glencorrie, Dufftown, in 1876, when he bought from Sir George Macpherson Grant the cow Deveron Lass 1416, of the Rothiemay Miss Morrison family, for 45 guineas, and from Mr Skinner, Drumin, the two-year-old heifer Matrimony 2214, of the Lucy family, for 50 guineas. Deveron Lass had previously suffered severely from foot and mouth disease, which somewhat disfigured her. Still she cost a good price, and her breeding has not been affected; while her constitution, and that of her stock, is excellent. Her calves at Glencorrie have been two heifers and four bulls. The heifers have been retained, and the bull calves have been sold, realizing from 25 guineas to 57 guineas. The latter price was paid for her calf of 1881, Deveron Lad, who was bought by the Earl of Seafield, and was considered the finest bull in the sale hall at Aberdeen in 1882, when he realized the highest price of the 81 sold. Matrimony has had two heifers and four bull calves. The latter sold at 24 and 25 guineas. In 1875, Mr Petrie bought at Mr Tayler's sale at Rothiemay, when not in calf, Annie of Inchcorsie 1840 for 39 guineas. She was a large cow of fine quality, but a bad milker, and for that reason she was sold after breeding Nellie of Glencorrie 4004, by the Lucy bull Victor of Glencorrie 850. This cow is a good milker, taking her milking property from the family of her sire. Nellie has had four bull calves, which have been sold at 25, 33, and 41 guineas. In 1877 was bought at the Tullochallum sale the cow Beauty 3rd of Drumin 3574 at 41 guineas. She was then two years old, and belonged to the oldest of the Drumin Beauty family. Beauty 3rd has had three bull and two heifer calves. Medea 3890, by the Queen bull Constantine 1180, was bought at the Aboyne dispersion for 60 guineas. She is a very true breeding cow, and is grand-daughter of Madge 1217, the first-prize winner at Kilburn. She has had a bull calf by the 155 guinea sire Warrior since she came to Glencorrie. There is in the herd a Rosie family, descended from Rosie 1st, bred at Glencorrie, who had calves by the Pride bull Major of Tillyfour 509, and Victor of Glencorrie 850, which were kept for breeding. The sires used in the herd have been Victor of Glencorrie 850, bought from Mr Skinner, Drumin; Ratepayer 1377, bought from Mr Hannay, Gavenwood; and First Lord 1641, a son of Judge 1150, and of The Lady Fanny tribe, bought from Sir George Macpherson Grant. The sire now in use is King

James 1877, bred at Easter Skene after Paris 1473, and
out of Tibbie Fowler 4020. The herd numbers about 30
head. The bulls in it have taken a good position at the
local shows, but no females have been exhibited. The bull
calves from Glencorrie realized the highest average, and
the highest individual price, at the Aberdeen joint sale in
the spring of 1882.

Greystone.

Mr Reid, Greystone, one of the largest and most successful exhibitors of Scotch cattle at the English Christmas
shows, has a very good herd of pure-bred cattle. Polled
stock have been at Greystone for a long time, a few animals
from Mr Reid's herd having been entered in vol. i. of
the 'Herd Book,' but it is only recently that particular
attention has been given to registration. The present lot
of cows and heifers are descended from various herds. The
Jannet family traces from Lottie of Clova 3176, by Jim
Crow 5th 769; the Kate family from Kate 3rd, bred at
Greystone; the Lady Haddo family from Lady Haddo 3rd
4735, by Jim Crow 5th 769, bred at Clova; the Bella
family, from a cow by Panmure 51; the Pride family,
from Pride of Clova 3rd 3175, by Jim Crow 5th 769, bred
at Clova. The herds represented in the female line are the
Archballoch, Ementeer, Tillyfour, Clova, Inverernan, Ardhuncart, etc. Much benefit has been derived from the use in
the herd of the wonderful old bull Major 3rd 662, bred by
Mr Bowie, Mains of Kelly, calved in 1870, after Jim Crow
3rd, and out of Martha 2nd 906. This bull was bought by
Mr Reid from the late Mr Forbes, Ruthven, Tarland, and
has been in profitable service for ten years. He is justly
regarded as one of the best stock bulls of the breed, and
has been a splendid getter of heifers. Mr Reid has renewed
most of his cows since he obtained Major 3rd. They are
all in good breeding condition, and not many of them over
seven years old. Most of the heifers have been sold or

mated with other sires, and Mr Reid has thus been able to
use Major 3rd with excellent results for a very long time.
He lately bought from Mrs Reid, Craskins, the bull
Tullochallum, bred at Tillyfour. He is a very nice fleshy
animal, and is leaving fine stock. As a proof of the
excellence of the stock got by Major 3rd, we may remark
that Mr Reid has sold of his produce one three-year-old
cow to Mr Bell, to go to New Zealand, for £200 ; three
females to Messrs Gudgell & Simpson, Kansas, U.S.A., each
fetching about £100 ; three yearlings to Mr Henry, Kansas,
at good prices ; a heifer to Mr Matthews, Kansas, for 100
guineas ; and a heifer to a local buyer. At the Royal
Northern show last year, Mr Reid was first for two-year-
old heifers ; first for pairs of two-year-old heifers ; third for
yearling heifers ; and first for pairs of yearling heifers.

Guisachan.

The herd belonging to Lord Tweedmouth at Guisachan
Home Farm, Beauly, is one of the most fashionable that
exists. It was established in October 1878, and in the
course of three years there has been gathered together a
grand collection of polled cattle, representing many of the
choicest families, and comprising individuals of the highest
merit. The purchases were made by Mr Samuel Davidson,
Lord Tweedmouth's manager ; and it having been resolved
to procure the finest specimens of the breed that could be
obtained, the additions were made without regard to price.
As the starting of a valuable herd of polled cattle in the
district was to some extent an experiment, we are glad to
learn that the animals have thriven exceedingly well, and
that the breed is considered specially adapted for that part
of the country. We will best convey information concerning the composition of this splendid herd by noting the
various purchases made. At Tillyfour, in 1878, Charmer
2d 1797, of the Charmer branch of the Queen tribe, was

bought for 76 guineas; Pride of Aberdeen 11th 3255, out of Pride Mulben 3d 3249, and Princess of Auchlossan 1140, were secured at the same sale.

From Mr Wilken, Waterside of Forbes, there were purchased Brucklay Princess 2310 for 50 guineas, and Waterside Stella 3210. Three animals were purchased privately from Mr Skinner, Drumin, viz. Melody 3338, of the Beauty family; Rosebud 3d 3339, of the Rose family; Heather Bell 3d 3340, of the Rose family. The bull Ethelred 1440, after Judge 1150 and out of the Erica cow Ethel 1415, was acquired from Mr Robertson, Aberlour Home Farm, and was retained in the herd as stock sire. At the Earl of Aberdeen's sale in 1879 the following purchases were made:—Kate of Haddo House 2261, Rosalind of Haddo 2262, Alice of Haddo 2d 3675, Mayflower of Haddo 3680, Ishbel 2d 3995, Lawn of Guisachan 4399, Rosamond of Guisachan 4400, Grace of Guisachan 4401, and Freak 4402. At the Aboyne sale in 1879 were bought—Dewdrop 2581, out of the first-prize Highland Society's cow Dora of Aboyne 1282, of the Daisy branch of the Queen tribe, for 95 guineas; Doris 3280, of the Westertown Duchess branch of the Queen tribe, for 63 guineas; Pansy 3275, of the Kinnochtry Princess tribe, for 46 guineas; Foxglove 4615, of the Kinnaird Fanny tribe, and Delilah 3283, of the Duchess tribe, for 81 guineas. Some very valuable animals were bought at the Tillyfour dispersion. They were the bull Heir of Glory 1746, out of the 270 guineas Pride cow; Pride of Aberdeen 9th 3253, for 135 guineas; Witch of Endor 3528, of the Easter Tulloch Mayflower tribe, and a member of the Paris group, for 155 guineas; Pride of Aberdeen 15th 3273, for 105 guineas; Pride of the Seine 4513, of the Baads Sybil tribe, for 73 guineas; and Jersey Lily 4514, out of Witch of Endor, for 49 guineas. At the Balquharn sale in 1881 that beautiful cow Pride of Mulben 3d 3249 was bought for 225 guineas; and Pride of Aberdeen 18th 4321, out of the Pride cow Regina 1179, for

160 guineas. Pride 18th was the second-prize two-year-old heifer at Kelso and Carlisle in 1880, and gained for Lord Tweedmouth the third prize as a cow at the Highland Society's show at Stirling in 1881. Heir of Glory was retained as stock sire, and is assisted by Tip Top 1828, out of Pride of Aberdeen 15th. Lord Tweedmouth, it will be seen, owns a rare group of Prides, and some valuable specimens of other branches of the Queen tribe. The herd has not as yet had an opportunity of doing much either in the show-yard or sale ring, but a brilliant future may safely be predicted for it.

Haddo House.

As already noticed, there was a fine herd at Haddo House, which was dispersed in 1861. A herd was again commenced by the Earl of Aberdeen in 1870 by purchases at Castle Fraser and Tillyfour. At Portlethen in 1873, Frances 3d 901, of the Kinnaird Fanny family, and Ida 6th 900, of the Portlethen Ida family, were bought for 51 guineas and 44 guineas respectively; Alice 1243, of Mr Brown's Victoria family, was bought at Westertown in 1874 for 55 guineas; and the bull Archbishop 787, of the Duchess branch of the Queen tribe, cost 48 guineas as a calf. Rosalind 1805, of the Grizzle family, was bought from Mr M'Combie of Easter Skene in 1874. Ellen 1st 2353 was bought at Mulben, and the Erica bull Heritor 1277 was acquired at the Corskie sale in 1877. Purchases were also made at East-town and East Kinmonth. The herd was largely reduced by a draft sale in 1879, when 39 animals averaged £25, 5s. In the following year attention was again given to breeding, and some valuable additions were made by purchases on Lord Aberdeen's behalf by Mr Douglass, factor. The herd now numbers about 30 breeding animals. Among them may be named Pride of Mulben 2d 2359, bought at the Aboyne dispersion for 67

guineas, and representing one of the best branches of this
fashionable family; Halt 2d 3527, bought at the Tillyfour
dispersion for 61 guineas, winner of the first prize and gold
medal in the heifer class at the Paris Exhibition in 1878,
and a member of Mr M'Combie's Champion group; Gitana
2578, of the Pride tribe, purchased at Tillyfour; Alice
4th 3683, of the Westertown Victoria family; Lady
Catherine 3d 4316, bred at Haddo House; Green Lady
4689, from Fyvie Castle; Sybil 3d, after the Queen bull
Dragon 1178, and out of Mr M'Combie's Champion cow
Sybil 3524; and Charming Queen, of the Charmer branch
of the Queen tribe, being out of Charmer 3d 3251, sold for
150 guineas. Sybil 3d and Charming Queen were bought
at the Tillyfour dispersion in 1880. The young stock in
the herd are after Baron Morven 1580, of the Kinnochtry
Princess family, Warrior 1291, and Heir of Paris 1917.
The last named, bred at Balquharn, and out of Pride of
Aberdeen 9th 3253, the 270 guineas cow, is the bull at
present in use.

Hatton Castle.

Mr Garden Duff of Hatton established his herd in 1877
by the purchase of two cows at Mr Hannay's sale at
Corskie. One of them — Fred's 4th Darling 1923,
of the Ballindalloch Sybil tribe—was bought for 98
guineas, and she herself and eight of her descendants
are in the herd. Mr Duff has since made purchases at
the draft sale of Lord Aberdeen's herd in 1879, at the
Aboyne draft sale in 1879, and at the Tillyfour dispersion
in 1880. At the Tillyfour dispersion was bought the
Pride cow Royalty 3053 for 80 guineas. The herd now
numbers 38 head, consisting of 3 Prides, 8 of other
branches of the Queen tribe, 10 Ballindalloch Sybils,
4 Kinnaird Fannys, and 3 Aboyne Livelys, etc. It will
thus be seen that in a comparatively short time Mr
Duff has collected specimens of some of the very best

tribes of the day, and the rapid increase is due to the
fortunate circumstance that the produce of the herd has
been almost entirely females. The stock sire is the
Erica bull Viscount 2nd 1743, half-brother on the
dam's side to the celebrated Young Viscount 736. Prizes
have been taken at the local shows, but Mr Duff has not
up to the present time exhibited elsewhere. Three
yearling bulls of last year were sold for a little over £33
each.

Haughton.

Over twenty years ago, Mr Farquharson of Haughton
purchased a polled cow off the Tillyfour stock, which he
named Leochel Lass, and from her has sprung the best of
his herd. Leochel Lass 2nd 1861 is still in the herd,
and although now sixteen years old, she keeps her shapes
as well as ever. She has been a regular breeder, and is
a heavy milker. Her daughter, Leochel Lass 3rd 1863,
gained the second prize at the Vale of Alford show as a
cow, and was sold for £40. Leochel Lass 4th 1864 won
the first prize at Alford in 1876, and was afterwards sold
to Professor Brown, of the Ontario Agricultural College,
Canada, for 70 guineas. From her has sprung a sub-
family of Heather Bells. Heather Bell 1st of Haughton
2295 won first prizes at Alford and Insch, and was sold
to Mr Mackessack, Earnside, for 80 guineas. Heather
Bell of Haughton 2nd 2496, after gaining many high
honours at Alford, was sold with her calf for £100.
Another daughter of hers, after Victor of Kelly 3d 854,
Heather Bell 3d 3953, bids fair to surpass her dam in
merit, and there is in the herd a very fine heifer from her
by The Black Knight 1809. There are other three cows
of the same blood. These go by the name of Marias.
They are good breeders, and their stock have brought
satisfactory prices. Others of the same line might be
mentioned as very promising. In the herd this season

there are a lot of very nice calves after the Pride bull The Black Knight 1809, an animal of great substance, good shapes, and quality. Mr Farquharson is very particular in having in his place bulls of the best pedigree, combined with individual merit. One of the first bulls used was an animal of splendid breeding and superior style and quality. He was Garibaldi of Haughton 707, after Rob Roy Macgregor 267, and out of Pride of Aberdeen 581. Mr Farquharson exhibited him at the International Show at Battersea in 1862, where he gained the second prize as a two-year-old. Victor of Kelly 3rd 854, of the Victoria branch of the Queen tribe, came from Mains of Kelly; Emir 1498, out of that excellent milking cow Miss Macpherson 1252, of the Erica tribe, from Balquharn; and The Black Knight 1809, of the Pride family, from Mr Pearson of Johnston. There are usually from ten to twelve cows in the herd, and they are all used as dairy cows, their calves being hand-reared.

Hill of Skilmafilly.

In 1863 a heifer out of Fyvie Flower 1516 was purchased by the father of Mr George Fraser, the present tenant of Hill of Skilmafilly, from Colonel Gordon of Fyvie. He made subsequent additions until 1867, when Mr George Fraser took over at valuation the farm stocking, with the exception of a two-year-old heifer, out of the animal purchased in 1863. In 1868 Mr Fraser bought a bull and three heifer calves at Fyvie Castle, and made a number of other additions from the same herd. In 1879 the heifer Annie Lawrie of Skilmafilly 4253 was bought from Colonel Gordon. Of these animals, Belle of Skilmafilly 4535 is still in the herd, although fourteen years old. She was in February last at the drop, her nineteenth calf, although she was thirty-five months old at her first calving, having had twins four times. After using until 1872 the bull bought at Fyvie Castle in 1868, Mr Fraser bred the next two sires used in the herd, one from a cow at Fyvie Castle descended from the Keillor stock, and the other from the cow his father reserved on leaving the farm in 1867. In 1876 was bought at the Shevado sale the bull calf Andrew Lammie 2nd 1166, bred by the late Mr Dingwall Fordyce. In 1879 Mr Fraser bought the bull calf Macer 1659 from Mr James Argo, Cairdseat. He is now the property of Mrs Hay, South Ythsie. In January 1882 was purchased the bull Baron Morven 2nd from the Earl of Aberdeen. The number in the herd at present, including calves, is twenty. Of these, twelve are registered, or eligible for entry, in the 'Polled Herd Book.' Mr Fraser has for the last eight years been buying and selling from 200 to 500 herd of cattle annually, and it would thus be difficult to give an account of all his transactions in polled cattle. Sales have been made to Mr James Hay, Little Ythsie; Dr Ligertwood, Auchencrieve; Mr Wilken, Waterside; Mr Metcalfe, Mains of Auchmunziel, etc. A good many prizes have been gained at local shows by animals from the herd.

Hillockhead.

Mr Duff's herd at Hillockhead has become very famous in connection with one or two of the best show and breeding cattle of the day. His first purchase was Cupbearer of Ballindalloch 451 and Erica 3rd 1249, a son and granddaughter of the celebrated Ballindalloch cow Erica 843. These animals were bought from Sir George Macpherson Grant, Bart., in 1868. Cupbearer gained several prizes, among them the second at the Royal Northern and Highland Society's shows. He was sold to Colonel Fraser of Castle Fraser, and Mr Duff bought from that breeder Matilda 1250, of the Mina family, and her bull calf Hampton 492. Hampton was put to Erica 3rd 1249,

and the produce was Young Viscount 736, who was sold
as a calf to the Earl of Fife, and after winning the
first prize three years in succession at the Highland
Society's shows, went to Sir George Macpherson Grant for
225 guineas. Among the other bulls used have been
Statesman of Hillockhead 1209, bought from Mr M'Combie
of Tillyfour in 1876, after he had gained the third prize
at the Highland Society's show; Nicholas 1210, bought
from Mr Hannay, Gavenwood; Vanguard 1415, of the
Montbletton Mayflower family, bought from Mr Hannay;
and Erichtonius, bought from Mr Robertson, Aberlour
Mains, after the Erica bull Whig 1867, and out of the
Erica cow Elf 3751. The females, which number about a
dozen, are all descended from Erica 3rd 1249 and Matilda
1250.

Johnston.

Mr Pearson of Johnston started a herd in 1868. In
that year the cow Millicent 1207, by Legislator 489, out of
Mysinda 1230, was purchased at the Honourable Charles
Carnegie's sale at Arratsmill. Ashentilly 1029 was bought
from Mr Scott of Easter Tulloch, and calved Ada of Johnston 3553, by the Erica bull Emperor of East Tulloch 396;
and Levity 5th 3554 was acquired from the same breeder.
Animals were also secured from Portlethen. At the Corskie
sale in 1877 the fine cow Heather Blossom 1703 was
bought for 111 guineas, being the highest price paid for a
polled cow at a public sale up to that time. In 1874, at
Mr M'Combie's sale at Alford, Pride of Aberdeen 3rd
1168, a daughter of the original Pride of Aberdeen 581,
and after Black Prince of Tillyfour 366, was secured for
52 guineas. She had gained the second prize as a cow at
the Royal Northern show, and the third prize at the
Highland Society's show in 1868, and was one of the best
bred Prides in the country. At the same sale Mr Pearson
bought Lucy 2nd 1186, of the Drumin Lucy tribe, for 57

guineas. The bulls used have been Moudiewort 686, bred
at Tillyfour, after Jim Crow 3rd 350, and out of Charmer
1172, of the Queen tribe; M.P. 1250, bred at Johnston,
after Moudiewort 686, and out of Pride of Aberdeen 3rd
1168; and A.K.H.B. 1576, also bred by Mr Pearson, got
by Young Viscount 736, and out of Heather Blossom 1703.
The herd usually comprised from fifteen to twenty cows,
and among those in it in May last, when Mr Pearson gave
us our information, were—Pride of Aberdeen 17th 4078, a
choicely-bred Pride; Heather Blossom of Johnston 2nd,
out of Heather Blossom 1703, and after M.P.; Ada 3553;
Levity of Johnston, after Prussia 900, and out of Levity
5th 3554; Annie 1212, and various of her descendants,
specially Annie 4th 4868; Inchgarth 2061, and several of
her offspring; Lizzie 4th 4867; and Lucy 2nd 1186.
Private sales have been made of animals to go to various
parts of Scotland, England, and Ireland, one bull to
Germany, and some heifers to America. Stock from the
herd have been exhibited only at the Kincardine county
show, where prizes have been won, Ada having been twice
first as a cow, and Inchgarth once. Since writing the
foregoing we regret to learn that pleuro pneumonia got in
amongst the Johnston herd. Several valuable animals
had to be killed in consequence of the disease, and the
whole herd was ultimately slaughtered in June last. Mr
Pearson has the heartfelt sympathy of every breeder of
polled cattle in the extermination of his valuable herd, the
result of many years' careful breeding.

Kinnaird.

After the fatal rinderpest in 1865, referred to in chapter
vi., the Earl of Southesk abandoned rearing the native
breed of the county, feeling that he could not replace the
stock he had lost except by the expenditure of a larger
amount of time, energy, and money than he felt equal to

after so serious a rebuff of fortune. His lordship had seen
in England some admirable animals of the Hereford breed,
and decided to try the experiment as to how they would
do in Scotland. As far as concerned the breeding and
rearing of excellent stock, the Herefords were on the whole
a decided success, but there was little or no market for
bull calves, and it could not, in a herd of that value, pay
to rear steers. Lord Southesk therefore decided to give up
breeding altogether, sold the Herefords, and let the farm of
Haughs of Kinnaird.

In the autumn of 1880 it became desirable that Lord
Southesk should himself occupy the farm of Greenden
instead of putting it into the market, and he then decided
to re-enter the field as a breeder of polled stock. He had
before this bought, at the Glamis sale, a pure-bred bull
calf Enterprise 1757, meaning to use him for his dairy
cows. As, however, this animal, though good in his way,
was not quite superior enough for the stock bull of the
sort of herd Lord Southesk decided to acquire, he was
sold at the spring sale in Aberdeen in 1881. The first
purchases for the new herd were made at the joint sale
of cattle belonging to Mr Hamilton of Skene and Mr
M'Combie of Easter Skene, at Aberdeen in 1880. Here
Lord Southesk purchased from the former the yearling
bull His Grace 1721, and the cows Lady Love of Corskie
3387, Pride of Skene 3193, and Vine 2nd of Skene 3398;
and from the latter, the cow Tibbie Fowler 4020, the two-
year-old heifers Lizzie Lindsay 4027 and Barbara Allan
4024, and the yearling heifer Tabitha 4585, a daughter of
Tibbie Fowler by Paris 1473. These were bought at very
moderate prices. Lord Southesk then being desirous of
reviving the old Kinnaird strains, purchased the Erica
cows, Erica 8th 3550, from Mr Grant, Auchorachan, Glen-
livet, and Echo 2976, from Sir George Macpherson Grant
of Ballindalloch, the latter having been the second-prize
cow at the Highland Society's show at Dumfries in 1878,

besides winning many local honours. He also bought from
Sir George the Lady Fanny heifer Lady Fatima 3798, by
Elcho 595, thus, through Lady Fanny 971, by King Charles
236, getting the blood of Druid 225 and Kate 12. At this
time Lord Southesk heard that a very highly-pedigreed
bull, which had been sold as a calf to go to England,
was obtainable. He therefore decided to buy him from
character without seeing him, and disposed of His Grace
1721 to Mr Hugh Ferguson, for exportation to the Sandwich Islands. The bull thus bought back to Scotland was
named Kingmaker 1794. He was bred at Ballindalloch in
1879, after Elcho 595, and out of the Pride cow Kindness
of Ballindalloch 1412, who combines in her lineage two
streams of the Kinnaird Dora 333 tribe. When the bull
arrived he was a mere "bag of bones." A little more
condition, however, made him look more worthy of his
ancestry. Lord Kinnaird felt that his herd would not be
complete without going back to the old original Kinnaird
blood, and he therefore bought the calf Blush Rose 4586
from Mr Walker, Portlethen. His lordship was so much
pleased with this scion of the old race, that he subsequently
obtained Blush Rose's mother, Bunch of Roses 3350, with
a heifer calf at foot by Matador 1710. These all trace
directly back to Old Lady Anne 743. Lord Southesk also
bought at the public sale at Aberdeen, from Mr Walker,
the cow Anemone 2269, of one of the very best old Balwyllo families. At the same sale he bought, for use among
the dairy cows, a bull, bred by Mr Scott, Easter Tulloch,
who was named Llewellyn 1888. At the dispersion of Mr
Adamson's Balquharn herd, Lord Southesk acquired Sibyl
2nd of Tillyfour 3526, and her heifer calf Sappho Sibyl
5020. The price was high; but Sibyl 2nd had the record
of having been the first-prize cow at Carlisle, Kelso, and
Aberdeen in 1880, and of having been awarded the
M'Combie prize as the best animal of the breed at the
last-named show. A few days later Lord Southesk bought

Charlotte of Fyvie 1893, with heifer calf at foot, and her daughter Mary Grace 4066, of the Fyvie Flower family, at the sale at Fyvie Castle; and shortly before these sales he added another Erica to his herd in the shape of the yearling heifer Essence 4547, by Laird of Fyvie 934, out of Erica 9th 3822, purchased from Mr Hannay, Gavenwood. This heifer gained the second prize at the Highland Society's show at Stirling in 1881. A few other females were added; and at a long price the bull Saracen 1689, out of Sybil 2nd 3526, was acquired from Sir William Forbes, Bart. of Craigievar and Fintray.

The new herd has thus been formed from the very best available material. The farm on which the cattle now are has not the fine soil of the Haughs of Kinnaird; but with the addition of the grass parks near the Castle, and the advantage of the outrun of the deer parks, there is every reason to hope that Lord Southesk's new herd may be a worthy representative of the old one, the destruction of which, by the cruel rinderpest, was characterized by the late Mr M'Combie as a " national misfortune."

Kincraig.

This herd, belonging to Mr Macgregor, has been in existence for about thirteen years. It was commenced by the purchase of young cows and heifers from Mulben, Westertown, Rothiemay, Ballindalloch, Bognie, Earnside, Burnside, and Johnston. The first bull used in the herd was from Drumin. Thereafter bulls were got from Westertown, Rothiemay, Earnside, etc. In 1877 Mr Macgregor, finding his herd becoming too large, resolved to reduce it, and over 40 animals were sold; but as too many had even then been retained, the herd was again considerably lessened in 1879. It is now composed of 20 cows and heifers with their calves. The animals are chiefly of Bognie, Ballindalloch, Westertown, and Johnston blood,

and, with the exception of two dairy cows, every animal
on the farm is purely bred, and in the 'Herd Book.' The
most numerous family now at Kincraig is that of which
Miss Carnegie 8th 1676 is the ancestress. This cow was
purchased at the Bognie dispersion, and has proved an
excellent breeder and a good milker. Another Bognie
family originated with Corskie 30th 1277, also bought at
the Bognie dispersion. A third family of three animals is
from the Ballindalloch cow Elaine 2989, descended from
the Drumin herd. She has done well at Kincraig, although
her first calf was a disappointment. A fourth family of
four animals is from Leddy 3556, a good handsome cow
from the Johnston herd. She was purchased in 1879 at
the Aberdeen sale, and has turned out a very valuable
acquisition to the herd. The fifth family is descended
from the excellent cow Adelaide 3501, of the Westertown
Victoria family, selected by Mr Macgregor from the late
Mr Brown's splendid herd, and purchased at what was in
these days considered a very long price. Unfortunately
Adelaide's progeny have been chiefly bulls, and her
present representative in the herd has as yet followed
her example. This has been very disappointing, for
Adelaide 2nd 2457 is a particularly handsome cow. The
stock bull Chieftain 1847 is her calf, and is now two
years old.

The climate of Badenoch, in which district Kincraig is
situated, is exceedingly severe in winter. This is a great
disadvantage; but in reducing his herd to its present
limits, Mr Macgregor has endeavoured to retain only such
animals as appeared most suitable, and the result has
been very encouraging. The chief difficulty is to provide
food in spring in a locality in which vegetation is very
late, and on a farm where a large stock of several thousand
blackfaced sheep is kept. There is also the drawback of
being generally obliged to sell the surplus stock in comparatively low condition, which always reduces the price

very much; but after full consideration, the practice of giving no artificial food is strictly adhered to. The cattle get just a moderate allowance of straw and turnips— nothing else.

Kinnochtry.

The herd of Mr Thomas Ferguson, now in Kinnochtry, Coupar-Angus, was founded at Ashmore about the year 1835. Between that year and 1839 Mr Ferguson received several black polled cows from the stock of his father, the late Mr Thomas Ferguson, who was then and had for years been tenant of the farm of Claywhat, near Bridge of Cally, in the parish of Blairgowrie. The late Mr Ferguson had got several of his cattle from the late Mr Chalmers of Netherton of Claywhat. Among Mr Thomas Ferguson's earliest recollections is his having seen Netherton's fine black polled cattle, of which the owner and the people in the district spoke as "Angus Doddies." The last Mr Chalmers of Netherton, who died in 1855, said his father had kept "Angus Doddies" as far back as he could remember, and that his grandfather also kept them. As long as Mr Thomas Ferguson recollects, there was also a herd of polled cattle on the contiguous farm of Milton of Drimmie. In fact, Mr Ferguson says the "Doddies" were sixty years ago, and previous to that time, common enough all over the district. In addition to the cattle Mr Ferguson thus obtained from his father, he occasionally bought in the locality other polled cows and heifers, supposed to be of about the same breeding.

Mr Ferguson soon discovered that the Keillor cattle were superior to those he had started with, and in 1839 he bought from Mr Hugh Watson the heifers Young Favourite 61, and Edinburgh 64, daughters of Old Grannie 1. Shortly afterwards he got the cow Favourite 2 from Keillor, and he then sold to Mr. Leslie, The Thorn, and others, the specimens of his father's strains. For many years he had in his herd descendants only of Young Favourite 61, Edinburgh 64, and Favourite 2. The families descended from Young Favourite 61 are the Princesses and Baronesses. These two families both trace to Prizie 586, bred by Mr Ferguson out of Young Favourite 61, and after Black Jock 3. The Princesses descend through Princess of Kinnochtry 914, calved in 1861, a daughter of President 3rd 246, and Prizie 586; and the Baronesses through Eliza of Kinnochtry 912, calved in 1860, after The Baronet 339, and out of Miss Scott 913, a grand-daughter of Prizie 586. From Edinburgh 64, a smaller family of Emily's is descended. The Kinnochtry Favourites are directly descended from Favourite 2. Mr Ferguson's present herd may therefore be said to have been founded by the three Keillor cows—Young Favourite 61, Edinburgh 64, and Favourite 2. Mr Ferguson, also, when he commenced to cultivate the Keillor families, purchased from Mr. Watson the bulls Black Jock 3, and Young Jock 4, and he obtained the use of the stock sires at Keillor.

With the exception of two heifers which he bought from Mr Mustard, Leuchland, in 1856, and which were that year shipped to Canada, along with Butterfly 71, a heifer of his own breeding, Mr Ferguson added no animals except from Keillor until 1871, when he purchased Young Mina 924, a calf, at Mr Leslie's sale at The Thorn. He bought other two bulls from Mr. Watson, Hugh 130, and The Baronet 339, the latter bred by Sir James Burnett, Bart. of Crathes, out of the Keillor cow Beauty, and by the Keillor bull Strathmore 5. He also purchased a cow at the Keillor final sale in 1860 for £58, 10s., but she died of dropsy soon afterwards. In consequence of an accident to a Princess bull, Mr Ferguson acquired, about 1873, the bulls Lord Macduff 678, and Young Palmerston 982, from the Earl of Fife, but he has sold the whole of their progeny excepting one or two. In 1874 he bought from Mr M'Combie of Tillyfour the Pride bull Shah 680, who has proved a very good sire; and in 1876 he purchased Diana 1782, of the Daisy branch of the Queen tribe, at Lord Airlie's sale, for 61 guineas. Diana had been the highest priced animal at the Tillyfour sale in 1874, when she was bought by Lord Airlie for £79, 16s. Subsequently Mr Ferguson bought Diana's heifer calf, Pride of Kinnochtry 3289, after Juryman 404, from Lord Airlie. In 1877, at Mr Hannay's sale, was secured Heather Blossom 2nd 3395, of the Rothiemay Victoria family, and after Young Viscount 736. In 1879, at Mr Cartwright's sale at Melville, he bought the heifer calf Eugenie of Kinnochtry 4338, obtaining in her, after an interval of twenty-five years, a representative of one of the late Mr Ferguson's tribes. In the autumn of 1881 Mr Ferguson bought at the sale at Guynd the cow Nannie of the Guynd, sire Arthur of the Guynd 2nd 1168, dam Rose of Guynd 2598. He recently purchased a Pride bull, out of Pride of Aberdeen 17th 4078, from Mr Pearson of Johnston, for the purpose of mating with his Queen females. Among other recent additions to the herd were three Daisy heifers from Ballunie, three lively heifers from Corston, two heifers from Stone o' Morphie, four heifers of various families from Mr Pearson of Johnston, and eight or ten from other breeders. The herd at present numbers over one hundred head.

A few remarks about the sires used at Kinnochtry will be interesting. The first notable sires used were the early Keillor Jocks, as already mentioned. Both Black Jock 3 and Young Jock 4 were Mr Ferguson's property. They were as good as most of the bulls to be seen at the time present, and both were splendid getters. After them came Hugh 130 from Mr Watson, who had been using him. Hugh was the last calf of Old Grannie 1, and was also a very superior bull, leaving some excellent stock. The last Keillor stud bull President 3rd 246, bred at Balwyllo after President 2nd 54, and out of Isabella of Balwyllo 423,

was also used. He was a long, level, stylish bull, and a
prize-winner at the Highland Society. The Baronet 339,
bred at Crathes, but from Keillor stock, was also used.
He was quite equal to President 3rd as a getter, and was
kept for a good many years. In 1863, when eight years
old, he gained the first prize at the Scottish Midland Agricultural Society's show, and at Perth.

Young Hugh 131, after Hugh 130, and out of Prizie
586, was then used, being about the most gay and
stylish bull Mr Ferguson ever had. He was never
fed for showing, but in 1861 he was exhibited at the
Perth show of the Highland Society, and although in lean
condition was highly commended. Young Hugh carried
all before him at the local shows, and was sire of
the cow Princess 2nd 916, now sixteen years old, and who
has twice in lean condition beat Highland Society prize
cows. It was, Mr Ferguson informs us, mainly from this
bull that the Kinnochtry Princesses got their high-bred-
looking and characteristic heads. Young Hugh was sold
to Mr William Watson, who was then engaged breeding
polled cattle at Binns, near Dundee. After The Baronet
339 and Young Hugh 131, Crathie Jock 340, calved in
1865, was used. Bred by Mr Ferguson, he was out of
Princess of Kinnochtry 914, and got by The Baronet 339.
He gained a large number of prizes, and was a remarkable
instance of early maturity. Meeting with an accident
when under three years old, he was sold by weight to
Mr Young, Whitelawstone, near Dundee, when his four
quarters were found to weigh 132 stones dead weight.
After Crathie Jock, Crathie 2nd 342, also bred by Mr
Ferguson, was used. Crathie 2nd was got by The Baronet
339, out of Miss Scott 913, by Hugh 130; g.d. Beauty of
Kinnochtry 595, by Young Jock 4; g.g.d. Prizie 586, being
thus of the Baroness family. In Mr Ferguson's possession
he gained the first prizes as a yearling at the shows of the
Scottish Midland and Stormont Union Agricultural Societies

in 1868. He was sold when two years old to Mr William Owen of Blessington, County Wicklow, and in Mr Owen's possession won the first prize as a two-year-old at the National Show in Ireland in 1879, the first prize at the Royal Dublin Society's spring show in 1870, and the first prize at the Irish National Show the same year. Crathie 2nd was a lengthy, gay, fine handling, stylish bull, and Mr Owen kept him a long time. Mr Ferguson believes that this bull gave an impetus to the breeding of polled cattle in Ireland, leaving excellent stock in Mr Owen's herd, as he had done at Kinnochtry.

Alfred of Kinnochtry 341 calved 1868, out of Miss Scott 913, being thus a Baroness bull, and Keillor 2nd 433, out of Princess 914, a Princess bull, were then used. Keillor 2nd was out of Princess of Kinnochtry by her own son Crathie Jock, and Alfred was also by Crathie Jock, and out of Miss Scott 913, the same cow who bred Crathie 2nd, so that Mr Ferguson was at that time carrying out the principle of line breeding very decidedly. He has still a considerable number of the closely-bred cows in his herd by these two bulls, and they are all good, especially in respect of quality, style, and uniformity. Keillor 2nd 433 gained the first prize at the Scottish Midland show at Kinross in 1870, and the first prize at the Stormont Union Society's show at Meiklour. He was also highly commended at the Highland Society's show at Dumfries the same year. He was sold for 50 guineas to Mr Farrell of Moynalty, County Meath, and in his possesson gained several first prizes. Mr Ferguson considered him superior even to Crathie Jock, his sire. The bull Alfred was lame and was never shown, but he was a very excellent getter. He was sold to the West Indian Company, and was shipped to Demerara along with four other bulls—a Hereford, Devon, Shorthorn, and Ayrshire. Some of the other bulls died on the voyage, and all of them succumbed in that trying climate, except Alfred, who remained for several

R

years quite healthy and vigorous. Afterwards came Lord
Macduff 678, calved in 1872, and Young Palmerston 982,
calved in 1873, from Lord Fife. They did not give Mr
Ferguson satisfaction, and, as already stated, he has disposed
of most of their offspring.

In 1874, Shah 680, of the Pride tribe, joined the
herd. He left some excellent stock, and Mr Ferguson
has seven or eight five-year-old cows by him that are
of very high merit. Shah gained the first prize at
the show of the Royal Northern Agricultural Society in
1873, first prize and silver cup as the best bull in they ard
at the Stormont Union Agricultural Society's show in 1877,
first prize in the class of aged bulls at the Highland
Society's show at Dumfries in 1878, and the gold medal
in the class of extra stock at the Highland Society's show
at Perth in 1879. After him was used Prince of the
Realm 1695, got by Shah, and the sixteenth calf produced
by Princess of Kinnochtry 914. He is a fine server and as
good a getter as Mr Ferguson ever had. Prince of the
Realm was the first prize yearling at the Stormont Union
Society's show at Meiklour in 1879, the first-prize two-
year-old at the Highland Society's show at Kelso in 1880,
the second-prize aged bull at the Highland Society's show
at Stirling in 1881, and the same year he won the first
prize in his class and silver cup as best bull in the yard at
the Stormont Union Society's show at Alyth. Mr Ferguson also used Baron Balgersho 1696, previous to selling
him to Mr J. J. Rodgers, Angus Farm, Illinois, U.S.A., in
1881. The bulls chiefly used at Kinnochtey during the past
season were Prince of the Realm and his son Baron
Wharncliffe, the latter out of Mary of Kinnochtry 1770, of
the Baroness tribe.

After the foregoing minute account of the materials on
which the Kinnochtry herd is based, we need scarcely point
out that its striking feature is the large representation of
Keillor blood which it contains. When Mr Ferguson

communicated to us a note of the animals in his herd, he had no fewer than 50 descendants of Keillor families, made up as follows :—16 Princesses, 24 Baronesses, 7 Favourites, and 3 Emilys. Not only is the bulk of the herd descended from animals bred by Mr Hugh Watson, but the sires used have also partaken largely of Keillor blood. A short analysis of the pedigrees of Mr Ferguson's stock bulls will show this clearly. The first three bulls used— Black Jock 3, Young Jock 4, and Hugh 130—were bred by Mr Watson. The fourth, The Baronet 339, was, as we have seen, of Keillor blood. In President 3rd 246, a very judicious outcross was taken. This animal had in his veins an almost equal proportion of Keillor and Ardovie blood. Of the existing stock at Kinnochtry, his descendants are confined to one strain in the female line, that tracing to his daughter Princess of Kinnochtry 914, the foundress of the Princess tribe; but his blood has also been perpetuated in a more modified form in the male line by Crathie Jock 340, out of Princess of Kinnochtry 914, his two sons, Alfred of Kinnochtry 341, and Keillor 2nd 433, and Prince of the Realm 1695, a son of Princess of Kinnochtry 914, all of whom were used in the herd. Young Hugh 131, and Crathie 2nd 342, were of pure Keillor blood. The President blood thus so skilfully and sparingly introduced, has doubtless contributed to the preservation of the vigour and health of this closely-bred herd. The two bulls Lord Macduff 678, and Young Palmerston 982, failed perhaps more on account of dissimilarity of blood than owing to any individual deficiency. Scarcely any of their produce were retained, and none of their blood has been spread over the stock, so that their influence on the herd was in a permanent sense infinitesimal.

In Shah 680, Mr. Ferguson secured a bull marked by personal excellence, a member of the most celebrated show-yard tribe of the breed, and not entirely without connection with the predominant strains in his own herd; for while,

of course, Shah had all the early concentrated Panmure
and Ardovie blood, it will be found by working out his
pedigree to its terminations, that there occur in it the
names of Mr Watson's bulls, Grey-breasted Jock 2, Old
Jock 1, Angus 45, Pat 29, Strathmore 5, Adam 39, and
Maynooth 58. Prince of the Realm 1695, again, was a son
of Shah 680. The other sire used by Mr Ferguson last
season, Baron Wharncliffe, continues the slightly diluted
blood by his sire Prince of the Realm, while on the dam's
side his pedigree presents a remarkable concentration of
the Keillor strains. The close affinities on which the herd
has been raised is shown in another way. Since 1839,
Mr Ferguson has used, leaving aside the bulls Young
Palmerston and Lord Macduff, thirteen sires. Of these,
nine were descended from Old Grannie 1, one from
Favourite 2, one from Mr Watson's Beauty, while one each
have belonged to the Balwyllo Isabella and the Pride
tribes. It will be seen that practically the only decided
outcrosses resorted to by Mr Ferguson during his career as
a breeder, extending over forty years, have been those
introduced by President 3rd and Shah, and the dilution
must have been necessary, in the circumstances under
which the herd was kept, to prevent sterility and unhealthi-
ness.

Mr Ferguson has held no public sales, but he has disposed of polled cattle privately for the last forty-five years,
and of course a full account of transactions extending
over that long period would be impossible. A note of the
chief sales may, however, be given. Mr Ferguson has bred
about 400 bulls. The great majority of these were never
registered, but went to ordinary rent-paying stocks throughout the country. About the year 1850, fifteen heifers were
sold in one lot to a gentleman who had formerly kept the
inn at Castletown of Braemar, and was then a grazier in
the north of Scotland. About the same time twelve or
fourteen heifers were sold to Mr James Leslie, The Thorn,

and with these he founded his herd. They were, as already mentioned, descended from the stock obtained by Mr Ferguson from his father. In 1855 Mr Ferguson took the best portion of his herd from Ashmore to Kinnochtry, and during a few years subsequent to that date it was perhaps larger than it has been before or since. From the years 1855 to 1860, a great many pure-bred heifers and cows were sent from Ashmore to the fat market, higher average prices being then got for bulls than for females. By the time the lease of Ashmore expired in 1864, that farm was mostly stocked with ordinary keeping cattle. Previous to 1866, sixteen or seventeen cows and heifers, with some bulls, were sold to Mr Scott, Easter Tulloch.

During the last twenty years, a good many bulls have been sold to Ireland at prices ranging from 30 to 60 guineas. Amongst those in Ireland who have been supplied with bulls from Kinnochtry, were Mr. Owen, Blessington, County Wicklow; Mr. Farrell, Moynalty, Kells, County Meath; Sir Charles Knox Gore, Bart., Beleek, County Mayo; Mr S. E. Collis of Tieraclea, Tarbert, County Kerry. In 1875 two yearling Princess heifers were sold to the Marquis of Huntly, and the following year a yearling heifer of the Princess family, and one of the Favourite family, were sold to Sir W. G. Gordon Cumming, Bart. of Altyre. During the last twelve or fourteen years, no females of the Princess, Baroness, or Favourite families have been sold at a lower price than 60 guineas, the animals of these families disposed of being mostly yearlings. Since 1876 no females of these tribes have been sold in Scotland, excepting a Favourite heifer calf to Lord Airlie. At the Highland Society's show at Perth in 1879, three yearling heifers and a a yearling bull were sold to Mr F. B. Redfield, Batavia, New York, U.S. The heifers were Princess 8th 3298, 3rd Baroness 3294, and Favourite 9th 3295, while the bull was Field Marshal 1778 of the Baroness family. In the

spring of 1881, a yearling bull and two heifers were sold
to the Honourable J. J. Dowsett of Honolulu, Sandwich
Islands. The bull was of the Baroness family, and the
heifers were of the Mina family. In the spring of 1881,
nine bulls and seven heifers were shipped to Mr Redfield.
At the same time, three animals were shipped to Mr. J. J.
Rodgers, Angus Farm, Knox County, Abingdon, Illinois.
They were the cow Favourite 6th 3118, the heifer Baroness
8th 5039, and the bull Baron Balgersho 1696. In the
spring of 1882, twelve yearling heifers and two bulls were
sold to Mr Rodgers. The heifers were sold at very high
prices, and chiefly represented the Princess, Baroness, and
Favourite tribes.

Mr Ferguson has gained most of the prizes for polled
cattle at the shows of the Stormont Union Agricultural
Society since its establishment in 1854. During the time
the Scottish Midland Agricultural Society was in existence,
he also won nearly all the prizes offered by it. He has
on various occasions gained prizes at other local shows
and sales. Recently he has exhibited at the Highland Society's shows, and we have already indicated the
prizes won by him for bulls at these. In 1878 he gained
the first prize for yearling heifers with Princess 6th 3296.
At Stirling in 1881 he was awarded the gold medal for the
cow Princess of Kinnochtry 914, who was twenty-one
years old when exhibited. In 1877 and 1881, when
champion prizes were offered at the Stormont Union shows,
they were won by Mr Ferguson, in 1877 with a heifer out
of Mr Brown's Duchess of Westertown 927, and in 1881
with Princess 7th 3297.

Mains of Advie.

The Mains of Advie herd is worthy of special notice on
several grounds. It has achieved distinction in the local
show-yards ; it is almost entirely descended from one cow ;

it is characterized by great concentration of blood; and its history reflects credit on the Ballindalloch herd, from which it was derived, and on which it has been mainly built up. The herd was started by Mr Charles Grant about twenty years ago, at a time when it was doubted whether, for a farm like Mains of Advie, situated at a high altitude, without much shelter, and in a late, cold, and inclement district, any breed except the shaggy Highlanders could be reared with profit. Mr Grant's success in his enterprise undoubtedly stimulated the breeding of polled cattle in the district; and it is probable that to his efforts more than to any other circumstance may be ascribed the transformation that has occurred in the class of stock now found in the Grantown markets, which are resorted to for store cattle from many quarters of the north of Scotland. In 1862 Mr Grant purchased a polled cow from the herd of Sir George Macpherson Grant at Ballindalloch. Few people then paid much attention to pedigree, and Mr Grant asked for no information regarding the animal acquired by him, being quite satisfied that, coming from Ballindalloch, her breeding must be satisfactory, and that individually she was of more than ordinary merit. This cow was entered in vol. iv. of the 'Herd Book' as Old Rose of Advie 3104, calved 1859, bred by Sir George Macpherson Grant, sire Craigo 260, dam a pure polled cow. Craigo, we may recall, was after a bull bred at Balwyllo, and out of a cow bred at Keillor. When purchased, Old Rose was in calf to King Charles 236, bred at Kinnaird, a son of Druid 225 and Kathleen 339. The produce in 1862 was Rose of Advie 3105. In 1866 Rose 3105 was sent to Ballindalloch and mated with the famous bull Trojan 402, a half-brother on the dam's side to Pride of Aberdeen 581, being out of the Paris cow Charlotte 203, and after Black Prince of Tillyfour 366. From this union came Dandy of Advie 3106. Dandy is now fifteen years old, is still in the herd, and has bred some wonderfully good stock. She is

a massive cow, very thickly fleshed, well haired, and
short legged. Nearly all her calves have been prize-
winners, and to some of them we shall briefly allude.
Before doing so, however, we may mention the more important sires used in the herd, and thus show how closely
and ingeniously the herd has been bred.

The first sire used was Conqueror 1190, bred at
Drumin. He was after Disraeli 401, and his dam was by
Defiance 397 (got by Rob Roy Macgregor 267, the sire of
Black Prince of Tillyfour, who, as already remarked, was
the sire of Trojan), and out of Charlotte 203, Trojan's dam.
Then followed Elcho 595, bred at Ballindalloch, out of
Erica 843, and after Juryman 404, whose sire Bright 454
was a son of Black Prince of Tillyfour, and whose dam Jilt
973 was a daughter of Black Prince of Tillyfour. Elcho,
who is renowned in the annals of the breed as a heifer
getter, left more than sixty calves in the herd, and
thoroughly stamped upon it the Ballindalloch characteristics. After serving at Advie for three years, he was sold
back to his breeder Sir George Macpherson Grant, and
subsequently went to the Glamis and Cortachy herds.
The next sire used was none other than Elcho's sire Juryman 404, who had been for some time in Forfarshire. He
was bought at Lord Airlie's sale in 1876 for £60, and was
used for one season in the herd. The bulls First Fruits
1325, of the Westertown Victoria family, and First Attempt
1324, of the Westertown Rose family, both bred at Altyre,
were then introduced. They were both after the Sybil
bull Senator 863, a son of Scotsman 474. Highland Chief
1590, after Judge 1150, a son of Jilt and Scotsman, and
out of Miss Fanny 3111, by Juryman 404, was then used.
Another son of Judge, Baronet, was the next sire, his dam
being Maid of Aven 2995, who was after Elchies 563 (a son
of Juryman 404 and Eisa 977), and out of Bertha 980, by
Trojan. The present stock bull is Etonian 1658, after Elcho
595, and out of the Erica cow Eva 984, whose dam was Eisa

977, by Trojan 402. The selection of sires thus presents some features of considerable interest. The concentration of Erica and Queen blood will be observed, and scarcely less noteworthy is the close relationship of the animals.

The success of the system of breeding adopted by Mr Charles Grant, and followed by his son Mr John Grant, who now manages the herd, has been unquestionable. Of Dandy's calves, Emily 3110 was a famous prize-winner at Elgin, Grantown, and Inverness. Mayflower 3108; Violet, sold to Lord Lovat; Edith, sold to Mr Hannay; Evelyn 4119, sold to Lord Strathmore; and Young Juryman, sold to Mr Reid, Baads, were also very superior. Other specially good representatives of the Rose family were Miss Emily, sold to Mr Whitfield, America; Florence 3587, a frequent prize-taker at Grantown, Elgin, and Dingwall; Duchess 3585; Mayflower 4th 4439; Maggie May; Daisy 3586; Blanche 3588, etc. There are also in the herd a few specimens of other strains, but the bulk is of the Rose family. Important sales have been made to Sir George Macpherson Grant, Lord Lovat, Mr Hannay Gavenwood; the late Earl of Strathmore, Mr Whitfield, Rougemont, Ontario; Mr Hine, Ohio, etc. The herd, as we have indicated, has figured prominently in the show-yards at Grantown, Inverness, Elgin, Keith, and Dingwall, and has frequently won prizes for groups—perhaps the best testimony to the merit of a breeding stock.

CHAPTER XIII.

MAINS OF KELLY—Oldest existing pedigree herd—Founded in 1809 or 1810
—Mr Bowie's system of breeding—The Jenny, Martha, Lizzie, Ardestie,
Jennet, Guinea Pig, Victoria, and Wattie families—Celebrated bulls
bred at Mains of Kelly—Cupbearer 59, Hanton 228, Logie the Lairds,
Majors, Jim Crows, Victors, etc.—MELVILLE—Dandys, Prides, and
Mayflowers—METHLICK—The Mabel branch of the Pride family—
MINMORE—MONTBLETTON—Commenced in 1831—The late Mr Robert
Walker and the tenant of Wester Fintray—The Victoria, Charlotte,
Mayflower, and Isabella families—Sires used—Fame of the Mayflowers
—MONTCOFFER—MORLICH—The Windsor branch of the Queen tribe
—PITFOUR—Logie the Laird 3rd 862—PITGAIR—PORTLETHEN—
Established about 1818—The early animals in the herd—The Nackets
and Brown Mouths—Families now represented—The Mayflowers,
Miss Scotts, Lucys, Fannys, Nightingales, Livelys, Pansys, Julias,
Idas, Madges, etc.—Bulls used in the herd—PORTMORE—POWRIE—
Easter Tulloch Mayflowers—Madge of Portlethen 1217, and Monarch
1182.

Mains of Kelly.

THE oldest existing pedigree herd of polled cattle is
that belonging to Mr Alexander Bowie, Mains of Kelly,
Arbroath, and few have been more instumental in improving
the breed. Mr Bowie gives us the following account of
the foundation of his herd : " The herd was formed by my
father in 1809 or 1810, by the purchase of the cow Boysack from Mr Henry Lindsay Carnegie of Kimblethmont,
Arbroath. My father, when he came from Cockpen, near
Dalkeith, at once took a liking to the *blackskins,* and

purchased the best black bull he could find. This bull he mated with the cow Boysack, who, by the way, was thoroughly dodded, although she had a little white on her belly." Under the entry of the cow Lady Margaret 40, in vol. i. of the 'Herd Book,' the line of breeding pursued by Mr Bowie is very succinctly described: "Lady Margaret 40 and Jenny 55 were selected by Mr Bowie from his father's well-known herd (originated about 1810); and by breeding from the Old Jock 1 strain of blood and Panmure 51, some of the best stock bred at Mains of Kelly have been originated." The Old Jock strain was obtained in two forms, first by the purchase of Pat 29, bred by Mr Hugh Watson, after Old Jock 1, and out of Favourite 2; and by the purchase of Old Favourite, the dam of Old Jock 1, at the Keillor sale in 1848. The Panmure strain was introduced by the purchase of Earl Spencer 24 at Mr Fullerton's sale in 1844, and of Black Meg, the dam of Panmure 51. Earl Spencer was a son of Panmure 51, and Milkaway cf Ardestie 668. These then, briefly stated, were the chief materials on which Mr Bowie has built up his herd. It would be an endless task to mention all the celebrated animals bred by Mr Bowie during his long career, and this is the less necessary as unfortunately, owing to a protracted struggle with rinderpest and pleuro pneumonia, the existing representatives of the herd, although of great and widespread influence, are comparatively few in number. Mr Bowie's was one of the few large Forfarshire herds that emerged from the desolating period of cattle plague; but its owner suffered very severely, his stock having been reduced from ninety-three to twenty-one.

The fame of the Mains of Kelly herd has been chiefly acquired by the large number of splendid sires produced and used, with the most gratifying results, in it and other stocks; but before mentioning some of the more famous bulls bred by Mr Bowie, we may first briefly note the leading families that have been cultivated in the herd.

The oldest of these is that tracing to Jenny 55, who, as already mentioned, was selected by Mr Bowie from his father's herd. This strain is known as the Jenny family. The Martha family is descended from Mary, bred at West Scryne, her dam Black Meg having been the dam of Panmure 51. The Lizzie family was founded by Lizzie 227, as to whom we are able to give some information supplementary to that contained in the 'Herd Book.' Lizzie 227 was first called "Hanton," after the name of Mr Bowie's servant, from whom he bought the cow. Although it is stated in vol. i. of the 'Herd Book' that the age and breeder of Brunette 745 (the dam of Lizzie) were unknown, Mr Bowie informs us that she (Brunette) was bred by Mr Webster, farmer, Auchrenny, who had invariably sent his cows to the Mains of Kelly bulls. The Ardestie family had its origin in Bubona 762, bred by Mr Lyall, Old Montrose, after a bull bred by the Earl of Southesk, the first of the sort owned by Mr Bowie having been Ardestie 1183, bred by Mr. Fullerton, Ardovie. A family of Jennets was formed by the purchase from Mr M'Combie of Jenny of Tillyfour 353, after Hanton 228, and out of Young Jenny Lind 207, the first-prize two-year-old heifer at the Highland Society's show at Berwick in 1854. The Guinea Pig family traces to Cynthia 761, bred by Mr Fullerton.

The Victorias, which are the most prized female strain at Mains of Kelly, go back to Queen Mother 348, bought from Mr M'Combie at the Highland Society's show at Inverness in 1856. She bred in Mr Bowie's possession one calf, Victoria of Kelly 345, and it is from her that Mr Bowie's Victorias spring. The Watties are descended from Wattie 2243, bred by Mrs. Lyall, Arrat, after Rob Roy of Arrat 277. A family of Lucys has sprung from Lucy of Portlethen 287, bred by Mr Walker, Portlethen, after Fyvie 13. Mr Bowie, as we have noted, bought Old Favourite, the dam of Old Jock 1 and Angus 45, at Mr Watson's sale in 1848, but she left no female descendants at Mains of

Kelly, where, however, her blood is preserved in the male line by her son Earl Spencer 2nd 25. Lola Montes 208 also went to Mains of Kelly in her old age, and left a bull calf, Lurgan 429, but the strain has not been perpetuated there. The Raniston family, descended from Raniston 352, bought from Mr M'Combie, is now best known in connection with the Drumin and Mulben herds. The cow, Matilda Fox 302, bred by Mr. Bowie, went to Portlethen, and became the dam of Mr Walker's celebrated Fox Maule 305.

It is a notable circumstance that nearly all the Mains of Kelly families have produced a number of famous bulls. From the Jenny family came the well-known Cupbearer 59, after Pat 29, and out of Rose of Kelly 828, a daughter of Jenny. Rose of Kelly had only one calf, and at four years old, having missed service, she was killed. She gained three first prizes as yearling, two-year-old, and cow at the East Forfarshire Association's shows. Cupbearer won numerous prizes, among them first in the two-year-old and aged classes at Highland Society's shows. Mr Bowie informs us that this famous bull was a bad server until two or three years old; but after Lord Southesk got him, "he very soon filled Aberdeenshire with his stock, and was accordingly kept on by his lordship until he was eight years old, when he went off his legs and was killed for the butcher." For a description of Cupbearer and a record of his achievements, both at the stud and in the show-yard, we would refer our readers to the account of the first Kinnaird herd. Another famous bull of the Jenny family was Standard-Bearer 229, out of Lady Ann 2nd 346. He was bought by Mr M'Combie at Mr Bowie's sale at West Scryne in 1859 for £89, and gained the first prize at the Highland Society's show at Aberdeen the following year.

The Lizzie family has been wonderfully successful in bull breeding. From Lizzie 227 was bred in 1852 the

renowned bull Hanton 228, another son of Pat 29. He
gained the first prize at the Highland Society's show at
Berwick in 1854 as a two-year-old. Mr Bowie's herd was
admirably represented at this show, Cupbearer having been
first, Earl Spencer 2nd 25 second in the aged class, and
Hanton first in the two-year-old class. At the show Mr
M'Combie bought Hanton for the large sum of £105, and
his subsequent career is fully referred to in our notice of the
Tillyfour herd. The Lizzie family also produced a number
of bulls known by the name of Logie the Laird. The first
of these was sold along with Albert of Kelly 346, of the
Jenny family, to the Hon. Matthew Holmes, New Zealand.
The most distinguished bull of this tribe was, however,
Logie the Laird 3rd 862, purchased by Colonel Ferguson
of Pitfour for 100 guineas. After winning numerous
honours, among them the first prize in the aged class at the
Highland Society's show at Edinburgh in 1877, and doing
excellent service in the Pitfour herd, he was sold to
Captain Beedie, Pitgair. His portrait is given in vol. v. of
the 'Herd Book.' Logie the Laird 6th 1623, another bull
of the Lizzie family, was sold to Lord Airlie. The Jennet
family is associated with a race of bulls called Jim Crow.
Jim Crow 344, calved in 1861, after Young Panmure 232,
and out of Jenny of Tillyfour 353, was used at Mains of
Kelly, and gained the first prize as a two-year-old at the
Highland Society's show at Kelso in 1863. Jim Crow 3rd
350, after Leo 349 of the Lizzie family, and out of Jennet
904, a daughter of Jenny of Tillyfour, won the second prize
at the Highland Society's show at Edinburgh in 1869 as a
two-year-old. He was sold for 100 guineas to Mr
M'Combie of Tillyfour, and was used in the Tillyfour herd.

The Guinea Pig family has furnished several very fine
bulls, named Gainsborough. Gainsborough 596, out of
Guinea Pig 3rd 1182, and after Major 351, was first-prize
two-year-old and first in the aged class at Highland
Society's shows. He was sold to the Earl of Fife and

proved a valuable sire in the Duff House herd. His portrait appears in vol. iii. of the 'Herd Book.' Gainsborough 3rd 598, after Victor of Kelly 353, and out of Guinea Pig 3rd 1182, was sold to Mr M'Combie of Tillyfour for £80. From the Martha family, which, as already noticed, traces from Black Meg, the dam of Panmure 51, we have a lot of capital bulls named Major, among them, Major 3rd 662, after Jim Crow 3rd 350, and out of Martha 2nd 906, one of the most remarkable sires of the day. The Victoria family is well represented in the male line by the Victors of Kelly, while its female descendants are much valued, no less for their choice blood than their high individual merits. Mr Farquharson, East-Town, and Mr Hamilton of Skene, own a few fine specimens of this family. From the Ardestie and Wattie families the Ardo and Wallace of Kelly bulls are descended. The Lucys are more famous in the female line, and are well known both at Mains of Kelly and Drumin, but they also have begot a race of bulls named Leo. The best proof of the excellence of the Mains of Kelly bulls is found in the fact that, at seven shows of the Highland Society, the aged male class has been headed by animals bred by Mr Bowie. Mr Bowie has, since the introduction of Earl Spencer 24 and Pat 29, generally used bulls of his own breeding—mostly the Jim Crows, Logies, and Gainsboroughs. On two occasions, however, he went to Tillyfour for stock sires. He bought from Mr M'Combie Alford 221, calved in 1856, after Hanton 228, and out of Fair Maid of Perth 313; and his son Young Alford 1184 gained for Mr Pierson of The Guynd the first prize in the two-year-old class at the International show at Battersea in 1862. Mr Bowie also acquired from Mr M'Combie Young Panmure 232, after Hanton 228, and out of Crinoline 204, and with him won the first prize in the aged class at the Highland Society's show at Dumfries in 1860. Females from Mains of Kelly have very rarely been exhibited at the National shows, Mr Bowie entertaining strong opinions regarding the impolicy of pampering cows and heifers.

A sale of polled cattle was held by Mr Bowie at West Scryne in 1857, when some very high prices were realized. The average for twenty-four breeding animals was over £37, and twelve three-year-old bullocks averaged £30, 16s. 8d. At the joint sales the stock from Mains of Kelly have always been in demand. At Aberdeen, in 1876, a Victoria cow was sold for 106 guineas. Private sales have been made to Hon. Mr Holmes, New Zealand; Mr M'Combie of Tillyfour; the Earl of Southesk; the Earl of Airlie; Mr Smith of Benholm; the Earl of Fife; Colonel Ferguson of Pitfour; Mr Melville Cartwright; Mr Farquharson, East-Town; Messrs Anderson & Findlay, Lake Forest, Chicago, etc. The herd at present comprises 22 cows and heifers and 2 bulls, exclusive of calves, which are very numerous.

Melville.

The Melville herd, belonging to Mr T. L. Melville Cartwright, was started in 1871 by the purchase of a few animals at Mr Leslie's sale at The Thorn, near Blairgowrie. These animals included the bull Colonel of Castle Fraser 443, the third-prize yearling at the Highland Society's show that year. He afterwards gained the first prize at the Scottish Midland show, and at the Highland Society's show in 1872; and in 1873, at the Highland Society's show at Stirling, he won the first prize in the aged class. The animals acquired at The Thorn were afterwards supplemented by the purchase, in 1873, of a heifer Victoria 6th 1409 (bought privately from Mr Bowie, Mains of Kelly), of the Queen blood, from whom the Lily family at Melville is descended; and by some purchases at the Westertown dispersion in 1874, including the old cow Dandy 949, of the Empress branch of the Queen family. In 1878 a purchase was made at the

Rothiemay sale, viz. Nugget 1796 ; while the same year at Tillyfour, Pride of Aberdeen 12th 3254 was added, both these animals being of the Pride family. In 1879 two purchases were made at the Aboyne sale, viz. Marjorie 2574, of the Madge family, and Princess 2nd 2570, of the Kinnochtry Princess family. The latter turned out a bad investment, as she proved not in calf, and has never bred. In 1880 at Glamis, Blackbird of Corskie 4th 3769 was bought. In 1881 the cow Peep o' Day 3570, of the Rothie-may Georgina family, was secured at Mr Adamson's sale ; while at Mr Hannay's sale the grand old matron Black-bird of Corskie 1704, of the Montbletton Mayflower family, was added. In 1879 a large draft, consisting of nearly 60 head, were sold by auction. They comprised chiefly all the animals with short pedigrees—in fact, Mr Cartwright weeded out the stock of inferior pedigree ; but there were five sold of the Queen blood, and they averaged £45, 11s. per head, although one of them was a heifer calf only six months old, and she fetched £57, 15s. The present herd consists of about 30 head, of which nearly half are of the Queen blood. Mr Cartwright has exhibited very seldom, as he prefers to keep the herd in a thoroughly good breeding condition, and not to feed his cattle for exhibition. Besides the bull already mentioned, Colonel of Castle Fraser, Black Prince 1244 gained the first prize as a yearling at the Highland Society's show at Dumfries in 1878 ; the fourth prize at the Kilburn show in 1879, where he had to compete with aged bulls ; and the fourth prize at the Highland Society's show at Perth in the same year. The sires now in use in the herd are the aged bull St Clair 1160, of the Erica tribe, and a young bull bred by Mr Cartwright, The Moor 1753, of the Pride tribe.

Methlick.

Mr John Grant established a herd at Methlick in 1873

S

His first purchase was at the Easter Tulloch sale that year,
when he acquired the cow Alice of Methlick 1760, by
Lord Southesk's Theodore 393. The same year at Drumin
he purchased Mary of Methlick 1761, after the Tillyfour
sire Disraeli 401, and out of Daisy 952, of Mr Skinner's
Lucy tribe. At Portlethen, in October 1874, Mr Grant
bought Jackdaw 1982, of Mr Walker's Julia family, and
the bull Lauderdale 671, after Melrose 382, bred at Castle
Fraser, and out of Louisa 658, tracing to the Ardovie
herd. Lauderdale was used for some years as stock sire.
At the Bognie dispersion in 1874, Mr Grant was a large
purchaser of representatives of the Greenskares and
Beauty tribes, full of the blood of Lord Southesk's Odin
153. At Rothiemay, in the autumn of 1875, Glenaven
1491, bred at Drumin, was added to the herd for 47
guineas. Mr Grant's most important purchase, however,
was at the Tillyfour sale in 1874, when he secured, as a
heifer calf, at 25 guineas, Mabel 1801, of the Pride tribe.
Mabel is after Bismarck 428, and is a grand-daughter of
Pride of Aberdeen 581. The heifer turned out a most
profitable investment, for Mr Grant now owns ten female
specimens of this valuable family. Mabel has been a very
true breeder. Her calves have likewise bred well, and are
remarkable for family type, being evenly fleshed, with
beautiful polled heads. They grow to large sizes, and are
very easily kept. As stock sire Lauderdale 671 was succeeded by Knight of Aven 775, bred at Drumin, out of
Dandy 949, of the Queen tribe. He cost 70 guineas at
the Brucklay dispersion. At the Tillyfour dispersion Mr
Grant bought the Pride bull Knight of the Garter 1763,
a son of Pride of Aberdeen 5th 1174, and of the Daisy
bull Dragon 1178. The herd has been drafted by sales at
Alford and Aberdeen, and a considerable lot was sold at
fair prices at Methlick in 1880. That year two heifers
were sold privately to Mr Taylor, Reigate, near London,
for £30 each. In 1882 the Pride cow Mabel 3rd 3235

with her calf, and the bull calf Baron Formartine, were
sold to Messrs Bell & Henderson, New Zealand, for £210;
and the Pride heifer Mabel 6th 4295 went to Mr Wilken,
Waterside, of Forbes, at £105, for exportation to America.
The herd numbers 30 cows and heifers, with 20 calves,
and the stock sire.

Minmore.

The foundation of this herd was laid by Major Smith in
1876 by the purchase for 51 guineas, at the Ballindalloch
sale, of the well-bred cow Nonsense 2158, of the Keepsake
family, bred by Sir George Macpherson Grant. Nonsense
was a cow of superior quality, good shapes, and substance,
and was frequently a prize-taker at local shows. At
Minmore her first calf was in 1878, the heifer Verbena
4793; and her next calf was also a heifer, viz. Alicia
4794, both by the bull Victory 1364. They are both in
the herd, and are now fine, strong cows of excellent
quality. Verbena's calf of last year was a heifer by
Viscount Duff 1365, and she also is very promising;
while her calf of this year is a bull that looks exceedingly
well. Alicia has a fine cow calf at foot by Canute 1601.
Another and the last calf from Nonsense was Marigold
4798, sire Scobieleoff 1526, calved in March 1880, and she
promises to turn out as well as the rest of the family.
Nonsense then, not being in calf, was sold for fat show
purposes, and gained some prizes. Major Smith next
acquired the heifer Queen Mary 7th 4791, calved 1875,
bred by the late Mr Paterson, Mulben, and she has proved
an uncommonly good cow, a first-rate milker, and a
regular breeder. Her first calf was Queen Mary 14th
4792, calved March 23, 1878, after the Ballindalloch bred
bull Barrister 804. This cow is one of the best animals
in the herd, being an excellent milker, and of good shapes
and quality. She has a nice heifer calf at foot by
Viscount Duff 1365. Another of Queen Mary's calves

is Queen Mary 15th 4795, calved in April 1879, sire
Victory 1364, a very good-looking cow. Major Smith
bought at the sale at Ballindalloch, in 1879, the cow
Nosegay 3rd 2157, who produced, on 10th February 1880,
twin heifer calves to the prize bull Judge 1150; but
failing next year to have a calf, she was sent to the
butcher. Her two calves are now two years old, fine,
substantial, level heifers, doing credit to the good blood
they inherit from their sire and dam. In 1880 Major
Smith purchased at Burnside the heifer Honesty 5th
3761, bred by Mr Robertson, Burnside. She is of the
famous Drumin Lucy tribe, and is the best milker in the
herd. Her first calf in 1881 was a bull by Viscount Duff,
and this year she has a fine heifer calf by the same sire.
Major Smith this year bought from Mr Robert Bruce,
Great Smeaton, the capital cow Patience of Corskie 1932,
bred by the late Mr James Skinner, Drumin. She has at
foot a very strong, fine-looking bull calf by Challenger
1260. Patience, it will be remembered, was dam of Lord
Airlie's celebrated heifer Pavilion 3772. The sire bought
in 1882 for use in the herd was Whig 1867, bred by Sir
George Macpherson Grant, out of Elma 3368, and after
Editor 1460. Whig is thus strong in the fashionable
Erica blood, and has proved himself a sure getter of good
stock.

Montbletton.

An historic interest attaches to the herd at Montbletton,
founded by the late Mr Robert Walker in 1831. Mr
Walker was son of Mr David Walker, Blair of Fintray,
and nephew of Mr Robert Walker, tenant of Wester
Fintray and Suttie. In a former chapter we have alluded
to the fact that Dr Skene Keith, in his 'View of Agriculture in Aberdeenshire,' published in 1811, quotes, as
evidence of the early fame of Aberdeenshire cattle, some
exploits in feeding by Mr Walker, Wester Fintray. It is

established, we think, that these cattle were of the polled breed. Mr Walker, Wester Fintray, appeared at shows as a breeder and exhibitor of polled cattle; some of his stock were among the first introduced to the Tillyfour herd, and the late tenant of Montbletton recollected having seen at Blair, in 1826, a beautiful polled heifer sent from his uncle's farm at Wester Fintray. On entering Montbletton in 1831, Mr Walker brought with him polled cattle from Blair, and these doubtless had some connection with the stock at Wester Fintray. In the existing herd at Montbletton, the blood of the Wester Fintray polled cattle is directly represented. As we have indicated, therefore, the Montbletton herd possesses an interest beyond that excited by its own excellence, inasmuch as it can be traced to the herd of Mr Walker, Wester Fintray, one of the most famous, as it was one of the earliest, of improved polled stocks in Aberdeenshire.

Although Mr Walker commenced breeding polled cattle at Montbletton in 1831, the records of the present herd do not enable us to speak with precision about its members until 1849. The cause of the break was inattention to pedigree. There was then no 'Herd Book,' and it was not until the collection of materials for that publication was begun in 1850 that Mr Walker kept notes of the breeding of his cattle. The herd, which has always been of considerable dimensions, is descended from not more than half-a-dozen females. The first animal of which a record has been retained was introduced to the herd in 1849. This was Victoria of Fintray 607, bred by Mr James Collie, Middleton of Fintray, after Panmure of Middleton 37, and out of Lady Margaret of Fintray 785. She was the foundress of the Montbletton Victoria family. At the Tillyfour sale in 1850, the cow Young Charlotte 103, bred by Colonel Dalgairns, Balgavies, after Black Hugh 316, and the winner of the first prize at the Highland Society's show in 1848, was acquired for £35. From

her descends the Charlotte family at Montbletton. At
the Craigo sale in 1856, Lady Craigo 99 was purchased for
£42. She was in calf to Craigo 260, whose dam was bred
at Keillor. The produce was Mayflower 614, the foundress
of the best family at Montbletton. The next purchase
was Heiress of Balwyllo 461, of the Balwyllo Isabella
family, bred by Mr Scott, and bought at the Powis sale
in 1859 by Mr M'Combie of Tillyfour. Heiress was the
first-prize yearling heifer at the Highland Society's show
at Edinburgh in 1859, and Mr Walker gave 53 guineas
for her at Tillyfour in 1860. Laurel Leaf 1397, of the
Portlethen Lively family, was acquired at Portlethen in
1873. Coquette 3rd 1402 came from Ballindalloch in
1872 for 40 guineas; and Pride of Alford 1778, of the
Zara family, the first-prize yearling at the Highland
Society's show at Kelso in 1872, was bought at the
Tillyfour sale in 1874 for 60 guineas, along with her
heifer calf Pride of Montbletton 2204.

The earlier sires used were bred at Montbletton, but no
particulars regarding them can be obtained. Fintray 125,
bred by Mr Walker, Wester Fintray, was also used. A
daughter of his was put to Lord Southesk's Odin 153, and
the produce in 1857 was The Earl 291, one the best bulls
that has been in the Montbletton herd. He won the
second prize as a yearling, and first as a two-year-old, at
the Highland Society's shows in 1858 and 1859. At
Tillyfour in 1860 an important purchase was made. The
bull calf Tam o' Shanter 491 was then added at the high
price of 47 guineas. Tam o' Shanter was individually of
high promise, and his breeding was of the best, for he was
out of Lola Montes 208, the dam of the renowned Charlotte
203, and after the celebrated Hanton 228. The bull was
invincible as a yearling, standing first at the local shows,
at Aberdeen, and at the Highland Society's show at Perth.
He was also first at Aberdeen in 1862 and 1863, and did
excellent service in the herd. His son, Black Diamond

464, out of Heiress 461, was also used in the herd. Another good bull introduced from Tillyfour was Squire 436, after Disraeli 401, and out of Edith 1194, of the Zara family. Hampton 492, bred at Castle Fraser, and the sire of some famous animals, was also used at Montbletton. The bulls recently used have been bred at Duff House and Gavenwood. The principal stock sire at present is Young Hero 1837, bred by Mr Hannay, after Young Viscount 736, and out of Heroine 3016, of the Rothiemay Victoria tribe.

The favourite families at Montbletton are those descended from Heiress of Balwyllo 461, Lady Craigo 99, and Young Charlotte 103. Lady Craigo's descendants have been particularly successful as breeders and in the show-yard. Her first calf, Mayflower 614, won the second prize as a cow at the Highland Society's show at Perth in 1861; but the first-prize cow failing to breed, she obtained that honour. Mayflower's daughter, Mayflower 2nd 1020, who lived to the age of sixteen or seventeen, bred fourteen calves, some of them of great merit. One of these calves, Lady Ida 1021, carried numerous prizes, and is still in the herd, having proved herself one of the most useful matrons of the breed. When we heard from Montbletton, she was expected to drop her fourteenth calf. A very valuable race of cattle has sprung from Lady Ida. Her daughter, Blackbird of Corskie 1704, was acquired by the Earl of Fife, and produced Blackbird 2nd 3024, who, in 1879, stood first in the class of cows at the Highland Society's show at Perth. Innes 1934, Lord Fife's first-prize cow at the Highland Society's show at Aberdeen in 1876, was out of Jinny 1017, bred at Montbletton, so that both directly and indirectly this old-established herd has had a good share of the highest show-yard distinctions.

Since Mr Walker's death in 1880 the herd has been carried on by his niece, Miss Cruickshank. It numbers sixteen cows, with their calves, ten heifers, and two bulls.

Mr Walker held a public sale in 1862, when Mayflower 614 was bought by Mr M'Combie of Tillyfour for £63. Private sales of considerable importance have been made to the Earl of Fife, Mr Hannay, Gavenwood ; Sir George Macpherson Grant, and several breeders in the district ; while specimens of the herd are also to be found in England and America.

Montcoffer.

Mr John Strachan, on entering the farm of Montcoffer, on 15th May 1881, purchased from Mr Hannay nineteen polled animals, which formed an excellent foundation for his herd. Some of these ceased breeding, and from that cause and other accidents there are now in the herd only twelve of the lot. These are—Errolline 1698, by Duke of Cornwall 643, descended from the old Mains of Hatton herd; Guava 3836, by Laird of Bognie 935, from the same stock ; Islet 4833, by Blairshinnoch 1307, of the Rothie-may Victoria family; Damson 3835, by Laird of Fyvie 934, from the Mains of Hatton stock; Finery 4835, by Blairshinnoch 1307, tracing to Old Lady Jean 187 at Rothiemay ; Quince 3839, by Laird of Fyvie 934, from the Auchlin stock ; Queen Bee 4830, by Blairshinnoch 1307, descended from Old Lady Jean 187 ; Walnut 3840, by Laird of Fyvie 934, from the Auchlin stock ; Braw Bell 4832, by Blairshinnoch 1307, of the Rothiemay Victoria family ; Tansy 4834, by Blairshinnoch 1307, of the Rothiemay Victoria family ; Caranella 4837, by Young Viscount 736, of the Mulben Caroline family ; Branch 4836, by Blairshinnoch, sprung from the Arratsmill stock. In February 1881 there were purchased from Mr Steven-son, Blairshinnoch, Pansy 3rd 4660, by Nubian 1294, tracing to Old Lady Jean 187 ; Sabrina of Blairshinnoch 4310, by Nubian 1294, off Arratsmill stock ; and Lilly 2nd 4309, by Nubian 1294, tracing to Old Lady Jean 187.

From Mrs Morison of Mountblairy, in December 1881, were bought Flora of Mountblainy 4878, by Royal Hope 1207, of the Ballindalloch Sybil family; and Frisk 4417, similarly bred. At Mr Bow's sale at Newton of Mountblairy, in May 1881, the following additions were made:—Rosie of Newton 2307, by Andrew Lammie 3rd 1193, of the Fyvie Flower family; Milkmaid 3454, by Dr Livingstone 582, of the same strain; and Verbena of Mountcoffer. At the Aberdeen joint sale in 1881 Miss Rosa 3691, bred by Colonel Ferguson of Pitfour, after Duke of Perth 357, and from the Westertown Rose family, was bought; Coquette 4th 3497, of the Ballindalloch Coquette family, was bought at the Mountcoffer sale in 1881. Bella 3rd 4123, by Major 3rd 662, was bought from Mr Leggat, Midtown; Lady Fancy, out of Annie 2nd of Morlich 4257, of the Windsor branch of the Queen family, from Mr Leggat, Pitfancy; Halcyon 5012, of the Zara family, from Mr Cowie, Easter Montbletton; Beauty of Dyce, out of Beauty of Kinnochtry 1884, of Kinnochtry blood, from Mr Williamson, Standing Stones; and Waterside Rose 2405, from Mr Gibson, Bogside of Eden. Several of these cows have gained prizes at local shows. The stock sire is Editor 1460, bred at Ballindalloch, after the Paris bull Judge 1150, and out of Edith 2973, of the Erica family. He was used for some time in the herd at Ballindalloch. As a yearling he was second at Elgin, and commended at Dumfries; as a two-year-old second at the Royal Northern at Aberdeen, and highly commended at the Highland Society's show at Perth. He has also been first in the aged class at Elgin, Dufftown, Banff, and Turriff. Most of the cows mentioned have produced calves, and the herd numbers over forty head. This year Mr Strachan has sold seven bull calves at an average of £31, three of which have gone to America; and four heifer calves for £175, also to America.

Morlich.

Mr Cran, Morlich, Towie, has been breeding polled
cattle for a long time.   He was fortunate enough to procure from Mr M'Combie of Tillyfour the cow Beauty of
Morlich 2072, and she has proved a most fortunate investment.   Calved in 1854, she was got by Angus 45, and out
of that grand-breeding cow Windsor 202, of the Queen
tribe, the dam of Lord Southesk's Windsor 221, and of
Mr M'Combie's Rob Roy Macgregor 267.   Beauty of
Morlich 2072 has left a numerous and excellent progeny.
The strain is held in high repute, and worthily so no less
on personal merits than on account of the choice Tillyfour
blood which it alone in the female line preserves.   Mr
Cran does not show except at the local meetings at Tarland
and Kildrummy, and he had the honour of gaining on one
occasion the challenge cup presented by Her Majesty the
Queen with one of the descendants of Windsor.   Another
very lucky purchase by Mr Cran was the bull Balwyllo
Eclipse 781, bought at the Balwyllo sale in 1863 for 23
guineas.   He was after Sir William Wallace 308, and out of
Princess Royal 444, by Cupbearer 59, of the Victoria family
at Balwyllo.   This bull was used with satisfactory results
in the herd.   Among other sires introduced were Bogfern
901, bred by Mr Shaw, after the Highland Society's first-
prize bull Palmerston 374, and tracing on the dam's side
to the Keillor herd; and Marshal Var 1452, bred by Mr
Hannay, got by Young Viscount 736, and of the Castle
Fraser Mina tribe.   Mr Cran has made a good many
sales privately, and his bull calves have always fetched
high prices at the Aberdeen joint sales.

Pitfour.

The foundation of Colonel Ferguson's herd at Pitfour
was laid in 1869, by the purchase of two heifers from

Easter Skene; and another heifer, Bella 1477, of the
Blanche family, was added at the Castle Fraser dispersion.
The next addition was Mysie by Bright 454, from Tillyfour. At the Rothiemay sale in 1872, Diana 1185, and
Deveron Banks 1492, were bought. Periwinkle 902,
descended from Mr Hugh Watson's cow Panmure 248,
was acquired at the Portlethen sale in 1874, and Buxom
Polly 2240, of the Easter Skene Queen of Scots family,
came from the Garthdee sale in 1875. In that year the
herd received a temporary check through foot and mouth
disease. Several of the above-mentioned cows slipped or
had dead calves, and three had to be fed for the butcher
in consequence of their udders spoiling. Rosemary 936,
of the Rose family, was bought at the Westertown sale.
Martha 4th 2254, of Mr Bowie's breeding, was obtained at
the joint sale at Aberdeen in 1876. Isla of Corskie 2999,
of Drumin descent, was bought at the Corskie sale. Tifty
of Fyvie 1527, of the Fyvie Flower family, was purchased
in 1879. The next purchase was Cumberland Lass 3970,
of the Rothiemay Victoria family, at the Tillyfour dispersion. Some of the strains noted have dropped out, only
the best having been kept and bred from. Among those
now in the herd, the Virtues, tracing from Mally 2299,
bought at Easter Skene in 1869, are perhaps the nicest,
although not the heaviest in the herd. They have always
come to the front at the local shows, and have been in the
prize lists at Aberdeen. The Dianas from Rothiemay
have been found a profitable rent-paying race, being large
fleshy animals, and mostly good milkers. From this sort
the prize cow Dulcet 4057 sprang. As a heifer and cow
she always stood first at the Buchan shows. When three
years old she was second at the Highland Society's show
at Kelso, and was first in the polled Derby at Keith. At
first the Mysies from Tillyfour were rather small, but
being crossed with the well-known bull Logie the Laird
3rd 862, they are coming out much larger in frame, while

retaining all the flesh of the matron cow. They are also
very good milkers, and there are of the family some promising youngsters. The family descended from Periwinkle
is also good, and likely to keep its ground in the herd.
The other families, particularly those from Cumberland
Lass and Tifty of Fyvie, promise well.

The first bull used was Aberdour 627. Sprung from a
very old race of cows, Aberdour, though small in size, was of
extra quality, and has left that characteristic on his offspring.
The most important acquisition to the herd was Logie the
Laird 3rd 862, from Mr. Bowie, Mains of Kelly, at £100,
considered a long price at the time. He was the stock
bull for four years, and raised the character of the herd
considerably. He had a very successful show-yard career,
having been first as a yearling at the Angus show at
Montrose; third at the Highland Society's show at Aberdeen as a two-year-old; first at the Highland Society's
show at Edinburgh in 1877, and first at the Royal Northern
the same year; while in 1878 he gained the challenge cup
as best polled breeding animal at Aberdeen. In 1881 he
was sold to Captain Beedie, Pitgair. Marischal Keith
1627, of the Lucy tribe, purchased from Mr Skinner,
Drumin, followed Logie in the herd. He was a massive,
lengthy bull, with a great amount of flesh, but perhaps
not so stylish as Logie. He did fairly well in the show-
yard, having been first yearling at Aberdeen, second at
Kelso, and second two-year-old at Aberdeen, and third at
Stirling. In consequence of an accident, he was sent to
the butcher in 1882. His calves promise well. The present stock bull is Lord Maurice 1881, bred at Rothiemay,
out of that fine Georgina cow Kate Darling 3573, and after
Sir Maurice 1319.

A few animals have been sold from the herd to go
abroad. Diana's yearling heifer was sold in 1878 to
Messrs Anderson & Findlay, Chicago. In 1879 the
yearling bull Virtuoso 1626, and one of the Mysies, was

sold to the agent for Senor Don Carlos Guenero, Buenos
Ayres, South America. These were the first of the breed
that were ever sent to South America. A year afterwards
the agent for the same gentleman bought one of the
Westertown Roses. The herd at present numbers fifty
to sixty pure-bred animals, comprising six Virtues from
Easter Skene, eight Mysies from Tillyfour, ten Dianas
from Rothiemay, seven Panmures from Portlethen, three
Westertown Roses, two Fyvie Flowers, four Pollys from
Easter Skene, and two Marthas from Mains of Kelly.

Pitgair.

The present herd at Pitgair, Gamrie, was founded by
Captain Beedie in 1865, by the purchase of Mayflower
2376, and other two polled cows, Mary and Polly, at the
displenish sale of his predecessor in the farm, Mr Sangster,
who had kept a black polled herd exclusively for at least
eighteen years previous to 1865, as he appears from the
records of the Highland Society to have been an exhibitor
at the show in 1847. Unfortunately, as in many of these
earlier herds, no record of pedigrees was made down to the
time that the animals came into Captain Beedie's possession. The bull in use at Pitgair when the dispersion of
the herd took place in 1865, and the sire of two of the
cows above mentioned (Mayflower and Mary), was Pitgair
952, bred by Mr Ruxton, Farnell, after Lord Clyde 249,
and out of Eva 450, by President 2nd 54. Captain Beedie
has added since, the cow Dandy of Glenbarry 1075, of the
Drumin Lucy tribe, purchased at Mr. Tayler's sale at
Rothiemay in 1872, the winner the first prize at the
Highland Society's show at Perth in 1871, as a yearling
heifer; Ellen 3rd 2365, from Mulben, bought as a two-
year-old at the dispersion of that herd; Shevado Gem
3032, bought a calf at the dispersion of the Brucklay herd;
Maiden 2nd 1743, bought at Mr Hannay's sale in 1877,

winner of the second prize at the Royal Northern show in
1874; and Bathy 1525, tracing through Miss Watson to
the Keillor cow Favourite 2. Bathy was acquired at the
Fyvie Castle dispersion in May 1881.

The earlier sires used were Duke of Cornwall 643,
and John Bright 642, winner of the first prize at the
Royal Northern show in 1874, and second at the Highland
Society's show the same year. The sires lately used have
been Jester 472, bred by Sir George Macpherson Grant,
out of Jilt 973, and winner of the fourth prize at the
Highland Society's show in 1874, also first at the Banff
and Turriff shows; and Gamrie Mhor 1240, of the Windsor
branch of the Queen tribe, bred by Mr Cran, Morlich,
winner of numerous first prizes, and four Highland
Society's medals at local shows. The present stock bull
is Logie the Laird 3rd 862, winner of the first prizes at
the Royal Northern and Highland Society's shows in
1877, and of the challenge cup, as best breeding animal in
the polled sections at Aberdeen. The herd numbers
thirty-seven animals, as follows:—nine descended from
Polly, bought in 1865; seven Pitgair Mayflowers; four
descended from the cow Mary, bought in 1865; seven
Lucys; two Fyvie Gems; and two Miss Watsons. Captain
Beedie sold in November 1879, by public auction, eleven
females; five cows averaged £25, 10s, 2 two-year-olds £26,
and 4 yearlings £17. Previous to that and since, he has
sold privately six animals, viz., Lass, out of Dandy 1075,
and Maiden, out of Maiden 2nd, to Mr Wilken for exportation; Mayflower 12th; May Morn, out of May 2557;
with two bulls to Mr. Findlay, Peterhead, for clients in the
United States. For the last three years the average for
bull calves has been—1880, £25; 1881, £28, 9s.; and
1882, £33, 5s. No animals have been fed for show
purposes or exhibited, except at the local shows, where
many prizes have been gained for males and females. The
cows are kept in a natural breeding state, and have bred

regularly. Mayflower 2376, calved in 1865, produced her
first calf when two years old, and bred every year afterwards up to 1881, when she was sold to the butcher at
sixteen years old. With one exception, Captain Beedie
has never had a cow that missed calf.

Portlethen.

Among herds that have contributed most substantially
to the improvement and extension of the breed, that at
Portlethen occupies a high position. The first bull used
in the herd was Colonel 145, calved prior to 1818, being the
oldest animal, the date of whose birth is given in the
'Herd Book.' It was some years later, however, before
the late Mr. Robert Walker established the pedigree herd,
which rapidly acquired a great reputation not only in
Scotland, but also in France. Mr George J. Walker,
the present owner of the herd, furnishes us with the
following note regarding it:—"The first known to me
about the herd is the fact that in 1818 the bull in use was
called Colonel, a prize bull of his day, and Porty his son.
At that time there appears to have been two distinct tribes
—the Nackets, a short-legged, neat, black animal; and the
Brown Mouths, a lengthy beast, and coloured as named.
These are all gone. Bulls were got, as far as I can see, from
Mr Walker, Fintray, and Mr Hector, Fernyflatt—that is,
from 1826 to 1836. Later, they were obtained from
Crathes and from the produce of females brought from
Ardestie, Mains of Kelly, Kinnaird, etc. All our best
bulls of late years—say since 1856—have been home-bred.
Within my recollection none but polled cattle have been
kept at Portlethen. The first draft sale I remember was
in 1847. There was one, I think, in 1843, but I have no
record of it. Banks of Dee 12; the Andrews—Andrew 8
and Young Andrew 9; Raglan 208, for whom the late
Emperor Napoleon offered £230 at the Paris show in 1856;

Marquis 212, who there had second prize ; Fox Maule 305, and Palmerston 374, were perhaps the crack bulls. The herd at one time numbered 120 head. It is now only a little more than half, close on 70. A famous old cow called Duchess went to America when, I think, fifteen years old. This must have been about 1850. The first regular ' Herd Book' kept is dated 1840, at least this is the first of which I can find any trace."

Mr H. H. Dixon, when collecting information in 1865 for ' Field and Fern,' visited Portlethen and gleaned some facts about the herd. He says : " We were just in time to see the last of Fox Maule, by universal consent the best Angus bull that has been seen in Scotland for many a long year. He was by Mr Watson's Marquis 212, from Mr Bowie's Matilda Fox, by Cupbearer 59, a dam which never failed. Mr Martin had been there the day before, and declared that he never killed a heavier beast, save one, as he proved, at 13½ cwt. *plus* 13 imperial stones of fat. It was a rare treat to see him come out, with every point so beautifully fitted into each other and bevelled off, and that ' neat Roman head set on like a button ; ' but he was nearly five years old, and had been sadly chary of his duplicates ; and therefore the second-prize two-year-old bull at Stirling, the blood-like Jehu by Duke of Wellington 219, from Young Jean 295, by Captain of Ardovie 63, was captain in his stead. The herd was commenced by Mr Robert Walker in 1826, by Brown Mouths and Nackets, which were left him by his father. Porty by Colonel 145, from the tribe of Rosie, ' a dowry cow,' whose milking sort had been in the family since 1778, crossed well with both these tribes. Colonel was a Nackets bull, with rather a brown back, and so crusty that he had three years of penal servitude at the plough. There was no Aberdeen show in Porty's day, but, although he was rather small, his nice shape and peculiarly fine bone brought him up first at Inverurie, and a cross with his own sister helped

not a little to improve the quality of the herd. It was
with Marquis 212 and Raglan 208, by Young Andrew 9,
that Portlethen stood second and third to Mr M'Combie's
Hanton at Paris; and he valued the blood of Raglan so
highly in consequence of his dam Young Miss Alexander
(who died from inflammation of the brain through the
scratch of a thorn) having only left one other calf behind,
that he declined the imperial offer of £230, and priced him
at £400."

In the period that has elapsed since the establishment
of the herd, many strains that were cultivated at Portlethen
have become extinct. Mr. Walker has informed us of the
disappearance of the Nackets and Brown Mouth sorts.
It is gratifying to find, however, that at least a dozen
families associated with the Portlethen herd are still
represented. The oldest of these trace from Old Maggie
681, Miss Scott 679, and Miss Alexander 678. The
descendants of Old Maggie are known as the Mayflowers,
latterly at Easter Tulloch. The strain had the crosses of
the Portlethen bulls Porty 50, Stanley 14, and Duke of
Wellington 219, the cow Bamba 1200 having been acquired
by Mr Scott, Easter Tulloch. Young Andrew 9, referred
to by Mr Walker as one of the crack bulls at Portlethen,
was of this family; and its most distinguished representative in modern times was Witch of Endor 3528, one of
the Tillyfour Paris group. The Miss Scott family is still
reared at Portlethen, the early sires in the pedigree being
the prize bull Banks of Dee 12, bred by Sir Thomas
Burnett, and Young Andrew 9. From Miss Alexander
678 descends the well-known Lucy family at Drumin and
Mains of Kelly, Lucy of Portlethen 287, got by Fyvie 13,
a son of Old Jock 1, having been purchased by Mr Bowie.
The famous bull Raglan 208 was out of Young Miss
Alexander 16, the dam of Lucy of Portlethen 287. The
other families connected with the Portlethen herd trace
from animals bought by the late Mr Walker. Flora of

T

Portlethen 244, bred by the Earl of Southesk after Balnamoon 36, and out of Fanny of Kinnaird 330, was
purchased from her breeder in 1855 for £27, 10s. She
has left a large number of meritorious descendants, this
being one of the best branches of the Kinnaird Fanny
family.

Mr Walker purchased at Sir A. Burnett's sale at Crathes
in 1856 the cow Nightingale 262, and her daughter
Princess Philomel 269, representing the old herd at
Wester Fintray. Nightingale won the first prize of the
Highland Society as a cow at Glasgow in 1857. She was
subsequently sold to Mr M'Combie of Tillyfour. Her
daughter Princess Philomel 269, was sold to the Earl
of Southesk; and Mr Walker purchased at the Kinnaird
sale in 1861 Princess Philomel's daughter Perdita 848, by
Druid 225, a highly commended heifer at Battersea. It is
by Perdita's descendants that this family is now preserved,
and its excellence is sufficiently attested by the fact that
the two first-prize Highland Society's bulls Palmerston
374 and Adrian 439, bred at Portlethen, were both
produced by it. The Lively family was founded by
Lively 256, bred by the late Mr Fullerton, Ardestie, after
Earl o' Buchan 57. Jean 264, bred by Mr Ruxton,
Farnell, after the Keillor bull Adam 39, founded the Julia
family. The Pansy family had its origin in the cow
Panmure 278, bred in 1853 at Keillor after Old Jock 1.
The Balwyllo Victoria family is represented by the descendants of Alice Maud 724, out of Princess Royal 444,
purchased from the trustees of the late Mr Scott, Balwyllo.
The Idas spring from Ida 651, a daughter of Inchmarlo
Maggie 301, bred by the late Mr Patrick Davidson of
Inchmarlo. Madge of Portlethen 1217, a descendant
of the Keillor cow Favourite 2, was bought by Mr. Walker
at Tillyfour, and going into the possession of the Marquis
of Huntly, established a rather famous strain in the Aboyne
Castle herd. At the Honourable Charles Carnegie's sale

at Arratsmill, Japonica 864 was bought and has founded a family. Among the familles that are extinct in the female line we may note that of Matilda Fox. The cow Matilda Fox 302, bred by Mr Bowie, Mains of Kelly, had been sold to Mr M'Combie of Tillyfour, and in 1857 was bought by Mr Walker, in whose herd she produced the bull Fox Maule 305, one of the most renowned animals of the breed.

It would be difficult to enumerate the whole of the sires used at Portlethen during the sixty years the herd has been in existence, but a few additional facts may be given regarding some of the more celebrated animals. As already stated, the first bull owned by Mr Walker was Colonel 145, whose pedigree is thus recorded in the 'Herd Book:'—"Sire, an Aberdeenshire bull, bred by Mr Williamson at Portlethen Mains, dam Old Nackets." Another early sire was Porty 50. Andrew 8 was bred at Ardestie, being after Captain 2nd 156, and out Betsy of Ardestie 143. His son, Young Andrew 9, out of Young Duchess 2nd 32, was a useful stock sire. Banks of Dee 12, a famous show bull of his time, was bred by Sir Thomas Burnett. Fyvie 13, of whose calves eleven are registered, was bred at Fyvie, and was after Old Jock 1, his dam having been bred by Mr Watson, Keillor. Marquis 212 was a very impressive sire. Bred at Keillor, he was got by Old Jock 1, and there are no fewer than twenty-eight calves of his registered in the 'Herd Book.' He gained the second prize at Paris in 1856, and second at the Highland Society's show at Glasgow in 1857. Raglan 208, after Young Andrew 9, and out of Young Miss Alexander 16, gained a great number of prizes, and competing at Paris in 1856 against aged bulls when only a two-year-old, won the third prize. Duke of Wellington 219, after Marquis 212, and out of Lively 256, was a Highland Society's first-prize bull. His son Jehu 362 won three second prizes at Highland Society's shows. Fox Maule 305 was one of the best bulls bred at Portlethen, and besides gaining the first prize in the aged class at the Highland Society's show, carried off the challenge cup at the Royal Northern at Aberdeen. His half-brothers Fox Maule 2nd 370 and Fox Maule 3rd 372 were, although not so famous in the show-yard, more useful in the herd. The bulls Sir James 369 and Derby 377, bred at Tillyfour, and out of the Keillor cow Beauty of Tillyfour 2nd 1180, were also used; and Palmerston 374, a first-prize Highland Society bull, bred in the herd, got a great many superior stock.

We have already indicated that a large share of show-yard honours have fallen to the herd. Mr Walker first appeared as an exhibitor at the Highland Society's meeting in 1834, when he won a second prize for cows. At the Highland Society's show at Aberdeen in 1858 much attention was attracted by the fine lot of ten cows exhibited from the Portlethen herd, Mr Walker receiving a silver medal for this unique display.

Periodical sales have been held for many years, and specimens of the herd were thus distributed over the country. The private registers of the stock have been most carefully and accurately kept, the late Mr Walker having perceived the value of pedigree long before many polled breeders gave much attention to preserving records of the breeding of their herds.

Portmore.

Mr Mackenzie of Portmore, Eddleston, started a herd of polled cattle with the object of exemplifying to his tenants and neighbours, that for the more elevated districts of the south of Scotland they are more profitable to farmers than Shorthorns, both in the pure breed and also for crossing. As yet Mr Mackenzie's is the only herd of polled cattle in the south of Scotland. Mr Mackenzie commenced by purchasing in the end of 1880 two cows, bred by Mr

T. L. Melville Cartwright at Melville, viz., Lavender
4th 4247 and Rosamond 3853. In 1881 he purchased two
cows from Lord Airlie at Cortachy, viz., Favourite 7th
3651 and Francesca 3274 ; also three cows from Mr James
Bruce, Collithie, viz., Julia of Collithie 3671, Ida 9th 3670,
and Vine of Collithie 4507. This year he has purchased
two from Mr James Carnegie, Aytoun Hall, viz., Fortune
of Aytoun 4632, of the Mina family, from Melville, and
Necklace of Aytoun 4633, of the Bracelet family, also from
Melville. The bull in service is Josephus 1684, out of
the Jilt cow, Jewess 1916, and after Elcho 595, bred by
Sir George Macpherson Grant of Ballindalloch ; and Mr
Mackenzie has also lately acquired from Mr Carnegie a
young bull, Black Peter, by St Clair 1160, out of Mina
6th 3489. Last year there were five bulls calved and two
heifers from the seven cows Mr Mackenzie then possessed.
He sold the five bulls at Messrs Macdonald & Fraser's
sale at Perth in the spring of this year, at an average of
31 guineas. At the date of writing us (April 1, 1882), Mr
Mackenzie had got five calves in his herd, so that the
entire stock, of both sexes, numbered 16.

Powrie.

Mr Thomas Smith has at no little trouble and expense
collected a large and fine herd at Powrie, Dundee. His
first purchase was at Lord Airlie's sale in 1876, and since
that time he has acquired some excellent animals at Easter
Tulloch, Tillyfour, Gavenwood, Aboyne, Easter Skene,
Portlethen, etc. At the Tillyfour sale in 1878, Matilda
1175, of the Zara family, dam of the prize heifer Pride of
Alford 1778, was secured for 80 guineas ; Rosa Bonheur
2565, of the Rothiemay Victoria family, for 60 guineas ;
Ruby 2nd of Easter Tulloch 3520, of the Kinnaird Rebecca
family, for 42 guineas ; and Mayflower 2nd 3521, for 36
guineas. The last named, bred at Easter Tulloch, was dam

of Lord Tweedmouth's Witch of Endor 3528, bought for 155
guineas. Mr Smith also purchased from Mr Scott, Easter
Tulloch, other specimens of the Mayflower family as well
as members of the Levity, Duchess, Fanny, etc., strains,
full of good blood. From the Easter Skene herd came
Naomi 3730, by Bachelor 690, a very sweet cow. British
Queen, of the Charmer branch of the Queen tribe, was
obtained at the Tillyfour dispersion; while at Aboyne in
1881, 100 guineas were paid for that magnificent breeding cow Madge of Portlethen 1217. Among the stock sires
used have been Norman 1257, bred at Cortachy, after
Juryman 404 and Monarch 1182, the celebrated son of
Madge 1217. Several animals have been sold at high
prices to go to America.

CHAPTER XIV.

EXISTING SCOTCH HERDS—CONCLUDED.

ROTHIEMAY—The late Major Tayler and the breed—A famous polled bull
at Rothiemay about 1822 or 1823—Present herd dates from 1846—
The Georgina, Miss Morrison, and Victoria families—Sires used—Kate
of Glenbarry 2nd 1482—High prices at public sales—SKENE—SKILLY-
MARNO—SPOTT—Descended from old Braedownie herd—STROCHERIE
—A herd of 200 years' standing—Matildas and Ruths—SOUTH
YTHSIE—THE THORN—Traces mainly to the Ashmore stock—Flower
of Strathmore 479, and her son President 4th 368—THOMASTOWN—
WATERSIDE OF FORBES—Mr Wilken selects 200 polled breeding
cattle for exportation—Prides, Ericas, Fannys, Sybils, and Daisys—
Pride of Aberdeen 7th 1777, dam of Mr Auld's 270 guinea cow—Large
sales to foreign purchasers—WELLHOUSE—Mr Anderson's herd started
in the end of last century—Ruth of Tillyfour 1169—WESTER FOWLIS
—WESTSIDE OF BRUX—OTHER HERDS.

Rothiemay.

The late Major Tayler, father of Mr Tayler of Glenbarry,
was in the habit of breeding animals, mostly polled and
either black or brindled, ever since Mr Tayler can recollect,
and he particularly remembers that his father had at
Rothiemay, about 1822 or 1823, a well-known brindled
polled bull, then considered a very fine animal. The
foundation of the present Rothiemay herd may be said to
have been laid by the purchase by Major Tayler of two
black polled cows named Old Lady Jean and Miss Mor-

rison, from the late General Hay of Rannes, and a bull named Fintray 125, from the late Mr James Walker, Wester Fintray, about the year 1846. The cows were very large and strong. Their descendants have been regularly retained and bred from, and in the 'Herd Book' the pedigrees of the strains established by these fine animals trace from Old Lady Jean 187, and Miss Morrison 833. Another cow early added to the herd was Victoria of Glenbarry 534, calved in 1855, after Black Jock of Mulben 104. She was acquired from her breeder, Mr Paterson, Mulben. From Old Lady Jean the Rothiemay Georgina tribe has sprung, through Georgina of Rothiemay 532, by Fintray 125, calved in 1852; from Miss Morrison the Rothiemay family of that name descends, and a third family comes from the Mulben cow Victoria of Glenbarry 534. This then was the material on which Mr Tayler's fine herd has been reared. For many years no females were added besides those bred in it, and much of its success is due to the careful selection of sires. At Mr M'Combie's sale at Tillyfour in 1857, the bull Napoleon 257 was bought for 40 guineas. Napoleon was out of Bloomer 201, a daughter of Queen Mother 348, and after Hanton 228. He was described by Mr M'Combie in the sale catalogue as being "got by the best bull, and out of the best cow in the world in the opinion of the exposer." Napoleon was also individually a first-class animal; he won the second prize as a two-year-old at the Aberdeen show of the Highland Society in 1858, and was used in the herd for a considerable time. The next sire used was Damascus 495, bought when a calf at the Earl of Southesk's sale in 1861. After the Queen bull Windsor 221, he was out of Deodora 1232, of the Kinnaird Dora family. Damascus was a splendid bull, and left excellent stock. By these two bulls some of the best blood in the country was infused into the herd. Napoleon was very strong in the Tillyfour Queen blood, which was also continued by the sire of Damascus; while the dam of the latter was after a son, and out of a daughter of Cupbearer 59, through whom the Keillor and Mains of Kelly strains were introduced.

Then followed Elector 427, bred by Colonel Gordon, winner of the third prize at the Highland Society's shows in 1870 and 1871, and second in 1872. The other sires used were Bon Accord 446, bought from the Earl of Fife in 1871, winner of second prize at the Highland Society's show at Kelso in 1872; Canmore 626, bought in 1874 from Mr Elmslie, Cardenston; Waterside King 870, after Mr Bowie's Major 3rd 662, and of the Kinnaird Fanny family, purchased in 1876 from Mr Wilken, Waterside of Forbes, and Sir Maurice 1319 of the Fyvie Flower family purchased at Colonel Gordon's sale in 1876 when a calf for 42 guineas. Waterside King gained the second prize in 1878 at the Highland Society's show at Dumfries, while Sir Maurice was first-prize two-year-old at the same show, and has been twice second and once third in the aged class at Highland Society's meetings, besides gaining all possible first prizes at local shows. Sir Maurice is still doing good service in the herd, and retains the superior points that have made him one of the best-known show bulls of the time. At least three distinguished bulls have been bred in the herd, viz. Clansman 398, of the Miss Morrison family, third prize-winner at the Highland Society's show at Inverness in 1865, second at the same Society's show in 1868, and first at Edinburgh in 1869; Sir Roger 702, of the Georgina family, who was second-prize one-year-old at the Highland Society's show at Glasgow in 1875, and died when rising two years old; and Sir Wilfrid 1166, of the Georgina family, first-prize one-year-old at the Highland Society's show at Aberdeen in 1876, and second-prize two-year-old at Edinburgh in 1877. The most famous cow bred in the herd was Kate of Glenbarry 2nd 1482, the winner of the first prize at the Highland Society's show at Inverness in 1874, when 21 cows

were exhibited, as well as many other first prizes and
challenge cups.

As formerly remarked, comparatively few females have
been introduced to the herd. Among these, however, may
be named Fashion 982, and Nosegay 2nd 2156, from Sir
George Macpherson Grant, and Crocus 2nd 3765, from
Mr Hannay. Mr Tayler has succeeded in rearing three
families of much merit—the Georginas, Miss Morrisons, and
Victorias. From what we have already said, it will be seen
that the members of these families have proved themselves worthy of the attention bestowed on them. Of the
Georgina family particularly, some splendid animals have
been produced, such as Kate of Glenbarry 2nd, Kate Duff
1837, sold at Mr Tayler's sale in 1881 to Sir George Macpherson Grant for 155 guineas; Kate Darling 3573, the
second-prize cow at Stirling in 1881; Lily of the Nile
4576, first-prize yearling at the Royal Northern show in
1881, and third at Stirling the same year; Moonlight
1479, the dam of Sir Roger and Sir Wilfrid; Apricot 1490;
Moonshine 4584, etc.

The principal sales of breeding stock have been public
auctions in 1872, 1875, 1878, and 1881. The average for
32 animals in 1872 was £31, 16s. 6d., highest price £63;
the average for 24 animals in 1875 was £41, 7s. 9d., highest
price £73, 10s.; the average for 32 animals in 1878 was
£41, 1s. 3d., highest price £96, 12s.; the average for 29
animals in 1881 was £38, 5s., highest price £162, 15s.
Four animals from the sale of 1878 went to Mr Egginton,
South Ella, Hull; and at the sale in 1881, Nosegay 8th
3914 was bought by Mr Wallis, Bradley Hall, Ryton-on-
Tyne, and Orange Plum 4133, by Mr Foote, New Jersey.

The number in the herd previous to the sale in 1881,
when it was considerably reduced, was from 50 to 60. The
tribes now represented are the Georginas, Ballindalloch
Ericas, Lady Fannys, and Nosegays, and the Montbletton
Isabellas. In addition to Sir Maurice, the bulls recently

used were Prince Leopold 1599, and Royal Victor 1780,
the last third-prize yearling at Stirling, and first at Banff
and Keith in 1881. The cows in the herd at present are
all good milkers. Among them is Nosegay 2nd 2156,
sixteen years old, who still maintains good condition and
breeds regularly.

Skene.

The foundation of the herd belonging to Mr Hamilton
of Skene was laid in 1874 by the purchase of Grace of
Indego 1847, Elf of Skene 2169, and Nellie of Skene
2172, all of whom have bred extremely well. From Elf,
after Prince of Wales 2nd 394, and descended from Bess
1161 by the celebrated bull Rob Roy Macgregor 267,
a family of Daisys has been reared; while Nellie 2172, by
Sir William 705, winner of the challenge cup at Aberdeen,
and similarly bred on the dam's side, a Nellie family has
sprung. The Pride cow Pride 3rd 1694 was bought in
1875. Several of the Mains of Kelly Victoria family o
the Queen tribe were bought, among them Victoria 7th
2256 by Gainsborough 596, who had been sold for 106
guineas. Some purchases were made from the Duff House
herd, and of these Mr Hamilton has several Marias, and
old Jinny 1017, the dam of the Highland Society's first-
prize cow Innes 1934. The first bull used was His Lordship 838, bred by the Earl of Fife, after Palmerston 374,
and out of Linnet 1706 of the Drumin Lucy family. His
Excellency 1271, after Young Viscount 736, and out of
Violet of Montbletton 1399, of the Mayflower family, has
done splendid service, and has enabled Mr Hamilton to
bring forward several pairs of yearling heifers that have
taken good positions at the Royal Northern shows. His
Excellency won the second prize at the Highland Society
as a yearling, with other prizes at the National show; and
he, with other members of the herd, has made a creditable
appearance at the Royal Northern and local shows. In

1880 a draft sale was held at Aberdeen, when 19 head averaged £25, 15s. Since then, the herd has been largely reduced by sales to the Honourable Mr Cochrane, Canada, who obtained two cows, four two-year-old heifers, and three yearlings, the yearlings being a Victoria, a Daisy, and a Maria, all of whom were shown at Aberdeen in 1881.

Skillymarno.

This herd, belonging to Mr Ferguson, was founded in 1869 from two sources—the Crimonmogate and Castle Fraser Lily families. Lady Anne 1144, and Lady Mary 1145, were descended from the former, and Lovely 1146 from the latter. In establishing the herd, the bull Jamie Fleéman 437, from the Strichen Mains herd, was used. He was the winner of the Kinmundy cup at the Buchan Society's show at Mintlaw in 1871. The females in the herd are wholly descended from the two strains named. The bulls introduced have been Miller 716, bred by Mr Tayler of Glenbarry, who proved unsuccessful, and Garvock 1221, bred by Mr Adamson, Balquharn. A few calves were sired by the noted Highland Society bull Logie the Laird 3rd 862, and by Marischal Keith 1627, both owned by Colonel Ferguson of Pitfour. The sire at present in use is Young Prince of Wester Fowlis 1897, bred by Mr Strachan, Wester Fowlis. The herd comprises about twenty cows and heifers, with calves. The cows are all good milkers. Mr Ferguson has been breeding more for the butcher than the show-yard, and has endeavoured to develop the beef-producing qualities of the stock. The females in the herd have, however, had a fair share of prizes at local shows.

Spott.

Mr William Whyte's herd of polled cattle is kept at

Spott, in Glenprosen, a high outlying glen in the county
of Forfar, and was founded about 1852 by animals got
chiefly from his father, whose polled herd at Braedownie
had been in existence ever since Mr Whyte remembers,
which would be nearly fifty years ago. The late Mr
Whyte's cattle were closely allied to the Kinnaird herd,
as he latterly generally obtained his sires from the Kin-
nordy and Shielhill herds, which were of the same strains.
The first bull Mr William Whyte used on his own account
was one bred by the late Mr Watson, Keillor, and bought
from Mr Alexander, then at Mains of Glamis; but as he
did not turn out so well as expected, he was not kept long.
The next bull used was bought from Mr Lyell, Shielhill,
being Heather Jock of Shielhill 278, sire Mariner 148,
grandsire Cupbearer 59. He was not only the best bull
Mr Whyte ever had, but one of the best he ever saw in
the county, and he has often since regretted selling him
to the butcher. After Heather Jock, Mr Whyte used
Pioneer 326, bred at Balwyllo, Othello 319, The Fenian
418, Baronet of Leys 419, Engineer 571, Juryman 404,
Juror 908, Johnston 1360, Man o' the Mearns 1483,
and Elcho 595, and for the last three years he has chiefly
used Khan 1260. The last-named, now the property of the
Earl of Strathmore, is a very fine specimen of the Pride
family to which he belongs. Mr Whyte never added many
females, only one occasionally when opportunity offered,
and his herd has been mainly reared with the cows that
came from the old-established stock of his father, crossed
with the excellent bulls we have named. The herd numbers about a score of breeding cows, with their followers.
Till lately Mr Whyte fed nearly all his heifers, selling
one or two now and then. The Earl of Airlie has a considerable number of Mr Whyte's breeding in his herd, and
some of them are very good milkers. Mr Whyte never
made a practice of exhibiting, unless at the county shows,
where he has generally been pretty successful.

Strocherie.

The ancestors of Mr George Barclay, now in Strocherie, King Edward, who are known to have been farmers at Yonderton and Auchmill for considerably over 200 years, during that long period bred the native cattle of Aberdeenshire. They were not at first all polled, several having been horned; nor were they all black, there having been also red, brindled, and brown, with a red stripe from top of tail to shoulder. It is now fifty years since the horned cattle disappeared. There are still in the herd descendants of the original stock, but they are not, perhaps, the best in it. By some very judicious purchases representatives of three of the best-known families of the breed are now in creditable numbers at Strocherie. At the sale at Tillyfour in 1860, Mr Barclay paid 32 guineas for the one-year-old heifer Matilda of Yonderton 1712, after Hanton 228, and out of Lola Montes 208, being thus a half-sister on the dam's side to the famous Paris cow, Charlotte 203. Matilda has founded a valuable race of this branch of the Queen tribe. At Mr M'Combie's sale in 1874, Mr Barclay bought Ruth 2nd 1783, out of Ruth of Tillyfour 1169, descended from the Keillor cow Favourite 2, for 70 guineas. She has also bred well. At the same sale, Naomi 2445, from the Easter Tulloch stock, was purchased. Carina 3379, representing the Ballindalloch Sybil tribe, was bought at Mr Hannay's sale in 1877. At the Fyvie dispersion in 1881, three good cows were purchased. Sires have been got from Tillyfour, Easter Skene, Mountblairy, Westertown, Balwyllo, Mulben, etc. One of the latest used was Albany 1354, bred at Easter Skene, after Bachelor 690, and out of Young Grizzle 1807. There are usually from twenty to twenty-five cows in the herd, which has been most carefully managed since Mr Barclay took charge of it thirty-five years ago.

South Ythsie.

This small herd, belonging to Mrs Hay, was started in 1877, when Mr James Hay bought from Mr Grant, Methlick, the cow Corskie 28th B 1065. She has been a good investment, having produced five females, all, except the calf of 1879, being now on the farm. Mr Hay also bought from Mr Grant a granddaughter of this cow, Wild Rose 3402, calved in 1877. She cost £36 at an Aberdeen sale, and has produced three female calves. From Mr John Morrison, Hattonslap, was purchased the cow Tollo 2nd 1832, bred by the late Colonel Gordon of Fyvie. She was a very fine cow, but unfortunately she was lost in 1879. Two calves of hers, Tollo 3rd 3698, and Tollo 4th 3699, were bought from Mr Morrison. They have been very regular breeders, and their stock have plenty of hair, good straight backs, and are well fleshed. The cow Julia 3rd 1896 was also in the herd, but left only one calf, a very promising heifer named Julia of Ythsie. The herd numbers twenty-one females, and the stock sire is Macer 1659, bred by Mr Argo, Cairdseat, and bought from Mr Fraser, Hill of Skilmafilly. Macer is a very good, well-fleshed animal.

The Thorn.

Mr James Leslie, The Thorn, Blairgowrie, owned a large and fine herd, which produced some noted prize animals. When Mr Ferguson, Kinnochtry, began to confine his attention almost exclusively to descendants of the Keillor herd, he disposed of most of the Ashmore stock tracing from his father's herd to Mr Leslie. He also sold him Grannie 473, out of Lady Panmure 59, a daughter of Panmure 51, and Lady Eleanor 474, out of Eliza 65, tracing to Old Grannie 1. The cattle sold by Mr Ferguson to Mr Leslie were nearly all after Black Jock 3, bred at

Keillor. Mr Leslie also acquired the cow Flower of
Strathmore 479, bred by Mr Ruxton, Farnell, after Cup-
bearer 59, and out of Flora 59 from Mr Fullerton's herd.
Other additions made in the female line were Mina 1009
from Castle Fraser, and Bracelet 1010 from Tillyfour.
One of the first sires used was Hanton 4th 31, bred at
Mains of Kelly, out of Lizzie 227, the dam of Hanton 228.
President 3rd 246, bred at Balwyllo, and used in the
Keillor herd, was bought at Mr Watson's sale in 1860
by Mr Leslie, and retained in the herd, as was also King
Henry 390, bred at Kinnaird after Windsor 221, and out
of Kathleen 339. One of the most celebrated animals bred
at The Thorn was President 4th 368, after President 3rd
246, and out of Flower of Strathmore 479. He was the
first-prize yearling at the Highland Society's Stirling
show in 1864, and was sold to Mr M'Combie of Tillyfour,
in whose herd he was used, and to whom he gained the
first prize as a two-year-old at the Highland Society's
show at Inverness in 1865. Colonel of Castle Fraser 443
was also bred by Mr Leslie, being after Jamie of Easter
Skene 367, and out of Mina 1009. He won the first
prizes of the Highland Society in 1872 and 1873, and was
used in the Melville herd. Mr Leslie had a large sale in
1871, when thirty-two head averaged £27, 2s. At that
sale Mr Melville Cartwright purchased a good many
animals, comprising members of the Lavender, Bracelet,
Flora, and Mina families. Seventeen of the cattle sold in
1871 were descended from Mr Ferguson's Ashmore herd.

Thomastown.

Mr Craighead, Thomastown, Auchterless, began a herd
in 1876 by purchasing the bull Haddo 1394 from the Earl
of Aberdeen; the cow Miss Jeannie 2309, of the Fyvie
Miss Miller family, from Mr Dingwall Fordyce of Brucklay;
and the cow Duchess of Fyvie 2478, of the Miss Watson

family, from Colonel Gordon of Fyvie. He has since added Lily 2nd of Thomastown 3628, from Mr Walker, Westside of Brux; the bull P.R. 1395, from the same breeder; Mayflower of Pitgair 8th 4237, from Captain Beedie; Cannie Chiel 1662, from Sir William Gordon Cumming; Diana 3rd of Morlich 5036, from Mr Cran, Morlich; and Knight of Fyvie, from Colonel Gordon of Fyvie. The bulls we have named have been used in the herd. P.R., descended from the Keillor cow Jane of Bogfern 540, left very good stock, and improved the herd very much. Cannie Chiel, by the Sybil bull Senator 863, and of the Westertown Victoria family, a heavy, useful sire, also has left nice calves. Duchess of Fyvie has had two bull calves. Miss Jeannie is a regular breeding and excellent milking cow, and was second in the cow class at the Royal Northern show at Aberdeen. Lily 2nd has had four heifer calves, was commended as one of a pair at Aberdeen, and was first at Turriff. Mr Craighead sold Lily 4th 5034, winner of first prize at Turriff as one of a pair and her bull calf; Lily 5th 5035, second-prize heifer at Turriff; Lily 6th; Joan of Thomastown 5032, commended at Turriff; and Knight of Fyvie, out of the Fyvie Flower cow Miss Grace 4066, at from 30 to 60 guineas, to Mr Bell, for Mr Robertson, Waimea, New Zealand. Diana 3rd of Morlich and her bull calf were sold to Mr Wilken for exportation to America. The herd numbers about twenty head.

Waterside of Forbes.

Mr George Wilken, Waterside of Forbes, who has taken such a prominent part in connection with the exportation of polled cattle to America, having been entrusted by clients with the difficult and important task of selecting over 200 head of breeding stock for the other side of the Atlantic, commenced a herd in 1872 by purchases from the old Asloon stock. The herd was drafted in 1877, when

U

twenty head averaged about £30, the highest price being
61 guineas. After this sale the herd was very select; and
when it was dispersed at Tillyfour in 1878 it was much
admired, and brought an average of over £32. Since that
time Mr Wilken has been diligently collecting a fresh
herd, and has succeeded in gathering together a good many
descendants of his former stock, together with members of
other celebrated families. He now owns over ninety head.
There are in the herd specimens of such well-known
families as the Tillyfour Prides, the Ballindalloch Ericas,
the Tillyfour Daisys, the Kinnaird Fannys, the Montbletton
Mayflowers, the Ballindalloch Sybils, and the Kinnochtry
Favourites. At the head of the Prides may be placed
Pride of Aberdeen 7th 1777, bred at Tillyfour, now eleven
years old, a daughter of Pride of Aberdeen 581, and the
dam of Mr Auld's 270-guinea cow Pride of Aberdeen 9th
3253. Pride 7th was purchased cheaply at the Balquharn
dispersion, having then, it was supposed, ceased to breed;
but in May last she gave birth to a fine heifer calf. The
seven-year-old Pride of Aberdeen 14th 3272 was acquired
from Mr Hamilton of Skene. Another branch of the Pride
family traces from Kismet 1946, and of it there are four
specimens in the herd. Of the Ballindalloch Erica family
Mr Wilken has two representatives—Waterside Erica,
bred by Mr Robertson, Aberlour Mains, out of Editha 1737,
and after Souter Johnny 1615; and the bull Octavius
Eric 1797, bred by the Earl of Southesk, out of Erica 8th
3550, and after Editor 1460. Vine 8th of the Daisy
family went from Tillyfour to Kendal, and was bought by
Mr Wilken from Rev. T. Staniforth, Storrs Hall, Winder-
mere. There are four of this strain in the herd. Mr
Wilken's chief family, prior to the dispersion, was the
Kinnaird Fanny. He has now secured several specimens
of it by purchase from gentlemen who bought the animals
at his sale in 1878. Of the Montbletton Mayflower family,
Mr Wilken has the cow Lady Wilfrid 3818, bred by the

late Mr Walker, Montbletton; and the bull Black Standard 1541, out of Blackbird of Corskie 1704. Sybil's Darling 4050, a very fine cow of the Ballindalloch Sybil sort, came from Mr Argo, Cairdseat, at a high price. There are three of the Kinnochtry Favourite family. The Greystone, Rothiemay, Baads, Clova, Westertown, Auchorachan, East-Town, and other herds are also represented. The stock sires are Black Standard of the Mayflower family, and Octavius Eric of the Erica family already referred to.

Mr Wilken sold from his herd in 1881, forty animals to the United States and Canada. In 1882 he sold (up to June 1) forty-two head to Canada, the United States, New Zealand, and England.

Wellhouse.

The farm of Wellhouse, in the Vale of Alford, will always possess interest to breeders of polled cattle, from the fact that it was to it Mr Farquharson Taylor brought the celebrated bull Panmure 51 after the Dundee show in 1843. The present tenant of Wellhouse, Mr William Anderson, has also devoted great care to the rearing of a herd characterized by usefulness for breeding and feeding purposes. As previously noticed, Mr Anderson's father and uncle farmed land in the Vale of Alford and bred polled cattle in the end of the eighteenth century. They gained prizes for animals of the polled breed at the early shows of the Vale of Alford Agricultural Association, formed soon after 1830. When Mr Anderson came to take charge of the herd, he bought females from Mr M'Combie, Tillyfour; Mr M'Combie, Cairnballoch; Mr Taylor, Wellhouse; and Mr Barron, Moonhaugh,—all of whom were breeders of polled cattle. The sires he bred from were the best he could buy. Like many other breeders in these pre-'Herd Book' times, he, however, neglected to register pedigrees. The first registered sire he bought was Hero of

Boghead 417. This bull, the second-prize yearling at the
show of the Royal Northern Agricultural Society in 1871,
left some good stock, especially females. The next sire
was Bob Lowe 633, bred at Wellhouse. He also left good
stock, particularly animals for the butcher. A son of his,
King of the Valley 965, won the third prize at the Royal
English show at Kilburn in 1879. The next sire was
Laird of Tillyfour 956, bred by Mr M'Combie. After him,
Mr Anderson used Black Prince of Wellhouse 1312, who,
like Laird of Tillyfour, was a superior heifer getter; and
Fitz Haughton 1563. Besides these sires, Mr Anderson
has obtained service of other bulls—viz. Victor of Kelly
3rd 854, Duke of Fife 1592, and Knight of the Legion
1494. The splendid Pride bull Knight of the Shire 1699,
purchased for 165 guineas at the Balquharn sale in 1881,
has also been used in the herd, leaving excellent stock.

There was bought at Tillyfour in 1874 the cow Ruth
1169, descended from the Keillor cow Favourite 2, and
after the Queen bull Black Prince of Tillyfour 366. She
was the dam of Madge 1217, the foundress of the leading
and most distinguished tribe in the Aboyne herd. Mr
Anderson has now more females of this family than any
other breeder. He has the old mother cow, who, although
seventeen years old, is as fresh and full of flesh as a ten-
year-old, and produced a fine calf this year to Knight of
the Shire. He has also two of her daughters better than
herself, a two-year-old granddaughter, two other females,
and a bull, as well as a nice lot of Ruth calves. This is
the chief strain in the herd. In 1878 Mr Anderson
bought from Mr Wilken, Waterside of Forbes, Fairy
Queen of Portlethen 889, of the Kinnaird Fanny tribe,
and he has several promising descendants of hers. The
other sorts in the herd have been long bred by Mr Anderson, and are not so remarkable for the production of show
animals as of cattle possessing satisfactory breeding, milking, and feeding qualities. The herd usually numbers

about forty head, and for many years Mr Anderson has
given attention to preparing a top lot of polls for the
London Christmas market.

Wester Fowlis.

This herd was founded by Mr James Strachan in 1842,
but for many years no records were kept, and the first
animal bred at Wester Fowlis that was registered in the
' Herd Book' was Nelly 1136, calved in 1866, she having
been entered by Mr Pearson of Johnston to whom she
was sold. Long previous to that, however, Mr Strachan
never used any except black polled bulls; but not having
retained their pedigrees, he cannot trace them back. In
1863, Messrs Strachan, J. Dunn, and H. Shaw bought from
the late Mr M'Combie the bull Black Prince of Ennenteer
512. This bull gained a prize every year he was exhibited
at Leochel Cushnie, which was then the principal show in
the district for polled cattle. He left some good females,
but few of them were registered. In 1870, Mr Strachan
entered in the ' Herd Book' Bate 1952, Matilda 1953,
Beatrice 1954, and Lady 1955. Bate and Matilda, both
after Black Prince of Ennenteer 512, were among the best
cows he had, and they were sold at £140 in 1877 to
Morayshire. Bate's first calf was Beatrice 1954, sold to
go to England for £60. After this she had Prince
Albert of Fyvie 624, sold in 1872 to Colonel Gordon of
Fyvie when one year old for 36 guineas. Bate gained
numerous prizes at the local show. In 1868 was purchased Draco 3rd 733 from Mr Walker, Ardhuncart. He
left some very fine stock, and was sold to the butcher in
1872. That year was bought Sir William 2nd 748 from
Mr Reid, Greystone, who had purchased him from Mr
Shaw. He was the best bull that had been at Wester
Fowlis up to that time, and after being used two years,
was sold to go to Germany. He gained the first prize

at the Leochel Cushnie show. This show, we may remark, was organized in 1848, and the late Mr M'Combie of Tillyfour manifested great interest in it. In 1872, Mr Strachan sold the bull calf Black Prince of Wester Fowlis 619 to Mr M'Combie of Tillyfour for £50. He was the best bull calf he ever bred, girthing 6 feet 2 inches when eleven months old. He gained the third prize at the Highland Society's show at Stirling in 1873, besides several other prizes, and is sire of the fine cow Lilias of Tillyfour 1795.

In 1871 was sold the heifer Balvenie 1700 to the Earl of Fife, and she gained the third prize at Kelso in 1872. Several other animals were sold at various times to Lord Fife. In 1874 Mr Strachan sold the cows Isabella of Felcourt 2327, Elleana 2328, and Lady of Wester Fowlis 1955 to Mr Carter Wood, Felcourt, Sussex, at a long price. In 1877 he purchased Waterside Dandy 2nd 2071 from Mr Wilken, Waterside, for £70. She gained the second prize in a large class at Alford in 1876. Signet 2nd 3017 and her bull calf Prince Albert of Wester Fowlis 1492, by Young Viscount 736, were acquired from Mr Hannay, Gavenwood, and both frequently gained prizes at the Alford and Leochel shows. Surplus pedigreed females have been sold by private bargain. Bull calves were sent to the Alford sales, and latterly to the Aberdeen joint sale. Mr Strachan's highest price for these in 1881 was 33 guineas, and in 1882 34 guineas. In 1882 the cow Matilda 2nd 3613 was sold to Her Majesty the Queen at a long price. This cow was the best in the herd at that time, and won first prizes at Leochel. In 1881 six heifers were sold to Messrs Gudgell & Simpson, Kansas city, U.S., for 30 guineas of an average, and two were sold to Mr Bruce. In 1882 ten heifers were sold to Mr G. N. Henry, Kansas City, U.S., at an average of 30 guineas. The cow Isabella 2nd 3857 was sold to Messrs Gudgell & Simpson for £60. Three one-year-old heifers went to

Messrs Anderson & Findlay, Chicago. These twenty animals, sold for exportation, were all bred at Wester Fowlis, and after Craigievar 1397 and Prince Albert 1492. Craigievar left excellent stock, perhaps altogether the best Mr Strachan has ever had.

Westside of Brux.

A herd of long standing, belonging to Mr James Walker, exists at Westside of Brux, Kildrummy. It is chiefly descended from three cows—one bred in 1852 by Mr James Reid, Kirktown, Forbes; one bred by Mr George Fyfe, Upperbigging; and one bred by Mr Stephen, Govals, Auchindoir. Sires have been obtained from Castle Fraser, Upper Farmton, and Bogfern. Mr Walker has also had the use of the Ardhuncart bulls. The two sires most recently in service were Logie the Laird 4th 892 bred at Mains of Kelly, and Prompter 1872, bred at Balquharn by Mr H. D. Adamson, after Dragon 1178, and out of the fine Pride cow Pride of Aberdeen 7th 1777. Bulls from the herd have been sold at high prices, and Westside females are found in several herds both in Scotland and America. Mr Walker supplied to Dr Profeit, Commissioner for Her Majesty the Queen, the first animals bought for the Royal herd at Abergeldie. Stock has not been shown beyond the local meeting, but there they have obtained a good many prizes.

Other Herds.

Aquorthies.—Mr James Gerrard has a small herd at Aquorthies, Tarves, mostly descended from a cow tracing to the Crathes stock. This cow, Fern, by Black Prince of Ennenteer 512 of the Zara tribe bred at Tillyfour, was purchased seven years ago, and was a splendid beef and milk producer. Her first calf was

steered, and when twenty-two months old brought £32.
Her next bull calf was very successful at the Formartine
show, and was a good stock getter. Fern 2nd 4136, by
Colonel Gordon 3rd 1602, has had several calves, one
of them having been sold to Sir Thomas Gladstone for 32
guineas. Bess of Burnside 3776 was bought at the Tillyfour sale in 1880.

Auchindellan.—Mr John Stewart, manager to Sir
George Macpherson Grant of Ballindalloch, Bart., M.P.,
began a herd at Auchindellan, Clatt, little more than a
year ago. The herd now numbers thirty head, being made
up of an Erica—a one-year-old out of Esther of Aberlour
4843, by Souter Johnny 1615; Nosegay 12th 4582;
three of the Ballindalloch Miss Burgess family; Young
Nora 3317, of the Drumin Lucy family, and five of her
descendants; Maid of Orleans 2nd 1177, Gaiety 4th, out
of Mr Skinner's Lucy cow Gaiety 2219; Lizzie of Fyvie
2nd 4683 and her heifer calf, by the Erica sire Etonian
1658. The latest addition to the herd was the Pride cow
Lilias of Tillyfour 1795, the dam of the famous bulls
Challenger, Black Watch, and Proud Viscount. The bulls
in use are Kaiser 1253 and Viscount Loftus—two good
specimens of the Pride family.

Auchlin.—On entering the farm of Auchlin, King
Edward, Mr James Smith took over at valuation the
polled stock belonging to his predecessor, Mr John
Morrison. They were mostly descended from the old
Mains of Hatton herd. A number of them were disposed
of to Mr Hannay, Gavenwood. To the remainder Mr
Smith used the bull Black Standard 1541, after St. Clair
1160, and out of Blackbird of Corskie 1704, of the Montbletton Mayflower family. Several animals have been
sold for exportation.

Auchmaliddy.—Mr James Fowlie, Auchmaliddy, New
Deer, commenced farming in 1870, and bought a bull and
cow from his father at Upper Boyndlie, who never bred

anything but polled stock. The cow was named Rosy of Upper Boyndlie, but she is not entered in the 'Herd Book,' although she was purely bred, and descended from the Fyvie Castle herd. Most of her calves have been registered. Mr Fowlie has sold five bulls and a heifer from her, and has kept two bulls and a heifer. The first registered bull used was The Laird 1296, bred at Fyvie Castle, and bought for £50. He gained Colonel Ferguson's cup at the Buchan Agricultural Society's show in 1876. The next sire was General 1297, by The Laird, and out of Rosy of Upper Boyndlie. He also gained the cup at the Buchan show as a yearling in 1877, and was sold to Mr Morrison, Phingask, Fraserburgh. He afterwards passed into the hands of Mr Mackessack, Earnside, to whom he gained a number of prizes in Moray and Nairn shires. The next bulls used were Reformer 1275, bred at Fyvie; Hector 1713, bred by Mr Fowlie; and Prince Albert 4th 1673, bred at Baads. The last named, now in service, is leaving very good stock. Mr Fowlie sold two heifers last year to Mr Findlay, Peterhead, for exportation to America.

Aytoun. — Mr Carnegie, Aytoun, Newburgh-on-Tay, started a herd by purchases at the Melville sale, the animals selected being of the Mina, Bracelet and Westertown Rose families.

Balfluig.—Mr Alexander Adam's herd here comprises representatives of the Auchlossan, Brucklay and Lumgair stocks, to which the Mains of Kelly bull Victor of Kelly 3rd 854 has been used. The herd took a very creditable position at the show of the Vale of Alford Agricultural Society in 1881.

Balgreen.—Polled cattle have long been reared at Balgreen, King Edward, by Mr Mitchell and his father. Few additions have been made to the herd. Among these, however, may be noted two cows from Castle Fraser— Georgina 2447, and her daughter Delta 2448; the cow Barbara 2nd 989, from Easter Skene in 1871; Dandy 2nd

2239, of the Empress branch of the Queen tribe, from
Westertown in 1874; Kineddart 1702, from Corskie in
1877, and Winsome 2nd 3774, from Montcoffer in 1878.

Balhaggardy.—Mr Maitland, Balhaggardy, owns a herd
descended from an Archballoch cow, by March 2nd 1239.
Sires from Conglass, Portlethen, and Wester Corse have
been used.

Balvenie.—Mr J. S. Findlater has been collecting a herd
at Balvenie, Dufftown, during the last few years. At the
Corskie sale in 1877 he purchased Jinny 2nd 3009, paying
41 guineas for her as a yearling heifer. She was a half-
sister on the dam's side of the celebrated show cow Innes
1934. The same year Julia of Balvenie 3723, of the
Westertown Victoria family, was secured at the Tullochallum dispersion. Milly 3rd 3471, descended from the
Honourable Charles Carnegie's stock, was bought at Ballindalloch in 1879; and in that year Briony 3889, of the
Drumin Beauty family, was added from the Aboyne sale.
At the Burnside sale in 1880 Duchess 2nd of Easter Tulloch
3750, descended through the Kinnochtry herd from Old
Grannie 1, was acquired. The bulls used have comprised
Raman 924, bred at Drumin after Talisman 640, and out
of Catherine 961; Carpen 1420, bred in the herd, out of
Jinny 2nd 3009, and after Sir Wilfrid 1157 and Phœbus
1908, bred at Drumin, after Cupid 1410, and out of Sunshine 1693 of the Beauty family.

Bents.—Mr Reid, Bents, Alford, has a few polled cattle
descended from Rose of Westside 2035, bred by Mr
Walker, Westside of Brux. Her progeny have been
crossed with the highly-bred sires at Haughton, Victor of
Kelly 3rd 854, Emir 1498, etc.

Bogarrow.—Mr James Farquharson, Bogarrow, Ballindalloch, has had some polled cattle since 1833 or 1834,
and although he has only lately registered his animals in
the 'Herd Book,' they have been kept pure, and are excellent
milkers. They are mostly bred from Drumin and Mulben

sires. Mr Farquharson has gained a considerable number of prizes at local shows within the last four years. It was from his stock that the cow went to Auchlochrach, that became the principal foundress of the herd there, and progenitrix of the champion ox at Smithfield in 1872. This ox was shown by Mr Bruce, Burnside, Fochabers; Mr Macpherson, Auchlochrach, getting the gold medal as breeder.

Boghead.—Mr M'Knight, Boghead, Chapel of Garioch, entered some animals in vol. i. of the 'Herd Book,' among them Evelyn 453 of Balwyllo breeding, Charlotte 570, by Angus 45, and Miss Anderson 571, by Panmure of Wellhouse 119 (probably a son of Panmure 51). He used in his herd the well-known Highland Society bull Malcolm of Bodiechell 269, referred to in notices of the Fyvie, Mulben, and Conglass herds where he was also in service. The descendants of these are still at Boghead.

Brucehill.—In the formation of this herd Mr James Fowlie acquired some animals from Mr Shaw, Bogfern, and Mr Williamson, Standing Stones. From the latter came Beauty of Brucehill 3684, of a Kinnochtry family, and one of the Portlethen Livelys. The Campfield and Castle Fraser herds are also represented, and bulls from Haddo House and Waterside of Forbes have been in service. Many prizes have been gained at the local shows, and some important sales made to America.

Burnside, Kintore.—This herd, belonging to Mr Roger, is composed of Haddo House, Skene, Fyvie, and Campfield blood.

Cairnfield.—Mr Gordon of Cairnfield has recently started a herd, drawing stock from Tillyfour, Burnside, and Gavenwood.

Castle Craig.—Sir Wm. H. Gibson Carmichael founded a herd in August 1880, by the purchase of the cows Fairy 7th 4255, and Beauty of Tillyfour 2567, at the Tillyfour dispersion. These have bred very well, and there are now seven animals in the herd. The stock sire is Prince Arac

1902, bred by Mr Anderson, Mill of Wester Coull, after Aggressor 1241, and out of Mopsie 3598, descended from the Keillor cow Jane of Bogfern 540.

Cardney.—Mr A. B. Brooke, Cardney, Dunkeld, has had some very highly-bred cattle in his herd. From Mr Ferguson, Kinnochtry, he secured the cows Erin 2202, of the Kinnochtry Emily family, and Emerald 2201, of the Favourite family. At the Westertown dispersion he bought the Rose cow Rosedale 934; and at Ballindalloch, in 1876, he gave 80 guineas for the Erica cow Emma of Garline 1733.

Commieston.—A small herd was lately started at Commieston by Mr Stephen. It is larely based on Easter Tulloch blood.

Cullen House.—The Earl of Seafield has begun a herd here. Some purchases were made at Portlethen; and the highest-priced bull at the Aberdeen joint sale in April, bred by Mr Petrie, Glencorrie, was acquired for the herd.

Dalmore.—Mr Andrew Mackenzie, Dalmore, Ross-shire, bought at the Corskie sale in 1877 the cows Grange 1940 for 41 guineas, and Blossom 3rd 1930 for 51 guineas. He kept them pure, and they formed the nucleus of his herd. Grange had a bull calf by Young Viscount 736, and he was used as stock sire. Additions were made at the sale of the Kincraig and Biallid herds in 1881.

Daugh.—The name of Mr Robert Anderson, Daugh, Tarland, has figured very prominently in recent show-yard records as the owner of the magnificent bull Prince Albert of Baads 1336, who, during all his victorious career, was his property. Cows were bought at Culsh and Ruthven. A specimen of the Fancy branch of the Queen tribe was obtained; and at the last Rothiemay sale the heifer Flush 3918, by Sir Maurice 1319, was acquired.

Ecclesgreig.—The origin of Captain Grant's small herd at Ecclesgreig was the purchase of two very well-bred cows at the Portlethen sale in 1869. They were Alberta 1510, of

the Balwyllo Victoria family, for 38 guineas, and Favourite
2nd 858, of the Kinnaird Fanny family, for 41 guineas.
Rosa 1079, bred by Mr Fullerton, Ardestie, was also in
the herd. The sires have come from Mulben, Easter
Tulloch, Stone o' Morphie, and Cortachy. The principal
strain is that tracing from Alberta 1510, who turned out
an excellent breeder.

Heads of Auchinderran.—Mr John M'Connachie keeps
a few pure-bred cattle at Heads of Auchinderran, Keith.
They number about sixteen head, and are descended from
Queen of Auchinderran 3639, bred by Mr Paterson, Mulben,
of the Mayflower family, and Sweet Home 2228, bred at
Inchcorsie. The bulls used have been Guardsman 1402,
bred at Rothiemay, of the Miss Morrison family; Buchan
Laddie 1384, bred at Strichen Mains; Franklin 1901, bred at
Heads; and Knighthood 1767, bred by Mr Hannay, Gaven-
wood, after the Pride bull Challenger 1260, and out of
Kate of Glenbarry 1187, of the Georgina family. All
these bulls have won prizes at the shows of the Central
Banffshire Farmer Club.

Inchcorsie.—Mr Alexander Smith, who has for many
years successfully managed the herd of Mr Tayler of
Glenbarry, himself owns a few well-bred cows and heifers
at Inchcorsie, Rothiemay. He has had the use of Mr
Tayler's bulls. In all he has thirteen females of very
good pedigree and shapes. Three are of the Fyvie Flower
tribe, two of the Rothiemay Georgina tribe, two of the
Ballindalloch Lady Fanny tribe, and five descendants of
the old Corskie tribe, which belonged to the late Mr G. G.
Robinson; some of them having six crosses of Highland
Society prize bulls on their pedigree.

Keilyford.—This herd, belonging to Mr W. D. Gray, is
wholly descended on the female line from Miss Miller
3908, bought from Colonel Gordon of Fyvie. There are in
the herd eleven of her progeny. Sires have been introduced from Waterside of Forbes, Morlich, Methlick, and

Haddo House. The bull from Methlick was Abercorn 1565, of the Drumin Lucy tribe; while the one from Haddo House now in use is Hartington, out of the Paris heifer Halt 2nd 3527, and after the Pride sire Knight of the Legion 1494. No females have been sold. The bull-calves disposed of have averaged over £30.

Keir.—The herd belonging to Mr Emslie, Keir, Belhelvie, is mainly composed of representatives of four strains—two from Kinnochtry, one from Portlethen, and one from Baads. The families from Kinnochtry are descended from Agnes of Keir 1433, of the Emily tribe tracing to Old Grannie 1; and Maud of Keir 1434, tracing to Lady Panmure 59, by Panmure 51. Both these cows were bred at Kinnochtry, and were bought at Easter Tulloch in 1873. The family from Portlethen was started by the purchase of Miss Walker 2nd 2200, of the Kinnaird Fanny strain. Bulls have lately been used from Inchgarth, Brucehill, Baads, Keilyford, and Greystone.

Kinbate.—Mr Thomas Fraser's herd at Kinbate is largely composed of representatives of the Montbletton stock. The cows, Fanny of Kinbate 3624, and Lady Ann of Kinbate 4661, both members of the Balwyllo Isabella family, were purchased from the late Mr Walker. Judith 4048, by Bachelor 690, came from Easter Skene; Young Breeze 3625, from Inchcorsie; Maud Mary 4046, from Westertown; Paleface 4079, from Portlethen; and Countess of Oakhill 4th 4362, from Oakhill. Sires have been introduced from Montbletton, Duff House, Nether Kildrummy, and Gavenwood.

Kinstair.—Mr Anderson, Kinstair, was the owner of two cows, got by the famous bull Panmure 51. They were Annie of Kinstair 3221, and Meg of Kinstair 3223, and they left some excellent stock. Bulls were purchased from Westside, Baads, Ballindalloch, etc.

Lewes of Fyvie.—Mr Mackie has here a small herd comprising specimens of the Portlethen, Fyvie, Easter Skene, and Oakhill stocks. The animals from Portlethen and Easter Skene are Sweetmeat 3348, of the Miss Scott family, and Young Grizzle 1807, of the Grizzle family. With these two cows Mr Mackie gained the second prize for pairs at the Royal Northern Show in 1881 ; and his stock bull Glenartney 1181, bred at Aboyne, after Duke of Perth 357, and out of Gem of Aboyne 1595, of the Pride family, was third on the same occasion.

Little Endovie.—In 1876 Mr Brown, Little Endovie, purchased from her breeder, Mr M'Combie, Upper Farmton, Lynturk, the cow Pride of Little Endovie 2393. She and her produce have been kept and bred from. In 1880 two calves were dropped to the Pride bull Petrarch 1258. One of these was a heifer, and was retained for breeding purposes. The other, a bull, went to Barra Castle. The calves in the herd this year are after Knight of the Shire 1699. Last year a two-year-old heifer was sold to Mr Wilken, Waterside of Forbes, for exportation to America.

Lyne of Carron.—The Tillyfour prize bull Standard-Bearer 229 left here a calf named Fanny, whose descendants, crossed with Mulben, Ballindalloch, Drumin, and Burnside bulls, have been carefully preserved by Mr M'Kenzie.

Mains of Ardlaw.—This herd was begun by Mr James Beedie a few years ago. An animal was purchased from Mr Morrison, Auchlin, descended from the Easter Tulloch herd. Additions have been made from Burnshangie, Brucklay, and Mains of Kelly. Bulls have been obtained from Montbletton and Mains of Kelly.

Mains of Wardhouse.—Mr Moir owns a few good cattle here, descended from the Clova and Bognie herds. From Miss Carnegie 3rd 2149, bred at Bognie, came the superior cow Hawthorn of Wellhouse 2467, a famous prize-winner at local shows, as well as at the Royal Northern and Highland Society's meetings. She won the third prize at Dumfries in 1878, and as the head

of a group she gained the prize for best family group at the
Royal Northern show. Bulls have been introduced from
Clova, Easter Tulloch, etc.

Midtown.—Mr Leggat has laid the foundation of a herd
here by purchases at Mr Bruce's sale at Keig in 1880, and
at Gavenwood in 1881.

Millhill.—For many years Mr George Bruce kept good
polled cattle at Wealthiton, Keig. The herd increased
until it numbered about thirty head in 1877. In October
1878 a fire occurred at the farm, and twenty-six valuable
breeding cattle were destroyed. These comprised first-
prize heifers at the Udny, Alford, and Garioch shows, and
eight bull calves. Mr Bruce's greatest success in the
showyard was gained in 1878, when he received the first
prize and gold medal for cows at the Paris Exhibition,
with Bella Mary 1503, of the Castle Fraser Blanche family.
On leaving Wealthiton, Keig, in 1880, Mr. Bruce sold the
few remaining polled cattle he had, four cows averaging
£33, and five yearlings £23. He has now eight or ten
pure polls, which are kept on the farm of Millhill, Tully-
nessle.

Mill of Wester Coull.—Mr John Anderson has at this
farm a few good polled cattle. Females have been acquired
from the Confunderland, Earnside, Bovaglie, and Bogfern
stocks. A cow named Frogneb 2468, bred by Mr Shaw,
Bogfern, traces to the Keillor herd, and she has bred
extremely well. The sire recently in use has been
Aggressor 1241, bred by Mr Hannay, Gavenwood, after
the celebrated Young Viscount 736, and out of Duchess
8th 1912, of the Duchess branch of the Queen tribe.

Milton of Kemnay.—Mr H. D. M'Combie maintains here
the descendants of the Cairnballoch stock. Females have
also been added from Wester Fowlis and Tillyfour, the
Queen cow Cream 1269 having been introduced from the
latter herd. The bulls have been got at Tillyfour, Morlich,
Tillychetly, Wester Fowlis, etc.

Monyruy.—Mr Beaton last year on entering the farm of
Monyruy, Longside, where Mr Hutchison had many years
previously kept some polled cattle, started a herd. His
principal purchases were made at the Balquharn and
Fyvie dispersions.

Mountblairy.—Mrs Morison continues at Mountblairy
the herd established there by the late Mr. Morison. The
materials are practically the same as were at Bognie.
Under notice of extinct herds, a few particulars will be
found regarding them. The strains represented at Mountblairy are the Susys, descended from the Tillyfour herd;
the Sybils, tracing from Fred's Darling 1055, bought at
Castle Fraser in 1870; the Southesks, from Southesk, bred
at Mountblairy; and the Hawkhalls, long at Bognie. At
Mountblairy, as at Bognie, the blood of the Kinnaird
bull Odin 153 has been strongly infused into the herd.
The bull recently used was Fitz Erica 1451, from Gavenwood, after Gainsborough 596, and out of Erica 7th 3019,
and he was followed by the Erica bull, Egbert 1443.

Nether Kildrummy.—This herd has lately taken a very
good position at the Kildrummy shows, where good
musters of polled cattle appear. The herd is small, and
the bulk of it descends from the cows Missie 2484, by
Reform 408, bred by Mr Taylor, Southbank, and Mary of
Ardhuncart 2013, by Draco 338, bred at Ardhuncart.
The Ardhuncart bulls have been used in the herd. The
sire lately in service was Socrates 1907, bred at Auchorachan, after Viscount Duff 1365, and out of the Sybil cow
Silvia 3073.

Novar.—Mr G. A Walker, Novar, commenced a herd a
year or two ago, by purchases from Mr Walker, Ardhuncart,
and Mr. Robertson, Burnside.

Oakhill.—Mr Manson's herd at Oakhill comprises specimens of the old Haddo House, Westside, Castle Fraser, and
Clova stocks. At the Corskie sale in 1877 two very nice
heifers were bought, viz.—Millstream 3389, for 33 guineas,

X

and Princess Dagmar 3rd 3233, of the Matilda branch of
the Queen tribe, for 35 guineas.

Raasay.—Mr. Herbert Wood of Raasay, Skye, started a
herd in 1880, by purchases at the Tillyfour dispersion.
The animals he then acquired comprised specimens of the
Pride of Aberdeen and Easter Tulloch Mayflower families.

Ruthven.—The herd here is one of the oldest in the
district, being descended from the Castle Newe stock.
Bulls have been introduced from Tillyfour, Mains of
Kelly, Auchlossan, and Aboyne Castle. A draft sale
was held in 1876, when an average of over £27 was
realized.

Semiel.—At Semiel, Strathdon, a herd was started about
sixty-six years ago, by the purchase, by the grandfather of
the present tenant, Mr Scott, of two polled heifers from a
farmer in Suiefoot, Gartly, Aberdeenshire. At that time
most of the cattle in this outlying district of the county
were horned, and there was some difficulty in obtaining
the services of a polled bull. However, there happened
to be a polled bull at Castle Newe, and the heifers were
mated with him. No cows were added, the produce of
these heifers being retained, and served with good polled
sires. In 1864 some of the best animals were bought by
Mr Scott, and he has also kept the strain pure, buying
sires from Tillyfour, Easter Skene, Whitehouse, Wester
Fowlis, and Nether Kildrummy. Two heifers were bought
from Ruthven, Logie Coldstone, and these, with the
descendants of the animals acquired in 1816, form the herd
at Semiel.

The Burn.—Colonel M'Inroy of The Burn has for many
years owned a herd of great purity, but owing to his never
having kept pedigrees, we are unable to give much information regarding it. He used to buy bulls from Kinnaird
Cavalier 411, after Windsor 221, and out of Kalliope 1234
having been one of them. The Earl of Airlie secured
some females from the The Burn herd, and from one of

them sprang the fine heifer Miranda 4204, first as a yearling and two-year-old at Highland Society's shows.

Tillychetly.—This is an old-established stock, and has been much improved by Mr. Charles M'Combie, the present owner. Among notable recent purchases were—Myrtle 1785, from Tillyfour in 1874; Lark 2nd of Easter Skene 3786, representing a very rare strain, tracing through Mr M'Combie's (Easter Skene) Mariana 622, and Lady Clara 4, to the Keillor cow Old Grannie 1; Pride of Aberdeen 16th 3302, and Vine of Tillyfour 1167, a grand old matron of the Daisy branch of the Queen tribe.

Turtory.—Mr Smith gathered together a number of specimens of some of the best strains at Rothiemay, and he also made some purchases at Standing Stones.

Wester Fordel.—This herd was founded by Major-General Kirkland, with animals of the Kinnaird Fanny, the Mayflower and Levity families from Mr. Scott, Easter Tulloch. The bull Morven 1502, bred by the Marquis of Huntly, out of Madge 1217, and after Duke of Perth 357, has been used.

Among other places at which polled cattle are reared are Strichen Mains, Clova, Firfolds, Cardenston, Milntorries, Knockollachy, Meikle Camaloun, Craskins, Dunnydeer, Invermarkie, Clockhill, Brunton, etc.

CHAPTER XV.

THE BREED IN ENGLAND AND IRELAND.

Polled cattle at the Battersea and Kilburn International Exhibitions—
Pride of Aberdeen 581 and Mr Richard Booth's Queen of the Ocean,
the two best females at Battersea—English herds—Baliol College—
Beechwood — Bradley Hall — The Ballindalloch Ericas — Ewell —
Felcourt—Goodwood—Horsted—Roos—Smeaton Manor—South Ella
—Studley Priory—Mr Henderson's experience with the breed—The
Breed in Ireland—Mr Hugh Watson's success at the early shows
of the Royal Irish and Royal Dublin Societies—Grey-breasted Jock 2
closed his career in the Emerald Isle—The herd of Mr Kirkaldy of
Hearnesbrook and Mr Seymour of Ballymore Castle—Lord Talbot de
Malahide and Lord Lurgan—Herds of Mr Owen, Blessington, and Mr
Collis of Tieraclea.

England.

ENGLISH agriculturists have had numerous opportunities
of inspecting the best specimens of the breed. Prizes have
been frequently offered for polled cattle at the shows of the
Royal Agricultural Society of England, while at the great
International Exhibitions at Battersea in 1862 and at
Kilburn in 1879, Aberdeen or Angus mustered in strong
force. At the former meeting a competent authority
bracketed Mr M'Combie's polled cow Pride of Aberdeen
581 with Mr Richard Booth's famous Shorthorn Queen
of the Ocean as the two best females at the show. For
many years the Smithfield and Bingley Hall Fat Stock
Shows have had as one of their leading features the displays

of animals of the polled breed. Of scarcely less importance in spreading the fame of the breed in England have
been the magnificent lots of polled oxen annually exhibited
at the Christmas Market in London. It is only in recent
years, however, that herds of polled cattle have been started
in England. One of the first to do so was Mr Carter Wood
of Felcourt, Sussex, and during the past year there has
been a large accession to the ranks of polled breeders in
England. We give below a few notes on English herds :—

Baliol College Farm.—For several years before Mr
Stephenson, Baliol College Farm, Benton, near Newcastle, turned his attention to a breeding stock of polled
cattle, he showed some specimens of the breed at the fat
shows. In 1878 he won the first prize at Smithfield with
a black polled heifer, while again at the same show in
1880 he had the best black polled heifer. Recognising
their great aptitude to fatten, he resolved to start a
breeding stock; and through Mr Robert Bruce, Great
Smeaton, laid the foundation of a herd in purchases from
Mr Bean, Balquhain. Good looks, combined with good
pedigree, were made two essential points in selecting his
females, and although he now has a great number of
strains or families represented in his herd, yet there is a
great uniformity of type and character running through
the lot. Of one thing he is very particular—he is
decidedly opposed to "scurs," and makes a true polled
head a cardinal point in the selection of his animals.
Having, as we have said, no large number of any particular family, Mr. Stephenson decided on buying an Erica
bull after seeing how impressive they had been in many
herds in the North of Scotland. A journey to Ballindalloch in the early autumn of last year, before North-country
breeders had begun to think of buying bulls, enabled him
to get, after one was drawn for home use, a pick of the
Erica bulls, and he was fortunate in choosing one which
he has since named Englishman from the favourite cow

Edith 2973, by the noted sire Young Viscount 736. A glance at the list of females in the herd shows that there is a great amount of fine material, so far as breeding is concerned, for the production of good animals, and the present lot of youngsters is sufficient guarantee that the dams have been well and carefully selected. There is one Erica in the herd, viz. Esther of Aberlour 4843, a very pretty specimen of the family, having all the characteristics of high breeding and the true Erica head. Since she came to England, Esther has produced a beautiful bull calf by the Jilt, sire Juval 1880. There are three female Prides—Pride of Aberdeen 16th 3302 and her two heifer calves (twins) from Gavenwood. The calves are by Challenger 1260, and they should turn out the foundresses of a valuable branch of this esteemed family. The other females in the herd include Lizzie of Morlich 4954, of the Windsor branch of the Queen tribe, with her yearling daughter Lizzie of Benton 4955, by Marshal Var 1452, a most promising animal; Lady Lizzie 4953 of a Kinnochtry family; Blooming Heather 2nd 3572; Lemon 2nd 2264, of the Portlethen Lively family, and her yearling daughter Lavish by Matador 1710; Rose of Boghead 1437 and her daughter Rose 5th 4958; Abbess 3rd, bred at Easter Tulloch, and her daughter Abbess 5th, by Serapis 998; Faithful 3rd 4957, of the Kinnaird Fanny family; Miss Carnegie 6th; Brunette 3rd, by Lowther 1388, of the Ballindalloch Miss Burgess family; Fanny of Boghead 3341 with her three-year-old daughter, Farewell, by Serapis 998; Gravity 4864, of the Montbletton Mayflower family; Ethelinda 3356, of the Tillyfour Ruth sort; and Bathy 3rd, of the Miss Watson family. Four females have been sold to Mr Geary, London, Ontario—viz. Miss Carnegie 5th; Brunette 3rd; Rose 5th 4958; and Lady Benton, out of Lizzie 4953. Two bull calves of last year have been sold—the one, Jock o' Benton 1894, from Lady Lizzie, to Professor Lawson, Halifax,

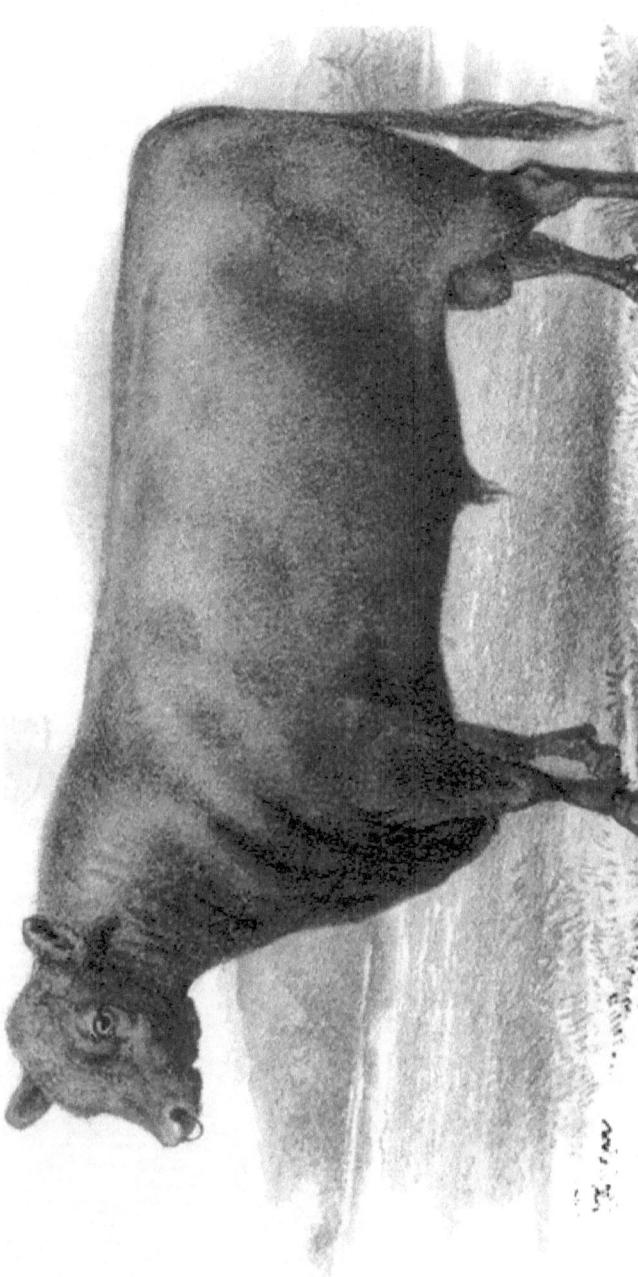

From Life by A M Gauci

Hanhart imp

"ENGLISHMAN" at 18 MONTHS OLD.

The Property of C.Stephenson Balliol College Farm Long Benton Newcastle on Tyne.

Nova Scotia, and the other, Laird o' Benton 1895, from Blooming Heather 2nd, to the Marquis of Londonderry for crossing purposes. The calves are allowed to suckle their dams, but are kept in a covered yard during summer, their dams being brought into them morning, noon, and night for a time, and afterwards night and morning. The heifers are put to the bull when about fifteen months old, and having been well kept are strong and well-matured. Mr Stephenson has allowed his neighbours the use of his bulls, and the result of the cross of the polled bulls on the ordinary cows of the district is very flattering to the polled breed. As a rule the cows in the district lack flesh, being kept principally for milk, and the polled bull not only gives this, but what is more noticeable, he is very impressive as to colour. A great proportion of the calves come black or nearly so, and seem to have many of the good characteristics of the polled breed, being full of flesh or muscle, and giving promise of being grand butchers' cattle.

Beechwood.—A very fine herd has been collected by Mr W. B. Greenfield of Beechwood, Dunstable, Bedfordshire. It was commenced in 1880 by purchases at the Glamis sale. On that occasion six animals were procured, five females from the Earl of Airlie and a bull from the Earl of Strathmore. The females comprised Rose of Guynd 2nd 2599 and her daughters, Gay Lass 3511, by Gainsborough 3rd 598, and Griselda 3877, by Timour 3rd 1287, the last-named having been the highest-priced animal at the sale (70 guineas). Rose of Guynd 2nd is a good milker, a splendid breeder, and since she went to Beechwood has produced Gay Lass 2nd 4723, the winner of the third prize as a calf at Peterborough in 1881, an animal of rare quality and style. Gay Lass 3511 is a strong, big, heavily-fleshed cow. Her last two calves were both heifers. Griselda is a beautiful specimen of a polled cow, with nice feminine head and splendid back and hind-quarters. She was the first-prize cow at Peterborough, and is an excellent breeder, her two calves being beauties. Another purchase from Lord Airlie was Manilla 4189 of The Thorn Flora family. Escape 3879, a strong, healthy cow and a deep milker, also came from Lord Airlie. The bull bought from Lord Strathmore was Bombastes 1548, from Beauty of Garline 1247, and after Neptune 1152. The first-prize yearling at Kilburn, he won in 1881 the prize of £20, presented by the Marquis of Huntly for the best bull of any age at Peterborough. He has been used as stock sire with success, his calves of this year being very promising. At the Marquis of Huntly's dispersion in 1881 some important additions were made. Mr Greenfield then secured the finest animal offered at that important sale in Vine 9th 3256 of the Daisy branch of the Queen tribe. She was the highest-priced yearling at the Tillyfour sale in 1878, and cost 115 guineas at Aboyne. A half-sister to the celebrated cow Dora 1280, she is an animal of beautiful symmetry and quality. At Aboyne, Mary 2nd 3851, of the Westertown Victoria family, and the grand breeding cow Daylight 1478, of the Rothiemay Georgina family, were obtained. The next additions were made at Mr Hannay's sale in 1881. They comprised Jinnes Gay 3771, a half-sister of the champion cow Innes 1934; Kilmeny 2nd 4780, of the Matilda branch of the Queen tribe; Challenge 4542 after Challenger 1260; the lovely heifer calf Benefit 2nd 5016, of the Montbletton Mayflower family, being out of the Highland Society's first-prize cow Blackbird of Corskie 2nd 3024 and Susanne 3rd of the Westertown Rose family, also a very handsome animal. Mr Greenfield has been very fortunate with his highly-bred herd, and the calves and heifers bred by him give promise of future excellence.

Bradley Hall.—While visiting Mr Stephenson's farm last autumn, Mr O. C. Wallis, Bradley Hall, was much struck with the polled cattle, and resolved to go into the

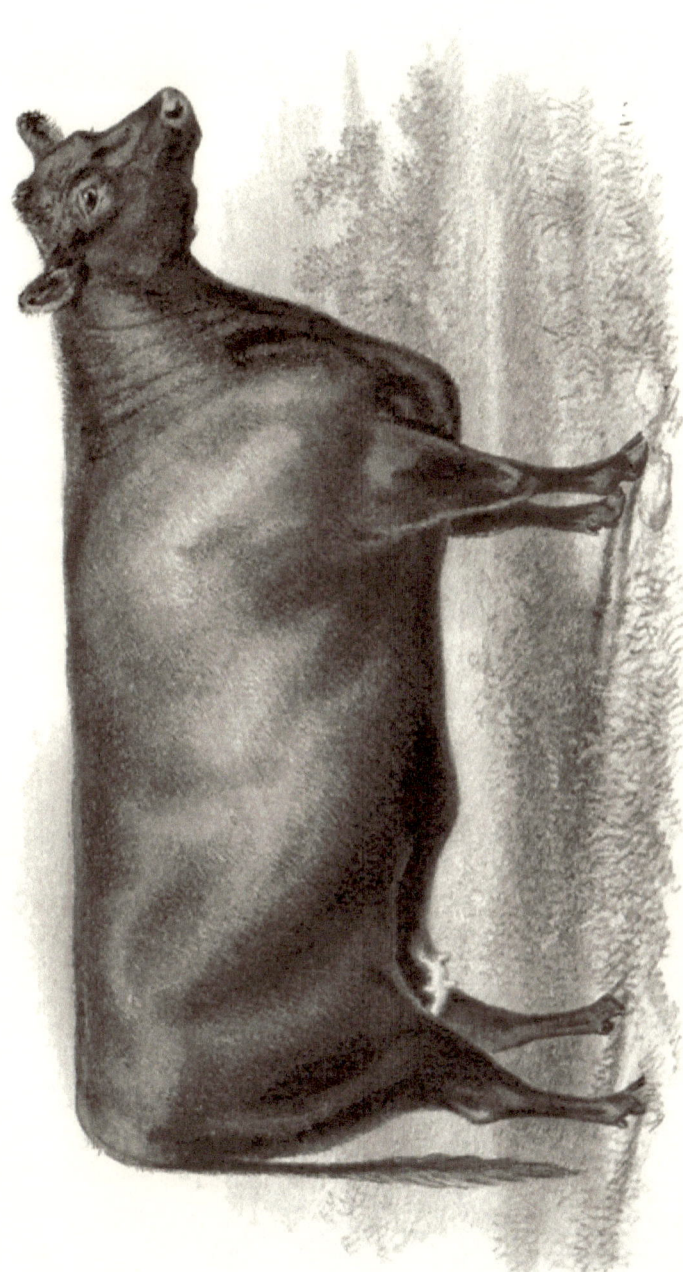

From Life by A.M Cauci.

Hanhart imp

"EASTER" (4540) at 3 YEARS OLD.
The Property of Owen.C.Wallis Bradley Hall Wylam-on-Tyne.

north of Scotland, accompanied by Mr Robert Bruce, Great
Smeaton, to see the principal herds. Being very greatly
impressed with the remarkable family-likeness of the
Ballindalloch Ericas, as well as with their beautiful heads
and other good characteristics, he determined on forming
a herd, and on getting as much of the Erica element as
possible. He bought the only female of this family obtainable at Ballindalloch, but from the list appended it will be
seen he has now in his possession thirteen females of this
tribe. The lot form a pretty family group, and there are
four particularly good ones,—viz. Eve 3355, Erica 6th 3023,
Era 3833, and Easter 4540,—while the heifer calf from
Ermin 3532, by the famous Pride bull Knight of the Shire
1699, may be mentioned as one of the most promising
youngsters of the breed. The other Ericas are Elina 4361
and her heifer calf, Editha 1737, Elf 3751, Errantine 4546,
Ermin 3532, with the heifer calves Esperanza, from Erica
6th, and Estella, from Easter. Of the Pride family, the
herd boasts of two specimens, both very pretty and good.
They are Khiva 4188, of the Ballindalloch Kindness branch
of the strain, and a heifer calf from the Gavenwood matron,
Lilias of Tillyfour 1795. Other three Ballindalloch families
are represented in the herd in Jemima of Ballindalloch
4172, of the famous Jilt tribe; Nosegay 8th 3914, of the
Nosegay tribe; and Frolic 4039, of the Lady Fanny tribe.
One of the best show animals in the herd is Patroness
4561, from the celebrated Patience of Corskie 1932, by
Proud Viscount 1264; while Heather Bell of Haughton 3rd
3953, from her great size and true outline, may be said to
be one of the best of the cows. In Smyrna 4571 and her
heifer calf, a well-known family is represented—viz. the
Miss Watsons of Easter Skene. The cow Penuel 3755,
bought from Mr William Robertson, is a very good
specimen of the old Burnside blood; while Mary of White-
side 3829, and her twin heifers, now two years old, represent
an old Clova family. Hecuba 3rd 3637, bought for the

dairy, though not a high-bred one, has good blood in her veins. As stock bulls, Mr Wallis has secured two splendid animals—a six-year-old and a yearling. The older bull is well known to all admirers of the breed. We refer to Challenger 1260, of the Pride tribe, whose portrait is given in vol. v. of the 'Herd Book.' The yearling named Sea King was bred at Ballindalloch from Sprite 3796, one of the best cows in Sir George Macpherson Grant's herd. Sea King has for sire the famous bull Justice 1462, while his dam's sire and grand-sire were the two champion bulls Judge 1150 and Juryman 404. From the material of which the herd is composed, containing, as it does, the very best blood obtainable, great things may be predicted of its future. Bradley Hall is beautifully situated on the banks of the Tyne, and its well sheltered pastures on a dry gravel subsoil ought to be a healthy, good home for the choice herd which has been gathered together at no little expense and trouble.

Ewell.—Mr John H. Bridges, yr. of Federate, has a few polled cattle at Ewell, Surrey. He bought two two-year-old heifers in 1878 from the late Mr Walker, Montbletton. Both were by Hampton 492, one being Mayflower 3rd 3411, and the other Duchess Marie 3410, and represented Mr Walker's celebrated Mayflower family. They had been first-prize winners as heifers at Turriff, and they carried respectively second and third prizes at the Royal show at Kilburn. The bull at present in use is Ebony 1261, own brother to Black Prince of Melville 1244, both bred by Mr Melville Cartwright of Melville. Prior to him, the bull used was Nicholas 1210, bred by the Earl of Fife. There are at Ewell four cows, a two-year-old heifer, two yearling heifers, and three bulls, besides a few steers. Mr Bridges finds the breed very hardy, and nothing seems to hurt them. He had some of his animals turned out on undrained meadows night and day last winter, with not even a shed to go into, and they always appeared to be well.

Felcourt.—Mr Carter Wood established a herd at Felcourt, East Grinsted, Sussex, in 1874, by the purchase of four animals from Mr Strachan, Wester Fowlis. There were: Beatrice 1954, by Draco 3rd 733; Isabella of Felcourt 2327, by the Highland Society's first-prize bull Palmerston 374; Elleana 2328, also by Palmerston; and Lady of Wester Fowlis 1955, by Draco 3rd. The produce of these cows have been retained and bred from, the sire used having been Lord Forbes 772, bred by Mr Walker, West-side.

Goodwood.—The Duke of Richmond and Gordon keeps a small herd at Goodwood, Sussex. It is mainly descended from stock obtained at the Westertown dispersion in 1874.

Horsted.—This herd, belonging to Mr F. Barchard, Horsted, Uckfield, Sussex, was begun in 1880 by purchases at the joint sale held by Mr M'Combie of Easter Skene and Mr Hamilton of Skene. From the former was bought Isabella of Easter Skene 2585, of the Miss Watson family; Lady Langtry 3804; Margaret, by Paris 1473; and Scota, by Paris; and from the latter, Lady Love 2nd, by His Excellency 1271, dam Lady Love 3387; Vine 3rd of Skene, by His Excellency, dam Vine 2nd of Skene 3329; and the bull His Worship 2nd 1889. At Lord Strathmore and Lord Airlie's sale at Glamis, in the same year, Mr Barchard bought from Lord Airlie Elmira 4208, Jessica 5th 4206, and Guinevere 4211, all by Potentate 1199. These have bred well, and as far as Mr Barchard can at present judge, the climate of the south of England is not unfavourable to the polled breed.

Roos.—The Roos herd was founded in October 1875, Mr Dickinson at that time being allowed the selection of the Tillyfour herd—four or five animals excepted. He chose Heather Bloom 1189, of the Rothiemay Victoria family, and her daughter Louisa of Tillyfour 1790, with the fine two-year-old heifer Lady Scott 1802, giving 100 guineas a-piece, then considered a high figure. At the same time he bought the first-rate old cow Naiad 978, of the Balwyllo Keepsake family. Mr M'Combie had acquired her at a sale of Sir George Macpherson Grant's, she being the highest-priced animal at the sale. Two or three others of lesser note were obtained at Tillyfour. A great milker, Mary of Kinnochtry 1770, was got from Mr Adamson, Balquharn, and a couple of cows from the Balquharn dispersion were added before Christmas of 1881. As stock bull, Mr Dickinson took from Tillyfour Blackleg 1350, bred at Easter Skene out of the well-known prize breeding cow Grizzle 995, and got by Moudiewart 686. Blackleg went to the butcher after a year's service, his place being taken by a promising yearling, Baron de Roos, out of Naiad, who was served when at Tillyfour by Altanour 641, being thus Tillyfour bred. This yearling was assisted by another of the same age, named Burton, out of Heather Bloom, who was in calf, when sold, to Sir Garnet 684. A bull from Mains of Kelly followed, and in 1880 Chard, out of Heather Bloom, sire Baron de Roos, was used. In 1881 he was assisted by a yearling named Heather Lad, also out of Heather Bloom, and by the Mains of Kelly bull. In addition to the progeny of the cows named, the Roos herd contains many good non-pedigree animals, which have gradually taken the place of cross-breds and dairy Shorthorns. Mr Dickinson finds that certain strains of polls give fully the average quantity of milk, the quality being second only to that of the Jersey. The polls are hardier and are easier kept than the dairy Shorthorn or cross-bred. The bulls show their potency, nine-tenths of the calves from cross-bred cows coming black and hornless.

Smeaton Manor.—Major Godman, who is improving and beautifying his property, recently took one of his farms into his own hands, and being favourably impressed with the polled cattle exhibited at the Carlisle show of the

Royal Agricultural Society of England, determined to found a herd in the very heart of the Shorthorn country. It may be interesting to state that the herd now grazes on land that was occupied by George Coates, the compiler of the Shorthorn 'Herd Book.' Major Godman's herd was started in August 1880 by the following six animals bought by Mr Robert Bruce, viz.:—May Queen 5th 4499, of the Easter Tulloch May Queen family; Pride of Altyre 3rd 4277, of the Pride family; Princess of Altyre 2nd 4280, of the Kinnochtry Princess family; Favourite of Altyre 3rd 4278, of the Kinnochtry Favourite family; Regia 2nd 4283, of the Montbletton Charlotte family; and Lena 3rd 4279, of the Westertown Lady Ann family. May Queen 5th 4499 was bought at the Tillyfour sale in August 1880, and since she went to Smeaton has had two bull calves, one, Knight of Smeaton 1879, by the prize bull Knight of the Garter 1763, having been sold to Mr Geary, London, Ontario. Pride of Altyre 3rd 4277, a pretty young cow, was bought from Sir William Gordon Cumming, Bart. of Altyre, and had, in 1881, a bull calf, The Proud Knight 1922, by the Westertown Duchess bull Dustman 1667. The Proud Knight succeeded Ludulph 1711, of the Portlethen Lively family as stock sire. Princess of Altyre 2nd 4280 was also bought from Sir William Gordon Cumming, and is an excellent representative of the family to which she belongs. She had in April 1881 a bull calf, Prince of Smeaton 1923, sold to Mr Geary, Ontario. The Altyre herd also supplied Favourite 3rd 4278, who has had two calves, a heifer and bull. Regia 3rd has had a heifer calf, Regina, by Black Watch 1242. Lena 3rd has had a heifer calf, Dusky Maid, and the pair were sold to Mr Geary. The cow Regia 2nd, a very good one, has gone into the dairy, the rest suckle their own calves. Regia is a wonderfully deep milker, and gives very rich cream. A good many farmers are sending Shorthorn cows to Major Godman's bulls, with exceedingly good results, some of the calves being very superior.

South Ella.—Mr Arthur Egginton, South Ella, Hull, started a herd in September 1878. In that year he purchased at Mr Hannay's sale at Montcoffer the cows Garland 3018 (since dead) and Pendant 1935; and at Mr Tayler's sale at Rothiemay, Charm 2436, Miss Ba-Rae 2311, Water Lily 2432, and Hallowe'en 2435. The first sire used was Kinsman 1444, bred by Mr Hannay, after Waterside King 870, and out of Kate of Glenbarry 1187 of the Georgina family. Then followed Scotter 1634, by Young Viscount 736, out of Pendant 1935, and Cupid 2nd, bought in October 1881. Mr Egginton informs us that he has found the polled cattle most satisfactory in every way — being wonderful feeders, very quiet and ornamental. His calving cows remain out all the winter, having sheds to go into when they like. They get a few turnips and some hay when snow is on the ground, but no cake is used, and it is wonderful to notice in what condition they keep. In fact, Mr Egginton says, they get too fat unless care is taken. They are most hardy, and the climate suits them admirably. Mr Egginton has killed steers under two years at 75 stones (14 lbs.) each. The calves are allowed to run with their dams during summer.

Studley Priory.—Mr Henderson, Studley Priory, near Oxford, supplies us with the following interesting account of his experience with polled cattle:—I made my first beginning in September 1879, when I purchased seven pedigree heifers and one pedigree bull, Royal Eric 1278, at the Earl of Aberdeen's sale in Aberdeen. Some of my neighbours advised me against attempting to rear polled stock. They believed there was something in the swedes of Aberdeen and Forfar shires which was not in English swedes, hence the breed could not develop in England so successfully as it had done in the north. The cattle

arrived at a most unfortunate time, as our grass was bad,
and partially flooded with the incessant rains, while a
most severe winter followed. The animals, however, got
nothing but what they could pick up, except a feed of
hay twice a day when there was snow on the ground.
They had only an open shed for shelter; still they kept in
good condition—better than my Shorthorns, which were
having plenty of mangels, etc. I felt so satisfied with my
short but trying experience of the polled breed that in
April 1880 I purchased other ten heifers, all pure bred.
Writing now in April 1882, I have had two seasons'
experience of the breed, and I find they do better on the
same grass land than the Shorthorns. They are more
contented, and they are a stronger and hardier race. I
find their calves are easier to rear. I do not use the
polled breed for the dairy, but I make every polled
mother suckle two calves—a foster calf in addition to her
own calf; and almost invariably the polled calf is much
stronger than the Shorthorn, both being suckled by the
same cow. No better test can be had of the superior
vitality and strength of the polled over the Shorthorn
breed, than the wonderful difference of the two breeds in
undergoing the painful operation of castrating the bull
calves. The strength and hardihood of the polled I have
observed to be amazingly greater. I have tried the experiment of crossing the Shorthorn heifer with the polled bull,
and this cross has produced very big, strong calves, hardier
and easier kept than the pure Shorthorn. I have still faith
in the "Blackskins" suiting my land and my roots, and
that they will be profitable to me. In these days of keen
competition, a farmer cannot afford to indulge his fancies
in breeding stock; he must find out what pays best, and
stick to that. Last week I was fortunate in securing, at
the Aberdeen sale, one of Mr James Argo's young bulls,
Icon, and I trust by another year to have made a start at
realizing some money from the herd, and begin to test

financially and practically the profit and loss from putting into practice my faith in the polled cattle.

A herd was established by the late Mr Postlethwaite, The Hollins, Cumberland, purchases having been made from Mr M'Combie of Tillyfour. On the death of Mr Postlethwaite the herd was dispersed in 1878, when Mr M'Combie bought several animals. At The Hollins sale Mr Thomson of Moresdale Hall, Westmoreland, acquired a few good polled cattle, and with some purchases made a short time previously at Tillyfour he had the nucleus of a herd, but we believe he has disposed of most of his stock. Mr Loder, M.P., Whittlebury, Towcester, procured several polled animals at the joint sale of the Earls of Strathmore and Airlie at Glamis in 1880.

Ireland.

The breed has long been favourably known in Ireland. Mr Watson, Keillor, used to include the Emerald Isle in his show circuit, not only as a judge, but also as an exhibitor; and it is partly from this circumstance that the great agricultural societies of the country, the Royal Irish and the Royal Dublin, have for many years offered prizes for polled cattle. It was in Ireland that Mr Watson's celebrated bull Grey-breasted Jock 2 closed his career, having been sold for 100 guineas, after his victory at Belfast in 1843, to Mr Kirkaldy of Hearnesbrook, Eyrecourt. It sometimes happened at these early shows that Mr Watson had to be content with minor prizes, having been occasionally beaten with his own stock, or their descendants in other hands. This was probably due to the fresh condition in which the Irish breeders were able to present their cattle compared with the jaded appearance of the Keillor animals after their trip across the channel. At the Royal Irish show at Belfast in 1843, when Grey-breasted Jock 2 was first in the class of aged bulls, Mr Thomas Seymour of

Ballymore Castle, Ballinasloe, was first for cows and heifers.
At the Royal Dublin show at Dublin in 1844, Mr Seymour
was first for aged bulls with a four-year-old, bred at Keillor,
Mr Watson being second with a bull named Saunders.
That year Mr Watson was first for two-year-old heifers,
with a pair bred by himself, after a bull named Black Jock.
At the Royal Irish show at Ballinasloe in 1845, Mr Kirkaldy of Hearnesbrook was first for aged bulls with Sambo,
bred by himself; and he was first for yearling bulls with
one bred by himself from the Keillor stock, probably a son
of Grey-breasted Jock 2. Mr Kirkaldy was also first for
cows with one bred by Mr Millar, Ballumbie, and Mr
Watson was first for two-year-old heifers. At the Royal
Irish show at Limerick in 1846, Mr Seymour gained all
the prizes, and at Londonderry in 1847 Mr Watson was
first for aged bulls with the famous Old Jock 1, who had
a very close fight for the Purcell cup as best bull in the
yard.

Lord Talbot de Malahide had a superior herd at Malahide
Castle, County Dublin, his animals being descended from
the Ardovie, Kinnaird, and Balwyllo herds. Lord Lurgan
also bred polled cattle, and possessed the well-known Kinnaird bull Monk 149, who left much fine stock in Ireland.
It will be seen from our notice of the Kinnochtry herd that
Mr William Owen of Blessington, County Wicklow, has
had many of Mr Ferguson's best bulls, and he has had
almost a monopoly of the prizes at the Royal Irish and Royal
Dublin shows for several years. Mr S. E. Collis of Tieraclea, Tarbert, County Kerry, has a very good herd, the
matrons of which are Sarah of Ruthven 2429, after the
grand old bull Major 3rd 662; Waterside Janet 3472, bred
by Mr Wilken, and got by the same sire; and Waterside
Daisy 2nd. He has used the bull Lord Kilmurrily 918,
bred by the Earl of Fife after Major of Bognie 444, and
out of the champion cow Innes 1934. Lord Kilmurrily
left some very good heifers, and has been succeeded by a

Y

highly-bred bull from Kinnochtry, after Shah 680, and out
of 2nd Baroness of Kinnochtry 3293, of Mr Ferguson's
Baroness family. The Earl of Carysfort and Mr. Farrell,
Moynalty, have also had some polled cattle. Although the
number of polled herds in Ireland is comparatively small,
the breed has had a considerable influence in improving
the cattle of the country. Mr Owen, for example, has
allowed farmers the use of his bulls, and their produce
shows great improvement as compared with the ordinary
stock of the country.

CHAPTER XVI.

THE Northern polls seem destined to have a wide distribution. Ten years ago little was known of them except by
reputation beyond the limits of their native country.
Within the past few years, however, large numbers of them
have been scattered over many foreign countries, including
the United States of America, Canada, South America,
New Zealand, France, Denmark, Germany, and other parts
of the European Continent. The breed was first introduced
into the grassy regions of the Far West by the late Mr
George Grant, who in 1873 sent three polled bulls to his
ranche on the Colony of Victoria, founded by him in Ellis
County, Kansas. These bulls were taken from the herd
of the late Mr George Brown, Westertown, Morayshire,
and were for several years used at Victoria among mixed
lots of native cows. In 1877 the writer saw two of them
(one had died previously) browsing near Mr Grant's resid-

ence, and well they seemed to enjoy their prairie life. They
were most prolific sires, and the great improvement in their
produce as compared to the ordinary cattle of the country
created no little sensation. All the cows were horned, and
yet a very large majority of the young stock were polled.
The choice quality and the early maturity of Mr Grant's
polled grades attracted considerable attention, and for his
surplus stock there was always a keen demand. By degrees
the fame of the polled breed made its way throughout
America, and the demand which has there sprung up for
them is so great that it would not be satisfied even if
every one of the race remaining in this country were sent
across the Atlantic. Probably over 500 head have gone to
the United States and Canada during the past two years,
and every month brings fresh commissions to the buyers
on this side.

The polls, we believe, have bright prospects in America.
Their excellent grazing, fattening, and maturing properties,
and their hardy constitution, fit them admirably for the
country, while the absence of horns also counts in their
favour. American cattle have long boat and railway
journeys to accomplish, and it is found that in these, horned
animals often inflict damage upon each other by goring and
bruising. From nearly every one who has had any
experience of the Scotch polls in America we have received
most favourable accounts, both as to the thriving of the
cattle and their future prospects on the farms and ranches
of the New World. As evidence of the interest aroused
in the breed on the Western Continent, it may be mentioned that steps are being taken to start a 'Polled Herd
Book' for America. This movement has been taken up
heartily by Mr F. B. Redfield and others, and is likely to
be carried out successfully.

The introduction of the Northern Scotch polled cattle
into Canada may be dated from 1876, when Professor
Brown, of the Ontario School of Agriculture at Guelph,

secured some very good specimens for that excellent institution, with which he has been long and creditably connected. There they have bred well, and for the young
animals which are offered for sale periodically there is an
active demand. From the other countries in which the
breed has been tried encouraging reports have also been
received. We append a few notes regarding the chief
foreign herds and importations.

United States of America.

Mr F. B. Redfield's choice herd at Wigwam Farm,
Batavia, New York, was founded in 1879 by the purchase
of three heifers and a bull from Mr Ferguson, Kinnochtry.
The purchase was made at the Highland Society's show
that year at Perth. The animals were—the bull Field
Marshal 1778, of the Baroness family, after the Pride of
Aberdeen bull Shah 680; and the heifers Princess 8th
3298, of the Princess family; 3rd Baroness of Kinnochtry 3294, of the Baroness family; and Favourite 9th 3295,
of the Favourite family, all after Shah 680. In March
1881, Mr Redfield imported sixteen additional animals—
nine bulls and seven heifers, as follows:—Bulls—Fandango,
of the Favourite family; Proud Knight, of the Daisy or
Vine branch of the Queen tribe; Favonius, of the Favourite
family; Falerino, of the Favourite family; Manfred, of
the Castle Fraser Mina family; Falconer, of the Favourite
family; Prince of Batavia 1898, of the Princess family;
Angus-bred Baron 1899, of the Baroness family; and
Manrico, of the Mina family. Heifers—Princess 10th
4339, Princess 12th 4345, 6th Baroness of Kinnochtry
4341, Favourite 10th 4336, Favourite 12th 4606, Maid of
the Mist 4344, and Mountain Mist 4346, these representing the Princess, Baroness, Favourite, and Mina families.
They were all bought from Mr Ferguson, Kinnochtry.
The three heifers Mr Redfield first imported were mated

in Scotland with the Princess bull Prince of the Realm
1695. In 1880 he used Field Marshal 1778. This bull,
now on a ranche in Kansas, left some very good stock,
including several excellent grades out of Shorthorn cows.
On the ranche he has proved most useful, and has thriven
admirably, keeping his condition well under severe climatic
trials. He was exhibited at the Fair at Hay's City last
year, and was greatly admired. For the bull calves dropped
to him by native cows, there was a spirited demand among
neighbouring ranche men. In 1881 and 1882 Mr Redfield used Manrico 1900. The herd numbered in April
1882 eleven head—four Princesses, three Baronesses, three
Favourites, and the stock bull Manrico 1900, a son of
the Erica bull St Clair 1160 a Highland Society first-
prize winner, and the Mina cow Mina 4th of Melville
3843, one of the best breeders at Kinnochtry. Mr Redfield's principal sales have been as follows :—In June 1881,
the bull Field Marshal 1778, went into the ranche of Mr
Robbins, Battell, Victoria, Ellis Co., Kansas. Shortly
after, the bulls Fandango and Proud Knight were sold to
Mr Jos. B. Eldridge, of Norfolk, Connecticut, for his ranche
in Ellis Co., Kansas. About the same time, Professor E.
M. Shelton, of the Kansas Agricultural College, visited
Wigwam Farm, and purchased the bull Falerino for the
College Farm at Manhattan, taking with him also a cow
purchased at the Ontario Experimental Farm, Guelph. In
addition to the above, Mr Redfield, sold in the summer
and fall of 1881, three bull calves bred from his imported
heifers—one to Mr J. J. Rodgers, Abingdon, Knox County,
Illinois; one to Messrs D. E. Fenn & Son, Tallmadge,
Ohio; and the third to Mr J. G. Tayler, Burlington, Kansas.
In January 1882 he also sold to Messrs D. E. Fenn &
Son, the heifers Maid of the Mist 4344, and Mountain
Mist 4346, with heifer calves. The only other sale was
that of the bull Falconer to Messrs D. J. & G. F. Whitmore, West Union, Iowa, in February last. Prices have

averaged about £100 a head. Mr Redfield exhibited
stock in 1881 at the Chicago Fair, the Illinois State Fair,
and the St Louis Fair, where he had much success, winning
in all about £200 in prizes. The cow Princess 8th 3298,
and the bull Manrico 1900, were particularly successful.
Mr Redfield gained the first premiums for young herds at
Chicago and St Louis with Princess 12th, Mountain Mist,
Maid of the Mist, Favourite 12th, and Princess A. Mr.
Redfield states that " the prospects are that the climate of
America will suit the polled Aberdeen or Angus cattle
perfectly. I hear favourable reports on this point from
all parts and extremes of the States and territories. I
believe they have constitutions of iron, so to speak, and
will stand very hard usage. The rough winter voyage on
deck of the steamer which my last lot, little more than
calves, endured without injury, was a severe test."

Mr A. B. Matthews, Kansas City, formed a herd within
the last two years by purchases in Canada and Michigan.
These were chiefly Galloways; but some Aberdeen or
Angus were also obtained, among them being Deeside
Lass, a daughter of Leochel Lass 6th 2096, bred at
Haughton. In the spring of this year, Mr Matthews
visited the North of Scotland, and selected an excellent
lot of 55 head, comprising 33 females and 22 males.
Among them were Bella 3rd of Greystone 4740, after
Major 3rd 662, from Mr Reid, Greystone, and full sister to
Bella 2nd, sold to go to New Zealand for 200 guineas;
Miss Fyfe 3rd 4841, after the champion bull Prince
Albert of Baads 1336, from Mr Anderson, Daugh, Tarland; Waterside Juliet, bred at Easter Skene, after Paris
1473, the first-prize bull at the Paris Exhibition in 1878,
and out of Juliet of Easter Skene 3808; a two-year-old
heifer Ray, after Fyvie 737, and out of Rompie 2298, bred
by Mr Smith, Burnshangie. From Mr Emslie, Keir, Belhelvie, were bought Cherry Princess 4930, of the Kinnochtry Emily family; and Keir, descended from Lady

Panmure 59, by Panmure 51. From Mr Scott, Easter Tulloch, were obtained Duchess 11th, of a branch of the Old Grannie strain, and Margaret 4th, of the same descent as the Easter Tulloch Mayflowers, from which Witch of Endor 3528 was bred. Several of the animals were selected from Mr Wilken's herd at Waterside of Forbes, and besides the herds mentioned, there were specimens of those at Balquharn, Gavenwood, Blairshinnoch, Campfield, Brucehill, East-town, Powrie, Skene, Kinbate, Baads, Balquhain, Nether Kildrummy, Oakhill, Haughton, etc. Two stock bulls were selected, the one bred by Mr. Ferguson, Kinnochtry, and the other bred by Mr Stevenson, Blairshinnoch. The latter is Strathisla 1816, of the Erica tribe, being out of Ella 1205, a daughter of Erica 843, and after Moraystown 1439, whose dam was the prize cow Forget-Me-Not 1685. Mr Matthews writes us:— "My herd now numbers 170 head. I have sold within the last two years about fifty head of cattle. They have nearly all gone to the plains in theWest. I have shown my cattle at the Kansas State Fair, where there was no opposition, and also at the Kansas City Exposition, where they received the first prizes in all classes shown. I also exhibited them at the great polled cattle show at St Louis last year, where seven herds were represented, and there took the herd premium, also several individual prizes. This was the greatest show of polled cattle ever held in America. I have fed a polled steer from November up to the present time (May 25, 1882), the average daily gain of which was about 3¼ lbs. per day, which I think very good. I am now also feeding a polled heifer, the average gain of which I cannot now give, but it is certainly much better than the steer. I could not expect animals to do better than mine have done during the time I have had them, and all parties to whom I have sold them write me most encouragingly of their hardiness, capability of caring for themselves under the most disadvantageous circumstances, and the ease with which they fatten when well fed. The prospect for the breed is beyond anything that I have ever known for any class of cattle."

Messrs Anderson & Findlay, Lake Forest, Illinois, have made three large importations. The first lot was landed at Quebec in August 1878, and comprised five females and a bull from the Westside of Brux, Brucehill, Pitfour, Burnshangie, and Waterside of Forbes herds. The bull then selected was Nicolis 1633, bred by Mr Walker, Westside, after Carlos 673, and out of Bess of Bogfern 1225, descended from the Keillor herd. Most of the animals had gained prizes at the local shows in Aberdeenshire. The next importation was made in August 1881, and included specimens from the Mains of Kelly, Wellhouse, Altyre, Blairshinnoch, Auchmaliddy, Earnside, and Bridgend herds. Among them were representatives of the Mains of Kelly Jennet, the Rothiemay Old Lady Jean, the Montbletton Charlotte, and the Westertown Victoria families. The bulls taken over at that time were Waterside King 2nd 1864, bred by Mr Wilken, of the Kinnaird Fanny family; and Basuto 1820, bred by Sir George Macpherson Grant, Bart., of Ballindalloch, after the Erica bull Editor 1460, and out of the prize cow Blackbird of Corskie 3rd 3766, of the Montbletton Mayflower family. The third import was made in the summer of 1882, and comprised 20 heifers and 10 bulls from various herds in the north of Scotland. Messrs Anderson & Findlay also purchased from Messrs Burleigh & Bodwill, Vassalboro, Maine their herd of polled cattle. Among these were the following:—the Erica cow Enigma 4176, bred by Mr Brooke, Cardney, Dunkeld; the Beauty cow Sunshine 3rd 3337, bred by Mr Skinner, Drumin; Snowdrop 2nd 4599, bred at Drumin; and the Nosegay cow Netta 4041, bred at Ballindalloch. There were also two heifers from the Mains of Advie herd—one out of Duchess of Advie 3585, and the other out of Norah

3107. The cows had calves at foot by a Jilt sire. The herd at Lake Forest is thus, it will be seen, composed of very good material, and has already taken a creditable position in the American showyards. Writing us in February 1882, Messrs Anderson & Findlay said:—" Our sales have been to T. R. Clark, Victoria, Ellis Co., Kansas ; Lee & Reynolds, Dodge City, Kansas ; J. J. Rodgers, Abingdon, Illinois ; Abner Royce, Naperville, Illinois ; P. H. Tompkins, El Paso, Illinois ; W. S. Crosby, Highland Park, Illinois ; George F. Whitmore, West Union, Fayette Co., Iowa. The animals sold were 6 bull calves, 2 heifer calves, a yearling and a two-year-old heifer realizing £660, or an average of £66 per head. The future is pregnant with promise to this breed in this country and North British America. We are unable to see any reason for breeding any other than the polled Aberdeen or Angus for plains and beef cattle, since for early maturity, weight, quality of beef, and hardiness of constitution they cannot be surpassed, to say nothing of the advantage of being hornless."

Mr J. J. Rodgers, Angus Farm, Knox County, Abingdon, Illinois, bought from Mr Ferguson, Kinnochtry, in the spring of 1881, three animals—viz., the cow Favourite 6th 3118, the heifer Baroness 8th 5039, and the bull Baron Balgersho 1696—these being of the Kinnochtry Favourite and Baroness families. In the spring of 1882 Mr Rodgers secured from the Kinnochtry herd twelve yearling heifers and two yearling bulls. These were of the Princess Baroness Favourite and Mina families. The list comprehended the following:—Princess Adelaide, by Shah 680, out of Princess 2nd 916 ; Princess Olga, by Baron Balgersho 1696, out of Theresa 1773 ; Princess Alberta, by Prince of the Realm 1695, out of Warble 922 ; Princess Louisa, by Baron Balgersho 1696, out of 5th Baroness 4333 ; Princess Maud, by Prince of the Realm 1695, out of Princess 3rd 1771 ; Princess Maria, by Prince of the

Realm, out of Georgina 3119; Dulciano, by Shah 680, out of Pride 3289; Blooming Belle, by Shah, out of Blossom, 3970; Melissa, by Prince of the Realm, out of Roxanna 3967; Everilda, by Prince of the Realm, out of Maggie 2nd 923; Minnie, by Prince of the Realm, out of Ruby 3964; Lizzie 5th, bred by Mr Pearson of Johnston Lodge, by A.K.H.B. 1576, out of Lizzie 4th 4867. Besides the twelve heifers, there also went from Mr Ferguson's herd two excellent yearling bulls, one being Faustulus, out of Louisa 1769, the other being Prince of the Blood, out of Princess 7th 3297. Both bulls were by Prince of the Realm.

Messrs Gudgell & Simpson, Missouri, Kansas, imported thirty animals last spring, supplementary to a previous importation. Thirteen of these were selected from the herd of Mr Wilken, Waterside, including the cows Blackcap 4042, bred at Ballindalloch, after the Erica bull St. Clair 1160, and from one of the Montbletton Mayflowers; Rosa Bonheur 2nd 3531, bred at Tillyfour, of the Rothiemay Victoria family; Myrtle of Tillychetly 3787, of the Drumin Lucy family, and calf at foot, by the Erica sire Etonian 1658. Besides a number of fine heifers obtained at Waterside, there were purchased two bulls— Polestar 1772, and Knight of St. Patrick, both of the Pride of Aberdeen family. The latter is a most valuable animal, bred by Mr Auld, Bridgend, after Knight of the Legion 1494, and out of Pride of Aberdeen 10th. The herd of Mr Reid, Greystone, furnished the cow Kate 6th 4733, a first-prize winner at Aberdeen; Pride 3rd 4744; and a two-year-old heifer. From the Old Morlich herd were secured the cow Jemima 2nd 4082, winner of the Queen's cup at Tarland, and a two-year-old heifer. The cow Rosella 3020 was bought from Mr Grant, Mains of Advie; the cow Isabella 2nd 3857, from Mr Strachan, Wester Fowlis. The other purchases were made from Mr Mackessack, Earnside; Mr Strachan, Montcoffer; Mr

Stevenson, Blairshinnoch ; and Mr George Bruce, Aberdeen.

Mr G. W. Henry, Kansas City, bought a valuable lot of twenty-three heifers and five bulls in the spring of 1882. From Mr Auld, Bridgend, was secured the cow Dandy 2nd 3266, of the Empress branch of the Queen tribe ; Tifty 5th 4575 of the Fyvie Flower family ; Dimple 3916 ; Dolly Douglass ; and Cymbeline. The herd at Greystone supplied Bella 4th, sister of the cow Bella 2nd, sold for 200 guineas ; Lady Haddo 7th ; and a yearling bull. A good selection was made from the herd of Mr Strachan, Wester Fowlis, all the animals from that herd—eight in number—having been by Prince Albert 1492, a son of Young Viscount 736. Three heifers were obtained from Mr Stevenson, Blairshinnoch ; two from Mr George Bruce, Aberdeen ; and one from Wellhouse. The bull Black Commodore was secured at Montbletton. He was after the prize bull Young Hero 1837, and of the Ballindalloch Coquette family. Bulls were also purchased from Mr Fraser, Kinbate ; and Mrs Hay, South Ythsie.

Mr J. V. Farwell of Chicago imported in the autumn of 1881, for his farm in Iowa, a bull and seven yearling heifers. The bull was Father Jack 1913, bred by Mr M'Kenzie, Lyne of Carron ; and among the heifers were specimens of the Westertown Rose and Mains of Kelly Guinea Pig families. Mr Farwell bought more recently, from Colonel Ferguson of Pitfour, a yearling bull out of the prize cow Dulcet 4057, and after Marischal Keith 1627 ; and two heifers. From other breeders in the North of Scotland eighteen heifers and a bull were secured.

Mr P. H. Tompkins, El Paso, Illinois, purchased a male and female,—the former being Black Hawk, and the latter Scottish Maid. The bull was purchased from Messrs Anderson & Findlay. Mr Tompkins says these animals wintered the easiest and best of any cattle he ever saw. Health and fatness appear to be their normal condition.

Mr J. F. Foote, New Jersey, made an importation in November 1881. The lot numbered twelve, and included a bull calf and yearling heifer from the Earl of Airlie; yearling heifer from Aboyne Castle; together with representatives of the Haughton, Pitgair, Old Morlich, Collithie, Skene, Tillychetly, Little Endovie, and other herds.

Mr W. H. Whitridge, of Baltimore, imported a bull and two heifers, selected for him by Mr Campbell Macpherson Campbell of Balliemore. They were the bull Sir Eustace, and the heifers Merrythought 4670 and Clarissa 4534.

Mr D. N. Hine, Milan, Erie Co., Ohio, laid the foundation of a herd by purchases from Mr Grant, Mains of Advie; Mr Maitland, Balhaggardy; and Mr Lumsden of Clova.

Mr Robbins Battell, 74 Wall Street, New York, and others, imported four females and two bulls in March 1881.

Mr F. W. Harvey, Chicago, imported two bulls and several heifers during the summer of 1882.

Mr Archibald Galbraith, of Messrs Galbraith Brothers, Janesville, Wisconsin, imported six animals in 1882 from the herds of Mr Bean, Balquharn Mains; Mr Grant, Methlick; Mr Beaton, Lethenty; and Mr Stewart, Knockollochy.

Canada.

In 1876 Professor Brown of the Agricultural College at Guelph, Ontario, paid a visit to Scotland, and selected for that institution three polled animals—the bull Gladiolus 1161 and the cow Eyebright 3001, from the herd of Mr Hannay, Gavenwood; and the cow Leochel Lass 4th 1864, from Mr Farquharson of Haughton, after she had taken the first prize at Alford the same year. In 1881 the bull Meldrum 1759, of the Madge family, was bought from the

Marquis of Huntly; and the cow Sybil's Darling 2nd
4611, of the Ballindalloch Sybil family, from Mr Argo,
Cairdseat. These animals have bred satisfactorily, and the
bulls have proved very sure stock-getters, having been put
with success to other breeds when other bulls failed to get
calves. Professor Brown writes:—"We can command
£60 to £70 for yearling bulls and heifers for the States
and Canada. Eyebright 3001 has given us a value in produce of £300 in five years. We have conclusively proved,
by extensive experiments, that the milk is very rich. We
are putting up a couple of grades (polled upon Canadian)
next winter against others in feeding. The polled cattle
do well in Canada—are hardy, splendid on pasture, good
searchers for food, kindly, good nurses, and evidently early
maturers. They are unquestionably, with Herefords, *the*
animal for our North-Western grazings."

Mr Mossom Boyd, Bobcaygeon, Ontario, founded a herd
in the summer of 1881 by the purchase of some very well-
bred animals. They comprised Pride of Findhorn 3rd
4758, of the Pride of Aberdeen family, and Mayflower of
Altyre 3rd 4763, of the Mulben Mayflower family, both
from the herd of Sir W. G. Gordon Cumming, Bart. of
Altyre; Wanton 4610, by the Erica bull Etonian 1658, bred
by Mr Argo, Cairdseat; Princess Alice 4829, descended
from the Keillor cow Old Grannie 1, bred by Mr Middleton, Waulkmill; Princess Dagmar 5th 4528, of the Matilda
branch of the Queen tribe, and Pauline 3672, bred by Mr
Bruce, Collithie; Waterside Queen 3208, of the Kinnaird
Fanny family, bred by Mr. Wilken, Waterside; and Caroline 2nd 3814, bred by Mr Reid, Nether Kildrummy.
These were to be largely added to this year. Mr Boyd
was using the bull Lord Macduff, bred at the Ontario
School of Agriculture, after Gladiolus 1161, and out of
Leochel Lass 4th 1864. Mr Boyd adds:—"I showed three
at our provincial exhibition last fall, and they were much
admired and curiously looked at, being the first exhibited,

and showing a marked superiority to the Galloways which stood alongside of them. Of the three I exhibited,—viz., Wanton 4610, Princess Alice 4829, and Pride of Findhorn 3rd 4758,—Wanton took precedence. She weighed 1040 lbs., being one year and 6½ months old. Having had so short an experience in handling the polled cattle, I cannot pronounce upon them further than to say that so far mine all look well and thriving, and I do not doubt will suit the climate admirably."

The Hon. J. H. Pope, Dominion Minister of Agriculture, Ontario, Canada, has made three importations through Mr Wilken, Waterside. The first two consignments were bought as an experiment, and consisted of fifteen heifers and a bull. These having proved satisfactory, a more valuable lot was selected last autumn. It included the beautiful cow Charmer 3rd 3251, of the Charmer branch of the Queen tribe, who had been sold at Tillyfour for 150 guineas, and was purchased at the Aboyne dispersion in September 1881 for 100 guineas; Pride of Montbletton 3rd 3418, of the Zara tribe; Melon 3837, of the Castle Fraser Mina tribe; Princess Dagmar 6th 4827, of the Matilda branch of the Queen tribe; and Fair Flower 4726, of the Ballindalloch Lady Fanny family. The others were from the Ardhuncart, Tillychetly, Cairnballoch, and Waulkmill herds.

The Honourable M. H. Cochrane has founded an excellent herd at Hillhurst, Compton, Canada. In March 1881 he bought some superior animals at high prices in Forfarshire. They comprised Beauty of Glamis 3515, by the Erica bull Elchies 563, from the Earl of Strathmore, for 120 guineas, and three yearling heifers from the same breeder, after Elcho 595. From Mr Thomas Smith, Powrie, there were obtained the cow Naomie of Powrie 3730, bred at Easter Skene, for 100 guineas; Rosa Bonheur 2565, and calf at foot, for 100 guineas, together with three two-year-old heifers. Since then Mr Wilken, Water-

side, selected twenty fine animals, comprising Blackbird of
Corskie 2nd 3024, the first-prize cow at the Highland
Society's show at Perth, and representing the Montbletton Mayflower family. We are informed that she
cost 200 guineas. Mabel 6th 4295, of the Pride family,
bred by Mr Grant, Methlick, was secured at a long
price. Vine 2nd 3329 was bought from the Earl of
Southesk, and was in the prize list at the Highland
Society's show at Stirling. The Pride heifer Pride 20th,
bred at Tillyfour, was acquired from Mr Auld. Animals
were further obtained from the East-Town, Altyre, Skene,
Dunnydeer, Cardney, Kinstair, Guisachan, and Thomastown herds. The bull Paris 3rd, out of Proserpine 3807,
a second-prize heifer at the Highland Society's show, and
after Paris 1473, the first-prize two-year-old at the Paris
Exhibition, was purchased from Mr M'Combie of Easter
Skene for 150 guineas. He was the first-prize yearling at
the Royal Northern and Highland Society's shows in 1881.
The herd contains specimens of the Pride, Easter Tulloch
Mayflower, Mulben Ellen and Mayflower, Kinnochtry
Favourite, Advie Rose, Indego Grace, Mains of Kelly
Victoria, Tillyfour Charmer and Windsor, Rothiemay
Victoria, Drumin Princess, Westertown Victoria, Drumin
Lucy, Kinnochtry Emily, and other well-known families.
Twenty-five bulls were also selected for the Cochrane
Ranche Company. Writing us in April last Mr Cochrane
said:—"I have at present in my herd thirty-three cows
and heifers, three stock bulls, and eleven calves of both
sexes. They have done well during the past winter. I
am in every way pleased with them, and they are greatly
admired by all who see them. The manager of our Ranche
Company in the North-Western Territory also speaks in
the highest terms of the nine young bulls which I purchased
at the Perth auction sale."

Three very fine lots have been imported by Mr George
Whitfield, The Model Farm, Rougemont, Quebec. The

animals were selected by Mr John Grant, Bogs of Advie, and among them were a few of the best-bred and best-looking cattle in the country. The first importation included two bulls from Ballindalloch, one of them Judge 1150, a frequent prize-winner in Scotland, and the first-prize bull at the Paris Exhibition, when an offer of 300 guineas was refused for him; and Rougemont, out of Siren 1915, of the Sybil family, and after the celebrated Young Viscount 736. The second importation, in the summer of 1881, comprised three of the Erica family, from Mr Robertson, Aberlour Mains—Etta 2225, with heifer calf, and Effie 4847. From Ballindalloch went the two-year-old heifer Maid of Cyprus 4177, by Elcho 595; and from Auchindellan, Gipsy 4006, after Judge 1150. In 1882 eleven animals were imported. They included four from the herd of Sir George Macpherson Grant, viz. Rose-blossom 4173, by Elcho 395, of the Rose family at Westertown; Lais 4178, of the Victoria branch of the Queen tribe; and two bull calves by Julius 1819, of the Jilt family. From Mr Hannay, Gavenwood, was purchased the cow Corriemulzie 2nd 3415, of the Montbletton May-flower family, a first-prize winner at the Royal Northern, and second at the Highland Society's shows; also Aivrin 4551, of the Rothiemay Georgina family; and Rosereyn of the Westertown Rose family. Three animals were selected from the herd of Mr Grant, Mains of Advie, representing the Advie Rose and the Drumin Lucy families. A heifer was bought from Mr Mann, Ballin-tomb. Mr Whitfield also procured twenty-four unpedi-greed polled females for crossing purposes.

Mr Geary, London, Ontario, imported in the summer of 1882 a lot of eighteen. Nine of these were from the herd of Mr Hannay, Gavenwood, comprising Patria 4549, by Challenger 1260, of the Drumin Rose family, a half-sister to the beautiful heifer Pavilion 3772; Caledonia 4550, by Challenger, and of the Rothiemay Georgina family; Oslin

4552, also of the Georgina family; Muscatel 4553, of the
Advie Rose family; Blue Ribbon 4554, by Challenger,
of the Montbletton Mayflower family, being out of the first-
prize Highland Society's cow Blackbird of Corskie 2nd
3024; Rosy Dream 4545, of the Westertown Rose family;
Flower o' the Forest 4568; Daydawn 4583; and a heifer
out of Henrietta 3912, of the Rothiemay Miss Morrison
family. Four females, representing Kinnochtry, Bognie,
Boghead, and Ballindalloch families, were obtained from
Mr Stephenson, Long Benton, Newcastle-on-Tyne; and
two females and two males from Major Godman, Smeaton
Manor. The bulls were of the Kinnochtry Princess and
the Easter Tulloch Mayflower families. The two-year-old
bull Rosebery, out of Rose Leaf 2993, of the Westertown
Rose family, and after the Erica sire Elchies 563, was also
purchased from the Ballindalloch stock.

Professor Lawson, Halifax, recently imported a lot of
polled cattle.

Other Countries.

An importation of polled cattle was made to New Zealand about twenty years ago; and at the Tillyfour dispersion the Honourable Mr Holmes bought two well-bred bulls.
He had previously bought several animals from Mr Bowie,
Mains of Kelly, and Lord Southesk. The most important
importation, however, was made in 1882 by Mr R. W. Robertson, Waimea House, Gore, Otago. Among the animals
selected by Messrs Bell & Henderson for this gentleman
were the following:—Bella 2nd of Greystone 4739, after
Major 3rd 662, first-prize two-year-old at the Royal
Northern show, and second at the Highland Society in
1881, purchased from Mr Reid, Greystone, with heifer calf
at foot, for 200 guineas; Mabel 3rd 3235, of the Pride
family, with heifer calf at foot, and a yearling bull, bought
from Mr Grant, Methlick, for 200 guineas. The Waterside
and Thomastown herds were also drawn on, the former

supplying a yearling bull Waterside Eric, out of the Erica cow Ermin 3532, and after the Pride bull Knight of the Shire 1699. His price was 100 guineas.

Senor Don Carlos Guenero, Buenos Ayres, South America, imported some animals, the selections being made from the Pitfour, Gavenwood, and Monthletton herds.

The Honourable J. J. Dowsett of Honolulu, Sandwich Islands, bought a bull of the Baroness family, and two heifers of the Mina family, from Mr Ferguson, Kinnochtry, in the spring of 1881.

CHAPTER XVII.

THE LEADING FAMILIES.

In the chapters on the various extinct and existing herds, and in other parts of the work, the breeding and career of the leading families have already been pretty fully set forth. To facilitate reference, however, it may be well to present here a few notes regarding those strains that have attained the highest celebrity.

The Queen Tribe.

In the Queen tribe there is a monument to Mr M'Combie's skill and success as a breeder. We have in it the result of the combined efforts in cattle-breeding of Mr Fullerton and Mr M'Combie, but chiefly of the latter, as the material was manipulated by him during a period of no less than thirty-seven years. In examining the career of the Queen tribe, the first point that excites notice is the illustration which it affords of Mr M'Combie's remarkable faculty of instantly and with unerring accuracy perceiving the inherent qualities and possibilities of development in an animal. This rare acquirement was undoubtedly perfected when he was transacting his immense business in buying and selling store cattle. It came to his aid on the occasion when he attended the late Mr Fullerton's sale at Ardovie in 1844, and made purchases that have become historical in connection with the polled breed. In that year Mr M'Combie brought to Tillyfour, from Ardovie, two young heifers Queen Mother 348, and Jean Ann 206, full sisters, both out of Queen of Ardovie 29, and after Panmure 51. The breeding and achievements of these animals have already been described. There was something in their appearance and in their pedigree which fascinated Mr M'Combie, and he determined on securing more of the same sort. He obtained, after considerable trouble, the bull Monarch 44, who was got by Panmure 51, and out of Julia 671, the latter after Panmure 51, and having for dam Susanna, a full sister of Queen of Ardovie 29. With the produce of these closely-allied animals Mr M'Combie resolved to risk his fame as a breeder, and he had no reason to regret the choice, for the strain has made a reputation second to none in the annals of the breed.

Monarch was twice put to Queen Mother, and the produce in 1847 was Lola Montes 208, and in 1849, Bloomer 201, both of which became celebrated prize cows. The following shows the pedigree up to this point:—

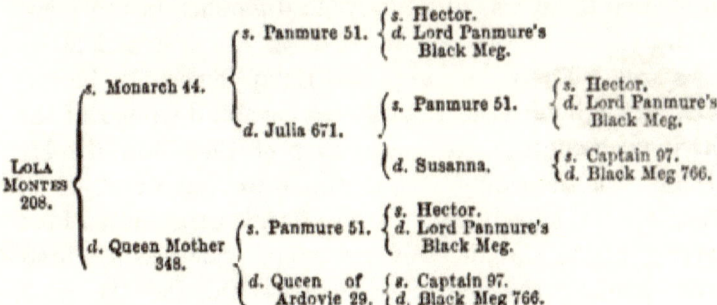

It has already been explained that Mr M'Combie having, according to his own published ideas on the subject, carried in-and-in breeding to an extreme point, sought an out-cross, and procured from Mr Watson, Keillor, the bull Angus 45, one of the best-bred and best-looking sires reared in that herd, he having been out of Old Favourite, and after the celebrated bull Old Jock 1, who was also out of Old Favourite. Lola Montes produced in 1852 a calf by Angus 45, which attained very high fame by her achievements in the show-yard, and also as the foundress of the branch of the Queen tribe which Mr M'Combie himself held in greatest favour, and which is now specially associated with his name. The calf referred to was Charlotte 203, known from her victory in the gay capital in 1856 as the "Paris cow." Charlotte's calf in 1857 was Pride of Aberdeen 581, got by Hanton 228, who may also be termed the "Paris bull," he having gained the corresponding honour in the male class at the French exhibition in 1856 to that obtained by Charlotte in the female section.

A somewhat nice point arises here. Pride of Aberdeen 581 had two full sisters, Empress of France 578, and Daisy of Tillyfour 1165, and we have heard the question asked, "In what consists the superiority of the Pride of Aberdeen branch of the Queen tribe over the Dandy and Daisy or Vine branches, which trace respectively to Pride's full sisters Empress 578, and Daisy 1165?" Of course there was absolutely no difference in the blood of these three cows; but, while both Empress and Daisy were undoubtedly fine animals, Daisy especially having been a Highland Society first-prize cow, and winner of the challenge cup at Aberdeen, neither of them can display a show and breeding record equal to that of Pride of Aberdeen. Indeed, Pride of Aberdeen's career is without parallel in the chronicles of the breed. She was the first-prize yearling, the first-prize two-year-old, and the first-prize cow at the Highland Society's shows; she gained the challenge cup at Aberdeen; and she was the first-prize cow at the International show at Battersea in 1862, where she beat her dam Charlotte, and was referred to as being, with Mr Richard Booth's celebrated Shorthorn cow Queen of the Ocean—designated by Mr Carr, the historian of the Booth Shorthorns, "a superb Shorthorn, a queen of cows"—the best female animal on the ground. Nor was this all. Pride of Aberdeen must have possessed, along with the most perfect shapes and quality, an extraordinary constitution. Few females of any breed have been able to stand three years of the forcing process necessary to keep in the front rank in the show-yard, and crown a career of unsurpassed success in exhibition, by no less distinguished performances as a breeder. Pride of Aberdeen produced seven female calves and four male calves that have been registered. The bulls were useful in the herds to which they were introduced, while from each of the females has sprung a race of valuable cattle.

An examination of the circumstances therefore proves that it was no mere fancy that led Mr M'Combie to maintain that the Pride of Aberdeen family was the most precious branch of the Queen tribe. The favour in which the Prides are regarded has certainly not been gained by that rarity which results from infecundity. We have counted the number of female descendants of Pride of Aberdeen 581 registered in vols. ii., iii., iv., v., and vi. of the 'Herd Book,' and find there are no fewer than 78. The estimation in which the Prides are held by breeders is illustrated by the fact that nine of the best representatives of the family sold publicly, in 1880 and 1881, realized an average of £140 each, one cow (Mr. Auld's Pride of Aberdeen 9th) bringing £283, 10s.

The Prides are distinguished in individual appearance by long, square, handsome frames, length of quarter, great size, substance, and wealth of flesh; while they are

known to be robust in constitution, with wonderful aptitude
to mature early, and to lay on flesh and fat on the better parts.

As has been observed, the Daisy or Vine and the
Dandy branches of the Queen tribe are descended from
full sisters of Pride of Aberdeen. The Crinoline branch
springs from Crinoline 204, out of Charlotte 203, and
after Victor 3rd 193. The Duchess branch, in which
there is a wonderful concentration of Queen and Panmure
blood, traces from Favourite 1237, whose sire was Hanton
228, and whose dam was Lola Montes 208. The cow of
this branch that went to Westertown was Duchess of
Westertown 927, by Rob Roy Macgregor 267. Mr
Brown infused the Queen blood into his herd in the male
line very strongly; and an analysis of the pedigree of
Baron Settrington 356, a son of Duchess 927, shows that
Panmure's name occurs no fewer than thirty times.
Another branch of the Queen tribe is that tracing from
Matilda of Yonderton 1722, by Hanton 228, and out of
Lola Montes 208. Fancy of Tillyfour 1195, by Hanton
228, out of The Belle 205, has also founded a small
family. The Charmer branch traces from another daughter
of The Belle—Lovely of Tillyfour 1166, by Rob Roy
Macgregor 267.

The cow Windsor 202, out of Queen Mother 348, and
after Victor 46, was very closely bred, as will be seen
from the following :—

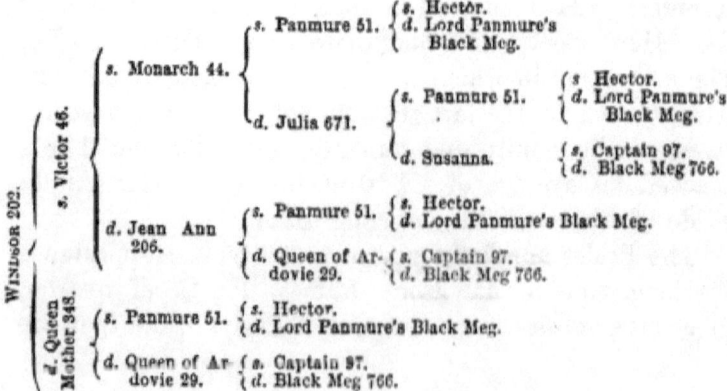

Windsor 202 was the first prize-yearling heifer at the show of the Royal Agricultural Society of England at Windsor in 1851, and, besides numerous other honours, won the first prize as a cow at Berwick in 1854. She was the dam of two splendid bulls—Windsor, 221 and Rob Roy Macgregor 267, full brothers, both having been after Hanton 228. These remarkable animals are referred to at length in connection with the Tillyfour, Westertown, and Kinnaird herds. Windsor 202 is represented in the female line only by stock tracing from her daughter Beauty of Morlich 2072, by Angus 45. This animal was sold to Mr Cran, Morlich. We know little concerning her individual appearance, but good stock has been bred from her.

Another branch of the Queen tribe is that descended from Victoria of Kelly 345, bred by Mr Bowie, Mains of Kelly. She was out of Queen Mother 348, who went to Mains of Kelly in her old age, and after Cupbearer 59.

The Ballindalloch Ericas.

No family of polled cattle has in recent years taken a more distinguished position in the show-yard than the Ballindalloch Ericas. Since 1870 they have not been absent from the prize lists of the Highland Society's shows excepting on two occasions. We have compiled the following list of prizes gained at the Highland Society's shows by specimens of this fashionable strain:—

1870, Dumfries: Cupbearer 451, out of Erica 843, second-prize two-year-old bull; Eisa 977, out of Erica 843, second-prize cow. 1871, Perth: Eisa, first-prize cow; Enchantress 981, out of Erica 843, first-prize two-year-old heifer. 1872, Kelso: Enchantress, second-prize cow. 1874, Inverness: Young Viscount 736, out of Erica 3rd 1249, first-prize yearling bull; Eva 984, out of Eisa, 977, third-prize cow. 1875, Glasgow: Young

Viscount, first-prize two-year-old bull; St. Clair 1160, out of Erica 4th 1697, first-prize one-year-old bull; Ethel 1415, out of Enchantress 981, second-prize two-year-old heifer. 1876, Aberdeen: Young Viscount, first-prize aged bull; Bacchus 607, out of Eisa 977, very highly commended aged bull; St Clair, first-prize two-year-old bull; Eva, second-prize cow; Erica 6th 3023, out of Erica 4th 1697, fourth-prize heifer. 1877, Edinburgh: St Clair, third-prize aged bull; Cluny 1283, out of Eva 984, highly commended two-year-old bull; Eva, second-prize cow; Echo 2976, out of Eisa 977, highly commended cow; Erica 6th, third-prize two-year-old heifer; Edina 2987, out of Enchantress 981, third-prize yearling heifer. 1878, Dumfries: Editor 1460, out of Edith 2973, commended one-year-old bull; Echo, second-prize cow; Edina, third-prize two-year-old heifer. 1879, Perth: Editor, highly commended two-year-old bull; Eva, fourth-prize cow. 1881, Stirling: Express 1821, out of Eleanor 3376, fourth-prize yearling bull; Essence 4547, out of Erica 9th 3822, second-prize yearling heifer.

We have referred to the Erica family at such length in notices of the Kinnaird and Ballindalloch herds that little remains to be said here. Erica 843, the foundress of the family, was bought by Sir George Macpherson Grant at the Earl of Southesk's sale in 1861 for fifty guineas, her sire having been Cupbearer 59, and her dam Emily 332, by Old Jock 1, bred by Mr Watson, Keillor; the sire and grandsire having thus been two of the most renowned show bulls of the breed. The following displays the material of which Erica's pedigree was composed:—

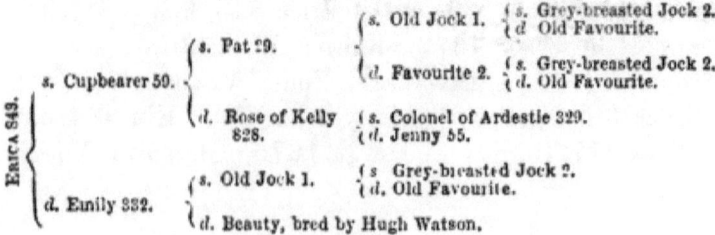

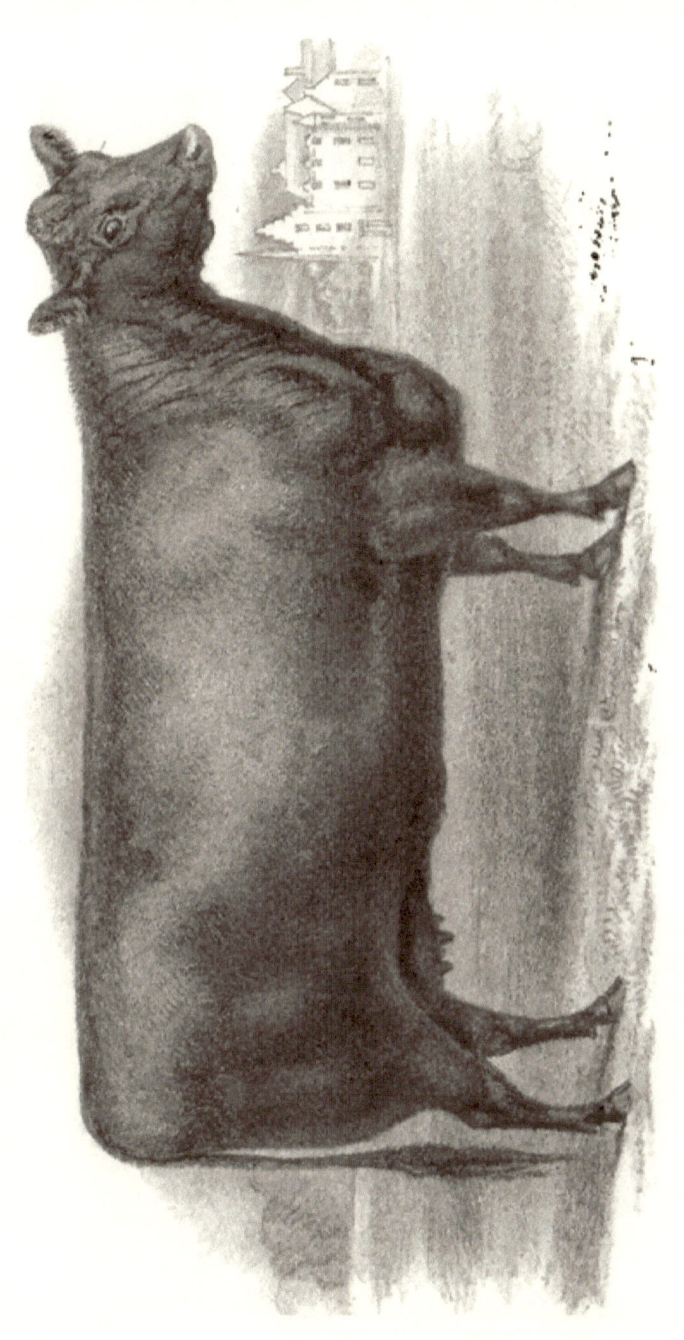

All the existing female specimens of the Erica family are descended from either of four calves, as follows :—

ERICA 843.

Erica 2nd, 1284, c. 1865, by Chieftain 318.	Eisa 977, c. 1867, by Trojan 402.	Enchantress 981, c. 1869, by Trojan 402.	Ella 1205, c. 1870, by Kildonan 405.

As previously explained, Erica 3rd, out of Erica 2nd 1284, and Ella 1205, were sold, the former to Mr Duff, Hillochhead, and the latter to Mr Macgregor, Garline. Eisa and Enchantress were retained in the herd, and the family, as bred without interruption at Ballindalloch, accordingly traces from these two daughters of Erica, got by the admirably-bred Queen bull Trojan 402. The Erica sires that have been used in the Ballindalloch herd were— Elchies 563, out of Eisa ; Elcho 595, out of Erica ; Editor 1460, out of Edith 2973 ; and Young Viscount 736. The last named is at present the stock bull, being assisted by Justice 1462, a son of Elcho 595. Very few female Ericas have been parted with from Ballindalloch since the family acquired its reputation, and it is thus difficult to indicate with precision the market value of the tribe. Young Viscount fetched 225 guineas in public competition, and a female Erica was sold publicly in 1877 for over 100 guineas. We have heard of several female specimens of the tribe having been sold privately at considerably over 100 guineas, and Sir George Macpherson Grant has lately had submitted to him an offer of 500 guineas for the first female Erica he can spare from his herd. The Ericas show striking uniformity of type, and display undoubted indications of high breeding. They are deep, broad, compact, low - set cattle, with short fine legs, excellent ribs and loins, beautiful quality, graceful head, and very rich cover of flesh.

Princesses, Baronesses, Emilys, and Favourites.

These four valuable and handsome families, cultivated

by Mr Thomas Ferguson, Kinnochtry, are the most closely-
bred of polled cattle. They are descended from the
Keillor cows Old Grannie 1 and Favourite 2, and, as we
have already stated, there can be no doubt that Mr Hugh
Watson practised in-breeding to a large extent, although,
owing to the inexact manner in which the Keillor herd
records were kept, it is difficult to give precise particulars.
In 1839 Mr Ferguson purchased from Mr Watson, Young
Favourite 61, out of Old Grannie 1, the foundress of the
Princess and Baroness families, and Edinburgh 64, also
out of Old Grannie 1, the foundress the Emily family.
Shortly afterwards he acquired Favourite 2, from which
the Kinnochtry Favourite family is derived. The following exhibits the line of descent of the Princess, Baroness,
and Emily families :—

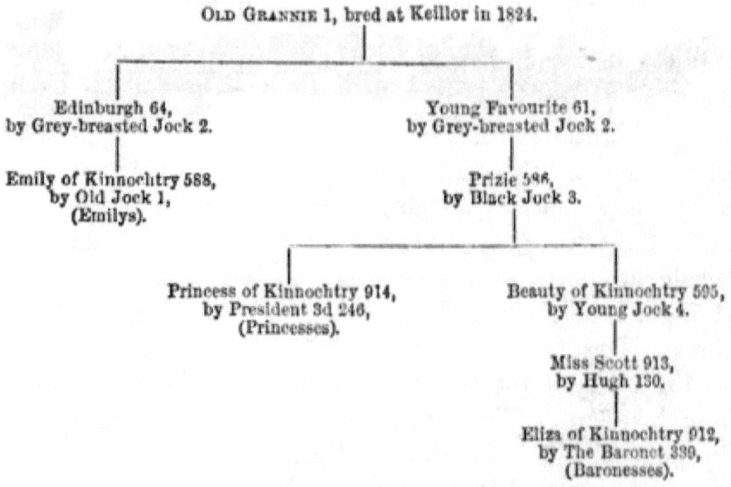

Old Grannie 1, bred at Keillor in 1824.

Edinburgh 64,
by Grey-breasted Jock 2.

Young Favourite 61,
by Grey-breasted Jock 2.

Emily of Kinnochtry 588,
by Old Jock 1,
(Emilys).

Prizie 586,
by Black Jock 3.

Princess of Kinnochtry 914,
by President 3d 246,
(Princesses).

Beauty of Kinnochtry 595,
by Young Jock 4.

Miss Scott 913,
by Hugh 130.

Eliza of Kinnochtry 912,
by The Baronet 339,
(Baronesses).

The Favourite family traces directly from Favourite 2.
Not only were the cattle at Keillor bred closely, but the
same system has been continued by Mr Ferguson, sires
having as a rule been obtained from Mr Watson, or bred
from the Keillor stock at Kinnochtry. It will be unnecessary here to enter into a detailed examination of the

pedigrees of the Kinnochtry families, as that has been done with some minuteness in the notice of the herd.

In the pedigree of Mr Ferguson's cow Eliza of Kinnochtry 912, from whom his Baroness family is descended, we have an excellent example of the concentrated breeding of the purest of his cattle, all of which are noted for handsome proportions, length of frame, wealth of flesh, and vigour of constitution. The pedigree analysis is as follows:—

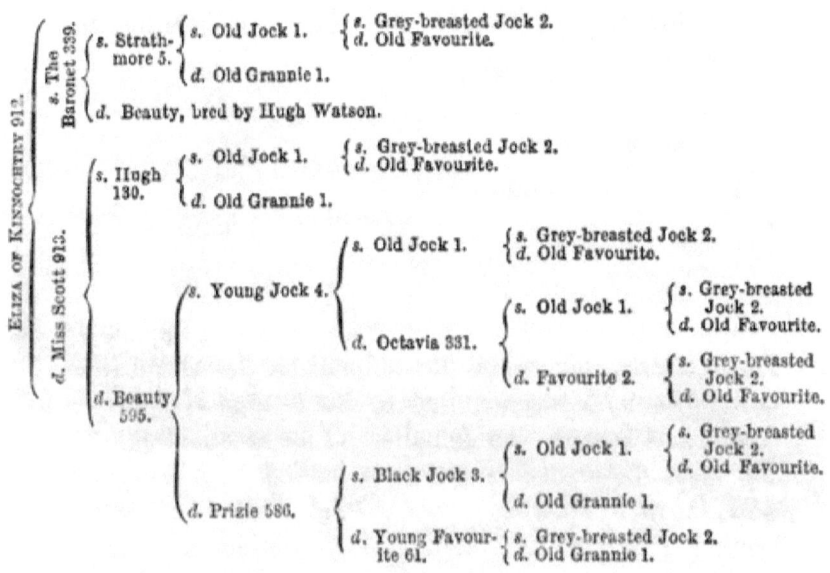

Miss Watson, Jilt, and Ruth Families.

The late Mr M'Combie of Tillyfour purchased at the Keillor sale in 1860 the cow Beauty of Tillyfour 2nd 1180, and her heifer calf Miss Watson 987, and from these animals three valuable families descend. The following table shows the strains established by Beauty 2nd:—

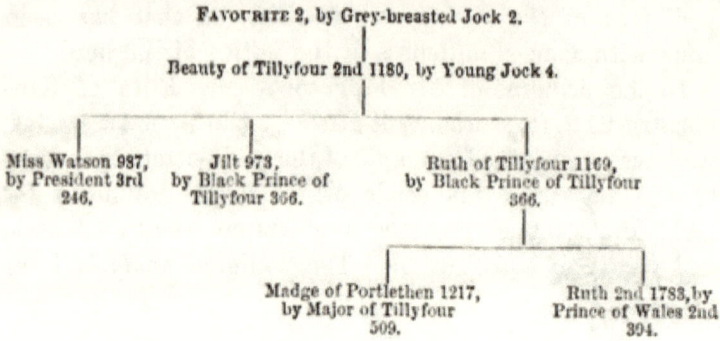

The breeding of Beauty 2nd will be seen from the annexed :—

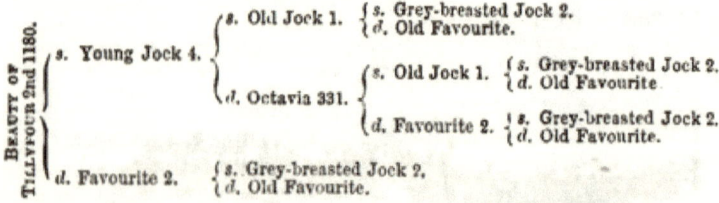

Miss Watson 987 was purchased by Mr M'Combie of Easter Skene, and several fine animals are descended from her. Jilt 973 was acquired by Sir George Macpherson Grant, and became the foundress of an excellent family, the most distinguished members having been Juryman 404, Judge 1150, and Justice 1462. Ruth 1169, before leaving Tillyfour, bred Madge of Portlethen 1217, the progenitrix of the Marquis of Huntly's well-known Madge family, and Ruth 2nd 1783, bought by Mr Barclay, Strocherie. In 1874 Ruth 1169 was sold to Mr Anderson, Wellhouse, Alford, and has produced some excellent stock there. It is a notable circumstance that these animals have all lived to extraordinary ages. Jilt 973 and Miss Watson continued breeding until they were sixteen years old; Ruth is still alive and breeding regularly, although eighteen years old; and Madge was sold for 100 guineas when over ten years old.

Kinnaird Fannys.

This family is valuable not only on account of the individual merit of its members, but also because by it is preserved one of the oldest and finest Kinnaird tribes. It is perhaps the case that it represents the earliest polled strain of which records exist. The first animal of the family registered in the 'Herd Book' was Old Lady Ann 743, and there is evidence that she was calved about 1820, four years prior to the birth of Old Grannie 1. The family is represented by two branches, thus :—

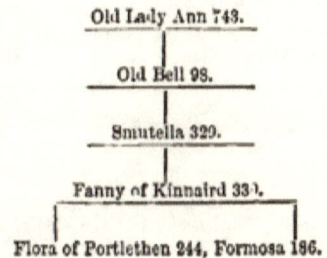

Old Lady Ann 743.

Old Bell 98.

Smutella 329.

Fanny of Kinnaird 33?.

Flora of Portlethen 244, Formosa 186.

Flora of Portlethen 244 was sold to Mr Walker, Portlethen ; and Formosa 186 was sold to Mr Scott of Easter Tulloch. The following shows the composition of the Fanny pedigree :—

FANNY OF KINNAIRD 330.			
	s. Southesk 34.	*s.* Colin 35.	*s.* Wattie 135. *d.* Lucy 670.
		d. Old Bell 98.	*s.* Bred by Mr Mustard, Fithie *d.* Old Lady Ann.
	d. Smutella 329.	*s.* Colin 35.	*s.* Wattie 135. *d.* Lucy 670.
		d. Old Bell 98.	*s.* Bred by Mr Mustard, Fithie. *d.* Old Lady Ann 743.

Old Lady Ann 743, we may here remark, is also represented by the Lavender family at Melville, Lavender of Kinnaird 1007 having been her great-grand-daughter, and also by the Rebecca family at Easter Tulloch.

Drumin and Mains of Kelly Lucys.

The Lucy family, although now best known in connection with the Drumin and Mains of Kelly herds, is descended from one of the oldest tribes at Portlethen. They are of the same strain as the bull Raglan 208, for whom Mr Walker, Portlethen, refused an offer of £230 from the Emperor Napoleon in 1856. The following exhibits the composition of the pedigree :—

```
                         ┌ s. Old Jock 1.    ┌ s. Grey-breasted Jock 2.
             s. Fyvie 13.│                   └ d. Old Favourite.
LUCY OF      {           │
PORTLETHEN 287.          └ d. Bred at Keillor.
             {
             d. Young Miss ┌ s. Sir Alexander ┌ s. Banks of Dee ┌ s. Rob Roy of Leys 158.
               Alexander 16.│      10.        │      12.        └ d. Harriet of Leys 260.
                           │                  └ d. Portlethen Mustard 171.
                           └ d. Miss Alexander 678.
```

Baads Sybils and Kates.

The wonderful show-yard success of those two families is commented on in the notice of Mr Reid's herd at Baads. The striking fact about the breeding of Mr Reid's cattle is that Sybil 1st of Tillyfour 3524, and Halt 3525 (out of Kate 1947, the dam of Prince Albert of Baads 1336), were respectively after a son and out of a daughter of President 4th 368. Isla 1965, another famous Baads cow, was a full sister of Sybil 1st 3524. We need not here repeat the statements made in the account of the Baads herd as to the prizes won by these cattle, or the high prices members of the Sybil and Kate families have realized in the public sale rings. In both respects they have established for themselves a position in the front rank of polled stock. There will, of course, be some regret that the recorded pedigree is so brief; but it must be remembered that several excellent and fashionable families of other breeds have sprung into repute with quite as

short a registry. An inspection of the animals belonging to
the two Baads families—their remarkable family likeness,
their true polled character, and their uniform excellence,
—must have the effect of liberalizing opinion and supplying a rebuke to those who may be inclined to maintain
that meritorious specimens of the breed can be produced
from only two or three lines.

Other Ballindalloch Families.

The most distinguished families associated with the
Ballindalloch herd are the Ericas and Jilts, to which
reference has previously been made. Sir George Macpherson Grant has, however, succeeded in rearing many
animals of other strains that have attained no little
celebrity. The cow Sybil 974, bred by Mr Shaw, Bogfern, and purchased from Colonel Fraser of Castle Fraser,
had earned renown before she went to Ballindalloch.
She produced there some good stock, although none of
them have yet equalled the old matron's fame. The
Coquette family represents the old Ballindalloch stock, the
dam of Coquette 1417 having been bred by the late Sir
John Macpherson Grant. Crossed with the celebrated
sires at Ballindalloch, it has produced good animals. At
Ballindalloch is also preserved the Balwyllo Keepsake
family, tracing from a somewhat famous cow, Keepsake
427, by President 205, bred at Balwyllo. The Lady
Fanny family had its origin in Grannie 131, bred by Mr.
Grant, Carnousie, the first of the sort that went to Ballindalloch being Young Mary 527, bred in 1852 by Mr
Grant of Carron. This animal produced Lady Fanny 971,
by King Charles 236. The Miss Burgess family, which
has supplied two first-prize cows at Highland Society's
shows—Bertha 980, and Maid of Aven 2995—springs
from Miss Burgess 1198, by King Charles 236, this
animal's dam having been bred by Mr Burgess, Slack of

Ballindalloch. The Nosegay family is another old Ballindalloch variety tracing from Nettle by Craigo 260. It is specially noted for its milking properties.

Portlethen Families.

In addition to the Lucys and Fannys, several other families have been successfully reared by Mr Walker, Portlethen. The Ida family traces from Ida 651, by Fortitude 28, of the Kinnaird Fanny family, Ida's dam having been Inchmarlo Maggie 301, bred by Mr Patrick Davidson of Inchmarlo. The Julia family had its origin in Jean 264, bred by Mr William Ruxton, Farnell, and after the Keillor bull Adam 39. The Lively family springs from Lively 256, bred by Mr Fullerton, Ardovie, and after Earl o' Buchan 57. The Mayflower family, now chiefly at Easter Tulloch, is descended from one of the oldest Portlethen strains, the first registered member of which was Old Maggie 681. Bamba 1200, fourth in descent from Old Maggie, went to Easter Tulloch, and bred, among other good animals, Mayflower of Easter Tulloch 3519. The Miss Scott family is another of the old Portlethen sorts, tracing from Miss Scott 679. The Nightingale family was founded by Nightingale 262, bred by Sir A. Burnett, out of Mary of Wester Fintray 21, and after Strathmore 5, bred at Keillor. The Pansy or Panmure family came from a cow Panmure 278, by Old Jock 1, bred by Mr Watson, Keillor. A branch of the Balwyllo Victoria family has also been preserved at Portlethen through Alice Maud 724, a great-grand-daughter of Mr Scott's Victoria 45.

Montbletton Families.

The best-known family at Montbletton is the Mayflower. Lady Craigo 99 was bought from Captain

Carnegie of Craigo, when in calf to Craigo 260, of Keillor and Balwyllo blood. The produce was Mayflower 614, who stood second as a cow at one of the Highland Society's shows; but the animal placed before her having failed to produce a calf, she actually obtained the first prize. A numerous and valuable family has sprung from Mayflower. Her daughter, Mayflower 2nd 1020, by The Earl 291, lived till she was seventeen years old, and had a progeny of fourteen. Mayflower 2nd's daughter, Lady Ida, a famous local prize-winner, is still alive and breeding, last season's calf having been her fourteenth. To this fine sort belonged Blackbird of Corskie 2nd 3024, the first-prize cow at the Highland Society's Show at Perth in 1879. The first of the Charlotte family at Montbletton was Young Charlotte 103, the first-prize cow at the Highland Society's Show in 1848. She was bred by Colonel Dalgairns, but came to Montbletton from Tillyfour. At Montbletton she produced twin calves— Twin Charlotte 609, and Twin Queen 610, by the Wester Fintray bull Fintray 125. These animals were prize-takers, and have each established a family. The Balwyllo Isabella family—tracing from Isabella of Balwyllo 423, bred by Mr Fullerton, after Earl o' Buchan 57—is maintained at Montbletton through the descendants of Heiress of Balwyllo 461, who was purchased by Mr M'Combie of Tillyfour, and sold by him to Mr Walker. Heiress was a first-prize heifer at the Highland Society, and the strain she represented furnished the last stock bull at Keillor— President 3rd 246, a half-brother of Heiress. From the cow Jane of Montbletton 1268, by Black Diamond 464, sprung the dam of Innes 1934, the first-prize cow at the Aberdeen show of the Highland Society in 1876. The Victoria family at Montbletton traces from Victoria of Fintray 607, bred by Mr James Collie, Middleton of Fintray, and doubtless inheriting the Wester Fintray blood.

Mains of Kelly Families.

The Victorias and Lucys, cultivated at Mains of Kelly, have already been alluded to. The other families reared by Mr Bowie—the Marthas, descended from the dam of Panmure 51; the Ardesties, from the Old Montrose herd; the Guinea Pigs, from Mr Fullerton's stock; the Jennets, tracing to Mr M'Combie's Young Jenny Lind 207; the Lizzys, going back to Brunette 745; and the Watties, from the Arrat stock—are fully dealt with in the notice of the Mains of Kelly herd, and their great achievements, the production of celebrated bulls, is detailed at length in that portion of the work.

Easter Skene Families.

Mr M'Combie's Miss Watson family has been noticed. Unfortunately several of the other Easter Skene strains are extinct. The one now most numerously represented in the herd is the Grizzle family, descended from a cow bred at Mulben. From it a great many prize stock have been bred. There also exist—although we believe not at Easter Skene—descendants of Mr M'Combie's cow Mariana 622. Mariana was after the Keillor bull Old Jock 1, and her dam Lady Clara 4 was after Grey-breasted Jock 2, and out of Old Grannie 1. The Miss Fraser family is descended from Miss Fraser 985, bred at Castle Fraser, her daughter Queen Mary 990 having been by the Kinnaird Dora sire Dalaware 457. The Queen of Scots family springs from Queen of Scots 72, a daughter of the famous Panmure 51.

Drumin Families.

The leading family at Drumin is probably the Lucys, to which allusion has been made above. At the same time that the foundress of the Lucy family was introduced to Drumin, Mr Skinner purchased Young Raniston 948, from Mr Bowie, Mains of Kelly. From her descends the Beauty family, among whose members was Sunshine 2nd 3333, a celebrated prize heifer, whose portrait appears in vol. v. of the 'Herd Book.' The Princess family at Drumin is descended from Princess of Drumin 950, bred by the late Mr Robertson, Burnside. The Rose family had for foundress, the cow Fortune 945, early purchased for the Drumin herd, but the pedigree of which was not ascertained. From this line was bred the famous heifer Pavilion 3772. The Catherine family traces from Grace 946. All these families of course owe much of their excellence to the splendid sires used at Drumin.

Castle Fraser Families.

Each of the Castle Fraser families has produced at least one celebrated prize-winner. From the Blanche family came Bella Mary 1503, Mr Bruce's first-prize cow at the Paris Exhibition; Lily 1114, the foundress of the Lily family, was the first-prize cow of the Highland Society in 1868; Mina 1009, the foundress of the Mina family, won the Challenge Cup at the Royal Northern, and the first prize at the Highland Society in 1867; and Sybil 974, whose descendants are known chiefly in connection with the Ballindalloch, Mulben, and Mountblairy herds, was the first-prize cow of the Highland Society in 1870.

Rothiemay Families.

Mr Tayler of Glenbarry has three well-known families —the Georginas and Miss Morrisons tracing from a purchase by the late Major Tayler about the year 1846, and the Victorias, descended from Victoria of Glenbarry 534, bred at Mulben. Although these families have been bred very similarly, they each retain distinctive characteristics, preserving the qualities of the original foundresses. The Georginas are probably the most noted, having produced Kate 2nd 1482, the first-prize cow of the Highland Society in 1874. Of the other two families there have also been several celebrated animals.

Westertown Families.

It will be sufficient to name here the families that were principally cultivated by the late Mr Brown, Westertown, and refer for further particulars to the account of the Westertown herd. Mr Brown's families were the Duchesses of the Queen tribe; the Lady Anns descended from Colonel Dalgairn's stock at Balgavies; the Roses and the Victorias. In every case the blood of Panmure 51 and the Tillyfour Queens was very largely infused into these strains.

Easter Tulloch Families.

Among these must be specially noted the Duchesses, descended from the Keillor cow Old Grannie 1; the Kinnaird Fannys and the Portlethen Mayflowers, elsewhere referred to; the Kathleens, descended from Mr Ferguson's Ashmore herd, with a cross of Panmure 51; the Levitys, having for ancestress the first-prize cow at the Highland Society's show at Dundee in 1843, bred by Lord Panmure; and the Bluebells from the Upper Tulloch stock.

Mulben Families.

The Mayflower and Ellen families, bred by the late Mr Paterson, Mulben, will be found fully described in the notice of that herd.

Advie Roses.

This family was founded by Old Rose of Advie 3104, bred by Sir George Macpherson Grant, after Craigo 260. The early members of the strain were by the well-known bulls King Charles 236, and Trojan 402, and since, the Ballindalloch Erica and Jilt bulls Elcho 595, and Juryman 404, have been used, imparting the stamp of the Ballindalloch stock.

The Zara Family.

This family, originally produced in Mr Collie's herd at Ardgay, was rendered famous by some remarkable show heifers—such as Zara 1228, of Battersea fame; her daughter, Kate of Aberdeen; and her grand-daughter Pride of Alford 1778—all exhibited by Mr M'Combie of Tillyfour, and the last two bred by him.

Fyvie Flower Family.

This family is descended from Juno, bred by Mr Malcolm, Bodiechell, and after Angus 45. Fyvie Flower 1516 was by the prize bull Malcolm of Brodiechell 269, and was herself a prize-taker. The family is characterized by exceptionally good milking properties.

CHAPTER XVIII.

SYSTEM OF MANAGEMENT.

Little variety in system of management—Practice of various breeders—
Mr Bowie, Mains of Kelly; Mr William Fullerton; Mr Ferguson,
Kinnochtry; Mr Whyte, Spott; Mr Smith of Benholm; Mr Anderson,
Wellhouse; Mr Reid, Greystone; Mr M'Combie of Easter Skene;
Mr Auld, Bridgend; Sir George Macpherson Grant, Bart., of Ballindalloch; Mr Hannay of Gavenwood; Mr Tayler of Glenbarry—Experiments in crossing by Mr Wilken, Waterside of Forbes—Summary
of system of management—Methods of breeding—Desirability of
establishing a few line - bred families—Natural characteristics of
breed should be maintained.

THERE is not much variety in the general system of
management pursued by breeders of polled cattle. As a
rule it is simple and natural. In the preparing of show-
yard animals high feeding has of course been freely
resorted to, but the great bulk of the breed has received
little "pampering" or unnatural treatment of any kind.
It cannot be doubted that to this last fact the exceptional
fecundity, general soundness, good health, and hardiness
of polled cattle is in a large measure attributable. No
race of animals can long withstand unnatural treatment,
no matter how skilful it may be pursued.

Breeders, as a rule, aim at having their calves dropped
between the first of December and the end of March.
Many come later and some earlier, but these are not in
favour. There are important advantages in having early

calves, and breeders are now endeavouring to obtain as many as possible before the end of February. Mr Alexander Bowie, Mains of Kelly, the oldest living breeder, says the best calving season is from December to the end of April. Early calves generally bring most money when sold to the butcher. Mr Bowie rears most of his calves by the pail or "cog," giving daily at the outset one pint, and gradually increasing the quantity till it reaches seven or eight quarts. Small quantities of cake, corn, and turnips are ultimately given along with the milk. The better sorts, perhaps intended for showing purposes, are allowed to suckle their dams for longer or shorter periods, and when weaned are shut up in loose boxes and treated to all sorts of good things. Mr Bowie keeps his breeding cattle in moderately lean condition. He does not think it wise to serve heifers until they are two years old, as too early breeding checks their growth.

Few breeders of polled cattle were more methodical in the management of their herds than the late Mr William Fullerton. Writing in reference to the principles of selection which should be observed in a pure-bred herd, he says: "I would say breed in line of course. Study the docility of bulls and cows, and breed from good-natured beasts. You will know good nature in a calf—it is *frank*, so to speak, even as calf. A full eye is a fine sign of a beast too; also plenty of hair if not over fine: *flightersomeness* I don't like, nor a bull that needs two men to lead him. The touch of a beast's skin should be mellow and easy, and need not be very remarkably thin. Both cows and bulls should stand well on their legs. Over crooked hind legs are not pretty, neither are knock-knees. Very wide hooks are not an Angus point, still they show off a beast. Depressed loins used to be an Angus fault, but this is now greatly mended. As to the head, who can describe it? You know it when you see it good, to be good; but the neck has so much to do in

showing off the head, that both must be judged together,
keeping an eye to a full neck-vein and brisket. A full
thigh is good, but the animal should not be double-
hipped — a fault that has worn out. A neatly-laid-in
tail is a point of great beauty, but boxing-gloves at each
side of the tail-head is not good, and is not Angus. A
full rib is good, but it should not be like the side of a
drum. When a beast is in condition, if the point behind
the shoulder is low and naked, a prize by that beast is
not easily secured. The top of the shoulder is a splendid
piece of meat, and should be full; while the top all along
should be broad and level, and well covered, especially
over the sirloin, the roast of roasts. The ears should be
large, hairy, and not over wide set."

Mr Thomas Ferguson, Kinnochtry, states that his
calves suckle their dams till from six to eight months
old; and that after being weaned they get straw, turnips,
and cake or bruised oats, in covered courts. He feeds
the bull-calves in the same manner all the winter after
weaning, and generally sells them in spring when they
are a little more than a year old. After Mr Ferguson's
heifers are ten months old, they get little food, excepting
straw and turnips, until put upon the grass. Bulls are
used when about twelve months old, and heifers mated
when about two years old, seldom sooner. He feeds
liberally the bulls that are in use, but he keeps his cows
rather lean than fat. In winter his cows before calving
are fed in covered courts, with about 30 or 40 lbs. of
turnips per day along with barley-wheat or oat-straw,
generally either of the two former, as oat-straw is scarce.
After calving, they get three times as many turnips as
before; and in summer they are kept solely on the grass
fields.

Mr William Whyte, Spott, Kirriemuir, informs us that
his cows get a few turnips in the morning, and if the
weather permit they are sent out to a hillside during the

day, being treated in this fashion till near calving time, when they get a more liberal allowance of turnips. Most of them are late calvers, winter keep being generally scarce. Bullocks are kept in a thriving state, or as well as the keep will permit, until two years old, when they are removed to a different farm and receive better food; but they are never forced till the last three or four months. They are usually sold at about three years old, when they weigh from 8 to 9 cwt.

Mr William Smith of Benholm, Kincardineshire, likes to have calves in February and March. Calves are brought up on their dams, and are taken from them in August and September. Young bulls when taken from their dams are put into small covered courts and fed on grass and tares until turnips are ready. They also receive 2 to 3 lbs. of linseed cake a day. Mr Smith sells his bulls when about one year old. They should be ready for use at eleven to twelve months. Heifers are fed same as bulls, but do not get so much cake, and that only in winter. In summer they go out in the fields with the cows and calves, and do not get any extra feeding unless they are to be exhibited, when a little cake is given to put a gloss on them. He does not think they require any cake, etc., to put them into condition—they are so easily fed. Formerly the heifers were served in April, but now, if possible, Mr Smith mates them in March, when about two years old, so that the calves may come in December, when they can be shown in young classes; but for those who do not intend exhibiting, he thinks it would be advantageous to serve the heifers when they are, say, eighteen to twenty months old. At that age they are not so fat, and have more chance of getting in calf, and are quite strong enough for breeding. Cows, after the calves are taken from them in autumn, go at large in the fields until they are put on turnips and straw, and placed into a small court, loose,

with plenty of shelter. When within two weeks of
calving, they are put in stall and kept there with the
calf until the weather is mild enough for them to be
again turned into the court. In summer they are day
and night in the grass field. Show cattle are treated the
same as the others, with the addition of a little cake
before being exhibited. Mr Smith mentions an experiment in feeding. At one of Mr Hannay's sales he
bought a very small heifer calf at £10, 10s. When she
got to be nearly two years old, he did not think she
would make a good cow ; so, to see what she would do as
a feeding animal, he bought a two-year-old Shorthorn
heifer, and a very good one she was, being better when
bought than the polled. They were kept together under
the same treatment until the Christmas following, when
they were showed at the fat show at Dundee. They
gained the first prize, although under three years old,
against all of any age. When killed, the polled heifer
weighed 66 stones 6 lbs. Imperial, and the Shorthorn 60
stones. He always thought the Shorthorn consumed
more food than the polled. Mr Smith thinks polled
cattle should all be fat, and sold when three years old.
If sooner, so much the better. He believes they can
easily be made fat at that age with grass and turnips,
and a little extra feeding the last three or four months.

Mr William Anderson, Wellhouse, Alford, gives his
experience as follows:—" I have been a breeder and a
feeder of polled cattle from a conviction that they are
the best beef-producing breed in existence. The polled
animal produces beef of the best quality, and has the
best cover of meat—more than crosses or any other breed
—on the most valuable parts of the animal. You will
get cross animals to stand higher on their legs, and bulk
more largely to the eye than the polls ; but compare them
closely, and especially the rump, loins, and along the
well-padded back of the latter, and you will soon find out

why the butcher, who is the final and best judge, prefers
the polled bullock to any other, and will buy a well-fed
polled animal when crosses are a glut in the market. I
have never bred polled animals for mere fancy purposes,
and have never prepared them for breeding or fat-stock
shows, but it has always been my practice to prepare
a small lot of prime polled bullocks for the London
Christmas market. I now think it would have paid me
to have given rather more attention to specially preparing
show animals than I have done; but I was afraid of
spoiling my cattle for breeding purposes, and I have
never, in the management of my herd, allowed myself to
depart from commercial utility. In preparing bullocks
for the London Christmas market, the first thing to attend
to, after breeding from good, well-shaped, well-fleshed
dams and sires, is the nursing of the calves. The calf
should get milk for at least six months; but after it is
six weeks old, if it is fed with the hand, the milk should
be mixed twice a day with a small allowance of pottage
made from bruised linseed or bruised oil-cake. The
quantity may be increased as the calf grows older and
stronger. After the first six weeks the calf should also
have a daily supply of cut turnips and straw. For the
first fortnight the calf gets a small quantity of milk four
times a day. After that it gets milk three times a day,
on to twelve weeks at least; and after about that age it
gets milk twice a day, until it is weaned. It is then of
special importance to attend to the calf well. Before it
is weaned it should be learned to eat linseed-cake. It
ought to receive at least 1 lb. a day of linseed-cake until
it is a year old, after which decorticated cotton-cake may
be used with good results. In winter, turnips should be
given twice a day, and plenty of good oat straw. I give
no cake either to yearlings or two-year-olds on the grass.
They are pastured, and lie in the fields from about the
26th May till — in the case of yearlings — about 1st

October; but two-year-olds are tied up, to be specially
prepared for the Christmas market, about the end of
August or the first week of September. When two-year-
old bullocks are casting their teeth, they get their turnips
cut, and, along with the turnips, 2 lbs. a day of cotton-
cake until their teeth are up so that they can again eat
the turnips, either yellows or Swedes. It is when they
are rising three years old that I finally tie up my bullocks
to prepare them for the Christmas market. When they
are tied up at the end of August or beginning of September, before turnips are ready, I provide an abundant
supply of tares mixed with oats, pease and beans, to feed
with. Such a mixed food, after the oats have come into
the ear, is a very valuable diet. About the middle of
September, in favourable circumstances, early turnips will
be ready for use, and two diets a day will improve the
feed. When the tares are done, which is generally about
the beginning of October, I give 2 lbs. of cotton-cake a
day to each animal, and three small feeds of turnips. A
fortnight or three weeks later, a feed of bruised oats is
added to the cotton-cake. By the beginning of November
Swede turnips are ready for use, and that, along with a
slight increase of bruised oats, as the state of the animal
seems to require in order to thorough ripeness of fattening,
constitutes the feeding until the animals are either sold
or forwarded to the London Christmas market. I thus
sell my polled bullocks at two rising three years old.
My weights average from 8 cwts. to 8½ cwts., though I
have at times had animals as high as 9 cwts. or even
10 cwts. In my experience the polled Scot is the best
selling animal in good times, and the best selling animal
in bad times, and, as a rule, I get £2 a head, or even
more, for polled animals than for crosses of the same
weight; and I am given to understand that the butcher
can well enough afford that sum extra. I lately heard a
statement of a leading Aberdeen butcher, that he could

give 5s. more per cwt. for a fat polled animal than for
a fat cross, because in shop use the polled animal, on
account of smaller bone development, was a better cutting
beast. This, on an animal of 8 cwts., showed a difference
of value in favour of the polled bullock of £2 a head.
It may be asked if bullocks could be fed off at an earlier
age, and the answer is in the affirmative. By a more
liberal use of concentrated foods, and especially by giving
them cake on the grass, I could make black polls prime
fat at two years old; but it has been my habit to prepare
my best cattle for Christmas, and as a whole I find the
market at that time most safe and steady. In regard to
the milking qualities of the polled breed, I think breeders
have rather neglected their duty. We have endeavoured
to produce a model butcher's animal; and we have succeeded in that, but we have not so well attended to the
fostering of the milking qualities of the breed. It is an
undoubted fact—I remember examples myself—that the
old Aberdeen unimproved polled breed were excellent
milkers. There are among the breed good milkers still.
I have cows that suckle two calves, and I know other
breeders who have superior milkers also; but we have,
as already remarked, given ourselves more to producing
the meat than the milk yielding animal, and that is the
simple reason why the black polled cattle have not a
better name as dairy stock."

Mr James Reid, Greystone, Alford, whose experience
as a breeder, feeder, and exhibitor of polled cattle is of
an extensive and exceptional kind, says truly, that while
great care should be exercised in selecting and mating
cows and bulls, it is also necessary that close attention
should be given to the rearing of calves. The calf flesh,
he says, should be retained not by too much forcing food,
but by wholesome diet, and by housing in good time, so
as not to allow the hair to overgrow. The skin should
be kept clean by grooming. The young animal should

have plenty of exercise, and all food given in such quantities and at such times as that it may be eaten at once, and no portion of it left to get spoiled. If kept in a loose court or box, the animals should have a clean, dry place to stand upon at feeding time, while the bed should be dry and soft. It is well now and again to wash cattle with warm water and soft-soap, having them thoroughly well dried and rubbed afterwards.

Mr M'Combie of Easter Skene says the calves meant for commercial purposes are put on cake a month before being weaned, after which they are kept on cake all through the winter until next year's grass, which at Easter Skene comes away early. While being fed on the grass they do not get an allowance of cake; but when they come off the grass as two-year-olds, they are tied up in stalls for a few months, and are finished off with a liberal supply of turnips and straw, to which are added three or four pounds of linseed-cake, bruised grain, and linseed-meal daily. They are sold in the autumn or spring, weighing from $6\frac{1}{2}$ cwts. to 9 cwts. each.

Mr R. C. Auld, Bridgend, states that while early calving gives advantages in the way of strong yearlings, it incurs great expense in keeping cows and calves during the winter and spring, before the grass season comes round. He says that during the period of gestation cows should be kept on good pasture when outside, and fed on good food when inside; and that some days before calving it is well to take a small quantity of blood from them, as a preventive of milk fever; and to have them closed up by themselves in a calving-box. Just after calving, the cows should be kept quiet, well "bedded" with fodder, and get a drink of milk-warm water and oatmeal. The calf should be carefully watched until it "gets its legs;" and when the cow has been milked, a small quantity of the first milking should be given to the calf. He approves of cows being allowed to "lick" their calves,

and regards the process as useful to the cow herself, as a
medicinal corrective. He brings up the calves upon their
dams; but if the cows are heavy milkers, he milks them
dry now and again, until the calf is able to do so itself.
The first fortnight is a most critical time with calves, and
Mr Auld states that when he sees any sign of dulness or
inactivity in their system, he gives them a table-spoonful
of treacle dissolved in warm water. He finds that the
calves are fond of this, and that it operates beneficially. He
states that his late uncle, Mr M'Combie of Tillyfour, was
always most careful to have his calves muzzled during
the first fortnight, so as to prevent them attempting to
eat straw. As soon as they are old enough to be able to
take them, they should be taught to eat cake and turnips,
and should be allowed plenty of exercise. Mr Auld does
not approve of cows being mated sooner than six weeks
after calving. Weaning usually takes place about the
end of the grass season, and after that has been done, the
"cording" of the calves (putting setons into their dew-
laps) is carefully attended to. Young bulls and young
heifers, he thinks, should be liberally fed, and cows kept
in moderate condition.

In Sir George Macpherson Grant's herd at Ballindalloch, an admirable system of management is pursued.
The calving season is made up of December and three
following months, but it often happens that cows fall
behind. As a rule, the calves are allowed to suckle their
dams for about six months. When housed, most of the
cows are kept in loose-boxes, each cow having a box to
herself and her calf. At weaning, calves are very carefully attended to. They are generally trained to eat
linseed-cake before being weaned, and every possible
effort is made to retain the calf-flesh, and not allow them
to fall off after losing the milk of their dams. When
the cold autumn evenings commence, care is taken to
have all the cattle, at any rate all the young cattle,

brought into a house over-night; and this also helps to
maintain the condition of the stock. The young bulls
require and always receive special attention. They are
generally kept in an open court, where they have plenty
of fresh air, but no draughts, and where they can have
constant exercise. Their food consists of a liberal supply
of good yellow turnips, as much oat-straw as they can eat,
and about 2 lbs. of linseed-cake per day. It has been found
advantageous not to allow them to lie or rest on heated
dung, as that has a tendency to damage their legs. A
ready demand is found for the young bulls at the highest
current prices. Young heifers are treated much in the
same way as young bulls, except that, unless grass or
turnips are scarce, they get little or no cake. They are
served when two years old. Cows, as a rule, get a small
supply of turnips three times a day in winter and spring,
the three meals making about 80 or 90 lbs. Latterly it
has been found advantageous to give only about 40 or
50 lbs. of turnips, in two meals, supplemented by a mixture of about 1 lb. of bran, 1 lb. of crushed oats, and
1 lb. of linseed-meal, in a mash of cut straw or chaff.
For about three weeks before and three weeks after
calving, cows get about 2 lbs. of linseed-cake per day.
The over-feeding of breeding stock is studiously avoided,
and the result is that the herd has been more than
ordinarily prolific. Animals intended for showing purposes are of course treated more sumptuously than the
other cattle in the herd.

Mr Hannay of Gavenwood says: "I give nothing to
cows beyond a supply of turnips and straw until within
six weeks of their calving, when they get 3 lbs. of oilcake
daily, and this allowance is usually continued for a month
or so after calving. I endeavour to arrange so as to have
the calves dropped between the end of December and the
middle of April, as the early calves generally thrive best
on the grass, and as calving is less dangerous before the

cows get the full flow of the grass. I try, as far as I can, never to allow the animals to lose the calf-flesh, and with this view I give a little oilcake before and after weaning. The calves here are all suckled; and after they are ten days old they are never tied up, but are allowed to run about the byre as they choose, clean straw being spread out behind the cows for them to lie upon. I have never had a calf injured by this freedom being accorded to them. Heifers here are never put to the bull till two years old. I disapprove of the practice of having them served when only yearlings, as this, as a rule, dwarfs their growth and weakens the constitution, probably both of themselves and their descendants. It is the practice here to put, at even a very early stage, the bull calves and their mothers in fields separate from the heifer calves and their mothers. I am also opposed to the use of yearling bulls beyond three or four times during the season, as tending to lesson their size and destroy their symmetry, with a risk also of unsatisfactory produce. The stock bulls here are kept each in a loose-box, opening on an open court, concreted, and boarded around to a height of 7 feet. In addition to their access all day to these open courts facing the sun, they are from time to time walked out for exercise. They are plentifully but plainly fed. We store the turnips in December, and as they are always at hand and in good condition, there is the less need for supplementing the natural foods. Care should always be taken to keep cattle free from draughts, and to maintain their houses in a clean airy condition. I think a breeding-stock should be kept habitually from getting into what may be called poor condition, while over-feeding ought to be equally guarded against. Much caution is necessary so as not to over-fatten two-year-old heifers for showing purposes. Indeed, it is questionable whether they should receive any extra feeding until they are safely settled in calf."

In reference to the rearing of calves, Mr Hannay writes :—" I find that with highly-bred animals they generally get into a frantic state when the calves are suddenly taken off, and this has occasionally caused the best of cows to slip calf. Now when weaning time comes, I always tie up the calf *in sight of the mother* for about a week, by which time many of the cows are dry, and all risk is avoided. Sometimes calves become dry in the hair and hard in the skin after being weaned. In such cases I cause warm oil to be rubbed well into the skin. This I have found to answer well, and also in most cases to be a complete cure for rheumatism." Mr Hannay gives special attention to the cultivation of docility and gentleness of temper, which have thus become a distinguishing feature in his herd. He says : " From the big bulls down to the calves of two months old, the animals are used to be fondled and fed by all of us—even by quite young children,—and many of them come of themselves to 'speak' to us in the fields."

Mr Alexander Smith, manager to Mr Tayler of Glenbarry, says calves are dropped at Rothiemay from December to May, the best calving months being December, January, and February. The calves suckle their dams, and are weaned at from six to ten months. They get a full allowance of turnips and straw, with 1 lb. of best linseed-cake daily for the first winter. Young bulls are sold from ten to fourteen months old, and if calved in December and January they are quite fit for use in March of the following year. Mr. Smith gives young heifers the first winter after being weaned a full allowance of turnips, straw, and 1 lb. best cake daily. They run on the grass in summer, and the following winter they receive a limited quantity of turnips, straw, and water, with a run in a grass field daily if the weather is dry, as they are apt to lay on fat too quickly before the season of being mated, which is done in the latter end of

February or 1st of March. The cows get grass in summer; turnips and straw in winter, until within two weeks of calving, when they get 2 lbs. cake daily; and after calving an addition of a good feed of bran with a little nitre three times a week for three weeks. Bullocks are fed at two years old, and are sold off in the end of April or 1st May.

Mr George Wilken, Waterside of Forbes, Aberdeenshire, has conducted a few experiments in crossing. He has had heifer crosses from a polled cow with Shorthorn bull, from a cross cow with polled bull, and from a West Highland cow with Shorthorn bull. He had heifers from these three breeds in 1874, all calved at the same time, and he crossed the three heifers with a polled bull. The heifers were all fairly good, that from the polled cow and Shorthorn bull being the best, the one from the West Highlander next, and the one from the cross cow rather the worst. He served them all when one year old, and the result in calves was not very encouraging. The calf from the polled cow's offspring was best, that from the cross cow's offspring nearly as good, and the one from the West Highlander's offspring was a "weed." He did not manage to continue the experiment, as two of the heifers became too fat for breeding. In 1878 Mr Wilken bought three Ayrshire heifers, and served them with a polled bull. The result in 1879 was three very pretty black polled heifer calves. One of the cows was sold in 1879. Mr Wilken has had two calves every year from the other two Ayrshires, or in all nine calves. With the exception of one this year that had a white spot on its side, all have been black and polled. One is now in the dairy, a fair milker, not so good as her dam, and is a very pretty polled animal. "In fact," Mr Wilken says, "last year she went in the field with other nine pedigreed heifers, and not one single polled breeder could point her out, although all who visited the field or byres were asked to do so. A cow-dealer one day was asked to point her out, and without any hesitation did so. I have known her all along by the different shape from the back down to the flank or udder."

These general notes, obtained from leading breeders, indicate fully the system of management generally pursued, both as regards breeding and fattening animals. It will have been gathered that calves are, as a rule, dropped between the 1st of December and the end of April; and that the prevailing custom is to let the calves suckle their dams for six or eight months. A small quantity, from half a pound to a pound, of linseed meal is usually given to calves each day for some time before they are weaned; and after weaning, the allowance is increased. Young bulls are generally allowed 1 or 2 lbs. of linseed cake daily, along with turnips and fodder or grass, until they are sold, at the age of from twelve to eighteen months. Heifers are similarly treated, except that they get less cake. In fact, in many cases after they have got beyond the stage of calves, they never taste cake until they commence to breed. Most breeders give their cows 2 or 3 lbs. of cake, or some equivalent, for a few weeks before and after calving; while stock bulls are always well fed during their active season. In some herds heifers are mated when about eighteen months old, but the prevailing plan is to delay serving another six months. Too early breeding undoubtedly checks the growth of animals. We also think it would be advisable not to use yearling bulls quite so freely as they are used at present.

In other portions of the work the method of breeding pursued in the more celebrated herds has been set forth pretty clearly. It has been shown that in several cases the deeper and more subtle principles of breeding have been employed judiciously and successfully in developing and maturing fixed and well-considered purposes. The

choice and uniform merit displayed by most of the
leading tribes affords ample proof of the ingenious and
methodical manner in which they have been reared.   But
while much has been done in the way of establishing
tribes of high character, it is very desirable that more
attention should be given to the building up of distinct,
well-defined families of as pure line-breeding as may be
found practicable.   It seems to us that it would be well
for the interests of the breed if there existed several
herds or strains which could be regarded as refined and
reliable fountains of that mysteriously beneficial influence
which may be generated by skilfully concentrating and
assimilating the ever-present forces of heredity.   Without entering upon a discussion of the question of in-and-
in breeding, we may remark that we believe it to be a
most powerful agent either for good or evil.   In competent hands it is perhaps the surest and shortest
pathway to the highest pinnacle of a breeder's success.
Unwisely employed, it becomes simply the broad road to
ruin.   We would not, therefore, desire that in-and-in
breeding should be pursued by the general body of
breeders.   We would, however, rejoice to see a few of
those best able, intellectually and financially, to under-
take the work, following the example of Thomas Bates,
the Booths, and other noted Shorthorn breeders, and
establishing distinct line-bred families.   We should like to
see a few families reared in such a way as that they would
not only be uniform in shape and character, but would
also be possessed of one strong, unbroken, unadulterated,
unvarying family current.   We believe in the doctrine
that "like begets like;" but if we breed from composite
animals—animals containing several conflicting family
currents, perhaps the living influence of dead ancestors—
we can have little confidence in the result.   We cannot
know which *likeness* may be produced—that of the immediate, or of more remote ancestors.   Practical experience

and scientific reasoning both teach that no animal is so
likely to reproduce an exact copy of itself as one that
has been in-bred, or in other words, one that contains one
dominant, all-prevailing family current.   We therefore
think that the existence of a few well-defined in-bred
families of really high individual merit would help
greatly to maintain, and even still further improve, the
high character of the breed generally.   These families
would be as it were strong springs of rich, pure blood,
from which fresh draughts might be drawn from time to
time for the reviving and ameliorating of mixed herds.

We are pleased to know that the importance of the
point in question is being more clearly recognised than
it has ever before been, and that by several breeders the
higher and more scientific modes of breeding, to which
reference has been made, are receiving greatly increased
attention.   Efforts, wisely and energetically sustained, are
sure to produce excellent results, and we think we are
not over-confident in predicting for some of our noted
herds of polled cattle a future of great distinction and
usefulness.   While pressing these considerations upon
the notice of breeders, we would also urge them to keep
a jealous eye upon what are recognised as the established
natural characteristics of the breed.   We desire to see
maintained its well-known distinguishing features, its
typical symmetry and roundness of form, its hardiness
and robustness of constitution, and at the same time still
further developed its excellent beef-producing, early-
maturing, and milking properties, as well as to have
imparted to the breed generally, and especially to the
principal families, a little more true high-bred character.
All these are attainable objects, and with good men devoted to the breed the great promise of the future of the
celebrated polls of the North-East of Scotland can hardly
fail to be abundantly fulfilled.

CHAPTER XIX.

THE BREED IN THE SHOW-YARD.

Achievements of the breed in the Show-yard—The Highland Society's Shows—Unique group of Tillyfour first-prize cows in 1864—Features of polled classes at Glasgow Show in 1867; Aberdeen, 1868; Edinburgh, 1869; Dumfries, 1870; Perth 1871; Kelso, 1872; Stirling, 1873; Inverness, 1874; Glasgow, 1875; Aberdeen, 1876; Edinburgh, 1877; Dumfries, 1878; Perth, 1879; Kelso, 1880; Stirling, 1881.—The Fat Stock Shows—Black Prince, the champion at Birmingham and Smithfield in 1867—Polled animals champions at Birmingham and Smithfield in 1872—The Altyre Smithfield champions in 1881—Performances at French Exhibitions—Paris, 1856; Poissy, 1857; Paris, 1862, and Paris 1878—The champion group at Paris in 1878.

THE position which the polled cattle of the North-East of Scotland have taken in show-yards—local, national, and international—has been almost unique. Wherever the breed has been well represented, it has attained marked distinction. It cannot be doubted that the splendid triumphs achieved by polled Aberdeen or Angus cattle in the principal British and French exhibitions have done much both to foster the improvement of the breed at home and to spread its fame in foreign lands. By these means its rare intrinsic merit as a beef-producing race, and its truly handsome and uniform proportions, have been made known far and wide; while the sweets of victory in those hotly-contested fields in which the breed has won its chief laurels, have operated as a powerful stimulus to its patrons, who,

in rearing their beautiful tribes of glossy blacks, have
accomplished work of a noble character and lasting
national value.

Scotch and English Shows.

Regarding the achievements of polled Aberdeen or
Angus cattle in Scotch and English show-yards during the
past twenty years, we have been favoured with some
specially interesting notes by Mr William Macdonald,
Editor of the *North British Agriculturist.* These notes we
shall present in the writer's own words. Mr Macdonald
says :—" For several years prior to 1865 polled cattle, if
not the largest, was one of the most meritorious features
of the Highland and Agricultural Society's shows. The
Tillyfour herd was in those years in its best form. At
that time few could stand successfully against the late
Mr William M'Combie. Numerous were the honours
won by those remarkably fine animals, which traced their
descent to Queen of Ardovie 29, Charlotte 203, Angus
45, Hanton 228, etc. Quite a unique spectacle it was to
behold no fewer than five Tillyfour cows at the Highland
show in 1864, each forward for the gold medal in virtue
of former first honours in the cow class. Such a display
testified to a remarkable succession of showyard achievements on the part of the late Mr M'Combie. The following year at Inverness Highland show he crowned all his
former National Society performances by carrying off no
fewer than five of the six first prizes for polls. Than
some of the Tillyfour females of that period, good judges
maintain that nothing better and very little as good has
since been seen in the polled ranks. Pride of Aberdeen
581, for instance, when she came out at Aberdeen Highland show in 1858 with the first ticket for yearlings on her
head, made an impression which polled admirers have not
yet forgotten. Her head, ears and neck, shoulders, bosom,

and general character, stamped her at once in the estimation of experienced polled breeders as an animal of rare
merit.   It may be doubted if her equal has since or before
headed the yearling-heifer class.   And she maintained her
grand form for years, winning in her classes all through,
and doing something more—transmitting her characteristics in a notable manner to her progeny, the premier
Pride branch of the Queen tribe.

   " Rinderpest occasioned a suspension of the Highland shows from 1865 to 1867, and almost swept
the Angus and Mearns country of polled cattle.   That
disease was not so hard on the Aberdeen, Banff, and
Moray herds, but the demand for Shorthorns was then so
strong that polls narrowly escaped annihilation.   At the
Glasgow Highland show in 1867, polled cattle were very
easily accommodated.   Only fifteen in all the classes
were entered, and there was very little competition.
Lord Southesk's Jupiter 471 had easy work in the aged
bull class.   He was a big, lengthy, substantial bull, not
so nice as his sire, the celebrated Windsor 221, which
cost 180 guineas, the highest price which had up till
then been paid, publicly or privately, for a polled animal.
The younger bulls were not very remarkable, nor were
any of the females, except the fine cow Mina 1009, and
the first prize two-year-old heifer Lily 1114, from Castle
Fraser.   These two were compact, symmetrical, and
admirably brought out by Mr Hampton, and would have
held their own in much stronger competition, as they did
that and next year at Aberdeen in formidable company.
Mina and Lily founded two tribes of richly-fleshed, short-
legged, level, handsome cattle—the Minas and Livelys,
which have since furnished several prize-winners, and
have bred truly and regularly.

   " The following year, at the Aberdeen Highland show,
the polled ranks were again numerously filled, and breeders
and patrons of the black skins got into better spirits.   If

the quality in every class was not quite as good as it
afterwards became, there were numbers enough, and a
sufficiency of general merit to stimulate breeders of polls,
and from that period onwards the northern polled breed
has steadily risen in public favour and increased in
numbers over the country. For first honours in the old
bull class there was a keen contest between Odin 2nd
499, from Bognie, and Clansman 398, from Rothiemay.
The latter was the more lengthy, bigger bull of the two,
but the former was rather finer in bone and more compact, and won accordingly. Clansman, however, rather
improved during the next twelve months, and topped a
very good class of aged bulls at the Edinburgh Highland
show in 1869. He was a lengthy, level bull of great substance, with massive quarters, and a little white in the
underline. After several years of valuable service at
Rothiemay, he was transferred to Drumin, where he
proved a splendid 'getter.' Easter Skene triumphed in
the two-year-old bull class with Caledonian 2nd 409,
a straight shapely bull of Mr M'Combie's own breeding.
The yearling class was to some breeders specially
interesting in that it was headed by the first animal
that the late Mr George Brown, Westertown, exhibited
after his valuable herd had been reduced almost to complete annihilation by pleuro-pneumonia, caught at the
Dumfries Highland show in 1860. The animal referred
to was March 355, a bull of exceedingly fine bone, great
gaiety, well-covered rump, and deep hind quarters. He
was not, however, very successful in after years at the
Highland shows. His head was too short and thick for
the Angus taste, and, excepting second at the Dumfries
Highland show in 1870, he was not further noticed by
the Highland Society's judges. He stamped his deep
chest, strength of shoulders, perfection of hind quarters,
and, it must be added also, clumsiness of head, on his
numerous progeny, several of which, nevertheless, were

first Highland Society's prize-winners, including Baron Settrington 356, the first yearling at Dumfries in 1870, as well as leading two-year-old at Perth in 1871; Duke of Perth 357, second aged bull at Stirling in 1873, and first at Glasgow in 1875; and Duchess 4th 944, the first two-year-old heifer at Kelso in 1872.

"The three-year-old Castle Fraser cow Lily 1114, looking blooming and ladylike, took the lead worthily in a good class of cows at the Highland show at Aberdeen in 1868, where Mina 1009 got the gold medal, and would have been able for something more if permitted to try for it. The two-year-old heifer class was noteworthy, in respect that it contained the first animal that was sent from the Drumin herd of Mr Skinner to the Highland Society's shows. This was a remarkably good heifer, nicely rounded in rib, well slanted in shoulder, and displaying a beautiful head and neck. If not long pedigreed, she had all the polled characteristics, and was shown in very high condition. She won the first ticket; and since then, with a trifling exception or two, the Drumin herd has been annually one of the best contributors to the national show. The Aberdeen heifer did not by her breeding properties augment the herd. Her rare symmetry and quality captivated the late Mr M'Combie's eye, and she went to Tillyfour for fat show purposes, where, however, she was not after all very fortunate.

"At the Edinburgh Highland show in 1869 there was numerically a smaller turnout of blacks, but merit did not suffer thereby. Clansman 398, as already explained, took the coveted ticket for aged bulls to Rothiemay. In the two-year-old bull class there was a serious derangement of anticipations. March 355, from Westertown, who had just returned from first honours at the Manchester Royal show, was expected by several breeders to keep his place. But no. The judges—a majority of them old Angus men—would not have his head at any

price, and he was, to the astonishment of many, turned
ticketless to his stall, and the first prize bestowed on the
Mulben bred bull Madeira, from Dunmore, who was second
to March the week before at Manchester, as also at Aberdeen in 1868. Madeira had a stylish head and neck,
and stood higher than March, but he was not so well put
together nor quite so fine in the bone.

"It was a day of surprises. In the cow class the
heavy, handsome, level-fleshed Sybil 974, from Castle
Fraser, bred at Bogfern, was looked upon as a safe winner.
The Angus men, however, seemed to think her rather less
feminine-looking than Duchess 1st 930, from Westertown,
who, being in a comparatively unfed state, was preferred,
most unexpectedly by the lookers-on, for the coveted
ticket. When examined after the judging, her thoroughly
'cow character' and good milking properties, with nice
shoulders and neck, went far to satisfy the critics. Next
year she gained the challenge cup as the best polled
animal at Aberdeen, though beaten in her class by Sybil,
who, however, had gained that trophy in 1869, and was
not again eligible. A massive, thickly-fleshed, heavily-
coated heifer from Tillyfour topped the two-year-old
class at Edinburgh, but she also failed as a breeder, and
'finished' at the English fat shows.

"Sybil 974 lived to fight another day, and won in a
good class of cows at Dumfries in 1870, where she
looked her best, and was followed by the three-year-old
Erica cow Eisa 977, from Ballindalloch. Sir George
Macpherson Grant shortly afterwards brought Sybil to
Ballindalloch, paying 63 guineas for her at the Castle
Fraser dispersion in the autumn of 1870. In the two-
year-old heifer class Colonel Fraser's Lively 1164, out
of the prize cow Lily 1114, made a hard tussle to
repeat her first Edinburgh honours. She was rather
small in size, but exceedingly neat and feminine-looking,
and afterwards went at 67 guineas to found the valuable

but too short - lived herd of the Marquis of Huntly.
Eventually, however, she had to give way at Dumfries
to Fuschia 979, from Ballindalloch, a very deep, short-
legged heifer of rare quality under the hand. Mr
Skinner got to the front in the yearling class with
Heather Bell 962, a tidy, smart heifer, not big, but well
brought out, and displaying a little white in her face and
in the underline.

"In the bull classes the cream of the honours, so to
speak, went to Portlethen, Ballindalloch, and Westertown.
Palmerston 374 was the best aged bull. His hind legs
came rather far in below him when he stood 'at ease,'
and he had rather much of bone; but his quality and
wealth of flesh were remarkable, and he was a popular
first. After leaving Portlethen, where he, like many
other notable animals, was bred, he did good service in
Lord Fife's herd. The subsequently famous Juryman
404 of the Jilt tribe, from Ballindalloch, the place of his
birth, made his first appearance in the national show at
Dumfries. His frame was then, as always, just a trifle
narrow, and his hind quarters drooped rather too much;
but his quality under the hand, his head, neck, and
shoulders and chine atoned for any defects, and he was
popularly placed first, a Ballindalloch-bred bull from
Castle Fraser getting second honours. Baron Settrington
356, from Westertown, was a grandly furnished yearling,
and was not to be denied in his class any more than he
was at Perth in 1871, where Juryman, looking nobly
although rather restlessly,—he was nervous and keen,—
proved too heavy for a large class of old bulls. The
Ballindalloch herd made a complete sweep of the three
money prizes for cows on the South Inch of Perth in
1871. Eisa was easily first, and a remarkably sweet,
ladylike, evenly - balanced cow she was. Indeed, I
hardly think that for genuine cow-character, quality,
and symmetry combined, any of the Highland Society's

winners since would favourably compare with her. To
the Ericas yet another premier honour went on that
eventful occasion. Enchantress 981 of Ballindalloch,
an animal of no great substance or size, but of extraordinary sweetness, quality, and style, won the first
ticket in the two-year-old heifer class. A neat little
heifer, considerably under size, from Rothiemay, un-
popularly won in the yearling class. The favourite for
first honours was Duchess 4th 944, from Westertown.
She had revenge at Kelso the following year, where she
was clearly the first two-year-old. The Rothiemay heifer
had not growth enough to enable her to keep her place.

"The cow class at Kelso in 1872 was a very good
one. Six cows came from Ballindalloch on that occasion,
the like of which I have never at any other time seen
exhibited from one herd. They included Sybil and Eisa
for the gold medals, and four beauties headed by
Enchantress in the ordinary class. After a close pull,
however, substance prevailed, and a Tillyfour, Charmer
1172, was placed first. She was very thick through the
heart, and had a good, hardy-looking head, but she
lacked the sweetness of the Ballindalloch cows that
pressed her so closely. The Tillyfour herd was fortunate
that day, for it finished with the best of a hard struggle in
the yearling heifer class, the combatants having been Pride
of Alford 1778, from Tillyfour, and Kate 2nd 1482, from
Rothiemay. The former was as plump and as ripe as a
pear, but the latter had more feminine character and a
grand head and ears, and great promise. In fact, I considered her one of the best yearlings that have appeared
since Pride of Aberdeen came on the scene at Aberdeen
in 1858. The tables were turned as between these two
heifers at Stirling in 1873, and Kate 2nd finished her
National Society's career at the early age of three years,
with full honours in a good class of cows at Inverness
Highland show in 1874.

" Perhaps the most attractive specimen of the polled breed at Kelso in 1872 was the three-year-old bull Adrian 439, from Fasque, bred at Portlethen. He followed Baron Settrington at Perth, but improved so much that he won fairly enough on the banks of the Tweed. His build was true, and his symmetry and quality were very fascinating. His breeding days, however, were comparatively early at an end. Size and substance carried Colonel of Castle Fraser 443, from Ladybank, and Scotsman 474, from Ballindalloch, to the front in the two-year-old and yearling bull classes.

" At Stirling the Ladybank bull, handling sweetly, but sunk in the belly, and not symmetrical, won in the aged class, the more symmetrical but smaller Duke of Perth 357 ranking second. Mr Bowie sent in Gainsborough 596, a very well brought out, handsome bull, that won the first prize in the two-year-old bull class. Bertha 980, from Ballindalloch, with prominent shoulders, but splendid quality, was a fairly popular first among cows. A big, lengthy heifer, with a little white about the flank, from Easter Skene,—Young Grizzle 1807,— was preferred in the yearling class ; but she lacked the quality to keep her position afterwards, although she bred some very good animals at Easter Skene.

" The Inverness show in 1874 was remarkable for the first appearance in public of two animals which have with their progeny founded highly prized families. I allude to Sybil 1st of Tillyfour 3524, and Halt 3525 from the same herd, which were the first and second prize yearlings, and afterwards passed into the hands of Mr M'Combie of Tillyfour. The Sybils especially have become famous. The yearling bull class, too, was topped by an animal that turned out even a more noteworthy specimen of the breed,— Young Viscount 736,— the highest priced bull, and perhaps the best looking animal of the breed, that has yet been shown, saving possibly

2 c

Prince Albert of Baads 1336, first winner at Perth, Kelso, and Carlisle in 1879 and 1880. These two bulls have been the best looking of modern show-yard polled males at anyrate. Gainsborough 596, in virtue of his symmetry and quality, won at Inverness over the much heavier aged bulls John Bright 642 and Scotsman 474. While on the same principle Mr Scott's Bluebeard 468, from Easter Tulloch, won rightly enough in the two-year-old class.

"At the Glasgow Highland show in 1875 there was a select if not not a large display of the northern polls. The Marquis of Huntly's Westertown bred Duke of Perth 357, and Sir George Macpherson-Grant's Tillyfour bred Scotsman 474, were the only combatants in the aged bull class, and a protracted engagement they had. Scotsman was the bigger and the fatter of the two, and his head and neck, barring the objectionable 'scurs,' were decidedly better than his rival possessed. The Duke, on the other hand, had better symmetry and quality, with great neatness over the loin and hind quarter. Still the size, substance, and gayer head of Scotsman impressed themselves favourably on Mr Bowie, who, however, eventually gave way to Mr Ferguson and Mr Mackessack, and after nearly an hour's tussle the award was in favour of the Aboyne bull. Scotsman went from that show to the butcher, and the Duke returned to some years of useful service in Lord Huntly's herd.

"Young Viscount 736, in a fairly good class of two-year-olds, looking compact and shapely, though less striking than he afterwards appeared, was a clear first. Sir Thomas Gladstone's Adrian 2nd 622, of handsome proportions but rather hard hair, stood second, and was then transferred to Mr Skinner's herd at Drumin, where he begot several prize winners. In the yearling bull class Lord Fife's Erica bull St Clair 1160, sired by Palmerston 374, the first-prize bull at the Highland show at Dumfries in 1870, was a popular first. The best class of the breed in the show-yard was that of cows, and a noteworthy incident was that the Ballindalloch Ericas were turned away without a ticket, having been regarded by the judges as somewhat deficient in substance compared to some of the others. The Marquis of Huntly's Dora 1282, of the Tillyfour Vine or Daisy branch of the Queen tribe, was chosen for the premier ticket, closely pushed, however, by Lord Fife's very thick, deep, and rather short quartered cow Corriemulzie 1701. The Aboyne cow had skin and hair of marvellous quality. Indeed her coat was as soft and fine almost as a seal's. That, combined with evident milking and true breeding properties, pulled her through more perhaps than really inviting shapes, as was the case at Aberdeen the year before, when she gained the challenge cup as the best polled animal in the show, Corriemulzie then having been the 'runner up.' There was nothing very remarkable in the heifer classes. Mr M'Combie of Easter Skene, with one of those good all round animals for the production of which his herd has long been famous, headed the two-year-old class, the winner having been Blackberry 1813, who started well as a cow. Sir Thomas Gladstone led off in a moderate class of yearlings with a full sister of the second prize two-year-old bull.

"The Highland show of 1876 was held at Aberdeen; and there the turnout of blackskins was the largest, and, taken all in all, the best that had up to that time been witnessed. It then became the feature of the bovine sections of the yard, and made an exceedingly favourable impression upon visitors. It may be doubted if the large numbers and general excellence of the polled animals were after all the subject of most frequent comment among the visitors to the cattle classes. One thing more remarkable than even the excellence of the polls, was probably

the extraordinary success of the Earl of Fife's exhibits.
With one exception, Lord Fife and his factor, Mr Hannay,
carried all the first prizes for polled cattle—a most wonderful feature in such formidable company.

"Young Viscount 736 here looked almost perfect in
form.   Deep, square, and level, he lacked length of neck
a trifle, but he had no other fault, and was 'head and
shoulders' above his compeers in the aged class.   The
shift to Drumin did not prevent Adrian 2nd 632 from
again following Young Viscount.   For his position
Adrian 2nd was indebted to his remarkable depth of
fore-rib and great fore-flank development.   St Clair, also
from Duff House, had lengthened out considerably since
the previous year, and was a popular enough first in the
two-year-old class.   Mr Hannay, with Sir Wilfrid 1157,
a very strong yearling of Rothiemay breeding, and a
future 100 guinea purchase by Lord Strathmore, was a
creditable first in a large class, closely run by the
Ballindalloch bred Jilt bull Judge 1150 of Paris fame,
and also sold at a hundred guineas for exportation to
Canada.

"An immense class of cows was headed by Lord Fife's
four-year-old deep, massive, wealthy cow Innes 1934.
There was no denying her that position.   Shapely and
well brought out she was.   Eva 984, from Ballindalloch,
rather hardly dealt with the year before, got second
honours, leaving third to the Easter Skene's Blackberry
1813, first as a two-year-old at Glasgow, as noted above.
Mr Hannay won in a splendid class of two-year-
old heifers with Zingra 2471, a remarkably well
brought out, well proportioned heifer, bred by Mr Hunter,
Confunderland.   She never, however, did much as a cow.
Nor was the future showyard career of Mr Skinner's
winning yearling Gaiety 2219 more successful, although
she bred well, and is still a massive round-ribbed cow at
Drumin.   The favourite yearling heifer, with experienced

practical onlookers, was the third winner, the property of
Sir Thomas Gladstone.

" At Edinburgh in 1877 the superiority of the blackskins was maintained. Any falling off in numbers as
compared with Aberdeen was not at the expense of
quality or general merit. In a very strong class of aged
bulls, Colonel Ferguson's 100 guinea Mains of Kelly bred
bull Logie the Laird 3rd 862, from Pitfour, which had
run St Clair 1160 hard at Aberdeen the year before, had
his revenge. The former winner failed to grow so much
as was desirable, but he was neat. The Pitfour bull was
not only big but handsome, and won with general
approval, St Clair getting only a commended ticket. Sir
Wilfrid still kept his place with Judge, and they followed
each other in the two-year-old class, although both were
beaten, unfairly as many good judges thought, by Serapis
998, an Easter Skene bred bull from Fasque. The
winner had plenty of substance, but he was not so even
in the flesh over the ribs as could have been desired, and,
moreover, had rather prominent ' scurs.' A good yearling
bull class was headed by Warrior 1291, of Mr Hannay's
breeding from the 111 guinea Rothiemay bred prize cow
Heather Blossom 1703, and after the 225 guinea bull
Young Viscount 736. Warrior was thick, deep, and
shapely, with remarkably neat rump and handsome hind
quarters. A few months afterwards he became the
Marquis of Huntly's property at 155 guineas, and proved
a good stock getter as well as a prize-taker, although he
did not quite maintain his position at the national show.

" The Ballindalloch Erica cow Eva and the Baads-bred
Tillyfour cow Sybil 1st 3524, that made her first appearance in the Highland show at Edinburgh since her
victory in the yearling class at Inverness in 1874, had a
hard pull for priority in a splendid class of cows. During
the protracted struggle, the veteran owner of Sybil, seeing
that the real pull was narrowed to the two, remarked to

the writer, ' Mind you, I could not say anything although the judgment went against me there.' It was pretty much a toss up, but victory eventually went to Tillyfour, and without any complaints on the other side.

" In the two-year-old heifer class, however, a very decided mistake was made in the awards. A heifer, owned and bred by Mr Reid, Baads, was most unexpectedly placed first. She had a calf at foot, but except that she had begun to breed very early, she had no other claim to the position over the excellent heifers shown against her by the Earl of Fife and the Marquis of Huntly. Mr M'Combie's Sybil 2nd 3526, daughter of the first-prize cow, was considered by many to have been safe for the first premium in the yearling class, but the judges, or at least a majority of them, preferred the rather leaner heifer from Drumin named Sunshine 2nd 3333. By future development as a heifer Sunshine 2nd justified the choice, although Sybil 2nd proved the more meritorious cow.

" The year 1878 will remain memorable in the history of polled cattle. In that year the late Mr M'Combie of Tillyfour achieved for himself a crowning victory, and for the polls a great triumph, by gaining the champion prize at the Paris International Exhibition for the group of cattle of any variety, and also the champion prize for the best beef-producing group, with four females and a bull bred at Tillyfour. Sir George Macpherson Grant, Bart., of Ballindalloch, beat Mr M'Combie in some of the classes at Paris, and ran him hard in the group contest, so that the polled breed interest had, so to speak, on that important representative occasion, more than one string to its bow. Mr M'Combie's remarkable feat at Paris did more, perhaps, than any other single showyard performance to bring the North of Scotland polls into national repute. The quarantine restrictions on the return of animals from France interfered considerably with the

display of polled Aberdeen or Angus cattle at the
Dumfries Highland show in July of 1878. That circumstance was possibly not alone to blame for the comparatively small turnout at Dumfries. The distance of the
show-yard from the stronghold of the breed also affected
their muster prejudicially. In a moderately good class
of aged bulls, the Tillyfour bred bull the Shah 680, from
Kinnochtry, where he did good service, was a worthy first.
He was big, lengthy, and massive, with good cover of flesh.
In the two-year-old bull class Mr Tayler's Sir Maurice
1319, bred at Fyvie Castle, turned the tables on Warrior
1291, from Aboyne, who was second, closely followed by
the Aboyne-bred bull Monarch 1182, of whom more
anon. Size and substance more than character and
quality, pulled Mr Cartwright's Black Prince 1244 to
the front in the yearling bull class. Mr Reid's symmetrical, little, ladylike cow Isla 1965, from Baads, was
a distinct first in her class, and testified to the good
material in the Baads herd, of which exhibitors had a
taste in Inverness in 1874. Sunshine 2nd 3333,
from Drumin, led away very easily in the two-year-old
heifer class. She was really a grand two-year-old, far
better than she was as a yearling, or than she afterwards
appeared. Deep-quartered, round-ribbed, full of hair, of
excellent symmetry and quality, she was perhaps the best
northern poll at Dumfries—I say northern, because the
polled Galloways formed the leading feature of the bovine
sections at the Highland show of 1878. Mr Ferguson,
Kinnochtry, with a capital representative of his fine old
Princess tribe of Keillor descent, had a hard pull in the
yearling heifer class, with a well brought out heifer from
Easter Skene. To Kinnochtry ultimately the coveted
ticket was sent; and not unworthily so, for the Princess
heifer had a head, neck, and front generally that were
hard to get over.

" Before I come to the Perth Highland show in 1879,

I must glance at the polls exhibited at the International
Kilburn show in the end of June of that year. They
were necessarily few, but good. Young Viscount 736,
which the previous autumn had become the property of
Sir George Macpherson Grant at 225 guineas, was not to
be gainsaid. He, looking a little paunchy, but otherwise
remarkably well, gained the first prize in his class, and
the champion prize as the best polled animal worthily
indeed. All the bloom of youth and quality which the
three-year-old bull Monarch 1182, from Aboyne, could
command, failed to bring him in higher in such company than second. The Pitfour bull Logie the Laird
3rd 862, first at Edinburgh in 1877, having lost form
somewhat, was only commended. Madge 1217, from
Aboyne, the dam of Monarch, was the winning cow easily,
and also the best female.

" At Perth Highland show, three weeks afterwards,
Monarch was a sure first, followed by Sir Maurice, from
Rothiemay, which topped the two-year-old class the year
before, but had become less even and compact than
Monarch, who, barring a slight deficiency in thighs,
would have been very bad to beat. Monarch was very
well filled behind the fore-arm, and all over was much
more than an average specimen, having possibly been the
best animal from a showyard point of view bred in the
Marquis of Huntly's herd.

" The best polled animal at Perth, as at Aberdeen the
week before, was Mr Anderson's Prince Albert of Baads
1336, from Daugh, Tarland, bred at Baads. This bull
won very clearly in the two-year-old class, and was altogether an astonishingly good animal, big, handsome, and
quality all over—rare combinations. Sir George Macpherson Grant came to the front in a really good class of
yearlings with the splendidly brought out bull Justice
1462, the last calf from the seventeen-year-old Tillyfour
bred cow Jilt 973, of kindred breeding to the Madges

and Monarchs, all tracing back through the Tillyfour herd to that at Keillor. Youth, and consequent lack of depth of carcass and substance in the cow class were pitted successfully against good type, great wealth of flesh, and no little character. Three young cows had a hard run with Eva, from Ballindalloch, and Madge, from Aboyne. The judges ultimately left the elder pair in the background, but many looking on would have placed them in the order named first and second. Mr Hannay's four-year-old Blackbird 2nd 3024, of Montbletton descent, a sweet stylish animal, rather bare of flesh and light of scale, but full of bloom, was placed first, followed by Sunshine 2nd 3333, and Sybil 2nd 3526, the two latter retaining their Edinburgh positions of 1877. Symmetry and remarkable neatness pulled Sir George Macpherson Grant's Birthday 3373 to the front in a very large and fine muster of two-year-old heifers. She, however, failed to breed, and the prize ultimately went to Mr Hannay's second. If Mr Skinner's Gaiety, first yearling at Aberdeen in 1876, was unable to keep her place, she was able to produce a daughter to repeat the mother's performance. The daughter, a neater and also fatter heifer than the mother was at the age, topped a large and good class of yearlings at Perth in 1879, though, like her mother, she never did much more in breeding showyards.

" At Kelso in 1880, unlike the Perth and Aberdeen experiences, the northern polls did not form the best filled bovine classes. Numbers, however, were relatively shorter than quality. Prince Albert of Baads, after winning the first prize at the Royal English show at Carlisle a fortnight before, was an easy winner in the aged bull class. By this time he had developed into possibly the best polled animal that has been shown in modern times, if not indeed at any time. His shoulders were a trifle strong, but he had not another faults Justice, from Ballindalloch, through a little lightness

round the girth, was unable to keep the premier position
he secured at Perth. The more colossal proportions and
better filling up behind the shoulder possessed by Mr
Ferguson's Princess bull Prince of the Realm 1695,
from Kinnochtry, rightly enough weighed with the
judges, and the coveted ticket went to the Princess
instead of the Jilt tribe. Mr H. D. Adamson's Pride
bull Knight of the Shire 1699 easily repeated his first
royal honours at Carlisle in the yearling class, although
at Aberdeen the week before a Drumin bred Lucy bull
from Pitfour, here second, was put before him. The
last-named bull, although lengthy and stylish, was not
so good over the fore-rib as the Pride bull.

" Sybil 2nd, formerly referred to, had even before the
Perth show become the property of Mr H. D. Adamson.
And like every other animal that had constitution to
stand liberal feeding, she improved in his hands, and at
Carlisle Royal show she walked ahead of the Baads, Isla
and the Drumin Sunshine 2nd, and again at Kelso stood
easily first. Mr Skinner was in bad luck at Kelso as
well as at Carlisle, and the Perth winning yearling
had to be contented with a commended ticket on the
banks of the Tweed. Lord Airlie's Pavilion 3772, of
Mr Hannay's breeding and Drumin descent, the second
winner at Perth, when she obviously had more outcome
in her than the first, was invincible in the two-year-old
class at Kelso as well as at Carlisle. But unfortunately
she, like many other showyard heroines, died before she
was able to add to a herd's numbers. Lord Airlie was
also distinctly ahead of the others in the yearling heifer
class with an animal of his own breeding, that kept her
place next year at Stirling, and promises well for the
future. This is Miranda 4204.

" At the Stirling Highland show in 1881 the polls
were once more the great feature of the cattle department. Prince of the Realm and Justice fought their

Kelso battle over again, with a different result. The former, not having been so fat and so sweet-looking as the latter, lost his place ; but had his advocates for the first premium, although the extraordinary quality and the grand out-bringing of Justice left little or no room for cavil. Knight of the Shire 1699, by this time the property of Messrs Auld & Anderson at 145 guineas, kept his place in the two-year-old class, and looked compact and handsome. Mr M'Combie of Easter Skene had decidedly the best yearling bull in the out-coming specimen of that fine old herd. The cow class was not popularly judged. The Ballindalloch cow Maid of Aven 2995, placed first, had a beautiful skin, and looked her best, but her shoulders were rather prominent to win in such company as Lord Tweedmouth's Pride 18th 4321, of Tillfour descent. This three-year-old, which cost 160 guineas at Mr Adamson's sale the previous April, and was second to Pavilion at Carlisle and Kelso in 1880, was generally regarded as the best in the cow class at Stirling, although only placed third. The writer certainly considered her the best, with possibly a little to spare. Lord Airlie's Kelso yearling Miranda 4204 improved in the interval, and was clearly abreast of her opponents in the two-year-old class at Stirling. The yearling heifer from Glamis, a 110 guinea purchase at Mr Adamson's sale, and daughter of Sybil 2nd, was handsome, but too thick in the skin. I liked better the second heifer from Kinnaird Castle, Essence 4547, a very sweet Erica, that by a good judicial bench at the Forfarshire show a week afterwards was placed before the Glamis heifer. So much for the diversity of opinion among judges.

"In the leading national fat shows, as well as in breeding stock exhibitions, Scotch breeders and feeders of polled cattle have during the last twenty years done much to bring their cherished variety into popular favour. In 1867 the late Mr M'Combie occasioned no little

sensation by the exhibition of his ponderous four-year-old
ox Black Prince, who carried the championship at
Birmingham and Smithfield, and from whose sirloin the
Royal baron of beef for Christmas-day was cut. The
extraordinary scale, wealth of flesh, and symmetry of that
noble bullock showed the public what with time and care
the polls could be brought to. More important features
and qualities in the breed had, however, still to be
demonstrated. An impression got abroad that the polls
were show maturers. In 1872 that erroneous idea was
somewhat rudely shaken by the fact that the late Mr
M'Combie carried the Birmingham championship with a
three-year and some months old polled ox, bred at
Tullochallum, Dufftown; and that Mr Bruce, Burnside,
Fochabers, secured the Smithfield 'blue ribbon' with
a polled ox of the same age, bred at Achlochrach, Dufftown—five miles distant from the birthplace of the
Birmingham champion. The Tillyfour ox was level and
nice, but not so firm under the hand as could be desired.
Indeed, he was a lucky winner. The Burnside bullock
was riper, displaying more length, a grand back, but a
rather light underline. The judging struggle, which
eventuated in his favour at Islington in December 1872,
was the most protracted and exciting that I have yet
witnessed. It lasted over an hour and a half, and after
all the ordinary set of judges could not finish it. Their
breed partizanship apparently brought them to a dead-
lock. Three fresh men were chosen, and in a short time
they gave the fiat in favour of the Scot.

"Now and again since the polls have had a nibble at
the 'big things' in the fat shows, but the crowning
effort as regards both polled superiority and early
maturity was left to Mr Walker, Altyre, factor for Sir
William Gordon Cumming, Bart. Mr Walker accomplished the task only last December (1881), when with
a pair of polls little more than two and a half years old

he carried the special prizes as best male and female in
Smithfield; while for the 100 guinea champion plate
the contest ultimately lay solely between these two
beautiful animals, the heifer having been at last preferred.   That unexampled performance in the Smithfield
show history redounded to Mr Walker's credit, and also
to the credit of the early maturing and splendid flesh-
forming properties of the polled breed."

Performances at French Exhibitions.

In France the polled cattle of the North-East of Scotland have on four notable occasions displayed their
superiority over most other breeds—at the International
Exhibitions at Paris in 1856, 1862, and 1878, and at
Poissy in 1857.   In reference to the Exhibitions of 1856
and 1857, we have been favoured with some very useful
notes from the able and facile pen of M. F. R. de la
Trehonnais, the well-known agricultural authority, who,
by his valuable work, entitled *Revue Agricole de
l'Angleterre*, and by other means, has done much to
make his countrymen acquainted with agricultural
progress in the British Isles, more particularly in regard
to live-stock matters.   At the first International Exhibition at Paris in 1855, no polled cattle were shown
from this country, but one bull of the Aberdeen or
Angus breed was exhibited by Mons. Dutrone, who was
for many years a passionate advocate of polled cattle,
and who never lost an opportunity of extolling the
virtues of the northern Scotch polls.   The bull he
exhibited in 1855, which was awarded a premium, was
Monk 149, bred by Sir James Carnegie, got by Balnamoon 36, and out of Meg 708.

The Exhibition of 1856 was carried out on a liberal
scale.   In regard to it M. Trehonnais says:—"It was a
happy thought, for in my long recollection of similar

agricultural gatherings, both in England and abroad, I do
not remember anything more splendid and successful than
the great International Exhibition of 1856. It was held
beneath the glass roof of that marvellous palace of industry
erected in the most beautiful public gardens in the world,
those in the Champs Elysees. On that occasion the
Aberdeen or Angus breed appeared in all its excellence
and splendour. That great champion, the late Mr
M'Combie of Tillyfour, came forward with a lot of such
perfection, as that I doubt whether those he brought out
in the last International Exhibition in 1878 were of
equal merit. Certainly the last lot did not surpass the
former, and I well remember the laudatory and wondering
remarks of foreign visitors when passing round the stalls
where the stately masses of the polled cattle were drawn
in a black and imposing array, even and level, as if the
chisel of the sculptor had been plied over their grand
fleshy frames. It is sufficient to name the exhibitors to
give an idea of the excellent and complete representation
of the breed. In the front rank, as remarked above, was
Mr William M'Combie of Tillyfour. Then came Mr
Hugh Watson of Keillor; the Earl of Southesk, Kinnaird
Castle; Mr John Collier, Panlathie, Forfarshire; Mr
James Stewart, Aberdeen; Mr Allan Pollok, Ireland;
Mr Robert Walker, Portlethen Mains, Aberdeen; Mr R.
Wardlaw Ramsay; Mr Thomas Carnegie of Craigo; Mr
J. Anderson of Gillespie; Mr James Beattie; Sir George
Macpherson Grant, Bart., of Ballindalloch; Lord Talbot de
Malahide; the Executors of the late Mr Scott, Easter
Tulloch; Mr A. Bowie, Mains of Kelly; Mr John
Hutchison; and last, but not least, His Grace the Duke
of Buccleuch, who showed some very fine Galloways."

The muster of polled cattle, including a few Galloways,
at the 1856 Exhibition numbered no fewer than thirty-
nine animals—thirteen males and twenty-six females.
In the bull class Mr M'Combie of Tillyfour won the first

prize—a gold medal and 900 francs—with Hanton 228;
Mr Robert Walker, Portlethen, the second prize—a silver
medal and 700 francs—with Marquis 212; Mr Hugh
Watson, Keillor, Forfarshire, the third prize—a bronze
medal and 600 francs—with Strathmore 5; Mr James
Beattie, Dumfries, the fourth prize—a bronze medal and
500 francs—most likely with a Galloway bull; the Earl
of Southesk the fifth prize—a bronze medal and 400
francs—with Cupbearer 59; and Mr James Stewart,
Aberdeen, the sixth prize—a bronze medal and 300
francs. Commendations (bronze medals) were awarded as
follows: Very high commendation to Mr R. Walker, for
Raglan 208; the second commendation to Mr John
Collier, Panlathie; the third commendation to Mr R.
Wardlaw Ramsay, Whitehill, near Edinburgh; the fourth
commendation to Mr John Anderson of Gillespie; the
fifth commendation to Mons. Dutrone of Trousseauville,
near Dives, Calvados, France, for the bull Monk, already
referred to. It is thus seen that of the thirteen bulls
exhibited no fewer than eleven received official recognition
of their merit. Mr Hugh Watson's third-prize bull
Strathmore 5 was sold to the Emperor Napoleon for 50
guineas. Mr R. Walker's bull Raglan 208 was actually
placed third in the order of merit, but as, by the rules of
the exhibition, each exhibitor could take only one money
prize in each class, this fine bull had to pass down to the
position of the animal most highly commended.

In the female class, the first prize—a gold medal and
600 francs—was awarded to Mr M'Combie for Charlotte
203; the second prize—a silver medal and 500 francs—
to the Earl of Southesk for Dora 333; the third prize—
a bronze medal and 400 francs—to Mr John Collier; the
fourth prize—a bronze medal and 350 francs—to Mr R.
Walker for Daisy 261; the fifth prize—a bronze medal
and 300 francs—to Mr A. Bowie, Mains of Kelly; the
sixth prize—a bronze medal and 250 francs—to Lord

Talbot de Malahide; and the seventh prize—a bronze
medal and 200 francs—to the Executors of the late Mr
Scott, Balwyllo.   The commendations (bronze medals)
were awarded to the following exhibitors in the order
given—viz. to Mr M'Combie for Bloomer 201 and for
two other cows; to Lord Southesk; Mr James Beattie,
Dumfries; the Executors of the late Mr R. Scott; Mr A.
Bowie; and Mr James Stewart. Mr M'Combie's beautiful
cow Bloomer 201 stood second in order of merit in the
class, but for the reason already explained could not carry
off a money prize.   On the recommendation of the judges,
a special gold medal was awarded to Mr M'Combie of
Tillyfour for the *tout ensemble* of his collection of polls.

The judges, in their official report on the polled cattle
at the Exhibition in 1856, say: "The hornless breed,
hitherto little known out of England, must have drawn
attention in more than one respect. The specimens
brought to our notice possessed in fact the following
characteristic points : perfect homogenity of race, beauty,
richness, and regularity of form, softness of skin, mellowness in handling, the whole united to a muscular system
sufficiently developed. They presented, besides, a considerable mass of flesh supported by a comparatively
small volume of bone. We are aware, besides, that that
breed joined sobriety to a great aptitude to fatten, and
that it supplies the butcher's stall with beef of much
esteemed quality; that it produces milk in satisfactory
quantity, is of sweet temper, and is also endowed with
prolific qualities." Special mention is made in the report
of the fine animals shown by Mr M'Combie, Mr R.
Walker, the Earl of Southesk, and others, and this
interesting official document concludes by "demanding"
a "grand gold medal for Mr William M'Combie as a
testimony of particular distinction."

The Exhibition of 1856 was confined to breeding stock,
and the French Government, encouraged by its success,

resolved to hold at Poissy in 1857 an International Exhibition of fat stock. Prizes were offered for polled cattle in two classes—one for oxen above three years and another for bullocks under that age. In the latter class there were eight oxen, nearly all of the Aberdeen or Angus breed. Four belonged to the late Mr William M'Combie of Tillyfour—one was 33 months old, and weighed (live weight) 17 cwt. and 1 quarter; another, 34 months, and weighed 17 cwt.; another, 34 months, and weighed 15 cwt.; and another, age not stated, weighing 18 cwt. In this class Mr M'Combie won the first prize —a gold medal and 1500 francs—as well as the third prize—consisting of a bronze medal and 1000 francs; the second prize—a silver medal and 1200 francs—going to Mr James Stewart, Aberdeen, for a 35 months old bullock, weighing 15 cwts. The other exhibitors in the young class were Mr William Heath, Norfolk, and Mr J. Knowles, Aberdeen. In the class for oxen over three years old, there were four entries. Here Mr William M'Combie of Tillyfour showed two splendid oxen—one 53 months old, and weighing no less than 25 cwt., and the other 48 months old, and weighing 21 cwt. For these two he obtained the first and second premiums, the first consisting of a gold medal and 1200 francs, and the second of a silver medal and 1000 francs. The third prize—a bronze medal and 900 francs—was awarded to Mr James Stewart for a 49 months polled ox weighing 21 cwt. The other exhibitor in this class was Mr John Balfour of Balbirnie House, Fifeshire, who showed a 48 months ox of the Falkland breed, weighing 18 cwt. Commenting upon the awards at the Poissy exhibition, M. Trehonnais remarks: "Out of six prizes offered for polled oxen, Mr William M'Combie obtained four: viz. two firsts, one second, and one third, amounting in money to 4700 francs, or £178 sterling, with two gold medals, one silver, and one bronze medal. Never was there in any exhibition the name of any individual exhibitor so intimately associated with a breed of cattle as that of the late lamented Mr M'Combie on this memorable occasion."

An exhibition of fat stock was held at Paris in 1862, when the polled breed achieved a great victory. At that gathering a polled ox exhibited by Mr M'Combie of Tillyfour gained, besides the class prizes, the two great prizes of honour: viz. the great gold medal of France for the best ox in any of the classes of foreign stock, and the Prince Albert 100 guinea cup competed for between the two winners of prizes of honour for foreign and French oxen.

That great "crowning victory" of the polled Aberdeen or Angus breed at the Paris International Exhibition in 1878 has been more than once referred to in preceding portions of the work. There were only fifteen polled Aberdeen or Angus cattle shown on that occasion, and yet in this small collection the race was, in regard to general merit, remarkably well represented. The late Mr William M'Combie of Tillyfour exhibited eight; Sir George Macpherson Grant, Bart., of Ballindalloch, M.P., six; and Mr George Bruce, late of Keig, one. As evidence of the high and uniform character of the muster of polls, it may be stated that every one of the fifteen animals was awarded either a prize ticket or an "honourable mention"—distinction not attained by any of the other sixty-four varieties of cattle represented.

Then for the two £100 champion prizes—the one for the best group of cattle in the division foreign to France, and the other for the best group of beef producing animals in the exhibition. Mr M'Combie and Sir George Macpherson Grant practically had the contest to themselves. Each group had to consist of at least four females and one bull all bred by the exhibitor. The Tillyfour group was made up of a four-year-old cow, four heifers, and a yearling bull. The cow was Gaily 1793, that obtained an "honourable mention" in her class; while the heifers were the two-year-old Sybil 2nd 3526, winner of an "honourable mention" in the cow class; Halt 2nd 3527, first among yearlings; Pride of Aberdeen 9th 3253, and Witch of Endor 3528, on which "honourable mentions" were bestowed in the class for yearlings. Mr M'Combie's bull was Paris 1473, the first prize yearling. The Ballindalloch group comprised the six animals shown from that herd—two cows eleven and seven years old, two yearling heifers, a three-year-old and a yearling bull. The cows were Eisa 977 and Eva 984, both members of the celebrated Erica family, the latter the winner of the third prize, and the former of an "honourable mention." The heifers were Birthday 3373, and Maid of Aven 2995, to which were awarded respectively the second prize and an "honourable mention." The bulls were Judge 1150, first in the aged class, and Petrarch 1258, second in the yearling class.

These two groups, and a group of Shorthorns belonging to Lady Pigot, were drawn up for the final tussle for the £100 offered in the division foreign to France. The adjudicating bench, numbering 16, first voted as between the "blacks" and the Shorthorns, with the result that the former won by a large majority—14 to 2, we believe. Between the two groups of polled cattle no division actually took place, and the coveted premium was awarded to Mr M'Combie, whose beautiful young group had, as was evident to the on-lookers, captivated the eye of the Scotch judge, Mr H. D. Adamson, late of Balquharn, Alford, on whom, of course, the responsibility of the decision mainly devolved. A jury of 31 gave the award in the contest for the £100 for the best group of beef producing cattle in the exhibition. Mr M'Combie was declared the victor by a majority of 24 to 7. The minority voted for a group of French shorthorns belonging to Count de Massol of Souhey, Cote d'Or.

The preference of the Tillyfour group over that from Ballindalloch has been the subject of considerable discussion, and still, as at the time it was declared, the writer regards it as a point upon which there is ample room for difference of opinion. The Tillyfour group, as will have been gathered, had the bloom of youth on its side, while it was most skilfully and uniformly. The fine, gay young animals were arranged like steps of stairs, and the even proportions of the lot excited much admiration among the on-lookers. The Ballindalloch, group on the other hand, lost in appearance by the inequality in size of the animals composing it; but closely examined, its intrinsic merit, as representing a breeding herd, could not have been easily excelled.

In the polled cow class at the exhibition referred to, Mr George Bruce won the first prize with Bella Mary 1503, a very heavy richly fleshed cow, bred by the late Mr Dingwall Fordyce of Brucklay. Mr M'Combie stood second with the beautiful cow Sybil 1st 3524, bred at Baads. The second prize in the aged bull class fell to Cluny 1283, a three-year-old Erica bull of excellent quality.

CHAPTER XX.

" Senior Wranglers."

WE believe it will be found useful to have in collected form a note of the winners of the first prizes in the classes of aged bulls and cows at all the shows of the Highland Society at which prizes were given for polled breeding stock. A few remarks are added to assist in the identification of the various animals. These become more brief as regards the later shows, ample information being already given as to recent winners. For the title and plan of this part of the work we are indebted to the late Mr H. H. Dixon, who drew up a similar sketch of prize Shorthorns at the shows of the Royal Agricultural Society of England.

Perth, 1829.

Bull, BLACK JOCK, bred and exhibited by Hugh Watson, Keillor.

Cow, OLD GRANNIE 1, bred and exhibited by Hugh Watson, Keillor.

Black Jock has not been entered in 'Herd Book.' He was the sire of Grey-breasted Jock 2, and was the third bull named Jock used at Keillor.

Old Grannie 1, the prima cow of the 'Herd Book,' was

one of the most remarkable animals of the bovine race that ever lived. She attained to the great age of thirty-five years, and produced twenty-five calves.

Inverness, 1831.

Bull, bred by Mr Robinson, Mains of Eden, near Banff, exhibited by Peter Brown, Linkwood, Elginshire.

Cow, bred by Mr Aberdeen, Skene, Aberdeenshire, exhibited by Major Forbes Mackenzie of Fodderty, Cromarty.

Aberdeen, 1834.

Bull, exhibited by R. Findlay, Balmain, Kincardineshire.

Cow, bred by Mr Walker, Suttie, Aberdeenshire, exhibited by the Earl of Kintore.

Perth, 1836.

Bull, bred and exhibited by Hugh Watson, Keillor.
Cow, bred and exhibited by Hugh Watson, Keillor.

Inverness, 1839.

Bull, bred by Robert Colville, Balnabreich, exhibited by Hugh Watson, Keillor.

Cow, bred by George Leslie of Rothie, and exhibited by the Duke of Richmond, Gordon Castle, Fochabers.

Aberdeen, 1840.

Bull, bred by Mr Brown, Banchory, exhibited by Isaac Machray, Torry Farm, Kincardineshire.

Cow, exhibited by James Walker, Wester Fintray, Aberdeenshire.

Dundee, 1843.

Bull, PANMURE 51, bred by Lord Panmure, exhibited by William Fullerton, Mains of Ardovie, Forfarshire.

Cow, bred by Lord Panmure, exhibited by Colonel Dalgairns of Balgavies.

Panmure has been described as " the Hubback of the polled breed." Perhaps the complete accuracy of the phrase may be questioned by some; but of this, at all events, there can be no doubt, that Panmure 51 stands in the same relation to the polled herds north of the Grampians that Hubback holds in reference to the early Shorthorn herds. A full description of his breeding is given in another page. After his success at Dundee, he passed into the possession of Mr Farquharson Taylor, Wellhouse, Aberdeenshire, in whose herd he was eminently useful, and to whom he gained numerous prizes.

Colonel Dalgairns' first-prize cow has not been entered in the ' Herd Book.' A daughter of hers, Lady Ingliston 60, belonged to Mr. Ferguson, Kinnochtry. It was a striking testimony to the excellence of the stock bred by Lord Panmure, that in the very close competition at Dundee this year, animals bred by him secured the two leading prizes of the show.

At the shows at Glasgow in 1844 and Dumfries in 1845, prizes were offered only for oxen of the polled Aberdeen or Angus breed.

Inverness, 1846.

Bull, OLD JOCK 1, bred and exhibited by Hugh Watson, Keillor.

Cow, exhibited by Alexander Craig, Kirkton, Golspie.

Old Jock 1, of whom the official return of the Highland Society simply stated that he was " aged 3 years

and 5 months, bred by exhibitor," was regarded by Mr
Watson as the best bull he ever bred. In a note we
have from a well-known breeder he is described as "the
best polled bull he ever saw." Other testimony is equally
favourable to his merits. He was one of the most impressive of the Keillor sires, and the stock got by him,
which were numerous, have been of the highest celebrity.
In short, he and Panmure 51 stand in the front rank
among the early polled sires that have most contributed
to the improvement of the breed.

Aberdeen, 1847.

Bull, bred and exhibited by Hugh Watson, Keillor.
Cow, bred by William M'Combie of Tillyfour, exhibited
by Robert Scott, Balwyllo.

The first-prize bull is thus entered in the official
records of the Highland Society: "Aged 3 years and 5
months, bred by exhibitor." Unfortunately we know
nothing more about him.
The first-prize cow had for dam what Mr M'Combie
has described as "the first female of note at Tillyfour."
She was bred by Mr Wilson, Netherton of Clatt.

Edinburgh, 1848.

Bull, ANGUS 45, bred and exhibited by Hugh Watson,
Keillor.
Cow, YOUNG CHARLOTTE 103, bred by Colonel Dalgairns,
Balgavies, exhibited by William M'Combie of Tillyfour.

Angus was a pure Keillor bull, his sire being Old
Jock 1, and his dam Old Favourite, bred by Hugh Watson. He was calved in 1846, not in 1836, as stated in
vol. i. of 'Herd Book.' Mr M'Combie (whose Victor 46
was second at this show) bought Angus for £36, and he

became sire of those celebrated Tillyfour cows, Charlotte
203, The Belle 205, Young Jenny Lind 207, and Fair
Maid of Perth 313.

Of the pedigree of Young Charlotte nothing is known,
except that the cow was bred by Colonel Dalgairns, and
was after Black Hugh 316. The judges speak in high
terms of the animal. She was purchased at Mr M'Combie's sale in 1850 by Mr Walker, Montbletton, and a
valuable family trace to her through her twin daughters
Twin Charlotte 609 and Twin Queen 610, by Fintray 125.

Glasgow, 1850.

Bull, EARL O' BUCHAN 57, bred by William Cooper,
Hillbrae, exhibited by William Fullerton, Mains of
Ardestie.

Cow, bred and exhibited by Hugh Watson, Keillor.

Earl o' Buchan was bred by Mr Cooper, Hillbrae,
Aberdeenshire, and was bought by Mr. Fullerton as a
calf. His blood circulates through many good tribes as
the sire of Isabella of Balwyllo 423 (the dam of President 3rd 246) and of Lively 256, etc.

Mr. Watson's cow was a daughter of Old Grannie 1.
She was sold at the Keillor sale a non-breeder. Mr
Ferguson, Kinnochtry, bought a daughter of hers, Glas-
gow 58, but has now none of her produce.

Perth, 1852.

Bull, YOUNG JOCK 4, bred and exhibited by Hugh
Watson, Keillor (Mr Watson also won the sweepstakes
for best bull with Old Jock 1).

Cow, BLOOMER 201, bred and exhibited by William
M'Combie, Tillyfour.

Young Jock 4 was after Old Jock 1, and was bought
and used by Mr Ferguson, Kinnochtry. Of his sire, Old

Jock, the winner of the sweepstakes, the official report
of the Perth show remarks: "He was particularly reported
by the judges as an extraordinary animal, and unrivalled
for strength, symmetry, and quality, though now fourteen—[should be ten or eleven]—years old. In fact he
showed the perfection to which judgment and attention
can bring this valuable breed."

Mr M'Combie, with Bloomer 201, on this occasion
commenced in earnest that extraordinary run of show-
yard success with members of the Queen tribe which
has few parallels in the annals of cattle exhibitions.
Bloomer was out of Queen Mother 348, and after Monarch 44, a son and daughter of Panmure 51, being thus
an example of close breeding. The cow was regarded by
Mr M'Combie as one of his best. She bred some fine
stock, chief among which may be named The Belle 205
and Mr Tayler's famous bull Napoleon 257. "Bloomer
was larger than Charlotte 203, but not so level and sweet,
nor so fine in the bone."

It was this year that the polled Aberdeen or Angus
cattle elicited the highest encomiums of the directors of
Society, and their pronouncement undoubtedly stimulated
the extension and still further improvement of the breed.
"The directors rejoice that this and preceding shows
indicate a praiseworthy amount of effort and care on
the part of breeders of polled stock followed by a corresponding improvement in the stock. They cannot but
regard it as the most valuable breed of Scotland, combining as it does in a great measure the constitution of the
Highlander with the feeding properties of the Shorthorn."
On this historic occasion Mr Watson, as we have seen,
was first for aged bulls, and also gained the sweepstakes.
Mr Bowie was first for two-year-old bulls with Cupbearer
59. Mr M'Combie was not only first for cows, but also
for two-year-old heifers; Mr Scott, Balwyllo, being first
for yearling heifers.

As this is the last time Mr Watson's name appears in this list, we may note that he was able to send forward ten of our " Senior Wranglers."

Berwick, 1854.

Bull, CUPBEARER 59, bred by Alexander Bowie, Mains of Kelly, exhibited by Sir James Carnegie.

Cow, WINDSOR 202, bred and exhibited by William M'Combie, Tillyfour.

Cupbearer 59 is fully referred to elsewhere. He was the first of Mr Bowie's great champions, and his progeny are alike numerous and excellent. He was indeed not only a splendid-looking bull, but one of exceptional impressiveness. There are credited to him in vol i. of ' Herd Book ' no fewer than 38 calves. Mr Bowie had great success at this show, being first and second for aged bulls, and first for two-year-old bulls. The animals were Cupbearer, Earl Spencer 2nd 25, and Hanton 228.

Windsor, who derived her name from the fact that she was first at the Royal English show at Windsor as a yearling in 1851, was an in-bred Queen. She was from Queen Mother 348 (by Panmure 51 and out of Queen of Ardovie 29), and after Victor 46, whose dam, Jean Ann 206, was also after Panmure and out of Queen of Ardovie 29. As the dam of the bull Windsor 221, so famous in the Westertown and Kinnaird herds, and of Rob Roy Macgregor 267, the sire of that impressive Tillyfour bull Black Prince 366, she must hold a high place in the history of polled cattle.

Inverness, 1856.

Bull, HANTON 228, bred by Alexander Bowie, Mains of Kelly, exhibited by William M'Combie, Tillyfour.

Cow, CHARLOTTE 203, bred and exhibited by William M'Combie.

Again a Mains of Kelly bull heads the list. Hanton, the sire of numerous celebrated animals, demands only a passing reference here. He was out of Lizzie 227, who had the Panmure blood through her sire, Spencer's Son 154, and after the choicely-bred Keillor bull Pat 29, a son of Old Jock 1 and Favourite 2. Mr M'Combie bought him for £105, and he was kept till he was eight years old, winning the great gold medal at Paris in 1856. When sold fat he fetched £40.

Charlotte 203, got by Angus 45, and out of the Queen cow Lola Montes 208, stands in the first rank among polled matrons. After her victory here she was sent across to the Paris exhibition, where she carried the first prize and the gold medal as best of all the cows and heifers. On account of these distinctions, she is generally spoken of as the "Paris cow." "She was all over a sweet-looking, level, nice, touching cow, with fine temper. Whether lean or fat, she was always level without patchiness of any kind about her." Her most renowned offspring are: Pride of Aberdeen 581, Daisy of Tillyfour, Crinoline 204, and Empress of France 578. Pride, Daisy, and Empress were full sisters.

Glasgow, 1857.

Bull, DRUID 225, bred and exhibited by the Earl of Southesk.

Cow, NIGHTINGALE 262, bred by Sir Alexander Burnett, Bart., of Crathes, exhibited by Robert Walker, Portlethen.

Druid, one of the many celebrated animals of Cupbearer's get, was out of Dora 333, bred at Keillor. The strain seems to be extinct in the female line, but it was considered the best at Kinnaird. Druid and his sire

Cupbearer are illustrated in volume i. of 'Herd Book.' "As a two-year-old, there has probably never been a finer specimen of the breed. He combined large size with fine quality and a most excellent temper." Unfortunately he was not very useful at the stud, but the stock after him were uniformly good.

Nightingale was purchased at Sir A. Burnett's sale in 1856 for £32, 5s. On the dam's side she represented the old established Aberdrenshire herd of Mr Walker, Wester Fintray. She passed successively into the Tillyfour and Ballindalloch herds.

Aberdeen, 1858.

Bull, STANDARD-BEARER 229, bred by Alexander Bowie, Mains of Kelly, exhibited by William M'Combie, Tillyfour.

Cow, THE BELLE 205, bred and exhibited by William M'Combie of Tillyfour.

Standard-Bearer was after Hatton 30, and out of Lady Ann 2nd 346. The bull subsequently passed into the possession of Mr M'Kenzie, Lyne of Carron. His fame has not been perpetuated.

The Belle was out of Bloomer 201, of the Queen tribe, and after Angus 45. With her breeder she was a favourite cow.

Edinburgh, 1859.

Bull, WINDSOR 221, bred by William M'Combie of Tillyfour, exhibited by the Earl of Southesk.

Cow, FAIR MAID OF PERTH 313, bred by William M'Combie, Tillyfour, exhibited by John Collie, Ardgay.

Windsor, a son of the Queen cow Windsor 202 and Hanton 228, was bought from Mr Brown, Westertown, for £150 in money, and the bull calf King Charles 236.

He was a very fine animal, with grand fore-end and back, and left a great many good stock, both at Westertown and Kinnaird.

Fair Maid of Perth was out of Young Jean Ann 144, and after Angus 45. She was first prize cow at the Royal English show at Carlisle in 1855. Mr Collie bought her at the Tillyfour sale in 1857 for £86.

Dumfries, 1860.

Bull, YOUNG PANMURE 232, bred by William M'Combie, Tillyfour, exhibited by Alexander Bowie, Mains of Kelly.

Cow, PRIDE OF ABERDEEN 581, bred and exhibited by William M'Combie, Tillyfour.

Young Panmure was after Hanton 228, and out of Crinoline 204, a daughter of the Queen cow Charlotte 203. The first-prize cow of this year, Pride of Aberdeen, was one of the best of the breed. She was out of Charlotte 203, and after Hanton 228. As a yearling, two-year-old, and cow, she was invincible at the national shows. She was the best polled heifer that has yet been seen, and she founded a tribe that has acquired rare value.

Perth, 1861.

Bull, TOM PIPES 301, bred and exhibited by Thomas Lyell, Shielhill.

Cow, MAYFLOWER 314, bred by Alexander Paterson, Mulben, exhibited by John Collie, Ardgay.

This was the "Shielhill year." Tom Pipes having been the first-prize aged bull, and his half-brother Prospero 302, also belonging to Mr Lyell, the first-prize two-year-old. Both animals were after the Kinnaird bull Mariner

148, and their dams were descended from the early established Leuchland herd.

Mayflower was a descendant of the Mulben herd, established in 1842.

International, Battersea, 1862.

Bull, PROSPERO 302, bred and exhibited by Thomas Lyell, Shielhill.

Cow, PRIDE OF ABERDEEN 581, bred and exhibited by William M'Combie of Tillyfour.

Prospero and Pride of Aberdeen are referred to in notes on the Perth winners of 1861. The International show at Battersea is included here, as at that exhibition the Highland Society gave the prizes for Scotch stock, and did not hold their own show on account of it.

It was noted as regards this International exhibition, that the two best females shown in the various classes were Pride of Aberdeen, bred by Mr M'Combie of Tillyfour, and Queen of the Ocean, bred by Mr R. Booth of Warlaby. In one report of the exhibition it is stated : " Pride of Aberdeen, five years old, closely resembles the first-prize cow in the class for Shorthorns, Queen of the Ocean, three years old. The poll is, however, much fatter, and there is the difference of two years in favour of the polled cow. When measured, these two very symmetrical cows correspond as to girth, height, breadth across loins, length of quarters. Both possess that mellowness of touch and general levelness which distinguish the best specimens of both breeds."

Kelso, 1863.

Bull, FOX MAULE 305, bred and exhibited by Robert Walker, Portlethen.

Cow, NANCY, by Hanton 228, bred by William M'Combie, Tillyfour, exhibited by Erskine Wemyss, M.P., Wemyss Castle, Kirkcaldy.

Fox Maule was after Marquis 212 (bred at Keillor, a son of Old Jock 1, and the sire of 28 registered calves). His dam, Matilda Fox 302, was after Cupbearer.

We can give no further particulars than those stated regarding the breeding of Nancy.

Stirling, 1864.

Bull, PRINCE OF WALES 453, bred by George Brown, Westertown, exhibited by Alexander Paterson, Mulben.

Cow, DAISY 1165, bred and exhibited by William M'Combie, Tillyfour.

Prince of Wales was after Prince Albert of Westertown 237, a son of Windsor 221, and out of Paris Kate 309, bred by Mr Ruxton, Farnell.

Daisy was full sister of Pride of Aberdeen, and was the foundress of the Daisy or Vine branch of the Queen tribe.

Inverness, 1865.

Bull, CHAMPION, by Rob Roy Macgregor 267, bred and exhibited by William M'Combie, Tillyfour.

Cow, LOVELY 1166, bred and exhibited by William M'Combie, Tillyfour.

Champion has unfortunately not been registered. His sire, Rob Roy Macgregor, was after Hanton 228, and out of Windsor 202.

Lovely, also by Rob Roy Macgregor, was out of The Belle, the first-prize cow at Aberdeen in 1858. She was first-prize two-year-old at Battersea.

At this show Mr M'Combie gained five of the six first prizes offered.

Glasgow, 1867.

Bull, JUPITER 471, bred and exhibited by the Earl of Southesk.

Cow, MINA 1009, bred and exhibited by Colonel Fraser of Castle Fraser.

Jupiter was after Windsor 221, and out of Balwyllo Queen 445. "He was a bull of great size and substance, but, like many of the Balwyllo stock, was a trifle rough in the hair, not enough, however, to be a very grave defect."

Mina, by Black Jock of Tillyfour 365 (a son of Hanton and Empress of France), was out of Grace, descended from the Crathes herd, which was largely based on Keillor blood.

Aberdeen, 1868.

Bull, ODIN 2ND 499, bred and exhibited by Alexander Morison of Bognie.

Cow, LILY 1114, bred and exhibited by Colonel Fraser of Castle Fraser.

Odin 2nd 479, after a son of Lord Southesk's Odin 153, was from one of the Mountblairy Corskie tribe, which sprang from Mr Robinson's old stock at Corskie.

Lily, descended from the stock of Mr Walker, Westside, Kildrummy, was after the Queen bull Black Jock of Tillyfour 365.

Edinburgh, 1869.

Bull, CLANSMAN 398, bred and exhibited by William James Tayler of Glenbarry.

Cow, DUCHESS 1st 930, bred and exhibited by George Brown, Westertown.

Clansman was by Lord Southesk's Dora bull Damascus

2 E

495, and out of Magdelina 817, thus representing one of oldest families in the Rothiemay herd.

Duchess 1st 930, was a daughter of the foundress of the Westertown Duchess family of the Queen tribe. She was after President of Westertown 354, a son of Windsor 221.

Dumfries, 1870.

Bull, PALMERSTON 374, bred and exhibited by Robert Walker, Portlethen.

Cow, SYBIL 974, bred and exhibited by Harry Shaw, Bogfern, Tarland, exhibited by Colonel Fraser of Castle Fraser.

Palmerston was got by Jehu 362, and was out of Prima-Donna 851, being thus a descendent of Nightingale 262, the winner in 1857. He passed into the herd of the Earl of Fife, and was a successful stock sire.

Sybil was a very beautiful cow. She was after Black Prince of Bogfern 501, and out of Ann of Bogfern 539. Going into the possession of Sir George Macpherson Grant, Bart., M.P., she won many other prizes, and was the foundress of a well-known Ballindalloch family.

Perth, 1871.

Bull, JURYMAN 404, bred and exhibited by Sir George Macpherson Grant, Bart., of Ballindalloch.

Cow, EISA 977, bred and exhibited by Sir George Macpherson Grant, Bart., of Ballindalloch.

This was the "Ballindalloch year." Sir George Macpherson Grant was first for aged bulls and cows, also second and third for cows, and first for two-year-old heifers.

Juryman, out of Jilt 973, and after Bright 454, was

first-prize two-year-old. He was a remarkably good-looking as well as a most valuable stock bull.

Eisa 977 was a daughter of Erica 843, and Trojan—a cow of splendid quality and very beautiful feminine appearance.

Kelso, 1872.

Bull, ADRIAN 439, bred by Robert Walker, Portlethen, exhibited by Sir Thomas Gladstone, Bart., of Fasque.

Cow, CHARMER 1172, bred and exhibited by William M'Combie, Tillyfour.

Adrian was after Palmerston, the first-prize bull in 1870, and out of Prima-Donna 851, Palmerston's dam.

Charmer 1172 was after President 4th 368, bred at The Thorn, and out of Lovely of Tillyfour 1166, of the Queen tribe, the first-prize cow in 1865.

Stirling, 1873.

Bull, COLONEL OF CASTLE FRASER 443, bred by James Leslie, The Thorn, exhibited by T. L. Melville Cartwright, Melville House.

Cow, BERTHA 980, bred and exhibited by Sir George Macpherson Grant, Bart., of Ballindalloch.

Colonel of Castle Fraser was after Jamie of Easter Skene 443, and out of Mina 1009, the first-prize cow in 1867.

Bertha, after Trojan 402, and out of Miss Burgess 1198, represented an old strain at Ballindalloch which has produced many good cattle.

Inverness, 1874.

Bull, GAINSBOROUGH 596, bred and exhibited by Alexander Bowie, Mains of Kelly.

Cow, KATE OF GLENBARRY 2ND 1482, bred and exhibited by William James Tayler of Glenbarry.

Gainsborough 596, got by Major 351, and out of Guinea Pig 3rd 1182, was afterwards purchased by the Earl of Fife, in whose herd he did good service.

Kate of Glenbarry 2nd 1482 was after Elector 427, and out of Kate of Glenbarry 1187, of Mr Tayler's Georgina tribe, of which she was perhaps the most distinguished representative that has yet appeared, as she was certainly a cow of excellent shapes and style.

Glasgow, 1875.

Bull, DUKE OF PERTH 357, bred by George Brown, Westertown, exhibited by the Marquis of Huntly.

Cow, DORA OF ABOYNE 1282, bred by William M'Combie of Tillyfour, exhibited by the Marquis of Huntly.

A representative of the Westertown Rose tribe, Duke of Perth, was the highest priced animal at Mr Brown's dispersion. He was after March 355, and out of Rose 3rd 925.

Dora was after Bright 454, and out of Vine of Tillyfour 1167, of the Vine or Daisy branch of the Queen tribe.

Aberdeen, 1876.

Bull, YOUNG VISCOUNT 736, bred by William Duff, Hillockhead, Glass, exhibited by the Earl of Fife.

Cow, INNES 1934, bred and exhibited by the Earl of Fife.

Young Viscount, after Hampton 492, and out of Erica 3rd 1249, of the Ballindalloch tribe of that name; was also first as a yearling and two-year-old. He gained the champion prize at the International show at Kilburn, and was sold to Sir George Macpherson Grant for the highest price ever paid for a polled bull, 225 guineas.

Innes was after Lord Ornoch 445, and her dam Jenny 1017 was from the Montbletton herd.

At this show Lord Fife had five cows mentioned in the prize list, while his herd, and that at Corskie, subsequently amalgamated, secured no fewer than five first prizes. The first-prize aged bull, the first-prize two-year-old bull, and the second-prize cow at this show, were of the Ballindalloch Erica family.

Edinburgh, 1877.

Bull, LOGIE THE LAIRD 3RD 862, bred by Alexander Bowie, Mains of Kelly, exhibited by Colonel Ferguson of Pitfour.

Cow, SYBIL 1ST OF TILLYFOUR 3524, bred by George Reid, Baads, Peterculter, exhibited by William M'Combie of Tillyfour.

Logie the Laird 3rd was purchased from Mr Bowie for 100 guineas. He was after Gainsborough 596, the first-prize bull in 1874, and out of Lizzie 4th 2249, of the Mains of Kelly tribe of that name. This was the fifth time a bull of Mr Bowie's breeding was first in the aged class.

Sybil 1st of Tillyfour 3524, was after Sir William 705, and out of Fancy of Baads (a son and daughter of President 4th 368), a strain which rapidly acquired a high reputation in the show-yard and sale-ring. She was sold to Lord Airlie at the Tillyfour dispersion in 1880 for 110 guineas.

Dumfries, 1878.

Bull, SHAH 680, bred by William M'Combie, Tillyfour, exhibited by Thomas Ferguson, Kinnochtry, Coupar-Angus.

Cow, ISLA 1965, bred and exhibited by George Reid, Baads, Peterculter.

Shah was after Prince of Wales 2nd 394, and out of Pride of Aberdeen 5th 1174. He was the thirteenth specimen of the Ardovie and Tillyfour Queen tribe that flourished among the "senior wranglers;" a success perhaps unique in the annals of any family of any breed of cattle.

Isla was a full sister of Sybil 1st 3524, being after Sir William 705, and out of Fancy of Baads 1948.

Perth, 1879.

Bull, MONARCH 1182, bred and exhibited by the Marquis of Huntly.

Cow, BLACKBIRD OF CORSKIE 2ND 3024, bred by the Earl of Fife, exhibited by John Hannay, Gavenwood, Banff.

Monarch was out of the first-rate cow Madge of Port-lethen 1217, a descendant of the Keillor Favourite 2, and was after Pluto 602.

Blackbird 2nd is one of a race of splendid breeding cows at Montbletton, named the Mayflowers. She was after John Bright 642, and out of Blackbird of Corskie 1704.

Kelso, 1880.

Bull, PRINCE ALBERT OF BAADS 1336, bred by George Reid, Baads, Peterculter, exhibited by Robert Anderson, Daugh, Tarland.

Cow, SYBIL 2ND OF TILLYFOUR 3526, exhibited by Henry D. Adamson, Balquharn, Alford.

Prince Albert of Baads was after Bachelor, a son of Bertha 980, the Ballindalloch first-prize cow at Stirling in 1873, and out of Kate of Baads 1947, by President 4th 368. He was the first-prize bull at the Royal English show the same year, and was one of the finest polled bulls that has been seen in recent years.

Sybil 2nd of Tillyfour, out of Sybil 1st of Tillyfour 3524, the first-prize cow in 1877, and after Sir Garnet 684, was one of the Tillyfour champion group at the International show at Paris in 1878. She was sold in 1881 to Lord Southesk for 180 guineas. Both the senior wranglers this year were representatives of Mr Reid's herd at Baads.

Stirling, 1881.

Bull, JUSTICE 1462, bred and exhibited by Sir George Macpherson Grant, Bart., of Ballindalloch.

Cow, MAID OF AVEN 2995, bred and exhibited by Sir George Macpherson Grant, Bart., of Ballindalloch.

Justice 1462 was one of the three prize-winning sons of Jilt 973, the others being Juryman 404, the first-prize bull at Perth in 1871; and Judge, the first-prize bull at Paris in 1878. Justice was by the Erica sire Elcho 595.

Maid of Aven 2995 was out of Bertha 980, the first-prize cow at Stirling in 1873, and after the Erica bull Elchies 563.

THE ROYAL NORTHERN AGRICULTURAL SOCIETY.

Second in importance to the Highland Society's shows are those of the Royal Northern Agricultural Society at Aberdeen. Frequently indeed the national meeting has been little more than a repetition of that at Aberdeen, in so far as the sections for polled Aberdeen or Angus cattle are concerned. The most important competitions at the Royal Northern show are those for the Challenge Cup, the M'Combie prize, and the Family prize. On each of these we have had prepared information which will be interesting and useful :—

Challenge Cup.

(Value £50, to be won three years in succession.)

This cup was won in three consecutive years—1860, 1861, and 1862—by Mr W. M'Combie of Tillyfour, and it therefore became his property. The successful animals were Pride of Aberdeen 581, Charlotte 203, and Lovely of Tillyfour 1166.

A new Challenge Cup was obtained in 1863, and is still being competed for. The winners since that year have been—

1863. R. WALKER, Portlethen.
> Bull Fox Maule 305, bred by R. Walker; *s.* Marquis 212, *d.* Matilda Fox 302.

1864. W. M'COMBIE of Tillyfour.
> Cow Daisy 1165, bred by W. M'Combie; *s.* Hanton 228, *d.* Charlotte 203.

1865. W. M'COMBIE of Tillyfour.
> Two-year-old heifer Kate of Aberdeen, bred by W. M'Combie; *d.* Zara 1228.

1866. No show in consequence of Rinderpest.

1867. Colonel FRASER of Castle Fraser.
> Cow Mina 1009, bred by Colonel Fraser; *s.* Black Jock 365, *d.* Grace.

1868. No show in consequence of Highland Society's show being held at Aberdeen.

1869. Colonel FRASER of Castle Fraser.
> Cow Sybil 974, bred by H. Shaw, Bogfern; *s.* Black Prince of Bogfern 501, *d.* Ann of Bogfern 539.

1870. GEORGE BROWN, Westertown, Fochabers.

Colonel Fraser gained the first prize in the section for cows; but as this cow gained the Challenge Cup in 1869, she could not compete. The judges awarded the cup to the *second*-prize winner in section for cows, Duchess 1st 930. This is possibly the only occasion on record when a Challenge Cup has gone to a second-prize beast. Duchess 1st 930 was bred by Mr Brown; *s.* President 354, *d.* Duchess of Westertown 927.

1871. W. DINGWALL FORDYCE of Brucklay, M.P.

Bull M'Combie 430, 3 years, 5 months, and 18 days; bred by exhibitor; *s.* Bright 454, *d.* Miss M'Combie 1118.

1872. GEORGE BROWN, Westertown, Fochabers.

Bull Baron Settrington 356, 3 years and 3 months; bred by exhibitor; *s.* March 355, *d.* Duchess of Westertown 927.

1873. SIR GEORGE MACPHERSON GRANT, Bart. of Ballindalloch.

Cow Eisa 977, 6 years, 6 months, and 14 days; bred by exhibitor; *s.* Trojan 402, *d.* Erica 843.

1874. THE MARQUIS OF HUNTLY, Aboyne Castle.

Cow Dora of Aboyne 1282, 6 years and 4 months; bred by William M'Combie, M.P., Tillyfour; *s.* Bright 454, *d.* Vine of Tillyfour 1167.

1875. THE EARL OF FIFE, K.T., Duff House, Banff.

Bull Young Viscount 736, 2 years and 4 months; bred by William Duff, Hillockhead, Glass; *s.* Hampton 492, *d.* Erica 3d 1249.

1876. No SHOW in consequence of Highland Society's show taking place at Aberdeen.

1877. WILLIAM M'COMBIE of Tillyfour.

Cow Sybil 1st of Tillyfour 352, 4 years; bred by George Reid, Baads, Peterculter; *s.* Sir William 705, *d.* Fancy of Baads, 1948.

1878. LIEUT.-COLONEL FERGUSON of Pitfour, Mintlaw.

    Bull Logie the Laird 3rd 862, 4 years and 5 months; bred by Alexander Bowie, Mains of Kellie, Arbroath; *s.* Gainsborough 596, *d.* Lizzie 4th 2249.

1879. ROBERT ANDERSON, Daugh, Tarland.

    Bull Prince Albert of Baads 1336, 2 years, 4 months, and 9 days; bred by George Reid, Baads, Peterculter; *s.* Bachelor 690, *d.* Kate of Baads 1947.

1880. HENRY D. ADAMSON, Balquharn, Alford.

    Cow Sybil 2nd 3526, 4 years and 3 months; bred by the late William M'Combie of Tillyfour; *s.* Sir Garnet 684, *d.* Sybil 1st 3524.

1881. R. C. AULD, Bridgend, Whitehouse.

    Bull Knight of the Shire 1699, 2 years, 6 months, and 15 days; bred by H. D. Adamson, late of Balquharn, Alford; *s.* Dragon 1178, *d.* Pride of Mulben 3rd 3249.

The M'Combie Prize.

In 1877 a subscription was started in order to make some suitable testimonial to Mr William M'Combie of Tillyfour, M.P., by breeders and others throughout the county and elsewhere. A sum of over £300 was thus raised, and, at Mr M'Combie's request, the money was handed over to the Royal Northern Agricultural Society, in order to constitute a capital, the interest of which was to be paid as a prize every year. This special prize is styled The M'Combie Prize, and is awarded to the best breeding animal of the polled Aberdeen or Angus breed. A prize of the value of about £15 is at present awarded yearly out of this fund. The first competition took place in 1878 at the annual summer show of the Society. The following is a list of the owners, breeders, and pedigrees of the animals which gained this prize :—

1878. John Hannay, Gavenwood, Banff.

Bull Young Viscount 736, 5 years and 3 months; bred by William Duff, Hillockhead, Glass; *s.* Hampton 492, *d.* Erica 3rd 1249.

1879. Robert Anderson, Daugh, Tarland.

Bull Prince Albert of Baads 1335, 2 years, 4 months, and 9 days; bred by George Reid, Baads, Peterculter; *s.* Bachelor 690, *d.* Kate of Baads 1947.

1880. Henry D. Adamson, Balquharn, Alford.

Cow Sybil 2nd 3526, 4 years and 3 months; bred by the late William M'Combie of Tillyfour; *s.* Sir Garnet 684, *d.* Sybil 1st 3524.

1881. R. C. Auld, Bridgend, Whitehouse.

Bull Knight of the Shire 1699, 2 years, 6 months, and 15 days; bred by H. D. Adamson, late of Balquharn, Alford; *s.* Dragon 1178, *d.* Pride of Mulben 3rd 3249.

The Family Prize.

This Society, in 1879, commenced a section for family groups of the polled breed, the family to consist of a cow of any age, and two or more of her direct produce, male or female. In addition to ordinary premiums, special prizes, value £10 each, were given as follows: In 1879 by Lord Douglas Gordon, and in 1880 and 1881 by Earl of Aberdeen. The following are the winners, together with a list of the animals, in the successful groups:—

1879. The Marquis of Huntly, Aboyne Castle, Aboyne.

Madge of Portlethen 1217, 8 years, 3 months, and 20 days; bred by Mr M'Combie of Tillyfour; *s.* Major of Tillyfour 509, *d.* Ruth of Tillyfour 1169.

OFFSPRING.

Marjorie 2574, 5 years and 2 months; bred by Mr Walker, Portlethen; *s.* Florist 385.

Medusa 2577, 4 years, 3 months, and 19 days ; bred by
exhibitor ; *s.* Pluto 602.

Monarch 1182, 3 years, 4 months, and 7 days ; bred by
exhibitor ; *s.* Pluto 602.

Duke of Aboyne 1500, 2 years, 4 months, and 20 days ;
bred by exhibitor ; *s.* Duke of Perth 357.

Morven 1502, 1 year, 4 months, and 10 days ; bred by
exhibitor ; *s.* Duke of Perth 357.

1880. JAMES MOIR, Mains of Wardhouse, Insch.

Hawthorn of Wardhouse 2467, 5 years and 2
months; bred by exhibitor; *s.* Wallace of Wardhouse 983, *d.* Miss Carnegie 3rd 2419.

OFFSPRING.

Hawthorn 2nd 4031, 2 years and 6 months ; bred by
exhibitor ; *s.* Watchman 1533.

Black Chief, 5 months and 12 days ; bred by exhibitor ;
s. Bogfern 901.

1881. GEORGE REID, Baads, Peterculter.

Isla 1965, 7 years, 2 months, and 5 days ; bred
by exhibitor; *s.* Sir William 705, *d.* Fancy of Baads
1948.

OFFSPRING.

Isla 3rd 4376, 2 years, 3 months, and 20 days ; bred by
exhibitor ; *s.* Keillor 1280.

Isla 4th 5003, 1 year and 3 months ; bred by exhibitor ;
s. Young Juryman 1591.

Isla 5th, 2 months and 23 days ; bred by exhibitor ; *s.*
Prince Albert of Baads 1336.

CHAPTER XXI.

THE BREED IN THE SALE RING.

Lord Panmure's sale in 1841—Mr Fullerton's sale in 1844—Keillor sale in
1848—Mr M'Combie's first sale in 1850—The Auchtertyre sale in
1853—Crathes sale in 1856—Mr Bowie's sale in 1857—Inchmarlo
sale in 1857—Mr M'Combie's sale in 1857—Keillor dispersion in
1860—Mr M'Combie's sale in 1860—Kinnaird sale in 1861—Balwyllo
sale in 1863—Kinnaird sale in 1865—Tillyfour sale in 1867—Portlethen sale in 1869—Castle Fraser sale in 1870—Tillyfour sale in
1871—Recent public sales—Average for Prices—High prices for
Ericas—High prices for Baads Sybils—Prices for exported animals—
Prices at 82 public sales.

MUCH interesting and useful information regarding the
history of the breed is derived from a study of the
catalogues and price lists of important sales of polled
cattle. Of many of the early sales we are without
record. The first of which we have any notice is that
of Lord Panmure, held at Brechin Castle in October
1841, when Mr Fullerton purchased the celebrated bull
Panmure 51 for £17, 17s. The next sale we know of
was Mr Fullerton's, at Ardovie in 1844, when a number
of important transactions took place. Mr M'Combie of
Tillyfour bought at this sale the heifers Queen Mother
348 for £12, 10s., and Jean Ann 206. Mr Bowie,
Mains of Kelly, here purchased Earl Spencer 24, and
Mr Ruxton, Farnell, Monarch 44, both famous bulls. Mr
Watson had a sale at Keillor in 1848, but of it we have
been unable to procure a complete record. Mr M'Combie

of Tillyfour on that occasion purchased the bull Angus
45 for £36, and Mr Bowie bought Old Favourite, the
dam of this bull and of Old Jock, for 40 guineas. The
bull Old Jock 1 was also offered at Mr Watson's sale in
1848, and Mr Ferguson, Kinnochtry, informs us he was
taken in at 180 guineas.

Mr M'Combie of Tillyfour held his first public sale at
Bridgend on 26th September 1850, and through the
kindness of Mr Auld, Bridgend, we have obtained a full
price list of it.   Mr Walker, Montbletton, bought for
£35 the Highland Society's first-prize cow Young Charlotte 103, that founded a well-known family in his herd ;
Anabella, bred by Mr Walker, Wester Fintray, was bought
by Sir Alex. Burnett for 29 guineas; Matchless (out of
Matilda, bred by Mr Williamson, St. John's Wells) was
bought by Sir John Macpherson Grant, Bart., of Ballindalloch, for 30 guineas, and Sir John also acquired the
cow Young Mary and the bull Victor 2nd 47. Among
other purchasers at this rather famous sale were Mr
M'Combie of Cairnballoch ; Mr Taylor, Wellhouse ; Mr
M'Combie of Easter Skene ; Mr M'Innes, Dandaleith ; Mr
Brown, Westertown ; Mr Scott, Balwyllo ; Mr Morison
of Bognie ; Mr Ruxton, Farnell, etc.   The next sale was
at Auchtertyre in 1853, when Mr Hugh Watson disposed
of a number of fine animals.   Of this sale we have a copy
of the catalogue priced by Mr James Ferguson, Ballunie.
The highest price was paid by the Earl of Southesk for
lot 8 (Octavia 331), the dam of Mr Ferguson's Young
Jock 4.   The price was 44 guineas.   Lot 20 was a one-
year-old heifer, entered in the catalogue as "by Old Jock,
dam Beauty, the dam of Sir T. Burnett's famous bull."
Lord Southesk bought this heifer for 39 guineas, and she
was registered in the 'Herd Book' as Emily 332.   Emily,
as our readers are aware, became the dam of Sir George
Macpherson Grant's celebrated Erica 843.   Sir Alexander
Burnett, Bart., held a sale at Crathes Castle in May 1856.

At it Mr Walker, Portlethen, purchased for £32, 5s. the cow Nightingale 262 (entered in the catalogue as Jenny Lind), after Strathmore 5, and out of Mary of Wester Fintray 21. She had at foot the calf Princess Philomel 269. Nightingale was the first-prize cow at the Highland Society's show at Glasgow in 1857, and has left many noteworthy descendants.

Mr Bowie's sale at West Scryne, in 1857, was remarkably successful in its financial results, the average of for fifty-one animals exceeding £28. The highest priced cow was Caroline 562, bought by the Earl of Southesk for £67, and the highest priced bull was Standard-Bearer 229, bought by Mr M'Combie of Tillyfour for £89. This animal was winner of the first prize at the Highland Society's show in 1858. In 1857, Mr Patrick Davidson's herd at Inchmarlo was dispersed. Mr Paterson, Mulben, here obtained for £34, 15s., Jean of Inchmarlo 522, "after Mr Walker's (Portlethen) bull, and out of Calder by Mr M'Combie's bull." The cow was ancestress of the Mulben Ellen family. At Mr M'Combie's sale at Bridgend in 1857, Fair Maid of Perth 313 of the Queen tribe, a very successful prize cow, was sold to Mr Collie, Ardgay, for £86; Lady Clara 4 out of Old Grannie 1, to Mr Shaw for £20, her daughter Mariana 622 going to Dr Garden, Balfluig, for £27; Jenny of Tillyfour 353 (a yearling heifer, the foundress of the Mains of Kelly Jennet family) to Mr Bowie for £21; Napoleon 257, "out of the best cow and after the best bull in the world in the opinion of the exposer," was bought by Mr Tayler of Glenbarry, for £42; Young Panmure 232, afterwards the first-prize bull at the Highland Society's show at Dumfries in 1860, was purchased by Mr Bowie for £20, being then three months old. The Keillor herd was dispersed in 1860. The most notable transactions there were the sale of Beauty of Tillyfour 2nd to Mr M'Combie, and President 3rd to Mr Leslie, The Thorn.

Mr M'Combie's next sale took place at Dorsell in 1860.
Lord Southesk bought Empress of France 578, a daughter
of Charlotte 203 and full sister of Pride of Aberdeen
581, for 60 guineas.   Three wonderful old cows were
sold at this sale.   Lola Montes 208, one of the most
renowned of polled matrons, was offered, being then
fourteen years old, and was bought by Mr Bowie, Mains
of Kelly, for 29 guineas.   Windsor 202, her sister, as
famous as a breeder of bulls as Lola Montes was of
heifers, was sold in her tenth year to Mr Wemyss of
Wemyss Castle for 40 guineas.   Jean Ann 206, one of
Mr M'Combie's purchases at Ardovie in 1844, and that
had done good service at Tillyfour by producing the
Victors, was sold in her seventeenth year to Mr Watson,
Keillor, for 15 guineas.   Nightingale 262, that had by
this time been bought at one of the Portlethen sales for
£68, 5s., was now sold to Sir George Macpherson Grant
for 47 guineas.   Heiress of Balwyllo 461 went to Mr
Walker, Montbletton, at 53 guineas, and the money
proved to have been well invested.   Mr Barclay, Yonderton, took out at 32 guineas the yearling heifer Matilda
1712, after Hanton 228, and out of Lola Montes 208.
It was at this sale also Mr Brown, Westertown, acquired
for 19 guineas Duchess 927, the foundress of the Duchess
branch of the Queen tribe, the animal being then a mere
calf.   Two very fine bulls were sold; Garibaldi 707, out
of Pride of Aberdeen, going to Mr Farquharson of
Haughton for 33 guineas, and Tam o' Shanter 491, stated
in the catalogue to be out of Maid of Orleans 508, but
entered in the 'Herd Book' as out of Lola Montes 208,
to Mr Walker, Montbletton, for 47 guineas.

The Earl of Southesk had an important sale at Kinnaird
Home Farm in 1861.   Some excellent animals were disposed of; but it is a lamentable circumstance that only a
few of them are now represented in the female line.   This
is doubtless due to the fact that many of the cattle were

retained in Forfarshire, and became victims to rinderpest a few years afterwards. The highest-priced animal
at the sale was Erica 843, bought by Sir George Macpherson Grant for 50 guineas. The Balwyllo cow Keepsake 427 went to Mr Collie, Ardgay, for 30 guineas.
Perdita 848, by whom the Nightingale family at Portlethen is preserved, was bought by Mr Walker for 25
guineas. Among the bulls sold were five very superior
animals—Delaware 457, who went to Easter Skene;
Draco 338, to Ardhuncart; Don Fernando 514, to Tillyfour; Damascus 495, to Rothiemay; and King Henry
390, to Easter Tulloch. The first four were of the Dora
family. At Mr Walker's sale at Montbletton in 1862,
the highest price (60 guineas) was paid by Mr M'Combie
of Tillyfour for the prize - cow Mayflower 614, the
foundress of the Mayflower family. The remark in
reference to the Kinnaird sale of 1860 applies with even
increased force to the Balwyllo dispersion in 1863.
Alice Maud 724, the highest-priced cow, sold for 63
guineas, is almost the only animal that has living female
descendants. Eugenie 458, sold to Sir Thomas Gladstone, is also worthily represented in the Fasque herd.
Mr Cran, Morlich, bought at this sale the bull Balwyllo
Eclipse 781. The low prices at the Earl of Southesk's
sale in 1865 are explained by the fact that the auction
took place while rinderpest was raging in the county.
Empress of France 578, then eleven years old, was sold
to Mr Scott, Easter Tulloch, for 26 guineas. A more
fortunate purchase by Mr Scott was the cow Formosa
186, of the Fanny tribe. We should notice that at this
sale a cow named Ella, out of Emily 332, the dam of
Erica 843, and after Windsor 221, was sold to Mr
Alexander, Bent, for 23 guineas. An examination of
these Forfarshire sales awakens melancholy reflections as
to the havoc wrought to the breed by cattle plague.

At the Tillyfour sale in 1867, Mr Skinner, Drumin,

2 F

bought Dandy 949, of the Empress branch of the Queen
tribe, for 46 guineas; Sir George Macpherson Grant, Jilt
973, for 70 guineas (highest price of the sale); General
Forbes of Inverernan, Sylph 1774, of the Queen tribe,
for 45 guineas; Mr Walker, Portlethen, Chaff 855, of
the Crinoline branch of the Queen tribe, for 48 guineas;
Mr M'Combie of Easter Skene, Miss Watson 987, grand-
daughter of the Keillor cow Favourite 2, for 33 guineas.
Normahal 726, from whom descends the Zaras, went to
Mr M'Knight, Boghead, for 34 guineas; and Keepsake
427, to Sir George Macpherson Grant, for 27 guineas.
At the Portlethen sale in 1869, the Earl of Dunmore
purchased several of the highest-priced animals. Sir
Thomas Gladstone bought as a calf, for 27 guineas,
Adrian 439, that subsequently became a first-prize bull
of the Highland Society. The highest-priced animal at
the Castle Fraser sale in 1870 was Lively 1164, bought
by the Marquis of Huntly for 67 guineas. The famous
Sybil 974 was acquired by Sir George Macpherson Grant
for 63 guineas, her twin daughters going to Mulben and
Bognie. This sale is notable as furnishing the nucleus of
several distinguished herds, such as the Aboyne Castle,
Duff House, Brucklay, etc. At the Thorn sale in 1871,
Colonel of Castle Fraser 443 was sold to Mr Cartwright
of Melville for 48 guineas, and won the Highland
Society's first prize. Among the noteworthy sales at
Tillyfour in 1871, was that of Dora 1282 to the Marquis
of Huntly for 49 guineas. This cow afterwards gained
the first prize at the Highland Society's show. Here
Pride of Mulben 1919 was sold as a calf to Mr Paterson,
Mulben, for 29 guineas, and Madge 1217, as a calf, to
Mr Walker, Portlethen, for 15 guineas.

The highest average that had up to this time been
obtained was realized at Mr Tayler's sale at Rothiemay
in 1872, when 30 head made £32, 6s. The highest
price was 60 guineas, for the cow Nicety 1076, bought

by Mr Morison of Bognie. Heather Blossom 1703, of the Rothiemay Victoria family, was bought as a yearling by Mr Hannay, Gavenwood, for 30 guineas, her dam Heather Bloom 1809 being secured by Mr M'Combie of Tillyfour for 54 guineas. A few weeks later — in November 1872—the Rothiemay average was exceeded by over £3 at the draft sale at Ballindalloch. The highest price, 60 guineas, was given by the Earl of Fife for Erica 4th 1697, of the Erica family. At the Drumin sale in 1873, an average of over £40 was realized, Lord Huntly taking Gem 1595, of the Pride family, for 70 guineas, and Beauty 959, of the Beauty family, for 60 guineas. At Portlethen in 1874, Lord Huntly bought the famous cow Madge 1217 for 51 guineas.

The transactions at subsequent sales enter closely into the current history of the breed, and will be found detailed in the notices of the various herds. We may just note the outstanding features. The highest price paid for a polled animal at a public sale up to the date of its occurrence was got at the Westertown dispersion in 1874, when Lord Huntly gave 95 guineas for the bull Duke of Perth 357. The Mulben dispersion in 1876 was probably the first occasion when there was a decided run by breeders upon members of a particular family, four females of the Pride of Aberdeen family averaging over £68, while the general average of the sale was £32. High averages were obtained at the Ballindalloch and Drumin sales that year. At the Tullochallum dispersion in 1877, the Erica cow Miss Macpherson 1252 brought 90 guineas. The Erica cow Erica 4th 1697 made 101 guineas at the Corskie sale. Heather Blossom 1703 fetched 111 guineas; Warrior 1291, 155 guineas; and Sir Wilfrid, 100 guineas, this being the first sale of polled cattle at which prices went into the "three figures." At the Montcoffer sale in 1878, the Erica bull Young Viscount 736 was bought by Sir George Macpherson Grant for

225 guineas, the highest price ever paid for a polled bull at a public sale. The Tillyfour dispersion in 1880 realized an average of £48, 1s. 6d., and the highest price that has been paid for a polled animal was obtained for Pride of Aberdeen 9th 3253, purchased by Mr Auld, Bridgend, for 270 guineas.   Ten females of the Pride of Aberdeen family averaged at Tillyfour £86,16s. 8d.; three Charmers £88, 18., twenty-eight males and females of the Queen tribe averaging over £65.   The dispersion of the Balquharn herd (Mr Adamson's) in 1881 resulted in an average of £56, 4s. 8d., the highest on record for the breed.   Pride of Mulben 3rd 3249 fetched 225 guineas from Lord Tweedmouth, and the Baads Sybil cow Sybil 2nd 3526, 180 guineas from Lord Southesk.   Eleven of the Pride family of all ages and sexes averaged nearly £100. At the Aboyne dispersion in 1881, the average was £50, 6s.   At the Rothiemay sale in 1881 the cow Kate Duff 1837, of Mr Tayler's Georgina family, made 155 guineas.

In notices of several herds will be found references to the chief private transactions in polled cattle.   Perhaps the most important event of the kind was the large sale made by Mr Hannay of Gavenwood, to Mr Bruce, Great Smeaton, the amount being between £2000 and £3000.   Mr Wilken, Waterside of Forbes, who has exported many cattle to America during the last year, kindly supplies us with a note of the range of prices.   For yearling heifers the prices have ranged from 30 guineas to 100 guineas ; for two-year-old heifers from 45 guineas to 100 guineas; for cows from 44 guineas to 200 guineas, several having gone at from 100 guineas to 150 guineas.   Yearling bulls have been bought at from 25 guineas to 40 guineas for ranche purposes ; yearling bulls for herds at from 45 guineas to 100 guineas ; two-year-old bulls (only a few) at from 65 guineas to 120 guineas.   No bulls over two years old have been exported by Mr Wilken.   A cow was sold to an English breeder at 150 guineas.

As illustrative of the rise in price of males of the breed, we may note that while 31 young bulls were sold at the Aberdeen joint sale, in the spring of 1879, at an average of £19, 18s. 7d., 81 were sold in the spring of 1882 at an average of £31, 8s. 10d.

The following list of average prices, &c., at eighty-two public sales, shows the range in value of polled cattle over a period of more than thirty years:—

Exposer's Name.	Date of Sale.	No. sold.	Average.			Highest price.		
			£	s.	d.	£	s.	d.
William M'Combie of Tillyfour . .	1850	28	20	13	0	35	0	0
Hugh Watson, Auchtertyre . . .	1853	38	19	15	0	37	0	0
Sir A. Burnett, Crathes Castle . .	1856	20	17	17	0	30	5	0
Alex. Bowie, Mains of Kelly .	1857	51	28	1	10	89	0	0
Patrick Davidson of Inchmarlo . .	1857	20	19	13	3	34	15	0
Wm. M'Combie of Tillyfour . . .	1857	30	28	11	0	86	0	0
Wm. M'Combie of Tillyfour . . .	1860	29	31	17	7	60	0	0
Earl of Aberdeen, Haddo House .	1861	22	19	5	10	40	5	0
Earl of Southesk, Kinnaird Castle .	1861	32	26	17	8	42	0	0
George Barclay, Yonderton . . .	1861	16	14	12	9	22	1	0
Robert Walker, Montbletton . .	1862	18	21	19	6	63	0	0
Trustees of R. Scott, Balwyllo . .	1863	59	24	14	0	66	3	0
Robert Walker, Portlethen . . .	1863	34	19	12	6	34	13	0
Earl of Southesk, Kinnaird Castle .	1865	34	22	8	4	34	13	0
John Collie, Ardgay	1866	13	24	10	0	35	14	0
Wm. M'Combie of Tillyfour . . .	1867	48	31	5	2	73	10	0
Hon. Chas. Carnegie, Arratsmill .	1868	16	19	9	4	35	10	0
Robert Walker, Portlethen . . .	1869	31	27	6	8	52	10	0
Colonel Fraser, Castle Fraser . .	1870	27	37	18	4	70	7	0
James Leslie, The Thorn	1871	32	27	2	0	50	8	0
Wm. M'Combie of Tillyfour . . .	1871	46	29	15	9	63	0	0
W. J. Tayler of Glenbarry . . .	1872	30	32	6	0	63	0	0
Sir Geo. Macpherson Grant, Bart. .	1872	19	35	18	5	63	0	0
James Scott, Easter Tulloch . . .	1873	34	19	10	3	36	15	0
Robert Walker, Portlethen . . .	1873	23	28	16	6	53	11	0
Wm. M. Skinner, Drumin . . .	1873	28	40	15	5	73	10	0
Alex. Morison of Bognie	1874	27	27	13	9	46	4	0
J. F. Macgregor, Garline	1874	12	22	2	6	35	0	0
Robert Walker, Portlethen . . .	1874	27	29	3	4	53	11	0
Dr Robertson, Indego	1874	24	26	19	10	42	0	0
George Brown, Westertown . . .	1874	56	37	10	10	99	15	0
Wm. M'Combie of Easter Skene .	1874	17	24	19	0	42	0	0
Wm. M'Combie of Tillyfour . . .	1874	46	41	5	10	79	16	0
W. J. Tayler of Glenbarry . . .	1875	25	41	8	2	73	10	0
J. W. Barclay, Auchlossan . . .	1875	53	28	5	6	91	7	0

Exposer's Name.	Date of Sale.	No. sold.	Average.			Highest price.		
			£	s.	d.	£	s.	d.
Alex. Smith, Inchcorsie . . .	1875	7	27	19	0	40	19	0
George Greig, Middlethird . . .	1875	18	23	18	11	43	1	0
Arthur Glennie, Fernyflatt . .	1876	26	21	12	6	33	12	0
Wm. Forbes, Ruthven	1876	9	28	15	6	40	0	0
James Scott, Easter Tulloch . . .	1876	26	23	0	4	33	12	0
Alex. Paterson, Mulben	1876	54	32	2	5	95	11	0
Sir Geo. Macpherson Grant, Bart. .	1876	21	47	15	0	84	0	0
Wm. M. Skinner, Drumin . . .	1876	21	40	2	0	69	6	0
W. D. Fordyce of Brucklay . . .	1876	38	31	0	0	73	10	0
Colonel Gordon of Fyvie	1876	17	28	9	5	48	6	0
The Earl of Airlie, Cortachy Castle .	1876	26	35	8	4	73	10	0
Rev. G. I. Sim, Glenlivet, . . .	1877	8	29	16	7	54	12	0
George Wilken, Waterside . .	1877	20	29	4	10	64	1	0
George Gordon, Tullochallum . .	1877	32	34	1	2	94	10	0
Roderick Macgregor, Kincraig . .	1877	38	19	19	0	42	0	0
John Hannay of Gavenwood . .	1877	68	44	15	10	162	15	0
James Bennet, Marypark	1878	11	27	13	0	40	19	0
John Hannay of Gavenwood . .	1878	38	49	6	5	236	5	0
Wm. M'Combie of Tillyfour . .	1878	44	43	11	6	105	0	0
George Wilken, Waterside . .	1878	25	32	4	0	52	10	0
W. J. Tayler of Glenbarry . . .	1878	32	41	1	3	96	12	0
John Postlethwaite, The Hollins .	1878	40	24	11	4	63	0	0
James Scott, Easter Tulloch . . .	1879	35	19	3	3	37	16	0
R. Macgregor, Kincraig	1879	30	17	10	0	28	7	0
C. F. Gwyer, Biallid	1879	24	21	17	9	42	0	0
Sir Geo. Macpherson Grant, Bart. .	1879	37	24	12	0	52	10	0
Marquis of Huntly, Aboyne Castle .	1879	37	44	8	9	99	15	0
Earl of Aberdeen, Haddo House .	1879	39	25	5	10	48	6	0
T. L. M. Cartwright of Melville .	1879	51	24	14	1	64	1	0
Colonel Gordon of Fyvie	1879	11	22	15	3	42	0	0
Wm. Beedie, Pitgair	1879	12	21	14	10	34	2	6
Wm. Robertson, Burnside . . .	1879	31	28	7	8	43	1	0
George Bruce, Keig	1880	9	27	11	11	36	7	0
John Grant, Methlick	1880	27	18	9	6	37	16	0
Wm. M'Combie of Tillyfour . . .	1880	70	48	1	6	283	10	0
Earl of Strathmore, Glamis . . .	1880	22	35	18	9	63	0	0
Earl of Airlie, Cortachy	1880	43	30	3	7	73	10	0
Wm. M'Combie of Easter Skene .	1880	18	27	1	7	36	15	0
George Hamilton of Skene . . .	1880	19	25	15	7	42	0	0
H. D. Adamson, Balquharn . . .	1881	36	56	4	8	236	5	0
Colonel Gordon of Fyvie . . .	1881	32	30	7	4	91	9	0
Marquis of Huntly, Aboyne Castle .	1881	32	50	6	0	120	15	0
John Hannay of Gavenwood . .	1881	46	33	16	1	74	11	0
Mr Pierson, The Guynd	1881	19	22	17	8	52	10	0
W. J. Tayler of Glenbarry . . .	1881	29	38	4	8	162	15	0
Alex. Smith, Inchcorsie	1881	7	30	0	0	46	4	0

INDEX.

PRINTED BY WILLIAM BLACKWOOD AND SONS.

www.ingramcontent.com/pod-product-compliance
Lightning Source LLC
Chambersburg PA
CBHW032015110726
47901CB00004B/1093